Ideas with Consequences
The Federalist Society and the Conservative Counterrevolution

Amanda Hollis-Brusky

OXFORD
UNIVERSITY PRESS

Oxford University Press is a department of the University of Oxford. It furthers
the University's objective of excellence in research, scholarship, and education
by publishing worldwide. Oxford is a registered trade mark of Oxford University
Press in the UK and certain other countries.

Published in the United States of America by Oxford University Press
198 Madison Avenue, New York, NY 10016, United States of America.

Library of Congress Cataloging-in-Publication Data
Hollis-Brusky, Amanda, author.
Ideas with consequences : the Federalist Society and the conservative counterrevolution /
Amanda Hollis-Brusky.
pages cm
ISBN 978–0–19–938552–2 (hardback); 978–0–19–093374–6 (paperback)
1. Federalist Society for Law & Public Policy Studies (U.S.) 2. Law—Political aspects—
United States. 3. Judicial review—United States. 4. Conservatism—United States.
I. Title.
KF294.F43H65 2015
349.7306—dc23
2014011196

Dedicated to Nelson W. Polsby (*in memoriam*),
who brought this book to life with ten words.

CONTENTS

PREFACE TO THE PAPERBACK EDITION

The world into which *Ideas with Consequences* was originally released looked remarkably different from the one into which this edition lands. Barack Obama was president of the United States, Donald J. Trump was merely a bombastic reality show host and real estate mogul, and I was touring the country giving lectures and interviews about an organization that some had heard about but which had not yet captured the majority of the nation's attention—the Federalist Society for Law and Public Policy Studies.

Much has changed in four years. Almost a year to the day of the book's release, conservative justice Antonin Scalia—the Federalist Society's original faculty advisor and longtime hero—died suddenly, leaving a vacancy on the Supreme Court. Within minutes of the news reaching the public, Senate majority leader Mitch McConnell (R-KY) announced he would not even hold hearings for any nominee until after the November 2016 elections. The announcement meant that the presidential election would determine who would fill the vacant Supreme Court seat—a seat that could determine the balance of power on the high court for decades to come.

Over the next ten months heading into the election, it looked as if McConnell's gamble would backfire. Hillary Clinton would easily defeat Donald Trump and would fill Scalia's seat on the Supreme Court with a progressive along the lines of Ruth Bader Ginsburg or Sonia Sotomayor. This appointment would shift the ideological balance of the court to the left, bringing the "conservative counterrevolution" to a grinding halt and all but foreclosing avenues for Federalist Society influence on Supreme Court jurisprudence. In this alternative timeline, *Ideas with Consequences* would be relegated to historical curiosity, the chronicle of a few decades spanning the late twentieth and early twenty-first century when conservatives controlled the federal judiciary and successfully shaped constitutional meaning and understanding with the help of a then-powerful and influential conservative and libertarian legal network called the Federalist Society.

Instead, in this timeline, with Donald J. Trump as president of the United States, the Federalist Society for Law and Public Policy Studies has reached its zenith in terms of access and influence. Moreover, this access and influence is significantly more visible than it has been in past Republican administrations. Whereas the pages of this book chronicle the subtle, behind-the-scenes manner in which Federalist Society members worked in the George W. Bush administration to influence judicial selection and vetting, the Trump administration has openly and publicly handed over the reins of judicial selection to the Federalist Society network. Even before Trump was sworn into office, his campaign took the unprecedented step of releasing a list of 21 potential Supreme Court nominees—a list curated by multiple Federalist Society network members including Vice President of the Federalist Society Leonard Leo—two months prior to the election with the aim of wooing partisan Republicans who might otherwise be loath to vote for Trump (Hohmann 2016; Malcolm 2017). It worked.

As we political scientists are fond of saying, *elections have consequences.* While now-president Trump has broken, backtracked on, and dissembled about nearly every other promise he made on the campaign trail, he has made good on his promise to appoint judges "in the mold of Justice Scalia," repaying partisan republicans and the Federalist Society network for their loyalty (Adler 2017). With Federalist Society Vice President Leonard Leo at his side, advising him and helping to shepherd his nominees through confirmation, it is no overstatement to say that Trump has changed the face and the ideological balance of the federal judiciary, appointing young, conservative Federalist Society type judges for lifetime terms (Berenson 2018). At the time of writing this preface, just a month removed from the 2018 midterm elections, Trump could claim 84 Article III appointees on the lower federal bench. Again, elections have consequences.

Perhaps most consequentially, Trump has helped the Federalist Society for Law and Public Policy Studies secure a five-Justice majority on the Supreme Court for the first time in history. Just weeks into his term as president, Trump selected long-time Federalist Society member and conservative judge Neil Gorsuch to fill Scalia's seat on the Supreme Court (Gerstein 2017; Toobin 2017; Kruse 2018). In another Federalist Society–friendly twist of fate, in June of 2018, Reagan appointee Anthony Kennedy announced his retirement from the Supreme Court. In addition to being the Supreme Court's last remaining centrist or swing vote, Kennedy was the last remaining Republican-appointed justice on the Supreme Court with no ties to the Federalist Society. Kennedy was replaced with Brett Kavanaugh who, as was well-documented during his extremely controversial confirmation hearings, has long-standing and deep ties to the Federalist Society network (Kruse 2018; Grayer 2018; Swoyer 2018). Brett Kavanaugh joins Federalist Society brethren John Roberts, Clarence Thomas, Samuel Alito, and Neil Gorsuch to form a five-Justice majority conservative voting bloc on the Supreme Court (Feldman 2018). As the late Associate Justice William Brennan was reported to tell every incoming class of law clerks, the "Rule of Five" is the most important rule to learn in Supreme Court jurisprudence because "with five votes, you could accomplish anything" (Stern and Wermiel 2010, 196).

Two-plus years into our new political reality, as the timeline few expected and even fewer predicted continues to unfold, what lessons can scholars, citizens, students, and activists take away from *Ideas with Consequences*? One no longer needs to read this book to know that the Federalist Society has had a central role in judicial selection in Republican administrations. The media has done a thorough job of chronicling this, particularly over the past two years as the Federalist Society has tethered itself quite publicly and visibly to the Trump administration's judicial selection team via Leonard Leo (see, e.g., Toobin 2017).

But in order to truly understand its influence, it is important to recognize that the Federalist Society for Law and Public Policy Studies is more than simply a judicial selection outfit. Yes, it influences that critical part of the constitutional change equation, but as *Ideas with Consequences* demonstrates in painstaking detail, the Federalist Society is also hard at work shaping and influencing the other, less visible but equally as important parts of the equation—providing the ideas and scholarly scaffolding for revolutionary judicial decisions, functioning as a vocal and vigilant judicial audience to help keep conservative judges and Justices in check, and creating a climate conducive to constitutional change by reducing the stigma of once-radical ideas.

Ideas begins from the premise that five or six or even nine Supreme Court Justices cannot, on their own, remake law and constitutional understanding. In other words, William Brennan's "rule of five" is a necessary but not a sufficient condition for revolutionary constitutional change and development. As Charles Epp famously observed, judges cannot wave a wand and make cases appear before them "as if by magic" (1998). They need to wait for the right case, properly framed, to be appealed through the proper channels before they can even put it on their docket. They need lawyers, committed to finding, financing, and bringing the right cases to them. Additionally, as *Ideas* argues, the "giving reasons requirement"— the requirement that judges and Justices justify their decisions in written opinions—opens the door for academics to influence the content of judicial decisions by supplying scholarship or intellectual capital that helps judges support their decisions. So in addition to litigators, judges and Justices also need academics or scholars committed to this work operating outside of the courts to help them justify radical or revolutionary changes in constitutional meaning or development.

The heavy empirical lift of *Ideas with Consequences* is in demonstrating precisely how the Federalist Society, in addition to influencing the necessary condition of getting the right judges and Justices on the federal bench, has evolved to respond to these "supply side" needs to help bring about and facilitate the "conservative counterrevolution" now still under way on the Supreme Court. Instead of grinding to an abrupt halt, as would have happened in the alternative timeline under President Hillary Clinton, we can and should expect the "conservative counterrevolution" in Supreme Court jurisprudence to be pushed farther—that is, into areas it had not yet reached—and deeper into those areas where Kennedy's moderating influence kept decisions from dismantling too much of past precedent or jurisprudence.

How do we know which areas the "conservative counterrevolution" is likely to reach in the coming years with the "Federalist Society Five" now securely in place at the Supreme Court? This is another way in which *Ideas with Consequences* can be instructive. It encourages us to focus not just on the role of the Federalist Society in judicial selection but also on its role in agenda setting, idea generation and development, the testing and refining of legal strategies, and as a networking hub. It instructs us to pay attention not just to the comings and goings of Leonard Leo in the White House but also to Federalist Society conventions, conferences, practice group calls, and meetings. Repeatedly throughout the pages of this book we see how, through its events and programming, the Federalist Society brings together the litigators who will bring the revolutionary cases of the future with the academics whose scholarship will support and justify them with the very judges and Justices who will hear and decide those cases. *Ideas with Consequences* tells us that this is where and how the building blocks for the next phase of the "conservative counterrevolution" will be constructed and gives us some clues as to the shape and direction it might take.

There are other questions that, as exhaustive an analysis as it is, *Ideas with Consequences* does not address and still others it merely waves at. First off, as some reviewers have pointed out—a few with a discernible hint of disappointment—the book does not evaluate or critically interrogate the ideas of the Federalist Society network. It does not dissect them or take them to task. It merely traces the influence of these ideas on some of the most important Supreme Court decisions of the past three decades. I want to emphasize that presenting these conservative and libertarian ideas about the law and constitutional jurisprudence does not imply endorsement or uncritical acceptance of these ideas. However, that wasn't the project I undertook. For those interested in that project, there is a paper trail forty years long of constitutional scholars and theorists writing critiques of Originalism and conservative legal and constitutional jurisprudence and many others—principally those connected with the Federalist Society network—writing in defense of those ideas.

Finally, there are the normative questions I merely gesture at in the final few paragraphs in the Epilogue to *Ideas*. What should we think about the rise of the influence of the Federalist Society? Is it qualitatively different from how things have been done in the past? If so, is it different in a good or a bad way? What does it mean for democracy? I have given dozens of interviews on the Federalist Society and this is the question I have been asked most by reporters. Prior to the rise of Trump, I would recite to reporters what I suggest in the Epilogue of this book—that the Federalist Society is simply a more institutionalized and organized version of the kinds of informal legal networks that have always existed and exerted influence on judicial nominations and decisions. The Federalist Society was the first to figure out how to bottle lightning, so to speak, but the lightning has long been a force in American politics.

I am no longer satisfied with that answer. Something changed when the Trump campaign released its list of 21 potential Supreme Court nominees with the Federalist Society seal attached to it. This action affixed the Federalist Society brand to the Trump campaign—a co-branding made even more visible when Federalist Society Vice President Leonard Leo became the White House advisor for judicial selection. There is palpable discomfort with this alliance between the Trump administration and the privately financed, unaccountable Federalist Society, a self-professed "society of ideas" that is supposed to do no official lobbying or take official policy positions. Concerns about elite capture, which I gesture at in the Epilogue, should be discussed and debated with renewed vigor and attention. With the Trump administration, the Federalist Society is no longer simply bottling lightning, it is manufacturing electricity.

On the other hand, and I think this is the point that has received less attention, what I have just described is actually more transparent than the process has ever been. In the past, judicial selection has been very cloak and dagger, with little public input and knowledge until the nominee was announced. With the Trump administration, everything about judicial selection—from the voter-approved list to the not-so-hidden hand of the Federalist Society—is being done out in the open. This transparency comes with a price, however. Subjecting lists of judges to electoral referenda blurs the ever more tenuous divide between law and politics. It threatens the perceived independence of the judiciary, which will force citizens to question the legitimacy of the rulings that come down from a federal judiciary that is increasingly becoming populated with Trump and Federalist Society–affiliated appointees.

Many on the left have loudly and repeatedly decried the influence of the Federalist Society citing many of the same concerns I just outlined. At the same time, however, left-leaning lawyers have invested a significant amount of money and energy trying to replicate its influence and access with the creation of the American Constitution Society (ACS). As I write in the Epilogue, founded by a handful of liberal lawyers in the wake of the 2000 presidential election in which the Supreme Court by a one-vote margin effectively resolved the election in favor of George W. Bush, the American Constitution Society is identical to the Federalist Society in terms of its institutional form and machinery. For reasons I discuss in the Epilogue, ACS has not appeared to have the same visible influence on judicial nominations in Democratic administrations that its counterpart has had with Republican administrations.

Sometime in the pre-Trump era, at our annual political science conference, I was having a sidebar conversation with Yale Law professor Jack Balkin about the lack of discernible influence the American Constitution Society had on Obama's judicial appointments. He said that in order to rival the influence of the Federalist Society, he believed the left would need to leapfrog the right, be creative, come up a new institutional form rather than trying to replicate what the right has done with the Federalist Society. Professor Balkin's observation seems even more resonant now. Necessity, the mother of innovation, has forced many to reevaluate long-held assumptions, to think creatively about possibilities, to grapple with a game that has different rules or, at times, seems to have no rules at all. I hope scholars, students, activists, and citizens read *Ideas with Consequences* with this in mind. As I have said time and time again to my students, to reporters, to friends and family since the 2016 election, we are in a time of great political possibility, for better or for worse. Ultimately, it will be up to all of us to answer the question of what comes next.

ACKNOWLEDGMENTS

Origin stories about big scholarly projects can be difficult to tell. Scholars struggle to recount the nebulous beginnings, pinpoint the multiple sources of inspiration, and identify the major moments of transformation and revision. The origin story of this book, on the other hand, is rather easy to tell. In April 2006, I presented a paper to faculty and fellow graduate students at a mini-conference held on the University of California–Berkeley's campus. Inspired by a course I had taken with Shannon Stimson, the paper grappled with Stanley Fish's concept of an "interpretive community" as it applied to judges and constitutional interpretation. I wondered how one might operationalize the concept of an interpretive community—how was it bounded, what might it look like, how could we identify its influence? After the presentation, Nelson Polsby waved me over to his seat and uttered the magical words every graduate student longs to hear: "I have a dissertation topic for you." I was all ears. "You should study the Federalist Society as an epistemic community." I nodded, thanked him, and scribbled a note to myself to look up "Federalist Society" and "epistemic community" when I got home. Less than an hour of Internet searching and reading that evening confirmed that, as usual, Nelson Polsby was on to something big and important. Though he passed away less than a year later, this project benefited immensely from his insight, wisdom, and his approach to studying politics and people. The best parts of this book, I am confident, are a reflection of him.

Of course, the project has evolved in significant ways since those early days of graduate school due, in large part, to the helpful advice and suggestions I received from reviewers, conference discussants, and colleagues over the past eight years. In the project's earliest stages, several established scholars took the time to give this fledgling graduate student advice, comments, and encouragement. In particular, I want to thank Jeb Barnes, Thomas Keck, Carol Nackenoff, Lawrence Solum, Ann Southworth, Laura Hatcher, Howard Erlanger, Steve Teles, Cornell Clayton, Mitch Pickerill, Kevin McMahon, Mark Graber, Jonathan Simon, Malcolm Feeley, and Chuck Epp. I am forever grateful and I promise to pay it forward. In transforming this project from dissertation to article to book, I also received helpful comments and suggestions from Austin Sarat, Michael McCann, Laura Beth Nielsen, Jill Weinberg, Josh Wilson, Neil Devins, David Fontana, and Rick Hasen.

I want to thank the Charles and Louise Travers Department of Political Science at UC Berkeley as well as the Phi Beta Kappa Alpha Chapter of Northern California for their financial support. I am also deeply indebted to two important centers at UC Berkeley—the Institute for Governmental Studies and the Center for the Study of Law and Society. The Institute for Governmental Studies provided a home for me as an advanced graduate student and an accelerated education (almost through osmosis) about American politics. In particular, I want to thank my fellow carrel-inhabitants who taught me so much and made the Institute a vibrant and dynamic place to work: Dave Hopkins, Matt Grossman, Jill Greenlee, Rebecca Hamlin, Alison Gash, John Hanley, Mike Salamone, Ben Krupicka, John Henderson, Devin Caughey, Lee Drutman, Andrew Kelley, Chloe Thurston, Adrienne Hosek, Loan Le, Bruce Huber, Alex Theodoridis, Abby Wood, and Matt Wright. I was also fortunate to be awarded the Institute's Mike Synar Fellowship for Research in American Politics, which provided financial assistance for the researching of this book.

The Center for the Study of Law and Society was an invaluable resource for me throughout all stages of this project. Its workshops provided me with a crash course in socio-legal research approaches, ethnography, and interviewing—skills on which I relied heavily in carrying out the research for this book. The Center also gave me training in Atlas.ti, the qualitative data management program that I used to manage, code, and analyze the thousands of primary sources I gathered for this project. Finally, through the Center's Visiting Scholars program, I was able to spend my post-doctoral year on campus revising the dissertation, collecting additional data for the book, and connecting with scholars doing fascinating work in socio-legal studies. I want to say a special thanks to the Center's Executive Director Rosann Greenspan for continuing to support my affiliation with the Center, as well as to Calvin Morrill and Laurie Edelman for the education they provided me.

Beyond the institutional support I received at UC Berkeley, I owe an immeasurable debt to the faculty and fellow graduate students with whom I shared the campus. Shannon Stimson and Mark Bevir introduced me to material and readings that profoundly shaped my thinking about this project in critical ways early on. I am particularly grateful to Shannon for being such a wonderful advisor and strong professional role model. Daniel Farber's enthusiasm for the project gave me confidence that I was doing something important, and his connections helped open doors for me in the research process. I also benefited from comments and conversations with Jack Citrin, Terri Bimes, Eric Shickler, and Sean Farhang. Interactions with my fellow graduate student colleagues influenced this project in more ways than I can acknowledge. In particular, I want to thank my friend and colleague Veronica Herrera, who gave up so many late nights with her family to talk with me about this project and whose advice and suggestions always made it better.

When it comes to UC Berkeley, I am obliged here to single out and acknowledge two people who gave more to me and to this project than I could ever possibly have expected—Gordon Silverstein and Robert A. Kagan. Though they occupy different corners of the Public Law world, each of them has had a profound and identifiable impact on my thinking, my work, and my professional development. Studying under Gordon and Bob, I first discovered my love of constitutional law and legal institutions, respectively. I also learned the importance of thinking about law and politics together, rather than separately. As their teaching assistant, I learned how to be an engaged and dedicated teacher and mentor of students. As dissertation advisors, they were a perfect complement to one another— yin and yang. Bob, who has become legendary for his marginalia and detailed and thorough draft comments, gave an almost super-human amount of attention to the details of the thesis and challenged me to more rigorously support every claim I made. Meanwhile, Gordon encouraged me to think big and helped me pull my head out of the weeds long enough to recognize how my case studies informed broader themes and dynamics in American politics and constitutional development. I can say with absolute confidence that this is a vastly better book because I had the opportunity to work with both of them.

I also want to acknowledge my wonderful colleagues at the Claremont Colleges, in particular, David Menefee-Libey, Rachel Van Sickle-Ward, Heidi Haddad, and Pam Bromley, who took time out of their schedules to read drafts, provide suggestions, and act as ever-present sounding boards, and Susan McWilliams, whose mentorship and friendship has helped me navigate all things professional and political at Pomona College. And then there are my ever-impressive and inspiring students—I am so fortunate to be able to work with and learn from some of the best and brightest young men and women in the country. I owe a special thanks to all my research assistants ("Go Team HB!") who spent their summers and spare hours throughout the semester gathering and coding data for this book: Tommy Conkling, Danny Hirsch, Ethan Grossman, Larkin Corrigan, Evan Slovak, Sarah Laws, Christina Tong, Joanmarie Del Vecchio, and Jerry Yan. I also want to thank Pomona College, the Sponsored Research office, and the

Summer Undergraduate Research Program for generously funding all of these students to work on this project for the past three years.

My editors at Oxford University Press, David McBride and Sarah Rosenthal, handled the manuscript with care, respect, and professionalism at all stages of the process. I also want to thank the series editor Steven Teles for his careful attention to the manuscript, his responsiveness to requests and questions, and for seeking out and selecting terrific reviewers. Their suggestions and comments improved the manuscript by leaps and bounds, especially Chapter 1. I also have to take time to thank the Federalist Society and American Constitution Society members in Berkeley, Washington, D.C., Chicago, and San Diego who agreed to be interviewed as part of this project. In addition to giving me their valuable time, they entrusted their stories to me. I have done my best throughout the book to honor that trust and repay it through accurate and careful accounts. In particular I want to thank Steven Calabresi, David McIntosh, Randy Barnett, Chuck Cooper, Doug Kmiec, Michael Greve, Eugene Meyer, Edwin Meese, Robert Post, and Goodwin Liu for being so generous with their time and for making themselves available for follow-up questions after the initial interview.

Finally, I have to acknowledge my family. This book belongs to them as much as it does to me. My working-class parents inspired in their daughter grit, tenacity, a strong work ethic, and the ambition to pursue a college education. They lived beyond their means to keep me in good public schools and encouraged me every step of the way. I am also humbled and inspired by my brother, Staff Sargeant Jonathan Hollis, whose courage and service help me keep a perspective on the things that matter, and by my grandmother, Lee Hollis, whose strength and resilience never cease to impress me. Lastly, I am grateful for my husband, Sean, whose patience with and unwavering support for me and my career has made all of this possible, and for my brilliant daughters, Annabelle and Eloise, who fill me with pride and infuse everything I do with a profound sense of purpose and meaning.

Introduction

In 1948, conservative intellectual Richard S. Weaver published a 200-page treatise on the decline of Western civilization. He entitled this treatise *Ideas Have Consequences*.[1] Though the book's contributions to modern conservative thought were modest, the phrase "ideas have consequences" became an important and oft-repeated mantra for a group of young ideological lawyers who came to Washington, D.C., in the 1980s to help carry out the "Reagan Revolution." There, working alongside the attorney general and others, these young lawyers helped lay the intellectual groundwork for what would become the "conservative counterrevolution" in the law. Thirty years later, as a conservative majority on the Supreme Court ushers in an era of "conservative renaissance" (Avery and McLaughlin 2013, 7), the phrase "ideas have consequences" continues to be the calling card of the organization founded and led by this same group of lawyers to help bring that counterrevolution about—the Federalist Society for Law and Public Policy Studies.

Launched in 1982 by a small group of conservative and libertarian law students at Yale Law School and the University of Chicago Law School, the Federalist Society was founded to provide an alternative to the perceived liberal orthodoxy that dominated the law school curriculum, the professoriate, and most legal institutions at the time (Teles 2008, 138). Two of the principal founders—Steven Calabresi and Lee Liberman Otis—had worked on the Reagan campaign before coming to law school, and they had identified a profound mismatch between the conservative and libertarian views that had achieved political and electoral ascendancy and their elite law school campuses, which were still very left-wing and openly hostile to these ideas. It was in response to this frustration, and in the hopes of facilitating a friendlier environment for conservative and libertarian law students and ideas, that the first Federalist Society Student Chapters were organized. With modest funding and organizational support from a few other right-leaning law student groups, the chapters hosted a national symposium at Yale in the spring of 1982. The symposium brought together top conservative intellectual luminaries such as Robert Bork, Richard Posner, Charles Fried, Ralph Winter, Michael W. McConnell, and Antonin Scalia (at that time a law professor at the University of Chicago). The preface to the transcript, which reads like a call to arms for embattled conservatives and libertarians, is indicative of the tenor of the event: "At a time when the nation's law schools are staffed largely by professors who dream of regulating from their cloistered offices every minute detail of our lives... the Federalists met—and proclaimed the virtues of individual freedom and of limited government" (Hicks 2006, 652). *National Review* magazine—one of the leading conservative publications of the time—covered the event, which spurred phone calls from dozens of students at law schools across the country inquiring about how to set up their own chapter of the Federalist Society.

The founders of the Federalist Society Student Chapters quickly realized that they had tapped into a high-demand market. As Steven Teles describes it, "[c]onservative law students alienated in their home institutions, desperate for a collective identity, and eager for collective activity provided a ripe opportunity for organizational entrepreneurship" (Teles 2008, 139). Within the first decade of founding the national organization, the number of Student Chapters at law schools grew to just over 150, while the operating budget of the Federalist Society increased from roughly $100,000 to $1.6 million. Over the course of its second decade, responding in part to its law student alumni who had graduated and entered the legal profession, the organization actively extended its reach beyond the law schools. During that time, the Federalist Society established practicing Lawyers Chapters in every major city, launched its Practice Group program, and increased its operating budget to just over $6 million (Teles 2008, 148–149). As it enters its fourth decade, the Federalist Society has matured into a nationwide network of more than 40,000 academics, practitioners, judges, politicians, and law students dedicated to reshaping America's institutions to reflect conservative and libertarian values. With annual revenues around $10 million and with the continuing support of prominent conservative and libertarian foundations and donors such as John Olin, Lynde and Harry Bradley, Richard Scaife, and the Koch family (Avery and McLaughlin 2013, 16–17), the Federalist Society has constructed a formidable conservative and libertarian counter-elite—a network of individuals shaped by a common set of beliefs, a canon of shared texts, and a desire to reformulate the law and legal institutions in accordance with these beliefs.

To wit, at the Federalist Society's Thirtieth Anniversary Convention in 2012, Vice President Leonard S. Leo took stock of all that the conservative legal movement had accomplished since the 1980s, and the important role that the Federalist Society network had played in that movement. Reflecting on three decades of the Federalist Society, he remarked that its success could be attributed to the tens of thousands of members who "choose to be citizen-lawyers by taking up service in government or in the judiciary, by becoming active in pro bono litigation or public policy activity, by teaching, or simply by helping to generate this institution's important educational products."[2] A glance at the program for the Thirtieth Anniversary Convention confirms the prominence and prestige of many of the Federalist Society "citizen-lawyers" to whom Leo referred in his address. Among those donning tuxedos and gowns at the event were Supreme Court Justice Samuel Alito, United States Senators Ted Cruz (R-TX) and Mike Lee (R-UT), twenty United States Court of Appeals judges (notably among those were future Supreme Court Justices Brett Kavanaugh and Neil Gorsuch), one former solicitor general, and dozens of leading libertarian and conservative intellectuals. While not featured on the 2012 program, Supreme Court Justices Antonin Scalia, Clarence Thomas, and John G. Roberts, Jr., also have well-documented and long-standing ties to the Federalist Society network.[3]

While the list of prominent and powerful participants has prompted journalists and politicians on the left to refer to the Federalist Society as a "vast right-wing conspiracy," the Federalist Society itself actually does very little in terms of direct legal and political engagement. Animated by the belief that ideas *can* and *do* have consequences, the Federalist Society's focus has been on training and shaping its members through intellectual engagement, networking conservative and libertarian legal elites, and facilitating opportunities for members to put their shared legal principles into practice as "citizen-lawyers." Because of this, Steven M. Teles has argued that the Federalist Society should be understood as a "provider of public goods for the conservative legal movement" (Teles 2008, 136), while Ann Southworth has described it as a "mediator organization" for various cross-cutting coalitions within the movement (Southworth 2008, 130–148). While journalists, social scientists, lawyers, and politicians universally agree that the Federalist Society is an important organization, its method of indirect versus direct influence—training, educating, and networking versus lobbying, litigating, and endorsing political candidates—has made the scope of its influence difficult to pinpoint.

The social scientific framework that I develop in the pages of this book represents an innovative effort to capture and chronicle the kinds of influence that the Federalist Society network exerts and, further, to identify and explore the conditions that have enabled it to do so. It respects the fluid, network structure of the Federalist Society, as described in great detail in Southworth's work. It also provides a clear methodology and research agenda for investigating how particular Federalist Society members used the "goods" or "capital" (Teles 2008) generated by the Society to influence Supreme Court decisions in concrete cases. Additionally, it highlights the Federalist Society's role as a vocal and effective "judicial audience" (Baum 2006), keeping judges and Justices from drifting from their conservative and libertarian principles once on the bench. In so doing, this book provides a valuable framework for understanding the influence of the Federalist Society for Law and Public Policy Studies as well as similar organizations or networks—past, present, and future.

Ideas with Consequences extends previous work I have published on this topic (Hollis-Brusky 2013) that analyzed the conditions under which Federalist Society network members had been successful in diffusing ideas or *intellectual capital* to Supreme Court decision makers in federalism and separation of powers cases. The following chapters apply the same kind of analysis but expand the scope of the study to include cases on the Second Amendment ("the right to keep and bear arms"), and the First Amendment ("the freedom of speech"), as applicable to campaign finance regulations. My selection of these constitutional areas follows from the principal finding of my earlier work, which is that the Federalist Society network was most influential in cases where the Supreme Court took a big step away from their established constitutional framework; that is, cases where *doctrinal distance* was greatest (Hollis-Brusky 2013). Similarly, I find that in each of the landmark cases I examine in this book—cases that represent "critical junctures" (Pierson 2000) in constitutional jurisprudence—members of the Federalist Society functioned as active conduits for idea transmission. The intellectual capital they supplied through their legal briefs and written scholarship helped the Supreme Court majority justify these revolutionary constitutional decisions in their written opinions. As I argue, how these written opinions are crafted and justified is critically important for law and policy development because these opinions shape, constrain, and direct the behavior of future courts, lower courts, legislators, and other policy entrepreneurs in the American political system (Shapiro 2002; Silverstein 2009). Additionally, in Chapter 6, I show how the Federalist Society network helped foster and facilitate a climate conducive to constitutional change. In other words, not only did it take advantage of these critical junctures in constitutional jurisprudence by providing intellectual capital to decision-makers when they were ready to revise or reconstruct constitutional frameworks, this network also actively worked to bring about those critical junctures in the first place.

Chapter 1 details my research approach and lays out an argument for why a slightly modified version of the epistemic community framework—what I am calling a *political epistemic network* (PEN)—is the most appropriate for understanding and investigating Federalist Society influence. I argue that while the epistemic community framework captures the fluid network structure of the Federalist Society and places an appropriate emphasis on the ideas and shared language of its members as the means of tracing network connections and influence, it does not adequately account for the politically constructed dimensions of legal knowledge, legal authority, and the path-dependent nature of legal precedent. Further, the epistemic community model, as it has been developed and deployed, does not account for the Federalist Society's role as a powerful and vocal "judicial audience" (Baum 2006)—a role that has been important in keeping judges and Justices aligned with the network's views and shared beliefs once on the bench. Because of the path-dependent nature of law and the non-refutable disposition of legal and constitutional interpretations, this has also had the additional effect of further entrenching the network's shared beliefs. This added dimension of influence is more fully developed and captured in the PEN model. Chapter 1 also demonstrates how the Federalist Society is bound by a simple but powerful set of principles: *that the state exists to preserve freedom, that the separation of governmental powers is central to our Constitution, and that it is emphatically the province and duty of the judiciary to say what the law is, not what it should be.*[4] I use these same principles to structure and organize the narratives of Federalist Society network influence contained in the book.

THE STATE EXISTS TO PRESERVE FREEDOM

Chapters 2 and 3 examine the role that the Federalist Society network and its members have played in fundamentally redefining the constitutional relationship between the person (human or corporate) and the state in two important areas. These areas include the Second Amendment and the right to keep and bear arms (*District of Columbia v. Heller* (2008); *McDonald v. City of Chicago* (2010)), and the First Amendment and restrictions on political speech (*FEC v. Wisconsin Right to Life* (2007); *Citizens United v. FEC* (2010)). While dealing with different constitutional questions and issues, what binds these together for members of the Federalist Society network is a forceful critique of the role of the state vis-à-vis the person and the perceived erosion of freedom from strangling regulation. Chapter 2 details the decades-long campaign to lobby the Supreme Court to adopt, for the first time in history, a personal rights view of the Second Amendment's guarantee of the right to keep and bear arms. As the chapter illustrates in detail, the Federalist Society and its members helped support and sustain the campaign to reinterpret the Second Amendment in a radical manner, even when this interpretation was deemed "loony" or "off the wall" by many within the mainstream legal academy. Similarly, Chapter 3 examines how Federalist Society network members helped build the path that led to the revolutionary decision in *Citizens United* to extend First Amendment protections to corporations in the area of political speech—a decision that seriously weakened existing campaign finance regulations and opened the floodgates for money in elections.

THE SEPARATION OF GOVERNMENTAL POWERS IS CENTRAL TO OUR CONSTITUTION

Chapters 4 and 5 shift focus from the relationship between the state and the individual to constitutional concerns about the relationship between the federal government and the states. These chapters examine Federalist Society influence on one aspect of the "separation of governmental powers"—federalism. Federalist Society network members view our system of divided government in general, and of dual federalism in particular, as one of the most important safeguards for individual liberty built into the structure of our Constitution. In these chapters, I examine the extent to which the Federalist Society network has reshaped the Supreme Court's understanding of the federal commerce power (*New York v. United States* (1992); *United States v. Lopez* (1995); *United States v. Morrison* (2000)) and state sovereignty (*Printz v. United States* (1997); *NFIB et al. v. Sebelius* (2012)). Chapter 4 examines how key network members provided the intellectual capital for some of the most important cases in the Supreme Court's "New Federalism" revolution—cases that resulted in a meaningful narrowing of the federal commerce power for the first time in fifty years. Chapter 5 describes how many of these same network members helped fabricate out of whole cloth a new Tenth Amendment doctrine— the "Anti-Commandeering Doctrine"—that has had the practical effect of limiting the scope and reach of federal power to regulate the implementation of background checks for gun purchases and the expansion of Medicaid through the 2010 Affordable Care Act.[5]

IT IS THE DUTY OF THE JUDICIARY TO SAY WHAT THE LAW IS, NOT WHAT IT SHOULD BE

The final chapter of this book, Chapter 6, aggregates insights drawn from preceding chapters but also expands the scope of the analysis to situate these insights within a body of scholarship on constitutional change and on the role of "support structures" (Epp 1998; Southworth 2008; Teles 2008; Hollis-Brusky 2011a) in that process. It identifies some of the critical ways in which the Federalist Society network has both (1) shaped the content, direction, and character of constitutional revolutions by supporting, developing, and diffusing intellectual capital to Supreme Court decision-makers; and (2) helped foster the conditions that facilitate those constitutional revolutions in the first place by (a) identifying, credentialing, and getting the right kinds of judges and Justices on the bench, (b) acting as a vocal and respected judicial audience (Baum 2006) to keep those judges and Justices in check once on the bench, and (c) creating an intellectual and political climate that is favorable to the desired change by reducing the stigma associated with once-radical ideas or constitutional theories. In effectively performing this dual function, I argue, the Federalist Society has had remarkable success implementing the third prong of its statement of principles: *that it is emphatically the province and duty of the judiciary is say what* [they believe] *the law is, not what* [others believe] *it should be.* The Epilogue suggests an agenda for future research, focusing on how the insights presented in this book might comprise a tentative rubric for evaluating the influence of PENs in prior constitutional revolutions and also for evaluating the potential and prospective successes of the self-proclaimed progressive counterpart to the Federalist Society for Law and Public Policy Studies—the American Constitution Society for Law and Policy.

Ideas with Consequences is a book about the Federalist Society for Law and Public Policy Studies—about its ideas, networks, and influences. It is also, in part, an intellectual history of the "conservative counterrevolution" currently underway on the Supreme Court. It shows how the constitutional theories and intellectual capital used to undergird some of the most radical decisions of this counterrevolution were nurtured and developed over decades by intellectuals supported by and connected through the Federalist Society network. But, if this book can be considered an intellectual history of the current Supreme Court, then it must be viewed as a partial and incomplete history. For, as Vice President Leonard S. Leo reminded everyone at the Federalist Society's Thirtieth Anniversary Convention, the Federalist Society's army of "citizen-lawyers" is motivated, refreshed, and poised to push the counterrevolution deeper and farther in the years and decades to come.[6]

Finally, and most important, this is a book about the dynamics of constitutional change and the roles that "support structures" (Epp 1998) play in that process. Implicit in the narrative presented in the chapters that follow is a strong endorsement for scholars, students, and observers of

American law and politics to pay more attention to the sometimes subtle but always important ways that actors outside the Supreme Court (and, indeed, outside government altogether) can help bring about and shape constitutional revolutions. As I have argued elsewhere (Hollis-Brusky 2011a), supplementing the theories of constitutional change currently dominant in the academy with more attention to the activities and influence of groups and actors within the support structure will provide us with a better understanding of the processes of constitutional change. The question of how this happens—and who influences it—is of critical importance to scholars, citizens, and students of American politics alike, as the high-stakes outcomes of these processes ultimately determine what our Constitution, our statutes, and, in short, the structure of our political life itself will look like.

CHAPTER 1

Understanding Federalist Society Network Influence

[The Federalist Society has] trained, now, two generations of lawyers who are active around the country as civic leaders. Implicit in that is the Tocquevillian notion of lawyers being important for the community and society and so that's going to be untold ways in which notions of Originalism, of limited government, of the rule of law, are being implemented in thousands of decisions at various levels of government and the community outside of government. Putting them in place means we'll have fifty years of seeing what that actually means for impact.
  —David McIntosh, cofounder of the Federalist Society[1]

The Federalist Society for Law and Public Policy Studies does not fit comfortably into any of the social science boxes that students of American politics traditionally use to study the impact of civic groups on law and politics. Unlike a public interest law firm, it does not find, finance, or staff litigation campaigns (though its individual members do). Dissimilar from an interest group, it does not lobby Congress, support judicial or political candidates, or officially participate in litigation as *amici curiae* (though its individual members do). Moreover, unlike a think tank, it does not have a full-time staff of residents paid to publish position papers designed to advance or endorse a particular policy position (though its members do this, too). What the Federalist Society *does* do, as the excerpt from cofounder David McIntosh alludes to, is educate and train its members through sponsored events and conferences, to shape and socialize them intellectually and professionally in a particular way, and to encourage them to draw on this training as they carry out their work as legal professionals, academics, judges, government officials, and civic leaders. It is important to note that the Federalist Society Executive Office would not claim credit for how its members or alumni apply the intellectual training that it offers. This, as Steven M. Teles noted, has been an important part of the organization's strategy of "boundary mainte-nance" (Teles 2008, 152). At the same time, its founding and core mem-bers do not *dis*claim credit for what Federalist Society network actors and alumni do outside the walls of conferences and events. There are thou-sands of "untold ways" in which these individuals go on to shape legal doctrine and policy in accord with organizational principles and priori-ties. For example, cofounder Steven Calabresi described the Federalist Society's core purpose and impact to me in precisely these terms:

> I think my own goal for the Federalist Society has been... [to] have an organization that will create a network of alumni who have been shaped in a particular way....
> [B]ecause many of our members are right of center and because they tend to be inter-ested in public policy and politics, a lot of them go on to do jobs in government and take positions in government where they become directly involved in policymaking. So I think it's fair to say that Federalist Society alumni who go into government have tended to push public policy in a libertarian–conservative direction.[2]

It is this peculiar dynamic—the oft-blurred line between what the orga-nization does and what its members do—that has made the Federalist Society for Law and Public Policy Studies so resistant to the labels and boxes developed by students and observers of American politics and has prompted several of its own members to classify it as *sui generis*.[3]

While I take seriously the claim that the Federalist Society might be *sui generis*, this description of what the Federalist Society network is and what it does bears a strong resemblance to what scholars of international relations have referred to as an *epistemic community* (EC). A close cousin of Thomas Kuhn's concept of a "scientific paradigm" (Kuhn 1970) and Ludwig Fleck's idea of a "thought collective" (Fleck 1979), an EC has been defined as a network of professionals with expertise in a particular policy area bound together by a shared set of normative and principled beliefs, shared causal beliefs, shared notions of validity, and a common policy enterprise, who actively work to translate these beliefs into policy (Haas 1992, 3; Cross 2013, 20). Initially developed in the international relations literature to understand the influence of technocrats and scien-tific experts on the development and coordination of international policy (see, e.g., Haas 1992; Sebenius 1992; Yee 1996; Cross 2013), the EC con-struct is a good fit in some ways for understanding the influence of the Federalist Society network, but not in others.[4] Structurally, an EC and what I am calling a *political epistemic network* (PEN) look nearly identi-cal: an interconnected network of experts with policy-relevant knowledge who share certain beliefs and work to actively transmit and translate those beliefs into policy. This is why, as I will explain in a few paragraphs, the research design and logic of the EC model is still appropriate for investigating PEN influence on policy development.

The primary distinctions to be drawn between the EC and PEN models have to do with the kinds of knowledge networks each concept seeks to model (scientific/technocratic versus legal/constitutional). Law is not like science, and lawyers and judges are not like technocrats. Claims to legal knowledge are non-refutable, always politically contested, and depend more on the authority and power of the speakers and their institutional positions than they do on the persuasiveness or objective truth of the knowledge itself (see, e.g., Fish 1980, 1989; Balkin and Levison 2001). A scientific or technocratic EC can be proven wrong empirically and its knowledge claims refuted. Such evidence would not guarantee but would certainly increase the likelihood that ECs could supplant one another. As Haas writes in his seminal theoretical article on epistemic communities, "If confronted with anomalies that undermined their causal beliefs," ECs "would withdraw from policy debate, unlike interest groups" (Haas 1992, 18; Toke 1999, 99). This is not the case with a PEN, whose knowledge claims and authority are derived from contested interpretations of political texts and meanings, such as those found in the Constitution. A PEN temporarily can be displaced and rendered powerless by the emergence of a rival PEN whose members more effectively have infiltrated positions of political power and decision-making. However, that PEN can continue to contest from the outside, working to adapt and better legitimate and market its own knowledge claims while still actively trying to place its own network members into positions of power and authority. This also means that PENs can and do modify their beliefs so as to better achieve their normative goals and shared vision of the proper arrangement of social and political life—another important distinction between a PEN and an EC. Thus, beliefs ("principled," "causal," and notions of "validity") in the PEN model should be understood as strategic and instrumental rather than sincere and objectively grounded, as they are often characterized in the EC model (Haas 1992; Gough and Shackley 2001, 331–332; Dumoulin 2003, 595). What makes the PEN's beliefs widely held and shared among network members is acknowledged and agreed-upon political value. The addition of "political" to the PEN model recognizes this and highlights the heightened political dimensions of legal knowledge and authority. Moreover, the dropping of "community" in favor of "network" in the definition signifies the important role the PEN plays in actively and consciously credentialing and placing its members into positions of political power—a function that I examine in greater length in Chapter 6.

With those small but important conceptual distinctions noted, because of the structural similarities between the PEN and the EC, the basic logic of the EC approach and the general research design developed in the international relations literature to investigate EC influence are still appropriate and translatable to the American legal-political context. The logic is straightforward: as decision-makers face an increasing number of difficult or complex policy decisions, they will tend to seek support from experts as sources of authoritative knowledge. This opens the door for well-coordinated groups of knowledgeable experts—ECs or PENs, with formal or informal ties to decision-makers—to frame, filter, or shape the outcome of the decision-making process according to their own shared beliefs, principles, or values (Sundstrom 2000, 4). In this way, both ECs and PENs can be understood as "channels through which new ideas circulate from societies to governments," with their individual members acting as "cognitive baggage handlers" whose activities and movements inside and outside government make that transmission possible (Haas 1992, 27).

Importing this logic and applying it to the American legal-political context, we can see certain institutional and political characteristics that might facilitate inroads for PENs in the judicial policymaking process. As Steven M. Teles argues in the context of his own work on the rise of the conservative legal movement, the American legal enterprise has become increasingly "complex, technical, and professionalized," which also means that it has become "acutely sensitive to the increasing significance of ideas, information, networks, [and] issue framing" (Teles 2008, 9–10). Thus, to carry out their work, legal and judicial decision-makers often rely on the broader legal community for intellectual support. This is particularly so in the case of judicial decision-makers whose written opinions and decisions need to persuade legal elites—and, through them, the public at large—in order to be considered authoritative. Legal scholar Martin Shapiro famously referred to this as the "giving reasons requirement" (Shapiro 2002). Unlike legislators who simply vote according to their policy preferences, judges and Justices are required to issue written opinions explaining, supporting, and defending their decisions in the language of the law. In order to persuade an audience of similarly educated and trained lawyers and politicians that their decisions are legitimate, these opinions must situate the given decision within a line of established precedent—that is, within an accepted constitutional framework—or, alternatively, they must provide a convincing argument for why that framework should either be ignored, altered, or reconstructed entirely (Silverstein 2009, 64; Hollis-Brusky 2013, 165). Thus, the importance of the persuasive function of the court is heightened in cases where the Supreme Court is altering or reconstructing existing constitutional frames—cases where *doctrinal distance* is greatest.

By working to legitimize a set of ideas in the legal profession, PENs make it easier for judicial decision-makers who share these beliefs to articulate them in their opinions without the fear of being perceived as illegitimate. In this way, the PEN provides an important kind of "cultural capital" within the broader legal and political community (Teles 2008, 136). At the same time, the goal of the PEN is political infiltration; as a PEN consolidates its power within government by placing its members in key positions as advisors or as decision-makers, it stands to institutionalize its influence and ideas. As legal scholar Jack M. Balkin writes, "[t]he more powerful and influential the people who are willing to make a legal argument, the more quickly it moves from the 'positively loony' to the 'positively thinkable,' and ultimately to something entirely consistent with 'good legal craft'" (Balkin 2001, 1444–1445; Teles 2008, 12). This has the related consequence of making competing sets of beliefs, values, and techniques—which at one point might have been dominant within the legal profession—seem illegitimate. This function is particularly important in the context of law and legal interpretation, where the meaning and dominant understandings of texts like the Constitution are politically contested in perpetuity and are subject to interpretation. Hence, as I wrote earlier, authority cannot and does not derive simply from the objective meaning or truth of a PEN's claim, but rather from the position, power, and influence of the persons articulating that claim and translating it into policy and governing rules.

THE FEDERALIST SOCIETY AS A POLITICAL EPISTEMIC NETWORK

By modifying Peter M Haas's definition of an EC (see Table 1.1), a PEN can be defined as an interconnected network of professionals with expertise or knowledge in a particular domain, bound together by the following four characteristics: a shared vision of the proper arrangement of social and political life (shared principled and normative beliefs); shared beliefs, largely instrumental, about how to best realize that vision (shared causal beliefs); shared interpretations of politically contested texts (shared notions of validity); and a common policy project, broadly defined. In the paragraphs that follow, I demonstrate how the Federalist Society network realizes each of these criteria.

Who are the 40,000 plus conservative and libertarian legal actors currently affiliated with and connected through the Federalist Society's burgeoning professional network? About one-fourth of these individuals, 10,000 total, are law students and select other undergraduate and

Table 1.1 THE EPISTEMIC COMMUNITY AND MODIFIED POLITICAL EPISTEMIC NETWORK CRITERIA

		Shared principled/normative beliefs	Shared causal beliefs	Shared notions of validity	Common policy enterprise
Definition of *Epistemic Community* (EC)	Network of professionals with expert knowledge				
Modifications for *Political Epistemic Network* (PEN)	Same	Shared vision of the proper arrangement of social and political life	Shared beliefs (instrumental) about how to best realize that vision	Shared interpretations of politically contested texts	Same
The Federalist Society for Law and Public Policy Studies	The Society's chapter-based membership network, at 40,000 strong, extends to all levels of the legal community.	The State exists to preserve freedom; the role of the judiciary is to say what the law is, not what it should be.	The separation of governmental powers is central to the Constitution and a precondition for individual liberty.	Originalism is the only interpretive method consistent with a proper understanding of the nature of government and the structure of the Constitution.	To promote an awareness of conservative and libertarian legal principles and to further their application throughout all levels of the legal community.

professional students participating in one of 200 Student Chapter groups. With financial and programming assistance from the National Office, these chapters host on average 1,000 events annually that draw close to 48,000 students across the various campuses. The Lawyers Division of the Federalist Society, with its 75 chapters in all major cities, 15 professional Practice Groups, Faculty Division spin-off, and Speakers Bureau, is home to the other 30,000 members. As Steven M. Teles described, with the exception of its two national meetings, all of the Federalist Society's supported activities and events are conducted in its "student chapters (in law schools), lawyer chapters (by city), and Practice Groups (organized by functional interest)" (Teles 2008, 148).

As the Federalist Society website claims, their network of conservative and libertarian actors "interested in the current state of the legal order" presently "extends to all levels of the legal community."[5] Evidence gathered from speaker lists at Federalist Society National Meetings from 1982 to 2011 provides a more descriptive picture of what this network actually looks like. By coding the speaker lists for occupation and aggregating the results, we get a sense not only of the range of representation from different levels of the legal and political community at Federalist Society National Meetings but also of the relative rates of participation by conservative and libertarian actors occupying different career roles within the legal-political complex.[6]

Figure 1.1 provides a visual illustration of the results and corroborates the statement of the Executive Office as well as the impressions excerpted in the beginning of this chapter by cofounder Dave McIntosh that the

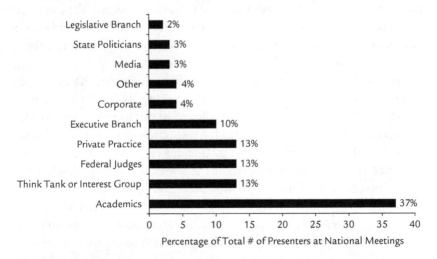

Figure 1.1 Presenters at Federalist Society National Meetings by Professional Occupation, 1982–2011

Federalist Society network, indeed, extends to all levels of the legal and political community. For an organization that started in 1982 as a small group of law students situated in what they perceived to be a "hostile institution, America's law schools" (Teles 2008, 137), the fact that academics still account for more than a third (37%) of presenters at Federalist Society National Meetings is unsurprising. The next four largest groups are legal and political actors representing a think tank or interest group (13%), federal judges (13%), lawyers in private practice (13%), and individuals working in the executive branch of government (10%). Finally, as can be seen from the graphic, Federalist Society National Meetings draw a much smaller but consistent number of actors representing corporate America (4%), conservative and libertarian press and media (3%), state or local politics (3%), and the federal legislative branch (2%).

On a very basic structural level, the Federalist Society for Law and Public Policy certainly satisfies the PEN criterion of being an interconnected network of professionals with expertise or knowledge in a particular domain—in this case, the law. With members situated throughout the legal-political community, including the relatively large number of participants representing the federal judiciary and the executive branch of government, the Federalist Society would seem to be in a good position to have the kind of functional PEN impact described earlier in this chapter. Indeed, when I asked member and frequent participant Gail Heriot to locate the source of the Federalist Society's influence, she simply responded: "Like Verizon, it's the network."[7] Showing that the Federalist Society has the requisite number of well-positioned "boots on the ground," as Federalist Society network member Michael Greve articulated it, is only the first step.[8] The more important task is to demonstrate that actors within this network are shaped by a set of normative and causal beliefs that would inform the actions and decisions of network members as they carry out their work as legal professionals.

The most logical place to start looking for evidence of shared beliefs among network members is the Federalist Society's official statement of principles: "[The Federalist Society] is founded on the principles that the state exists to preserve freedom, that the separation of governmental powers is central to our Constitution, and that it is emphatically the province and duty of the judiciary to say what the law is, not what it should be."[9] This sentence, co-authored by cofounders Lee Liberman Otis, David McIntosh, and Steven Calabresi in 1982 when the organization was still in its infancy, represents a short but powerful statement of conservative and libertarian legal principles. By unpacking this statement, we can see how it incorporates several important normative, principled, and causal beliefs shared by Federalist Society network members. Additionally, it alludes to the existence of a shared notion of interpretive "validity," which is yet another critical criterion for the existence of a PEN.

The first belief listed in the Federalist Society's statement of principles, that the "state exists to preserve freedom," represents a fusionist[10] understanding of the role and responsibility of government vis-à-vis the individual. Frank S. Meyer, the philosophical father of fusionism—and the biological father of Federalist Society Executive Director Eugene Meyer—was a "staunch individualist" who, believing that individual freedom was the primary end of political action, argued that "the State" had only three, limited functions: "national defense, the preservation of domestic order, and the administration of justice between individuals" (Edwards 2007, 2). This belief in a necessary but necessarily limited role for government, some conservatives have argued, was a principal concern of James Madison, the same Founding Father whose silhouette graces the Federalist Society for Law and Public Policy's logo. Madison's fusionist understanding of the role of government, founded on "a profound mistrust of man and of men panoplied as the state" (Edwards 2007, 3) is articulated most famously in *The Federalist 51* (Rossiter ed., 1961):

> "If men were angels, no government would be necessary. If angels were to govern men, neither external nor internal controls on government would be necessary. In framing a government to be administered by men over men, the great difficulty lies in this: you must first enable the government to control the governed; and in the next place oblige it to control itself."

This is also—perhaps unsurprisingly given the canonical status of James Madison among Federalist Society members—one of the most oft-quoted and referenced passages from *The Federalist* among Federalist Society participants.[11]

Placed in the context of this first principled belief, the second principle listed in the Federalist Society's statement, that "the separation of governmental powers is central to our Constitution," can be understood as a causal or instrumental belief derived from this fusionist understanding of the role of government. In other words, members of the Federalist Society believe that the separation of powers is the best and perhaps only condition under which their shared principled belief in limited government and individual freedom can be properly realized. Federalist Society participant and co-author of the Society's *Annotated Bibliography of Conservative and Libertarian Legal Scholarship*, Roger Clegg, articulated the relationship between these beliefs in the following manner: "One of the things [Federalist Society members] have in common is a strong belief in individual liberty and that's the reason we have the separation of powers and division of powers, federalism, is to protect individual rights and liberties."[12] Evidence of a strong concern for the preservation of the separation of powers is not difficult to find among other Federalist Society members. In questioning just over 40 key actors about the principles or priorities that unite members of the Federalist Society, a concern for the "separation of powers" received 13 mentions.[13] Articulated as a concern for the preservation of "federalism" or the "federal structure," this principle received another 23 mentions in interviews.[14]

The organ of government that has historically policed the boundaries between the separate branches of government is the subject of the final principled belief listed in the Federalist Society's short statement: "it is emphatically the province and duty of the judiciary to say what the law is, not what it should be." Echoing familiar language from Chief Justice John Marshall's famous opinion in *Marbury v. Madison*,[15] this statement reflects the belief among members that unelected judges, who incorrectly interpret constitutional and statutory text, exercise the lawmaking functions of elected legislators and run dangerously afoul of the separation of powers. This is also popularly referred to in shorthand among Federalist Society members as a concern with "judicial activism" or, conversely, a belief in "judicial restraint." For instance, when asked what attracted him to the Federalist Society in its fledgling years, former Reagan Justice Department official Charles J. Cooper responded that it was the Federalist Society's "belief in a restrained judiciary... the belief that the Constitution... should be interpreted to mean what it was intended to mean. I was and still am very concerned about judicial activism and its consequences."[16] This principled concern with judicial activism was expressed more than 20 times in interviews with key Federalist Society actors.[17] Additionally, the nature of the judicial role has been the headlining topic at no fewer than eight Federalist Society National Conferences throughout the years.[18]

The debate about the proper role of the judiciary is very old, and it gets to the heart of what the PEN believes to be a valid exercise of judicial power and how it goes about making that determination. For members of the Federalist Society, the answer to what makes an act of judicial power valid is consistent with the other normative and causal beliefs explored in this section. The relationship between these beliefs and the shared understanding by members of what makes judicial interpretation valid was articulated by Federalist Society Board member and mentor, the late Robert H. Bork, whose 1971 *Indiana Law Journal* article was cited multiple times by interviewees[19] as an important influence on their own beliefs:

> The requirement that the Court be principled arises from the resolution of the seeming anomaly of judicial supremacy in a democratic society. If the judiciary really is supreme, able to rule when and as it sees fit, the society is not democratic. The anomaly is dissipated, however, by the model of government embodied in the structure of

the Constitution, a model upon which popular consent to limited government by the Supreme Court also rests. This model we may... call "Madisonian".... it follows that the Court's power is legitimate only if it has, and can demonstrate in reasoned opinions that it has, a valid theory, derived from the Constitution.... If it does not have such a theory but merely imposes its own value choices, or worse if it pretends to have a theory but actually follows its own predilections, the Court violates the postulates of the Madisonian model that alone justifies its power. (Bork 1971, 2–3)

The "valid theory" that Bork refers to in his article, the one that solves the "Madisonian" dilemma, would later become known throughout the legal community as the theory of Originalism. Scholar Jonathan O'Neill has provided a good working definition of this theory:

Originalism is best understood as several closely related claims about the authoritative source of American constitutional law, that is to say, what it means to interpret the Constitution and what evidence interpreters may legitimately consult to recover meaning. . . originalism holds that although interpretation begins with the text, including the structure and relationship of the institutions it creates, the meaning of the text can be further elucidated by. . . evidence from those who drafted the text in convention as well as from the public debates and commentary surrounding its ratification. (O'Neill 2005, 1–2)

Long-time Federalist Society member Loren A. Smith, now a judge on the U.S. Court of Federal Claims, explained the relationship between Originalism and judicial restraint: "The more basic formulation [of Originalism] was the result of some of the actions of the courts... of the fifties and sixties and seventies where the judge was making the decision based on what the judge's view of social policy was." Smith continued that while the idea that "judges should stick to the Constitution" was not "original to Originalism," the theory articulated more clearly "why it was important to democracy to follow the text as [the] controlling principle that controls judges from going off and doing whatever they want."[20]

Executive Director Eugene Meyer commented that while they did not start the discussion of Originalism, the Federalist Society has worked hard to nurture and develop it over the past two and a half decades: "Specifically, when you talk about Originalism... our Student Chapters and our Lawyers Chapters and all our activities have fostered that to a great degree and I don't think the debate and discussion would be where it is were it not for us."[21] In addition to having the topic of "Originalism" headline two of its National Conferences,[22] institutional efforts to promote this theory within the Federalist Society include the web-published *Annotated Bibliography of Conservative and Libertarian Legal Scholarship*, which relies heavily on Originalist scholarship and sources,[23] an online debate series called *Originally Speaking* that typically pits one Originalist against one non-Originalist on a given legal or political topic of currency, and a recently published collection of Federalist Society debates edited by cofounder Steven Calabresi (with a foreword by Justice Antonin Scalia) entitled *Originalism: A Quarter-Century of Debate*.[24]

My interview data also corroborate the degree to which actors in the Federalist Society network have adopted Originalism. When I asked about the principles or priorities that unify members of the Federalist Society network, Originalism received 31 mentions, the most of any principle listed.[25] For example, as Federalist Society member Daniel Troy explained in our interview, "what the Federalist Society offers is an opportunity to interact with people who at least share your point of view about constitutional interpretation. . . people who have shared views about Originalism."[26] Similarly, Federalist Society member John Yoo emphasized in our interview that if he had to identify the single most important thing that the Federalist Society stood for, it would be "a commitment to Originalism."[27]

Originalism also provides a standard or metric by which other network members can keep judges and fellow members in the network in check, that is, to mitigate what conservative commentators and others have come to refer to as the "Greenhouse Effect" (Baum 2006, 139–145). The "Greenhouse Effect," named after *New York Times* Supreme Court reporter Linda Greenhouse, refers to the propensity of Supreme Court Justices to seek the approval—through their decisions—of the liberal media and the left-leaning "Georgetown set" (Baum 2006, 139). Several conservative commentators when discussing Republican nominees John Paul Stevens, Harry Blackmun, Potter Stewart, David Souter, and even Anthony Kennedy in part attribute the leftward drift of these Justices to their desire for approval from the Washington, D.C. elite circles (Baum 2006, 140–141). In helping to build a conservative and libertarian counter-elite around a shared belief in Originalism as the only valid mode of constitutional interpretation, the Federalist Society acts as a bulwark against this kind of judicial drift, holding members accountable for staying true to their principles. In the course of my interviews with key Federalist Society members, it became clear that they engage in this kind of feedback-loop with the Justices frequently—at Federalist Society conferences, at barbeques, through personal correspondence, and through scholarly publications.

As Federalist Society cofounder Steven Calabresi said in our interview, the growth of a conservative and libertarian counter-elite through the Federalist Society has "absolutely" helped keep Justices such as Scalia, Thomas, Roberts, and Alito in check:

I think it absolutely helps keep them in check. When one tries to think about what kinds of checks exist on officials as powerful as Supreme Court Justices I think the check of criticism by law schools, journalists, and conservative think tanks like the Federalist Society, criticism from those quarters is something that they notice. They may or may not be persuaded by it but I think they know it's out there and I think it is something of a check on them. Some of them may care more about being consistent than others. I think Scalia actually cares a lot about being consistent. He's no wall-flower so if you criticize him he's not necessarily going to wilt under the criticism; he may conclude that he was right and stand up for the position he originally articulated but I think he notices things like that and I think in general other conservative and libertarian judges and public officials notice things like that as well and I think it can have an effect on them.[28]

In this way, the Federalist Society elite is able to act as an effective "judicial audience" (Baum 2006), vocalizing their approval and disapproval of the decisions or the legal reasoning of fellow network members on and off the Supreme Court. As Lawrence Baum has written, judges, like people, are motivated and driven to act for many reasons—one of which, he argues, has to do with their desire to win approval from various "audiences" whose approval is valued not only strategically (as a means to promotion, selection to higher courts) but also "as an end in itself." For example, Baum writes in *Judges and Their Audiences*, people are not "interdependent solely because they want to get concrete things from each other. Rather, people's identities, their conceptions of themselves, rest fundamentally on their relations with each other. And the need for others to validate people's self-conceptions. . . continues throughout life" (2006, 26).

Working under this assumption, Baum argues, even a Supreme Court Justice who has reached the pinnacle of his or her career cares about and would have incentive to seek approval from people whom he or she respects and with whom he or she is personally and politically connected. Because interpretations of inherently subjective texts like the Constitution will always be politically contested (unlike scientific knowledge that can be refuted), the "validity" criterion within the PEN functions more as a barometer for how closely aligned a judicial decision or its reasoning is with the PEN's normative and principled beliefs about the proper arrangement of social and political life.

The final definitional characteristic of actors within a PEN is that they also share a common policy project to which they can apply their shared beliefs and interpretive understandings of politically contested meanings or texts. The Federalist Society lists as an institutional goal the desire to chip away at the dominant liberal ethic espoused in the academy, legal institutions, and the legal community at large by "reordering priorities within the legal system" and "restoring the recognition of the importance of [conservative and libertarian principles] among lawyers, judges, law students, and professors."[29] This multifaceted, ambitious policy project— which really comes down to an effort to reorient the legal culture—is, to recall the excerpt from cofounder David McIntosh, carried out in "untold ways" when conservative and libertarian principles are implemented by network actors and alumni in "thousands of decisions" at various levels of government and the legal profession. The Federalist Society's effort to reorder the priorities within the legal system involves not only shaping its members intellectually but also credentialing them professionally so that they might be in a position to have the kind of impact on the legal culture that the Federalist Society is trying to bring about. In our interview, former Federalist Society member and legal academic Thomas Smith recalled hearing the cofounders (including Calabresi) tell him very early on that it was

> crucial to credential young conservatives... and to build an alternative elite because [at] Yale Law School... and other elite schools, it's quite true that it wasn't just a point of view, it was a way of life; it was a network, it was a group of people, it was a way to talk, it was a set of books to read.... On the other hand, the conservatives didn't have that. They were this sort of rag-tag group of people from lots of different odds and ends and I think [within the Federalist Society] there has been a very conscious effort to sort of build up an elite, and I think [it has been] really quite remarkably successful.[30]

Federalist Society members recognize that this common policy project of restoring the recognition of conservative and libertarian principles in America's legal institutions requires the sustained efforts of thousands of network actors operating at times collectively and at other times separately, at different levels of government and the legal profession. After all, as one interviewee recalled hearing repeatedly at Federalist Society meetings of the effort to tear down the liberal orthodoxy permeating the legal profession and institutions of government, "Rome wasn't burned in a day."[31]

While on a very general level, the Federalist Society for Law and Public Policy satisfies the basic criteria of a PEN, it is perhaps more accurate to say that the Federalist Society network is composed of *multiple* PENs. The various coalitions and divisions within the Federalist Society reflect those within the conservative legal movement more generally (see, e.g., Paik, Southworth, and Heinz 2007; Southworth 2008). While the Federalist Society has managed to successfully navigate and "mediate" (Southworth

2008) these fissures within the conservative movement, it would be a bold claim indeed to say that all 40,000 members agreed on all the constitutional issues I examine in this book. Acknowledging the limitations of this approach—that is, the non-generalizability of what I detail to the entire network membership—I believe that the framework is still extremely useful for examining the influence of the various smaller PENs that have cohered within the Federalist Society network around key doctrinal areas—the Second Amendment, the First Amendment, federalism, and state sovereignty. The next section lays out, in detail, my research approach for this work.

TRACING THE INFLUENCE OF THE FEDERALIST SOCIETY ON THE CONSERVATIVE COUNTERREVOLUTION

In terms of conceptualizing influence, the PEN framework is consistent with the post-positivist tradition in social science.[32] As law and society scholar Michael McCann has put it, this tradition "begin[s] from the assumption that no contextual factor alone is determinative or autonomous, and, indeed, the conceptualization of factors as independent forces only impedes understanding of both their dynamic interactions and their cumulative significance over time for the subjects we are trying to understand" (McCann 1996, 462). Understood in this sense, Federalist Society network influence is not defined as its power to change the votes of Supreme Court justices in key cases. Rather, influence, as it is deployed in the PEN analysis, captures and chronicles the subtle, complex, and dynamic ways in which this network and its ideas helped shape the content, direction, and character of key Supreme Court decisions. It is also plausible, for reasons that I explore in greater detail in this book's final chapter, that the Federalist Society network, working systematically over the course of several decades, made it easier for the Justices to make the difficult decision to change constitutional course in the first place—that they helped foster an environment conducive to constitutional change.

The research techniques for demonstrating the influence of PENs on policy development are identical to those prescribed for the EC framework. The process involves "identifying community membership, determining the community members' principled and casual beliefs, tracing their activities and demonstrating their influence on decision makers at various points in time" (Haas 1992, 34). I should note that within the PEN framework, it does not matter whether or not these individuals are card-carrying and dues-paying Federalist Society "members" (in the same way that one is a member of a gym or a country club). What matters instead is the extent to which these individuals are active participants in Federalist Society network activities and programs. Thus, I refer to them in the pages of this book as "network members" rather than "members" of the Federalist Society. Because of this emphasis on activity versus membership (and because, from a practical standpoint, the Federalist Society maintains a strict policy against publishing their membership lists), I relied on speaker agendas for Federalist Society National Conferences (Student and Lawyers) from 1982 to 2012 to establish network affiliation. These speaker agendas furnished a list of 1,190 different individuals who have presented at Federalist Society National Conferences. In one respect, this data set is over-inclusive for determining PEN membership. It includes several speakers who are sometimes referred to as the "token liberals," such as Cass Sunstein, Louis Michael Seidman, Walter Dellinger, and Laurence Tribe. These individuals do not tend to share the Federalist Society's beliefs, notions of validity, or general policy project. For this reason, I have filtered them out of the subsequent case studies where I track network influence. In many respects, however, this list is highly *under-*inclusive. National Student and Lawyer Conferences account for just two of the thousands of events the Federalist Society sponsors nationally each year, including local Student Chapter meetings, local lawyer lunches and speaker events, student leadership camps, regional colloquia and symposia, faculty conferences, professional Practice Group meetings, and campus debates.[33] Further, this list does not take into account the tens of thousands of members who attend Federalist Society events each year but are not on the program. These constraints notwithstanding, I have found that these National Conferences attract some of the most high-profile Federalist Society participants, including leaders in the academy, in the legal profession, and decision-makers in government and on the judiciary.

While, for some network actors, the number of appearances at Federalist Society National Conferences is in the double digits, even an appearance on the program at one National Conference, as several interviewees confirmed, is viewed as an important credential and a great honor within the Federalist Society network—a signal of "true believership."[34] As evidence, in the context of discussions with former Federalist Society Student Chapter Presidents, presenters at National Conferences were referred to as the "rock stars" and the "Mick Jaggers" of the network.[35] Thus, though this network list represents less than 3% of the 40,000 members the Federalist Society boasts, these 3% can be understood as constituting the thought leaders of the network. Additionally, given the high profile of these conferences, these 3% are also likely to be among the most prominent and active "citizen-lawyers," to use Leonard Leo's term, within the network. Table 1.2 provides some evidence of this by listing the 13 most frequent participants at Federalist Society National Conferences and detailing their positions within the legal-political community.

In determining these network members' beliefs about the constitutional doctrines examined in this book, I relied on several different expressions of these beliefs, both institutional (transcripts of Federalist Society conference speeches and panels, Federalist Society Practice Group newsletters and articles, the Federalist Society's *Annotated Bibliography of Conservative and Libertarian Legal Scholarship*, Federalist Society– hosted online debates, Practice Group Teleforum calls and Podcasts) and non-institutional (law review articles and other scholarly publications, newspaper articles, archival data, and interview data).[36] I work to establish these beliefs in the beginning of each chapter, detailing the major Federalist Society members contributing to the PEN's dialogue on that particular set of doctrines while providing evidence of these beliefs from the sources just mentioned.

As the model in Figure 1.2 illustrates, ideas can be diffused from the PEN to Supreme Court decision makers through several pathways. The dotted lines represent network actors as "cognitive baggage handlers" (Haas 1992, 27), carrying the ideas of the Federalist Society into their roles as legal professionals, including judges, academics, executive branch officials, litigators, or friends of the court. Of course, the most direct mechanism of transmission is through political infiltration. In this case, political infiltration is achieved when network members have secured positions as Supreme Court decision makers and, to a lesser extent,

Table 1.2 MOST FREQUENT PRESENTERS AT FEDERALIST SOCIETY NATIONAL CONFERENCES 1982–2013

Name	# Nat. Conferences	Occupation(s)
Frank Easterbrook	32	Federal Judge
Richard Epstein	26	Academic
Edwin Meese, III	20	Executive Branch, Think Tank
Steven Calabresi	20	Executive Branch, Academic
Thomas Merrill	19	Academic
Lino A. Graglia	19	Academic
A. Raymond Randolph	19	Federal Judge
John McGinnis	19	Executive Branch, Academic
Theodore Olson	18	Executive Branch, Litigation
Lillian BeVier	16	Academic
Charles J. Cooper	16	Executive Branch, Litigation
John C. Yoo	15	Executive Branch, Academic
William H. Pryor	14	State AG, Federal Judge

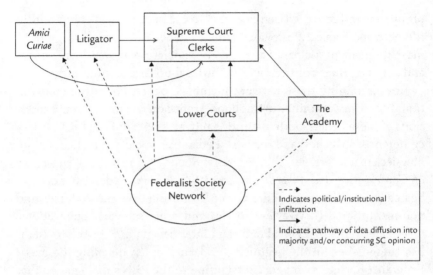

Figure 1.2 Political Epistemic Network (PEN) Pathways of Influence on Judicial Branch

Supreme Court clerks.[37] However, network ideas can reach decision-makers by several other paths. In Figure 1.2, these external paths of idea transmission are represented by solid lines. For example, ideas might travel through a lower court opinion authored by a Federalist Society network-member judge, a brief submitted by network-member litigator(s) and/or *amici curiae* ("friends of the court"), or through published scholar-ship authored by Federalist Society–affiliated scholars. Federalist Society network participation in all these capacities—as a Supreme Court deci-sion maker, Supreme Court clerk, lower court judge, *amicus curiae*, and litigator(s)—was catalogued in each of the cases examined in this book. Realizing that the reader will not have access to my complete database of Federalist Society network participants, the first time I identify a member of the network I have endeavored to make it clear in either the body of the text or with an endnote (or both) exactly how he or she is connected to the Federalist Society network (e.g., conference participation, Practice Group membership, affiliated scholar, etc.). Finally, the respective opinions and briefs were coded using Atlas.ti Scientific qualitative data management software.[38] Using references to Federalist Society scholarship and to the shared canon of Originalist sources as my primary indicators, I examined the extent to which Supreme Court Justices relied on the expressed intel-lectual capital of Federalist Society members in constructing their written opinions in each case.[39]

As I wrote in the introduction, the constitutional areas examined in this book were selected because of the distinct conservative turn each has taken over the past 30 years—a turn that is very much in line with the kinds of arguments that conservatives and libertarians have been making at Federalist Society meetings since the 1980s. As my previous work on the Federalist Society suggested, it is in these kinds of revolutionary Supreme Court cases, those in which the degree of *doctrinal distance* is greatest (Hollis-Brusky 2013), that the extent of reliance on outside intellectual capital should in fact be highest. Additionally, unlike the various cross-cutting issues that tend to routinely divide the conservative coalition and its lawyers (see, e.g., Southworth 2008), this book examines areas of constitutional law about which there seems to be—if not perfect agreement—a clear and identifiable consensus among the most prominent and active members of the Federalist Society network in terms of the kinds of arguments being made and how those arguments are being supported.

The next two chapters examine Federalist Society network influence on two constitutional areas that reflect the organization's first shared principle: *the state exists to preserve freedom*. Subsequent chapters examine network efforts, consistent with their second principled belief in the centrality of *the separation of governmental powers*, to rein in the federal commerce power and bolster state sovereignty, respectively. The final chapter aggregates insights from these narratives of influence and situates them in a broader literature on the dynamics of constitutional change and judicial policy development. In short, it shows how and why the Federalist Society network has been so successful in *saying what the law is*.

PART I

The State Exists to Preserve Freedom

CHAPTER 2

The Right of the People to Keep and Bear Arms

Lost and Found

U.S. Constitution, Amendment II
A well regulated Militia, being necessary to the security of a free State,
the right of the people to keep and bear Arms, shall not be infringed.

"The rights of the individual citizen would be little different today if the Second Amendment did not exist."[1] This provocative statement, first appearing in a 1965 *American Bar Association Journal* article entitled "The Lost Amendment," was intended to serve as a damning indictment of the Supreme Court's interpretation and application of the "right of the People to keep and bear arms" protected by the Second Amendment to the U.S. Constitution.[2] Penned by eventual Seventh Circuit Court of Appeals judge and Nixon appointee Robert A. Sprecher, the article accused the Supreme Court of misconstruing the right to keep and bear arms on two grounds. First, in a series of late nineteenth-century cases (*U.S. v. Cruikshank* (1876); *Presser v. Illinois* (1886); *Miller v. Texas* (1894))[3] the highest court in the land failed to apply the U.S. Constitution's Second Amendment protections against the states, arguing that like all provisions of the Bill of Rights at that time, the Second Amendment should be read as providing protection against the actions and encroachments of the federal government, not the states.[4] Second, in *United States v. Miller* (1939), the first case in a century and a half in which the Supreme Court had the opportunity to rule squarely on the nature of the right to keep and bear arms, the Justices indicated that the Second Amendment right ought to be understood to be collective in nature, as opposed to a right guaranteed to each individual. In upholding the constitutionality of the federal National Firearms Act (NFA) and writing for a unanimous court in *Miller*, Justice James Clark McReynolds wrote that "[i]n the absence of any evidence tending to show that possession or use of a 'shotgun having a barrel of less than eighteen inches in length' at this time has some reasonable relationship to the preservation or efficiency of a well regulated militia, we cannot say that the Second Amendment guarantees the right to keep and bear such an instrument."[5] The Supreme Court's reading of the Second Amendment in *Miller*—a reading that focused on the right in the context of its relationship to the guarantee of a "well-regulated militia"—was quite in line with academic and elite opinion on the subject. As one observer noted, nearly all legal scholarship at the time was supportive of "some variant of the collective rights reading" of the Second Amendment (Cornell 2006, 204). Moreover, lower federal court judges had reinforced the Supreme Court's holding in *Miller* by applying, almost without exception, a narrow collective rights reading of the Second Amendment[6] (Williams 2003, 106–107).

In Robert A. Sprecher's view, this double-barreled misconstruction of the scope and the nature of the right to keep and bear arms had turned the U.S. Constitution's Second Amendment into "The Lost Amendment." In addition to serving as an indictment of the Supreme Court's Second Amendment jurisprudence, Sprecher's article also contained a call to arms for then-present and future scholars to develop the intellectual underpinnings of a more robust understanding of the right to keep and bear arms and to pressure the Supreme Court to adopt this notion. He went on to say, "We should find the lost Second Amendment, broaden its scope and determine that it affords the right to arm a state militia and also the right of the individual to keep and bear arms" (Sprecher 1965, 669). Robert A. Sprecher served on the Seventh Circuit Court of Appeals until his death on May 15, 1982, and his call to arms, though eloquent and bold, went largely unanswered during his lifetime. According to two prominent Second Amendment scholars, as late as the early 1980s, there was little interest from legal scholars in challenging the Supreme Court's interpretation of the right to bear arms, which by that point had garnered a broad scholarly consensus (Barnett and Kates 1996, 1141). As Randy Barnett and Don Kates noted, even libertarian law professor Daniel D. Polsby went on the record with the *Chicago Sun Times* in 1981 and called the individual rights view of the Second Amendment "a lot of horsedung" (Barnett and Kates 1996, 1141). Still, the individual rights view of the Second Amendment was beginning to garner a fair amount of political support. In 1976, the language of the Second Amendment appeared for the first time in a Republican Party platform ("We support the right of citizens to keep and bear arms") (Spitzer 2001, 83). In 1980, as Robert J. Spitzer explains, the Republican Party used even stronger wording, stating, "We believe the right of citizens to keep and bear arms must be preserved" (Spitzer 2001, 83–84). This emphasis in the Republican Party's platform on the Second Amendment coincided with the party's nomination of Ronald Reagan, who had strongly endorsed the position of a group that was becoming a rising political force in Washington, D.C.—the National Rifle Association (NRA) (Langbein and Lotwis 1990, 430–434; Spitzer 2001, 84).

Around the same time that Ronald Reagan was catapulted into the presidency, the tide of academic and elite opinion on the Second Amendment was beginning to turn. One source of support for this shift would come from a fledgling group of law students and academics who would hold their first meeting in New Haven, Connecticut, in April 1982. The preface to the transcript of that first Federalist Society conference, reprinted in the *Harvard Journal for Law and Public Policy*, signaled their sympathy with and receptivity to the kind of arguments that Robert A. Sprecher and a few others had been advancing before this time with little success: "At a time when the nation's law schools are staffed largely by professors who dream of regulating from their cloistered offices every minute detail of our lives... the Federalists met—and proclaimed the virtues of individual freedom and of limited government" (Hicks 2006, 652). This emphasis on "individual freedom" was soon institutionally enshrined in the Federalist Society's statement of principles, which, if we recall last chapter's discussion, states that one of the Society's foundational beliefs is that *the state exists to preserve freedom.*[7] As the next section will detail, while the Society's openness and receptivity to this reading of the right to keep and bear arms was clear from the genesis of the organization, scholars and judicial decision makers affiliated with the Federalist Society network began aggressively advocating for an individual rights view of the Second Amendment in the early 1990s. These efforts accelerated after 1997, when Federalist Society member and hero Justice Clarence Thomas signaled in a Tenth Amendment case that the Supreme Court might be ready and willing to revisit the Supreme Court's five decades–old holding in *Miller.* In his concurring opinion in *Printz v. United States* (1997), (discussed at length in Chapter 5), Thomas pointed to "a growing body of scholarly commentary" that supported the individual rights view of the Second Amendment and mused hopefully that "perhaps, at some future date, this Court will have the opportunity to determine whether Justice Story was correct when he wrote that the right to bear arms 'has justly been considered as the palladium of the liberties of a republic.' "[8]

This "judicial signal" (Baird 2007) was received loud and clear by other members of the Federalist Society network. A decade after Justice Thomas's concurring opinion in *Printz*, in a 2008 opinion written by former Federalist Society advisor Justice Antonin Scalia, the Supreme Court would hold for the first time that the Second Amendment protected an individual, not just a collective right to keep and bear arms. A mere two years later, in 2010, in an opinion written by another Federalist Society member—Justice Samuel Alito—the Supreme Court would incorporate and apply that right for the first time to the states. These two cases, *District of Columbia v. Heller* (2008) and *McDonald v. City of Chicago* (2010), represented a seismic shift in the Supreme Court's Second Amendment jurisprudence. This chapter explores the role that the Federalist Society network played in providing the intellectual capital for this constitutional paradigm shift. The following section works to establish the arguments and authoritative sources relied on by Federalist Society network members at conferences and in their scholarship in support of an individual rights reading of the Second Amendment. I then examine Federalist Society network participation in *Heller* and *McDonald* litigation, working to tease out some of those "untold ways" in which the network effectively diffused ideas or intellectual capital to Supreme Court decision makers in these two revolutionary decisions. I close the chapter with an evaluation and assessment of the ways in which the Federalist Society network ultimately helped the Supreme Court find "the Lost Amendment."

THE FEDERALIST SOCIETY NETWORK ON THE SECOND AMENDMENT

As I mentioned in the previous section, the Federalist Society network had signaled its receptiveness early on to the kinds of arguments that would challenge the weak or watered-down version of the Second Amendment that the Supreme Court and the academic community at large had supported since the nineteenth century. Loren A. Smith, now a Federal Court of Appeals judge, was a frequent participant at some of the Federalist Society's earliest gatherings. He recalled for me, in our interview, the Society's early focus on the role of government, the perceived negative impact that government regulation was having on individual freedom, and the efforts within the Federalist Society to push back against the scholarly consensus about big government:

> [One unifying] idea was that government has gotten too big and infringes too much
> on individual liberties. . . . I think [the Federalist Society] has made it respectable

to debate whether government has gotten too big and whether judges, by their decisions, are undermining the Constitution. [That] wasn't really a respectable topic
when I was at law school, at least. You didn't hear any discussion by my professors of
whether government was too big or not.[9]

This sentiment was echoed by Federalist Society cofounder David
McIntosh, who said that the Federalist Society was established in part to
provide an alternative to the "dominant liberal ethic" in legal academia
that considered many views (including those about an individual rights
view of the Second Amendment) to be "outside of the mainstream" and
therefore out of bounds for serious scholarly consideration.[10] While this
hospitableness to unorthodox legal and constitutional views was apparent from the Federalist Society's founding, the Second Amendment did
not become a salient topic of discussion at National Meetings until the
early 1990s. In 1991, for example, the Federalist Society hosted its Tenth
National Student Symposium on "The Bill of Rights after 200 Years"
at Yale Law School. At that symposium, several participants lamented
the failure of the judiciary to enforce the safeguards of the Second
Amendment properly.[11] One particularly noteworthy lament came from
law professor Thomas W. Merrill. As he said, "[t]he judiciary in this country has done little to enforce the Second Amendment, perhaps because
intellectual elites, such as the American Civil Liberties Union, do not
really think it is a right." "Or," Merrill continued, "perhaps a judiciary that
lives by the pen is not terribly supportive of those who would live by the
sword. Nevertheless, and notwithstanding the complete judicial default
in enforcing the Second Amendment, we have rather widespread owner-
ship of firearms and other weapons in this country."[12] It is no coincidence
that the Brady Handgun Violence Prevention Act was being debated in
Congress, and ultimately passed, in the early 1990s.[13] Since that time, as
I show in detail in the next section, Federalist Society network members
have been active discussants of the Second Amendment both at conferences and in their scholarship.

In reviewing speech acts mentioning the Second Amendment at
National Conferences, in online debates, in Practice Group Newsletters,
and in scholarship recommended by the Federalist Society's *Annotated
Bibliography of Conservative and Libertarian Legal Scholarship* (hereinafter, the *Bibliography*), I identified just 27 speakers. Several of these speakers (e.g., Randy Barnett, Eugene Volokh, and Nelson Lund) are on the
record multiple times. The number 27 does not account for the hundreds
of attendees at conferences and events and other members who likely
share these intellectual sympathies but are not on the record as endorsing the Second Amendment views of these leaders. With these limitations

in mind, it is still important to note that of all the doctrinal areas examined in this book, the *political epistemic network* (PEN) that has cohered
around the Second Amendment within the Federalist Society network
is the smallest. Size notwithstanding, this group is noteworthy both for
the prominence of its members within the field more broadly and for the
extent of ideological agreement among its members. As attorney Alan
Gura explained on a Federalist Society Teleforum Call entitled *Gun Rights
Litigation Update*, "the Second Amendment field is very small."[14] That
being said, many of the most prominent and active attorneys and academics involved in Second Amendment litigation and intellectual development, such as Randy Barnett, Don B. Kates, Nelson Lund, Eugene Volokh,
Charles J. Cooper, Robert Levy, and Clark M. Neily are active members of
the Federalist Society network. Moreover, all of these speech acts (including all four sources recommended by the Federalist Society *Bibliography*)
endorse an individual rights view of the Second Amendment. The following sections provide an overview of the Federalist Society network's
support for and endorsement of the individual rights view of the Second
Amendment; that is, these sections provide evidence from conferences,
events, and scholarship of this PEN's long-standing support for this radical reinterpretation of the right to keep and bear arms.

An Originalist Reading of the Second Amendment Supports an Individual Right to Bear Arms, not a Collective Right

Critical to reinterpreting the Second Amendment as protecting an individual and not merely a collective right to keep and bear arms is the argument,
expressed consistently in Federalist Society speech acts on the subject,
that the "justification clause" of the Second Amendment ("A well regulated Militia, being necessary to the security of a free State") should not be
read to limit or constrain the "operative clause" ("the right of the people to
keep and bear Arms, shall not be infringed"). As Thomas W. Merrill put
it at the 1991 National Student Symposium, "[t]he Second Amendment
prefaces [the right to bear arms] with a reason why it is needed—to
maintain a well-regulated militia. It does not, however, suggest that the
right is limited to the implementation of that reason alone."[15] Member
Nelson Lund[16] writes in his 1996 law review article, "The Past and Future
of the Individual's Right to Bear Arms" (recommended reading in the
Society's *Bibliography*), that "when read properly," the legislative history
reveals that the "Second Amendment's prefatory language was perfectly
adapted to a purpose having nothing to do with limiting or qualifying

the grammatically inescapable language establishing an individual right to keep and bear arms."[17] Similarly, member Eugene Volokh[18] writes in his 1998 law review article, "The Commonplace Second Amendment" (also recommended reading in the *Bibliography*), that a close historical reading of state constitutions and other Originalist sources from the founding shows that "operative clauses are often both broader and narrower than their justification clauses, thus casting doubt on the argument that the right exists only when. . . it furthers the goals identified in the justification clause."[19] To put it another way, Federalist Society network members argue that an Originalist reading of the Second Amendment commands us to read it *backward*.

In doing so, Federalist Society network members give far more interpretive weight to the operative clause, emphasizing the Framers' selection of the phrase "the right of the people" rather than "the right of members of the militia." As Volokh writes:

> The operative clause says the right to keep and bear arms belongs to "the people." Given that "the right of the people" is likewise used to describe the right to petition the government, the right to be free from unreasonable searches and seizures, and the rights to keep and bear arms recognized in various contemporaneous state constitutions—all individual rights that belong to each person, not just to members of the militia—"the people" seems to refer to people generally.[20]

This same argument is made in each of the other three sources recommended in the Federalist Society's *Bibliography* under the Second Amendment. For example, in their 1996 law review article, "Under Fire: The New Consensus on the Second Amendment," members Randy Barnett[21] and Don B. Kates[22] argue, "the strongest support for the individual right view and against the. . . militia-centric view derives from the text of the Amendment itself. . . [which] uses the phrase, 'right of the people,' a term also used in the First, Fourth, Ninth and Tenth Amendments, and in the original Constitution, and used to denote the rights of individuals."[23] Nelson Lund, in his above-cited 1996 article, also emphasizes the overlap in language ("the right of the people") between the Second, First, and Fourth Amendments, pointing out that no one has "ever explained why the Framers of these three provisions would have used the identical language in a fundamentally different sense in the Second Amendment."[24] Lund echoed this same argument at the 1999 Federalist Society National Lawyers Convention in Washington, D.C., on a panel discussing "Firearms Litigation, Tort Liability, and the Second Amendment." There, he declared emphatically, "the Second Amendment protects the right of individuals to keep and bear arms, not some sort of collective states' right to maintain military organizations like the National Guard."[25]

Further underscoring the coherence of beliefs about the Second Amendment within the PEN is the shared canon of sources that network members have relied on in their scholarship and speech acts to construct the legal-intellectual scaffolding of this individual rights view. For example, the sources recommended by the Federalist Society's *Bibliography* under the "Second Amendment"—each of which is authored or co-authored by a Federalist Society member—draw in critical ways in their arguments on Blackstone's *Commentaries on the Laws of England*,[26] *Federalist* 29,[27] and *Federalist* 46.[28] Blackstone's *Commentaries* are mobilized by network members to support the proposition that the right to bear arms, as it relates to self-defense, is a natural and personal (not collective) right. As such, the network members argue, it cannot be taken (or regulated) away. For example, in Barnett and Kates's "Under Fire. . ." the authors cite the following excerpt from Blackstone: "Self-defense therefore, as it is justly called the primary law of nature, so it is not, *neither can it be in fact*, [emphasis added by Barnett and Kates] taken away by the law of society."[29] Alexander Hamilton's *Federalist* 29 is mobilized to deemphasize and shed a skeptical light on the "prefatory" language in the Second Amendment ("A well-regulated Militia. . .") and to justify shifting the analytical focus of that Amendment to what network members refer to as the "operative" clause. For example, in defending this analytical move in his article "The Past and Future of the Individual's Right to Bear Arms," Federalist Society member Nelson Lund writes the following:

> Some of the more liberal leaders of the founding generation probably thought that the republican ideal of the citizen militia amounted largely to romantic nonsense, inconsistent with the principle of the division of labor. Alexander Hamilton, for example, wrote that "[t]he project of disciplining all the militia of the United States is as futile as it would be injurious if it were capable of being carried into execution." THE FEDERALIST No. 29, 184 (Alexander Hamilton) (Clinton Rossiter ed., 1961) . . . Hamilton's views only confirm that while the Second Amendment may have embodied a *hope* for something impracticable, it *requires* something perfectly feasible [emphasis in original]. Indeed, Hamilton believed that something well beyond the requirement of the Second Amendment was feasible. In the midst of his strongest criticism of the militia ideal, Hamilton also wrote: "Little more can reasonably be aimed at with respect to the people at large than to have them properly armed and equipped; and in order to see that this be not neglected, it will be necessary to assemble them once or twice in the course of a year." (THE FEDERALIST No. 29, *supra*, 185)[30]

In addition to Hamilton, Federalist Society network members also mobilize their patron founding father James Madison, to emphasize the importance that the founding generation placed on the right to keep and bear arms. For example, Nelson Lund, in his Second Amendment entry in the *Heritage Guide to the Constitution* (recommended by the Federalist Society's *Bibliography*), includes a lengthy excerpt from *Federalist 46* to support the *"shared* assumption" [emphasis in original] of the Founding generation that "the federal government should not have any authority at all to disarm the citizenry."[31]

These are, of course, but three of the dozens of sources that Federalist Society network members mobilize in support of a robust and individual rights interpretation of the Second Amendment. However, as this section has aimed to show, these three sources were recognized as critical to deconstructing the collective rights framework and building the scaffolding of the individual rights interpretation that more than a decade after most of this scholarship was written would help revolutionize the Supreme Court's Second Amendment jurisprudence in *District of Columbia v. Heller* (2008).

The Second Amendment Should Be Incorporated and Applied to the States Through the Fourteenth Amendment's Privileges or Immunities Clause and/or Due Process Clause

As I wrote earlier in this chapter, Federalist Society network members and other sympathizers had a "double-barreled" agenda when it came to the Second Amendment. This agenda included goals to (1) supplant the collective rights view of the Amendment that had been the dominant view in Supreme Court jurisprudence since the late nineteenth century, and (2) argue for the incorporation of the Second Amendment as a protection against actions and regulations of the states rather than merely as a protection against actions by the federal government. In reviewing Federalist Society speech acts, it is clear there are two principal avenues that network members identify and endorse when it comes to incorporating the Second Amendment. The first, utilizing the Due Process Clause of the Fourteenth Amendment (Amend. XIV, Sec. 1, cl. 3),[32] is rather uncontroversial—it is the manner in which prior (mostly progressive/liberal) Supreme Courts have incorporated many of the other Amendments of the Bill of Rights against the states. The second, however, is rather radical. Building from the scholarship of former Reagan Justice Department appointee and first generation Federalist Society member John Harrison,[33] as well as that of network member Michael Kent Curtis,[34] several Federalist Society network members (including Justice Clarence Thomas), argue for resurrecting the Privileges or Immunities Clause of the Fourteenth Amendment (Amend. XIV, Sec. 1, cl. 2)[35]—a clause that was all but neutered by a set of Supreme Court rulings in 1873—and using this clause instead to incorporate the Second Amendment against the states. Each is considered seriously by fellow Federalist Society member Samuel Alito in his majority opinion in *McDonald v. City of Chicago* (2010) (examined later in this chapter); I will briefly review each set of arguments for incorporation in turn.

Nelson Lund, speaking on a Federalist Society National Conference Panel organized by the Society's Civil Rights Practice Group in 1999, offered a strong defense of using the Due Process Clause to incorporate and apply the Second Amendment against the states. Lund said, "If one applies the substantive due process principles on which the Court purports to rely in its modern incorporation cases, there can be no doubt that the Second Amendment will be applied against the states, just like almost every other provision of the Bill of Rights." Nelson Lund continued by adding that, "[i]n fact, the argument for incorporating the right to arms through the Fourteenth Amendment is actually much stronger than for such rights as free speech and free exercise of religion."[36] Lund's arguments for incorporation are fleshed out more fully in his various law review articles on the Second Amendment. For example, in Lund's 1996 law review article, "The Past and Future of the Individual's Right to Bear Arms" (recommended reading on the Second Amendment by the Federalist Society's *Bibliography*), he argues that the right to keep and bear arms is both "fundamental" and integral to a "scheme of ordered liberty" and thus satisfies the Supreme Court's criterion for incorporation under the substantive Due Process doctrine.

While Lund and many other conservative legal scholars are deeply skeptical about the substantive Due Process doctrine—the doctrinal foundation of the right to privacy, abortion, homosexual sodomy, and same-sex marriage—Lund concludes that "[i]f the Court has the slightest regard for doctrinal consistency, it will have no choice except to incorporate the Second Amendment."[37] This ambivalence about incorporating the Second Amendment through the Due Process Clause of the Fourteenth Amendment is echoed by various other Federalist Society members in their speech acts and scholarship. For example, network member Thomas Burrell, writing for the Federalist Society's Practice Group Journal, *Engage,* wrote in 2008 (prior to the *Heller* decision) that while he and others are skeptical of the Due Process doctrine, the right to keep and bear arms is "'fundamental' and thus protected by its understanding of 'due process' under the Fourteenth Amendment." Burrell continues to argue that "[t]he Court's refusal thus far to see the right to keep and bear arms in the Second Amendment as a 'deeply rooted' or 'fundamental' right is at odds with its own jurisprudence."[38] In other words, to summarize many of these network members' concerns, absent a more viable constitutional alternative, most members would lobby at least for "parity" in the Supreme Court's incorporation doctrine.[39]

Several prominent voices within the Federalist Society network, including Randy Barnett, Don Kates, John C. Harrison, Michael Kent Curtis, and Clarence Thomas, argue that there is, in fact, a more viable constitutional alternative—resurrecting the Fourteenth Amendment's Privileges or Immunities Clause and incorporating the Second Amendment as applicable to the states through that clause. This path is more viable, these voices insist, because it is the more constitutionally principled route; that is, it is more consistent with the original meaning of the Fourteenth Amendment. As John Harrison argues in his 1992 *Yale Law Journal* article, "Reconstructing the Privileges or Immunities Clause," a proper reading of the "Privileges or Immunities Clause accomplishes something very much like incorporation as the Republicans would have understood it. . . this would go a long way toward actually applying the first eight amendments to the states."[40] However, this route would involve asking the Supreme Court to overturn a 140-year-old set of decisions handed down in the wake of the ratification of the Fourteenth Amendment—the *Slaughterhouse Cases* (1873)[41]—that narrowly circumscribed the scope and reach of the Privileges or Immunities Clause. In brief, the Supreme Court had interpreted the "Privileges or Immunities" of national citizenship as encompassing only a few narrow rights—the right, for example, to leave a state without paying an exit tax, the right to use navigable waters of the United States, the right to demand protection of the national government when in a foreign country or on the high seas, and a few others.[42] Nowhere on the Supreme Court's truncated list of the Privileges or Immunities of national citizenship was the right to keep and bear arms. This omission, according to several scholars within the Federalist Society network, was a constitutional mistake—one that ought to be corrected by (to borrow the title of John Harrison's article recommended by the Federalist Society's *Bibliography*) "reconstructing the Privileges or Immunities clause"[43] using Originalism.

Randy Barnett and Don Kates's 1996 law review article "Under Fire. . ." (recommended by the Federalist Society's *Bibliography*) addresses the issue of incorporation by referring to the work of several scholars who have shown that "the Privileges or Immunities Clause of the Fourteenth Amendment was specifically intended to incorporate the personal right to arms."[44] Among those scholars whose work is cited as authoritative on this issue are Federalist Society members William Van Alstyne and Michael Kent Curtis. Van Alstyne, who participated in the Second Annual Federalist Society National Lawyers Convention in 1987 on "The Constitution and Federal Criminal Law,"[45] is a recommended authority on "Federalism" in the Federalist Society's *Bibliography* (see Chapter 4 of this book). As Barnett and Kates acknowledge in their article, Van Alstyne is also recognized within the Federalist Society network for his influential 1994 law review article entitled "The Second Amendment and the Personal Right to Arms."[46] In this article, Van Alstyne mobilizes evidence from the framing and ratification period of the Fourteenth Amendment to argue that the Privileges or Immunities Clause was specifically designed to incorporate and apply the Second Amendment to the states.[47] The other Federalist Society network scholar whose work is cited by Barnett and Kates in their Second Amendment piece is Wake Forest University School of Law professor Michael Kent Curtis, who argues in his book *No State Shall Abridge: The Fourteenth Amendment and the Bill of Rights* (1987) that among the rights that "Republicans in the Thirty-ninth Congress relied on as absolute rights of the citizens of the United States were the right to freedom of speech, the right to due process of law, and the right to bear arms."[48] Signaling Federalist Society network approval of this kind of argument, Curtis was invited to participate in his first Federalist Society National Conference the year after his book was published. The title of his talk, delivered at the 1988 National Student Conference, was (appropriately enough) "Privileges or Immunities, Individual Rights, and Federalism."[49] Curtis's 1988 talk at the Federalist Society, which outlines in abbreviated form some of the historical evidence mobilized in his book to support the incorporation of fundamental rights (including the right to keep and bear arms) through the Privileges or Immunities Clause, contains the following prescient statement: "The title of this panel is 'The Modern Role for the Privileges or Immunities Clause,' but there is almost no modern role for it. I will therefore look at the history of the Fourteenth Amendment; perhaps its future role may be found in the past."[50]

Michael Kent Curtis's aspirations, articulated at a 1988 Federalist Society talk, that a "future" Supreme Court might reconsider its Privileges or Immunities jurisprudence and align it with what he and other members considered the correct Original meaning of the clause might have seemed to be a bit of a fantasy at that time. But after 20 years of chipping away at the collective rights view through conservative and libertarian scholarship, the production and diffusion of intellectual capital, and—most important—the successful appointment of three additional Federalist Society member Supreme Court Justices (Thomas, Roberts, and Alito) presumably sympathetic to this view, it seemed that the time was ripe for both Second Amendment and Privileges or Immunities enthusiasts.

THE SECOND AMENDMENT AND
THE SUPREME COURT

As I wrote in the introduction to this chapter, at the time that Federalist Society hero and mentor Justice Clarence Thomas penned that fateful concurrence in *Printz* in 1997 (expressing hope that the Supreme Court might soon get the opportunity to reconsider its Second Amendment jurisprudence), the collective rights reading of the Second Amendment had been settled constitutional jurisprudence for over half a century. While I examine *Printz* in great detail in Chapter 5, it is worth excerpting from Thomas's concurrence here, to provide some context for the revolutionary process it would set into motion:

> This Court has not had recent occasion to consider the nature of the substantive right safeguarded by the *Second Amendment*. If, however, the *Second Amendment* is read to confer a *personal* right to "keep and bear arms," a colorable argument exists that the Federal Government's regulatory scheme, at least as it pertains to the purely intrastate sale or possession of firearms, runs afoul of that Amendment's protections. As the parties did not raise this argument, however, we need not consider it here. Perhaps, at some future date, this Court will have the opportunity to determine whether Justice Story was correct when he wrote that the right to bear arms "has justly been considered, as the palladium of the liberties of a republic." 3 J. Story, Commentaries 1890, p. 746 (1833). In the meantime, I join the Court's opinion striking down the challenged provisions of the Brady Act as inconsistent with the *Tenth Amendment*.[51] (emphasis in original)

Within six short years of Thomas sending this "judicial signal" (Baird 2007), members of the Federalist Society network would respond by filing a case in District Court that would eventually make its way to the Supreme Court in the form of *District of Columbia v. Heller* (2008); a case that would allow the Supreme Court (in Thomas's words) to "[re]consider the nature of the substantive right safeguarded by the *Second Amendment*."

District of Columbia v. Heller (2008)

This case challenged the constitutionality of the District of Columbia's "Firearms Control Regulation Act of 1975."[52] Proposed as part of an effort to improve the District of Columbia's government capacity to monitor firearms trafficking, this legislation sought to reduce the rate of gun-related crimes and violence within its jurisdiction by prohibiting the purchase, sale, transfer, and possession of handguns by D.C. residents.[53] The law excluded law enforcement officers and military members and included a provision for firearm owners registered under D.C.'s 1968 registration law to re-register their firearms within 60 days of the Act becoming effective, after which handguns became "unregisterable." The Firearms Control Regulations Act also made an exception for certain firearms, including rifles and shotguns, which re-registrants and prospective firearms purchasers could acquire after undergoing a required eligibility screening process.[54] Finally, the Firearms Control Regulations Act obliged owners to have their certificate of registration whenever possessing their firearms and required any firearm to be kept unloaded and either disassembled or secured by a trigger lock.[55] The legislation was catalyzed by a record number of homicides in 1974, more than half of which were committed with handguns, and an increasing number of reported cases of juveniles obtaining access to handguns.[56]

The *Heller* case was originally filed in the federal district court for the District of Columbia in February 2003, then known as *Parker v. District of Columbia*, on behalf of six plaintiffs. Robert A. Levy, who is chairman of the Cato Institute's board of directors and also sits on boards of the Institute for Justice, the Federalist Society, and the George Mason University School of Law, had a large role in developing, shaping, and supporting the case from conception. Taking sole responsibility of financing the case, Levy collaborated with Clark Neily, a staff attorney at the Institute for Justice, to handpick plaintiffs and select fellow Federalist Society member Alan Gura as the lead attorney on the case.[57] One of the strategies for building the case involved interviewing a number of prospective plaintiffs and ultimately choosing individuals who represented a diversity of ages, genders, races, incomes, and occupations.[58] The lead plaintiff, Shelly Parker, was a neighborhood activist who had been threatened by drug dealers, and the case sought to challenge the constitutionality of D.C.'s gun control laws under the Second Amendment.[59] In March 2004, federal district Judge Emmet Sullivan ruled in favor of the D.C. government, stating that the Second Amendment referred to persons in a militia, and consequently did not apply to the six plaintiffs. The case was then appealed to the federal Circuit Court of Appeals for the District of Columbia, which held that five of the six plaintiffs did not have standing for the lawsuit.[60] The court determined that the lone plaintiff with standing was Dick Heller, whose application to register a gun he owned and kept outside D.C. was denied by the D.C. Metropolitan Police Department. Upon rehearing the case, the panel ruled 2 to 1, in an opinion written by Federalist Society member Laurence Silberman, that the challenged gun control laws were unconstitutional under the

Second Amendment.[61] In September 2007, the District of Columbia petitioned for a *writ of certiorari* for the case, now *District of Columbia v. Heller,* which the Supreme Court granted in November 2007. Oral argument was held on March 18, 2008, and just a few months later, on June 26, 2008, the Supreme Court ruled in a 5 to 4 decision that the D.C. firearms control regulations violated the Second Amendment, holding for the first time that the Amendment protected an *individual,* not merely a collective, right to bear arms. The majority opinion in *Heller* was written by Justice Antonin Scalia.[62] Chief Justice John Roberts, Justice Anthony Kennedy, Justice Clarence Thomas, and Justice Samuel Alito were also in the majority. Of these five Justices, as I detailed in Chapter 1, four have deep and long-standing connections to the Federalist Society network. In addition to the network affiliations of these four Supreme Court Justices, as Figure 2.1 illustrates, the Federalist Society was well represented in other areas of the litigation effort. Six-time Federalist Society National Conference presenter Judge Laurence Silberman[63] wrote the Circuit Court decision in *Heller.* Further, three of the lawyers involved in masterminding the litigation strategy on behalf of Dick Heller et al., Clark M. Neily III,[64] Robert Levy,[65] and Alan Gura,[66] have active ties to the Federalist Society network. Finally, an impressive 21 members of the Federalist Society network signed on to eight different *amicus curiae* briefs submitted on behalf of Dick Heller.[67] Some of the more prominent signatories on these briefs include former Reagan attorney general and early

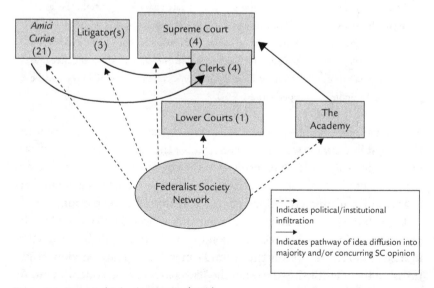

Figure 2.1 *District of Columbia v. Heller* (2008)

Federalist Society patron Edwin Meese III,[68] Eugene Volokh (whose Second Amendment scholarship is also recommended reading by the Federalist Society's *Bibliography*), and Nelson Lund, who chairs the "Second Amendment" Subcommittee of the Federalist Society's Civil Rights Practice Group.[69]

One *amicus* brief ("Brief for Amici Curiae Former Senior Officials of the Department of Justice in Support of Respondent")[70] is particularly noteworthy, because it contains 10 Federalist Society signatories, and was being drafted by several members of the network at the time I was interviewing them in 2008.[71] For example, in responding to a question about Federalist Society influence, former attorney general and Federalist Society mentor Edwin Meese cited this joint-brief as one example of the ways in which the organization has helped further the goals and principles of the Reagan Revolution. Meese said, "For example on the *Heller* case that's coming up, the gun case... we have a lot of people helping on that in various ways and other major cases today. I know I get importuned to help participate in various briefs for Supreme Court cases by people I worked with in the past there."[72] Similarly, former head of the Office of Legal Counsel and Federalist Society member Douglas Kmiec talked about how he came to be a signatory on that same brief:

> [Charles J.] Cooper called me about this one and said... "would you take a look at the brief filed by Janet Reno and the Solicitor General and tell me what you think." So this is a brief filed by... a pretty suspicious looking group: Ed Meese, Bill Barr, Bob Bork, Viet Dinh, Richard Willard, myself. You'll notice this is mostly [Office of Legal Counsel] people... but Chuck [Cooper] basically said he was going to take the laboring ore in terms of most of the writing and then he'd circulate drafts so that we could make changes and if we were satisfied enough we could sign on. And that happened I suppose because first the Federalist Society pulled us together as former colleagues and now on this current issue we have at least some common ground in seeing [the Second Amendment] properly interpreted.[73]

This is just one example of the ways in which the "social capital" that the Federalist Society network helps generate for the conservative legal movement (Teles 2008, 136) has resulted in the coordinated and effective diffusion of intellectual capital, or ideas, to Supreme Court decision makers in a way that, ultimately, helped effect a constitutional revolution.

Like all of the Federalist Society network scholarship outlined in the previous section on the Second Amendment, Justice Scalia's justification in *Heller* for (re)interpreting the Second Amendment as an individual right turns on the relationship between the "two parts" of the Amendment. As Scalia writes in *Heller*:

The Second Amendment is naturally divided into two parts: its prefatory clause and its operative clause. The former does not limit the latter grammatically, but rather announces a purpose. The Amendment could be rephrased, "Because a well regulated Militia is necessary to the security of a free State, the right of the people to keep and bear Arms shall not be infringed."... Although this structure of the Second Amendment is unique in our Constitution, other legal documents of the founding era, particularly individual-rights provisions of state constitutions, commonly included a prefatory statement of purpose. See generally Volokh, The Commonplace Second Amendment, 73 N.Y.U. L. Rev. 793, 814–821 (1998).[74]

As you will note above, Scalia relies on fellow network member Eugene Volokh's article to help support the Court's interpretation of the relationship between the "prefatory" and "operative" clauses of the Second Amendment. Later in the opinion, in further defending his Originalist (re)interpretation of the right to bear arms as not being limited to the militia, Scalia again enlists the help of Eugene Volokh, whose analysis of historical materials from the founding in a later law review article provided support for the Supreme Court's claim that the "natural meaning" of "bear arms" in the eighteenth century "enshrined a right of citizens to 'bear arms in defense of themselves and the state'" and was not limited to "carrying a weapon in an organized military unit."[75] Finally, a 2007 law review article by Volokh is mobilized by Scalia, to provide a rather expansive understanding of the meaning of "security of a free state" in the Second Amendment's prefatory clause: "The phrase 'security of a free state' meant 'security of a free policy,' not security of each of the several states as the dissent below argued." "It is true," Scalia continues, "that the term 'State' elsewhere in the Constitution refers to individual states, but the phrase 'security of a free state' and close variations seem to have been terms of art in 18th-century political discourse, meaning a 'free country' or free polity. See Volokh, "Necessary to the Security of a Free State," 83 *Notre Dame L. Rev.* 1, 5 (2007)."[76]

In addition to Scalia's frequent reliance on Eugene Volokh's Second Amendment scholarship, the majority opinion mobilizes an article by member Randy Barnett (a recommended author on the Second Amendment by the Federalist Society's *Bibliography*) to rebut the petitioner's argument that the phrase "bear arms" was used most often in the military context, not the personal or everyday context.[77] This 2004 law review article, entitled "Was the Right to Keep and Bear Arms Conditioned on Service in an Organized Militia?" was also cited by fellow member Nelson Lund in his *amicus curiae* brief submitted to the Supreme Court in *Heller* on behalf of the Claremont Institute.[78] The Barnett article provides a plethora of Originalist evidence to support an individual rights (not collective rights) reading of the Second Amendment. In fact, as Barnett explained to me in our interview in 2008, it was his move to Originalism in the scope of his work on the Ninth and Second Amendments that truly solidified his connection to and relationship with the Federalist Society network:

> . . . although the Federalist Society was always generous and warm to me in my deal-
> ings with them. . . it was when I made the move to Originalism that we became much
> closer, because before then we had this limited government idea in common and
> some other general cultural things in common possibly but what I was writing about
> was stuff that a lot of Federalist Society people disagree with. Once I made the move
> to Originalism, and not only that, became one of the leading theoretical spokespeo-
> ple and defenders of the method, we had a lot more in common and my relationship
> to the Federalist Society became much closer after that.[79]

Not only is Randy Barnett now a leading theoretician of Originalism, as he mentions in the excerpt above and as I detailed in the preceding sec-tions, he is one of the leading authorities within the Federalist Society network on the Second Amendment.

In addition to Federalist Society network scholarship, the major-ity opinion in *Heller* also mobilized some of the most oft-cited sources from the Originalist canon (examined earlier in this chapter) by network members defending an individual rights view of the Second Amendment: *Federalist* 46 (*595), *Federalist* 29 (*598 and *600), and William Blackstone's *Commentaries* (*582, *593, *594, *595, *597, *606, *609, *626, and *627). The Supreme Court majority's heavy reliance on this out-side intellectual capital developed over decades by scholars affiliated with the Federalist Society in *Heller* is noteworthy but, in the end, not all that surprising. As I wrote in Chapter 1, when the Supreme Court decides to either significantly alter or entirely reconstruct a constitutional frame (as it had to do with the Second Amendment in *Heller*), it cannot simply rely on its own authoritative precedent to do so. In *Heller*, as in other cases like this, the Court had to look for outside authorities to justify this radical reinterpretation of the Second Amendment. However, Federalist Society mentor Justice Scalia did not have to look too far or too hard to find the intellectual capital upon which to construct this new Second Amendment frame—a small but influential group of scholars had been hard at work, building it for decades. As this section has demonstrated, this intellectual capital was easily diffused by Federalist Society network affiliated litiga-tors, *amici curiae*, and clerks—individuals who became active conduits for the transmission of ideas and Originalist sources that supported this seis-mic Second Amendment shift.

McDonald v. Chicago (2010)

Initiated in the immediate wake of the Supreme Court's *Heller* ruling, this case challenged the constitutionality of several long-standing Chicago and Oak Park ordinances that prohibited people from possessing firearms unless they were holders of valid registration certificates.[80] The ordinances also prevented the registration of most types of handguns, effectively banning nearly all possession for private residents of the city.[81] The Chicago City Council approved the gun control law in March 1982, stating that the handgun ban was designed to protect its citizens "from the loss of property and injury or death from firearms."[82] The law was enacted during a national trend of increased handgun regulations prompted by events associated with the small suburb of Morton Grove, Illinois.[83] Following Morton Grove's passage of a ban on the possession of handguns by anyone but police officers and antique collectors, the city of Chicago joined approximately 400 cities and towns, from Massachusetts to California, in passing similar ordinances.[84]

The *McDonald* case was filed with the support of three gun rights organizations on behalf of a group of residents of the greater Chicago area. Otis McDonald, one of the petitioners, wanted to possess a handgun in his home for self-defense because he was in his late seventies and resided in a neighborhood with a high crime rate.[85] A community activist devoting substantial time to alternative policing methods with the intention of increasing neighborhood safety, McDonald often received threats from nearby drug dealers.[86] Another petitioner, Colleen Lawson, had been the victim of a home burglary and believed a handgun would protect her in the event of a future attack.[87] The petitioners owned handguns but were forced to keep them outside the city limits instead of inside their homes, due to the Chicago city ordinances.

Following the Supreme Court's ruling in *Heller*, the Chicago petitioners, the Illinois State Rifle Association, and the Second Amendment Foundation, Inc., filed suit against the City of Chicago in the U.S. District Court for the Northern District of Illinois, claiming Chicago's gun control ordinances violated the Second and Fourteenth Amendments to the U.S. Constitution. The National Rifle Association (NRA) filed an additional action challenging the Chicago ordinance, and joined two Oak Park residents in challenging the similar Chicago suburb law in the same District Court.[88] The three district court cases were assigned to the same judge who, citing Seventh Circuit precedent, rejected the plaintiffs' argument that the Chicago and Oak Park laws were unconstitutional.[89] The Seventh Circuit affirmed the decision based on three Supreme Court cases from the nineteenth century: *United States v. Cruikshank*,[90] *Presser v. Illinois*,[91] and *Miller v. Texas*.[92] This trio of cases was decided in the wake of the Supreme Court's narrow interpretation of the Privileges or Immunities Clause of the Fourteenth Amendment in the *Slaughter-House Cases*.[93] Although the Seventh Circuit, in an opinion written by Judge Frank H. Easterbrook, described the rationale of those cases as "defunct," recognizing that they did not consider "the question whether the Fourteenth Amendment's Due Process Clause incorporates the Second Amendment right to keep and bear arms,"[94] the court nonetheless felt obliged to follow the precedent established by the Supreme Court. The Supreme Court granted certiorari,[95] after which the petitioners argued on appeal that the right to possess handguns is among the "Privileges or Immunities of citizens of the United States" and that the Court should reject the narrow interpretation of the Privileges or Immunities Clause established in the *Slaughter-House Cases*. Additionally, the petitioners contended that the Fourteenth Amendment's Due Process Clause incorporated the Second Amendment right to keep and bear arms.[96] The Supreme Court ruled five to four, with Federalist Society member Justice Samuel Alito writing for the majority (and with fellow network members Scalia and Thomas both penning concurring opinions), that the local handgun bans were unconstitutional because the Fourteenth Amendment's Due Process Clause incorporated the Second Amendment.[97]

In addition to the four Federalist Society network Justices on the bench in *McDonald*, the network was represented by 11 *amici curiae* on seven briefs,[98] including Edwin Meese III, Clint Bolick,[99] and John C. Eastman.[100] Additionally, the network also boasted three litigators representing the petitioners Otis McDonald et al. (Paul Clement,[101] Alan Gura, and Kevin Martin[102]), one lower court judge, and 32-time Federalist Society National Conference participant Frank Easterbrook, who wrote the majority opinion for the Seventh Circuit decision. While not an impressively large number of Federalist Society network members participated in the *McDonald* litigation overall, those who did were both well-positioned to diffuse intellectual capital to Supreme Court decision makers and, consistent with the PEN framework, very ideologically coherent in their arguments and sources. For example, of the eight briefs (seven *amicus curiae* and Brief for Petitioner) that contained Federalist Society network signatories, seven of these argued for *exclusively* using the Privileges or Immunities clause to apply the Second Amendment to the states.[103] In fact, of the 30 *amicus curiae* briefs submitted in *McDonald*, only two briefs with non-Federalist Society signatories lobbied as aggressively and exclusively for using the Privileges or Immunities path.[104]

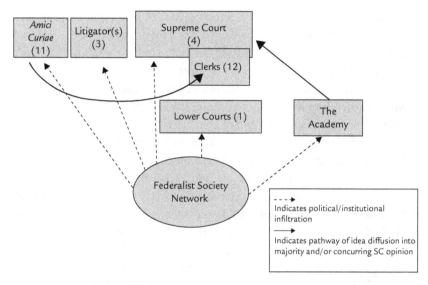

Figure 2.2 *McDonald v. City of Chicago* (2010)

Moreover, in constructing their arguments, each one of these Federalist Society network briefs relied on at least one source (and in most cases multiple sources) of Federalist Society network intellectual capital, including the scholarship of Michael Kent Curtis, Eugene Volokh, Randy Barnett, and John C. Harrison, which I reviewed earlier in this chapter. While, as I explain below, neither the Circuit Court nor the Supreme Court majority opinions would adopt this view of radically reinterpreting incorporation of the Bill of Rights through the Privileges or Immunities Clause, it would feature prominently in the concurring opinion in *McDonald* by fellow Federalist Society network member Justice Clarence Thomas.

Judge Frank Easterbrook's Seventh Circuit Opinion, while expressing sympathy for the views advocated for by fellow Federalist Society members lobbying for the resurrection of the Privileges or Immunities Clause, is more directly concerned with the judicial hierarchy and the notion of judicial restraint—the notion that his court has neither the authority nor the willingness to overturn or sidestep the *Slaughter-House Cases* and the controlling precedent regarding the applicability of the Second Amendment to the states. As he writes, "[a]lthough the rationale of *Cruikshank*, *Presser*, and *Miller* is defunct, the Court has not telegraphed any plan to overrule *Slaughter-House* and apply all of the amendments to the states through the Privileges or Immunities clause, despite scholarly arguments that it should do this." Easterbrook's opinion continues by stating that the question of incorporation needs to be one for "the Justices rather than a court of appeals."[105] This opinion is an excellent illustration of what Easterbrook has, at Federalist Society conferences and in other cases, consistently been preoccupied with—judicial activism. Purportedly captured and articulated in the Federalist Society's statement of principles, within the Federalist Society network, judicial activism has come to mean that judges should be confined to using their power of judicial review to say "what the law is" not "what [they think] it should be."[106] Since being invited to speak at one of the earliest Federalist Society conferences, a 1984 "Symposium on Judicial Activism: Problems and Responses," Judge Easterbrook has spoken on the topic of "judicial activism" or "judicial restraint" an impressive five additional times at Federalist Society National Conferences.[107] More recently, Easterbrook participated in the 2008 National Lawyer Convention's Showcase Panel at the Federalist Society's conference on "The People and the Judiciary."

Easterbrook is not alone within the Federalist Society network in thinking this is an important set of constitutional concerns. As a testament to how salient this conversation is within the Federalist Society, eight National Conferences have featured some variation of the judicial role or the problems of judicial activism as their dedicated and headlining theme.[108] This is also borne out in interview data. For example, in asking key members of the Federalist Society network about the shared principles or priorities of the Federalist Society, the idea of "judicial restraint" received the second most mentions, right behind a belief in, or commitment to, Originalism.[109] As Federalist Society member Gail Heriot explained in our interview, when asked about unifying principle(s) within the Federalist Society, "[o]ne thing, the most unifying thing. . . is that the judiciary's job is not to make law but to say what the law is. That is something that just about everyone agrees with up to a point." [110] This emphasis on judicial restraint helps provide some context for why Judge Easterbrook—the single most frequent participant at Federalist Society National Meetings since its founding (see Table 1.2)—would issue a decision that might seem to be at odds with the preferred outcome of Second Amendment enthusiasts within the Federalist Society network. It might also help explain why Supreme Court Justice Samuel Alito, a clear Second Amendment enthusiast who signed on to Scalia's revolutionary majority opinion in *Heller* rendering several long-standing Second Amendment decisions obsolete, would be hesitant to overturn another century-plus-old opinion (*Slaughter-House*) just two years later.

Like Easterbrook's Seventh Circuit opinion, Justice Samuel Alito's majority opinion in *McDonald* signals his intellectual sympathy with the Privileges or Immunities approach to incorporation, noting that "[t]oday, many legal scholars dispute the correctness of the narrow *Slaughter-House* interpretation" of that clause.[111] However, perhaps because of a belief in judicial restraint combined with the availability of an alternative (though admittedly less desirable to conservatives and libertarians) path, Alito sees "no need to reconsider that interpretation here," ultimately declining "to disturb the *Slaughter-House* holding."[112] Using the Due Process framework, the burden on the majority was still to show that the right to bear arms was a "fundamental right" in the context of the Supreme Court's precedent and understanding in this area. To do so, the Alito-authored opinion relies in part on the intellectual capital of Federalist Society cofounder Steven Calabresi, whose 2008 co-authored law review article "Individual Rights under State Constitutions When the Fourteenth Amendment Was Ratified in 1868"[113] mobilized evidence from the constitutions of several states that showed, according to Alito, that "[a] clear majority of the states in 1868, therefore, recognized the right to keep and bear arms as being among the foundational rights necessary to our system of Government."[114]

Fellow Federalist Society network member Justice Scalia writes separately in *McDonald*, first, to signal that he joins the Court's opinion "despite [his] misgivings about Substantive Due Process as an original matter,"[115] and second, to respond to dissenting Justice John Paul Stevens's criticisms of Originalism as an interpretive method in general, and of its application in this case.[116] Recall the discussion in Chapter 1: the Federalist Society as a PEN identified Originalism as the interpretive method embodying the Federalist Society's shared notion of validity— that is, as the only mode consistent with a proper understanding of the nature of government and the structure of the Constitution. Thus, Justice Stevens's attack on Originalism can be seen, in part, as an attack on the PEN itself. Given this, it is not surprising that the Federalist Society's founding advisor at the University of Chicago, Antonin Scalia—who also wrote the foreword to the Federalist Society's 2007 edited volume *Originalism: A Quarter-Century of Debate*[117]—would exert the intellectual energy to pen an impassioned defense of Originalism in his concurring opinion in *McDonald*. Scalia's response to Stevens, reminiscent of his own writings on Originalism and of early talks he gave at the Federalist Society prior to and since becoming a member of the Supreme Court,[118] defends Originalism not as a "perfect" method of constitutional interpretation, but rather as the "best means available" and, more pointedly, as better than the methodology of "'living Constitution' advocates":

> Justice Stevens' response to this concurrence, post, 3116-3119, makes the usual rejoinder of "living Constitution" advocates to the criticism that it empowers judges to eliminate or expand what the people have prescribed: The traditional, historically focused method, he says, reposes discretion in judges as well. Historical analysis

can be difficult; it sometimes requires resolving threshold questions, and making nuanced judgments about which evidence to consult and how to interpret it. . . . But the question to be decided is not whether the historically focused method is a *perfect means* of restraining aristocratic judicial Constitution-writing; but whether it is the *best means available* in an imperfect world. . . . I think it beyond all serious dispute that it is much less subjective, and intrudes much less upon the democratic process (emphases in original).[119]

Scalia's concurrence in *McDonald*, while not reflective of the PEN's specific beliefs and intellectual capital concerning the Second Amendment and incorporation, is a reflection of that community's most widely shared and deeply held beliefs about Originalism as the best (and, indeed, the only valid) method of constitutional interpretation.

Fellow network member Justice Thomas's concurrence, on the other hand, embodies nearly perfectly the Federalist Society network beliefs about Privileges or Immunities and Second Amendment incorporation. Spanning an impressive 29 pages in length and drawing on various sources of Federalist Society network intellectual capital—including the previously examined scholarship of member Michael Kent Curtis as well as non-network sources provided in Federalist Society-affiliated briefs— Thomas's concurrence in *McDonald* mounts an Originalist argument for overturning *Slaughter-House* and for declaring the right to keep and bear arms as one of the various privileges protected in his reconstructed understanding of the Privileges or Immunities Clause.[120]

In critical parts of his historical/Originalist argument for resurrecting the Privileges or Immunities Clause, five times in his opinion Thomas draws on the intellectual capital of Michael Kent Curtis,[121] who—as I wrote earlier in this chapter—laid out an argument for resurrecting the Privileges or Immunities Clause at the 1988 Federalist Society National Conference. Curtis's book *No State Shall Abridge* was also mobilized in every single one of the Federalist Society–affiliated briefs (*amicus* and counsel) that argued for incorporating the Second Amendment through the Privileges or Immunities Clause.[122] Thomas's concurrence mobilizes dozens of other historical and Originalist sources to support his argument, nearly all of which also are mobilized in Federalist Society–affiliated briefs submitted to the Supreme Court in *McDonald*. One *amicus curiae* brief is particularly noteworthy—that of the American Center for Law and Justice (ACLJ), with Federalist Society member Jay Alan Sekulow as counsel of record.[123] Jay Sekulow participated in the 2007 Federalist Society National Conference alongside Federalist Society stalwarts Eugene Volokh and Michael W. McConnell on a panel organized by the Free Speech and Election Law Practice Groups.[124] Not only does

Sekulow's brief mobilize several of the same sources as the Thomas concurrence, but it also deploys them in a very similar way. I excerpt (and abridge) two lengthier sections below that demonstrate this overlap between the ACLJ *amicus curiae* brief and Thomas's concurring opinion, beginning with the former:

The Privileges or Immunities Clause of the Fourteenth Amendment is better suited for incorporation the individual protections of the Bill of Rights, including the Second Amendment. In interpreting the Constitution, this Court is "guided by the principle that '[t]he Constitution was written to be understood by the voters; its words and phrases were used in their normal and ordinary as distinguished from technical meaning." *District of Columbia v. Heller*, 128 S. Ct. 2783, 2788 (2008). This reference to the phrase "normal and ordinary" should be read to include the way in which the terms were understood in contemporary legal discourse. . . William Blackstone recognized the true relationship between man's natural rights and the law of governments as their protectors. . . . Blackstone characterized these positive law rights as "civil privileges" and "private immunities." Blackstone supra, 125. Blackstone's undeniable influence over American legal thought imparted this understanding of privileges and immunities to the Founders. . . . [Alexander] Hamilton quotes Blackstone's position that the terms "privileges" and "immunities" referred to the sacred and fundamental natural rights of all men as guarded by the sentinel of positive political enactments. . . . This understanding of "privileges" and "immunities" is not inconsistent with prevailing case law at the time of the Fourteenth Amendment. . . . Of all the possible interpretations of the Privileges and Immunities of Article IV, the interpretation that dominated antebellum case law and commentary was a reading that; "require[d] [S]tates to grant visiting citizens *some* of the same privileges and immunities which the [S]tate conferred upon its own citizens." Kurt Lash, *The Origins of the Privileges or Immunities Clause, Part I: "Privileges and Immunities" as an Antebellum Term of Art*, 18 (Loyola Law Sch. Legal Studies Paper No. 2009-29, 2009. . . . Applying this history of the origins of the terms "privileges" and "immunities" to the text of the amendment, the terms "privileges" and "immunities" when paired together, "did not refer to the natural rights belonging to all people or institutions, but referred instead to rights belonging to a certain group of people or a particular institution." Lash, supra, 16; see also *Magill v. Brown*, 16 F Cas. 408, 428 (C.C.E.D. Pa. 1833) (No 8952) (privileges and immunities are "the rights of persons, place or property; a privilege is a peculiar right, a private law, conceded to particular persons or places, whereby a particular man, . . . is exempted from the rigor of the common law. . .").[125]

In interpreting [the Privileges or Immunities Clause], it is important to recall that constitutional provisions are "'written to be understood by the voters.'" Heller, 554 U.S., at ---. . . . Thus, the objective of this inquiry is to discern what "ordinary citizens" at the time of ratification would have understood the Privileges or Immunities

Clause to mean. 554 U.S. at ---, 128 S.Ct., 2788. At the time of Reconstruction, the terms "privileges" and "immunities" had an established meaning as synonyms for "rights." The two words, standing alone or paired together, were used interchangeably with the words "rights," "liberties," and "freedoms," and had been since the time of Blackstone. See 1 W. Blackstone, Commentaries *129 (describing the "rights and liberties" of Englishmen as "private immunities" and "civil privileges"). A number of antebellum judicial decisions used the terms in this manner. See, e.g., *Magill v. Brown*, 16 F. Cas. 408, 428 (No 8.952) (CC ED Pa. 1833) (Baldwin, J.) ("The words 'privileges and immunities' relate to the rights of persons, place or property; a privilege is a peculiar right, a private law, conceded to particular persons or places"). . . . Blackstone, for example, used the terms "privileges" and "immunities" to describe both the inalienable rights of individuals and the positive law rights of corporations. See 1 Commentaries, *129 (describing "private immunities" as a "residuum of natural liberty," and "civil privileges" as those "which society has engaged to provide, in lieu of the natural liberties so given up by individuals"). . . . The nature of a privilege or immunity thus varied depending on the person, group, or entity to whom those rights were assigned, See Lash, The Origins of the Privileges or Immunities Clause, Part I: "Privileges and Immunities" as an Antebellum Term of Art, 98 *Geo. L.J.* 12241, 1256–1257 (2010) (surveying antebellum usages of these terms).[126]

While the two do not map perfectly on to one another, there is an unmistakable overlap in terms of the logic and use of authorities to support and defend the radical reinterpretation of Privileges or Immunities that both Federalist Society network members propose.

In our 2008 interview, former head of the Office of Legal Counsel under Reagan and Federalist Society member Douglas Kmiec described Justice Clarence Thomas as "the jurist who is unafraid to explore originalist implications." Expanding on this thought, Kmiec added: "I think if you were looking for an honest statement of originalist jurisprudence, Thomas comes closest to the pure Federalist Society model."[127] Similarly, Federalist Society member and Second Amendment expert Randy Barnett described Justice Thomas as a Federalist Society "icon" and quiet "hero."[128] In the context of the PEN framework, Justice Thomas might be described more accurately as the best *consumer* of Federalist Society intellectual capital on the Supreme Court. As I demonstrate throughout this book, his Originalist analyses—often penned as concurring opinions in major cases—borrow heavily from Federalist Society–member briefs and scholarship (sometimes citing his sources, other times not). As Law Professor Sandy Levinson noted in a 1996 law review article in the context of evaluating Thomas's concurring opinion in *United States v. Lopez* (which I examine in great length in Chapter 4), "[t]he ordinary standards governing attribution of sources—the violation of which constitutes plagiarism—seem not to apply in Justice Thomas' chambers. Whether responsibility for this. . . is best assigned to the Justice himself or to his law clerks is known only to them" (Levinson 1996, 775). Either way, Kmiec and Barnett were correct in asserting that Thomas's opinions, including his concurrence in *McDonald*, do represent the Federalist Society model in its most pure form—in part, because these opinions are often constructed almost entirely using network member intellectual capital.

IDEAS WITH CONSEQUENCES: THE RIGHT TO KEEP AND BEAR ARMS

"The rights of the individual citizen would be little different today if the Second Amendment did not exist" (Sprecher 1965, 667). Nearly half a century later, thanks in part to the persistent and coordinated efforts of a small but dedicated group of academics, judges, and litigators connected through and supported by the Federalist Society network, the Supreme Court has (to borrow the words of the late Judge Robert A. Sprecher) finally "found" the "Lost Amendment." Nevertheless, as this chapter has demonstrated, constitutional frameworks are not simply "found" or rediscovered. They are consciously and systematically constructed and reconstructed, often over a long period of time with the help of key members of the "support structure" (Epp 1998; Southworth 2008; Teles 2008; Hollis-Brusky 2011a) working from the outside to develop, support, and diffuse the intellectual capital that will become the scaffolding for new Supreme Court frames. In his revolutionary opinion in *Heller*, former Federalist Society advisor Justice Antonin Scalia relied on several sources of Federalist Society network intellectual capital to help construct and support the personal or individual rights reading of the Second Amendment—a view that only three decades earlier was considered to be completely "off-the-wall" within academic, legal, and political circles. Still, with the properly framed case brought by Federalist Society–affiliated litigators and, just as importantly, with the intellectual capital nurtured and supported through Federalist Society conferences and events and further developed by network members in their scholarship, in *Heller* five Justices on the Supreme Court were able to reinterpret radically the Second Amendment's right to keep and bear arms as a personal, not a collective right. Federalist Society network members recognized the revolutionary and important nature of the *Heller* decision, and their post-decision reactions reflected their optimism about where this jurisprudence might lead. Second Amendment scholar and network member Randy Barnett called the decision "a great victory for gun rights—one that until a few years ago would have been unimaginable."[129] Similarly, Federalist Society network member Robert A. Levy wrote in the wake of the *Heller* decision: "Last week, apparently embarrassed by seven decades without a coherent explanation of the right celebrated during the Founding era as 'the true palladium of liberty,' the court rediscovered the Second Amendment."[130] George Will, who delivered an address at the Federalist Society's National Lawyers Convention in 2000, remarked in a *Washington Post* editorial in 2008, "[o]f conservatives' few victories this year, the most cherished came when the Supreme Court, in *District of Columbia v. Heller*, held for the first time that the Second Amendment protects an individual right to bear arms."[131]

Others within the Federalist Society network—including those who were involved most closely with the litigation in *Heller* and who continue to bring Second Amendment litigation in the post-*Heller* era—while recognizing the decision as an important step toward a more robust protection for the right to keep and bear arms, have expressed disappointment with Scalia's opinion in that case. For example, during a Federalist Society Teleforum Call sponsored by the Criminal Law and Procedures Practice Group on August 16, 2012, Nelson Lund said that Scalia's opinion in *Heller* was "unclear" and was generating significant problems in the lower courts, which in his view, were struggling to apply the case's holding properly.[132] As Lund and Gura noted during their Teleforum Call with fellow Federalist Society members, there have been some encouraging post-*Heller* decisions coming out of select lower courts—including decisions in *Ezell v. City of Chicago*, authored by Federalist Society network member Judge Diane A. Sykes,[133] in which the Seventh Circuit struck down part of a Chicago law prohibiting public firing ranges,[134] and in *Moore v. Madigan*, authored by Federalist Society network member Judge Richard A. Posner,[135] in which the Seventh Circuit relied on *Heller* and *McDonald* to strike down Illinois's total ban on concealed carry of firearms outside the home.[136] In hundreds of other cases that have been initiated in the wake of *Heller*, lower courts generally have been reluctant to strike down gun control laws.[137] As Alan Gura noted toward the end of that Teleforum Call, "we are at the very beginning of the post-*Heller*, post-*McDonald* process," and while there are a small group of individuals working hard to bring the kinds of "strategic civil rights cases" that have the "likelihood of shaping the law," the process is slow and will be continuing over the next decade. In other words, the process of building upon and, for Federalist Society network actors, entrenching these victories (or at least protecting them from being narrowed or eroded in the lower courts) is just now beginning.

Additionally, as we saw in the case of *McDonald*, which was initiated in the wake of the *Heller* litigation, the question of how and if to incorporate the Second Amendment against the states presented a critical opportunity for members of the Federalist Society network, who had been waiting for the right time and opportunity to aggressively lobby the Supreme Court to overturn *Slaughter-House* and resurrect the Privileges or Immunities Clause. While the practical effect of incorporating the Second Amendment through either the Due Process or Privileges or Immunities Clause would have been no different (as Randy Barnett wrote in a *Wall Street Journal* op-ed, regardless of the approach the Supreme Court chose, "the Chicago gun ban at issue will soon be consigned to the dust bin of history"),[138] the long-term and precedential effect of such a decision favoring the latter approach would have been nothing short of sweeping. Even still, as Randy Barnett wrote shortly after the decision, with Justice Thomas providing the crucial fifth vote in *McDonald* but doing so by incorporating the Second Amendment through the Privileges or Immunities Clause, there was no true majority for using the Substantive Due Process approach, only a *plurality*. As Barnett explains:

> . . . the fact that there was only a plurality for using the Due Process Clause means that the original meaning of the Privileges or Immunities Clause is not a part of constitutional law. Justice Thomas's uncontradicted analysis will enter into the casebooks from which all law students and future justices study the 14th Amendment. . . . Justice Thomas presented an extensive and detailed analysis of the original meaning of the Clause in the belief that "this case presents an opportunity to reexamine, and begin the process of restoring, the meaning of the Fourteenth Amendment agreed upon by those who ratified it." By declining to take issue with Justice Thomas's impressive 56-page originalist analysis, the other justices in effect conceded what legal scholars have for some time maintained— that the court's cramped reading of the clause in 1873 was inconsistent with its original meaning.[139]

Barnett concludes, in language that echoes that of the late Judge Robert A. Sprecher in describing the Second Amendment half a century earlier, "[t]his week the lost Privileges or Immunities Clause was suddenly found. And some day it may be fully restored to its proper place as the means by which fundamental individual rights are protected under the Constitution against abuses by states."[140] In short, while the Federalist Society network did not achieve its optimal goal in *McDonald*, its members did help push the doctrine significantly forward—laying one brick down on the path toward resurrecting Privileges or Immunities (and, according to Barnett's reasoning above, subtly chipped away at the authoritativeness of the despised Substantive Due Process doctrine). Ultimately, as the various narratives and analyses

throughout this book show, it is in this incremental fashion that constitutional change actually comes about. As Federalist Society network
member Lillian BeVier[141] said to me in our 2008 interview in response
to a question about changing the law (and changing the way people
think about the law), "[a] lot of times it's just like dripping water. You
know it can wear away a stone but it takes a lot of drips."[142]

CHAPTER 3

Judicial Activism, Inc.

The First Amendment, Campaign Finance, and Citizens United

U.S. Constitution, Amendment I
Congress shall make no law...
Abridging the freedom of speech

The Supreme Court's January 2010 decision in *Citizens United v. Federal Election Commission* (2010),[1] invalidating key campaign finance restrictions on election spending by corporations and unions, sent a shock wave through the American polity. Newspaper headlines shortly after the decision read, "Supreme Court Opens Floodgates for Corporate, Union Political Contributions,"[2] "Judicial Activism Inc.; The Supreme Court Tosses Out Reasonable Limits on Campaign Finance,"[3] and "Court Kills Limits on Corporate Politicking."[4] Every progressive politician from Nancy Pelosi (D-CA) to Barney Frank (D-MA) to Charles Schumer (D-NY) publicly decried the decision and vowed to pass an override or a constitutional amendment to fix this issue. Perhaps most memorably, on January 27, 2010, President Barack Obama used the bully pulpit of the State of the Union Address to chastise the members of the Supreme Court (seven of whom were sitting just in front of him) for issuing a decision that "will open the floodgates for special interests, including foreign corporations, to spend without limits in our elections."[5] The president then implored Congress to "pass a bill that helps correct some of these problems."[6] In response, the House of Representatives Subcommittee on the Constitution, Civil Rights, and Civil Liberties held a hearing called "The First Amendment and Campaign Finance Reform After *Citizens United*."[7]

The chairman, Jerrold Nadler (D-NY), opened the hearing with the following remarks on the Supreme Court's decision in *Citizens United*: "One of the things that strikes me. . . is the extent to which an extraordinarily activist Court reached out to issue this decision. The justices answered a question they weren't asked in order to overturn a century of precedent which they had reaffirmed only recently."[8]

Though the Court under the direction of Chief Justice Roberts was, to quote the subcommittee chairman, "extraordinarily activist" in how it orchestrated the *Citizens United* decision itself,[9] this is only half of the story. Having an activist Court is a necessary but not sufficient condition for revolutionary constitutional change. There also needs to be a set of litigators finding and bringing well-framed cases and a set of academics working to nurture and develop the intellectual capital that might be used to justify such a radical departure from existing constitutional frames. Put another way, there needs to be a well-developed, attentive, and attuned "support structure" (Epp 1998) to listen and interpret the "signals" from the Court (Baird 2007) and to respond by effectively supplying what the Justices need to enact sweeping change. In this case, as in many others detailed in this book, the Federalist Society, acting as a PEN, performed this important role for the Justices.

As this chapter details, the path to *Citizens United* began in earnest with two Supreme Court decisions issued in the late 1970s—*Buckley v. Valeo* (1976)[10] and *First National Bank of Boston v. Bellotti* (1978).[11] The constitutional campaign to deregulate campaign finance was accelerated in the mid-1990s with the institutional support and networks of the Federalist Society for Law and Public Policy Studies. The Supreme Court's decision in *Austin v. Michigan Chamber of Commerce* (1990)[12] and the momentum building behind campaign finance reform in Congress prompted actors within the Federalist Society network to organize around the issue and begin to build and develop the intellectual capital that would eventually allow a reconstituted Supreme Court in *Citizens United v. FEC* (2010) to reclaim, entrench, and extend the *Buckley-Bellotti* path. Most important, certain network members vocally urged the Justices to abandon judicial restraint—a principle the Federalist Society had championed since the 1980s—in the area of campaign finance jurisprudence in favor of a return to First Amendment first principles. For the two Federalist Society member Justices recently appointed to the Supreme Court (Roberts and Alito), this network nudging seems to have made a difference in terms of how they viewed their roles and the role of *stare decisis* in the area of campaign finance. To understand the full magnitude of the Federalist Society's influence in this area of constitutional law, we first must turn back the clock to the decade prior to the Federalist Society's founding.

Corruption-free government was the cry following the Watergate scandal in 1972. Opportunistic campaign finance reform advocates rode this wave of government distrust and proceeded to enact several significant amendments to the Federal Election Campaign Act of 1971. These amendments sought to reduce the role of money in elections, provide greater transparency for the electorate, and dispel the pall of perceived and real corruption that hung over current political affairs. Passed over President Gerald Ford's veto and enacted into law in 1974, the amendments were challenged in a lawsuit brought by Senator James L. Buckley of New York and others against Secretary of State Francis R. Valeo, an ex officio member of the newly constituted Federal Election Commission (FEC). Buckley et al. levied several constitutional challenges against the newly enacted amendments, but the most important test implicated campaign spending and contribution limits because they violated the First Amendment's freedom of speech.[13] *Buckley v. Valeo* (1976) was the resulting challenge. In a complex *per curiam* opinion, the Supreme Court majority upheld some provisions of the amendments (disclosure and reporting provisions and limits on individual contributions to candidates) but struck down caps and limits on overall contributions on behalf of candidates and spending caps for candidates themselves. In the course of doing so, the opinion in *Buckley* articulated the first important constitutional variable in the *Citizens United* equation: money is speech. The phrase "money is speech," while actually appearing only once in the opinion (in the partial dissent of Justice Byron White),[14] became shorthand for the majority's reasoning that money in the context of campaigns and elections can be understood as a form of important political speech and is therefore protected by the Constitution's First Amendment.

Just a few years after *Buckley*, the Supreme Court further entrenched the "money is speech" path in *First National Bank of Boston v. Bellotti* (1978). The Massachusetts legislature had established a criminal statute that prohibited corporations or banks from making certain kinds of expenditures for influencing the vote on state referenda. Justice Powell, writing for the majority, characterized the issue as whether or not the statute, "a prohibition directed at *speech itself*," could survive "the exacting scrutiny necessitated by a state-imposed restriction of free speech."[15] The majority in *Bellotti* reaffirmed the commitment to the "money is speech" path from *Buckley*. More important, however, through the course of its legal reasoning, the majority in *Bellotti* signaled that corporations, like individuals, should be afforded robust speech rights. This case provided the second important constitutional variable in the *Citizens United* equation: corporations also have speech rights. As Justice Powell wrote, "The inherent worth of speech in terms of its capacity for informing the public does not depend upon the identity of its source, whether corporation, association, union, or individual."[16] While not considered a landmark or particularly high-profile Supreme Court decision at the time it was issued,[17] as this chapter details, *Bellotti* came to play a central role 32 years later in the Supreme Court's landmark decision in *Citizens United.* [18] For this reason, former *New York Times* Supreme Court correspondent Linda Greenhouse named *Bellotti* "the most important Supreme Court case no one's ever heard of."[19]

Very little transformative Supreme Court litigation took place in the decade following *Buckley* and *Bellotti.* While lower courts were relying on the *Buckley* and *Bellotti* decisions to strike down campaign finance restrictions in various states,[20] the conservative legal movement did not mobilize and make a concerted effort to push the Free Speech agenda forward at the Supreme Court. One explanation for this was that the conservative legal movement did not exist in any meaningful sense prior to the mid-1980s. Absent a coordinated and sophisticated network of individuals and organizations to connect ideas and intellectual capital with litigation, financing, and strategies, coordinating and organizing litigation strategies would have been difficult. Additionally, it did not seem to be a priority for members of the conservative legal support structure who were organized during that time. In the decade following the *Buckley* and *Bellotti* decisions, for example, the Federalist Society hosted only one National Conference, in 1986, featuring organized panels on campaign finance and the First Amendment.[21]

The pace with which the courts traversed the path increased significantly in the last 15 years for a few reasons: the emergence of a robust conservative legal movement that brought the right kinds of cases framed in the right way to appeal to conservative members of the court and, second, the Supreme Court's surprising decision in *Austin v. Michigan Chamber of Commerce* (1990),[22] which marked the first major rejection of the *Buckley-Bellotti* path in over a decade, galvanizing a response among the conservative legal support structure to prevent the court from backpedaling any further. *Austin* addressed the heart of the expenditure-contribution distinction. The State of Michigan passed a law that prevented corporations from using funds from their general treasury for political expenditures. The Michigan Chamber of Commerce challenged the statute, asserting that it did not constitute a compelling state interest. The Court disagreed with the Chamber of Commerce and established a new compelling state interest. As the majority opinion stated, states have a vested interest in regulating "the corrosive and distorting effects of immense aggregations of wealth that are accumulated with the help of the corporate form and that have little or no correlation to the public's support for the corporation's political ideas."[23] The distinction the court drew in *Buckley* turned on the desire to prevent quid pro quo corruption—money for political votes. *Austin* expanded the Court's definition of corruption to accept influence, or political responsiveness, as a compelling state interest.

The conservative legal support structure did not present a robust voice in *Austin*, nor was it particularly concerned with campaign finance issues given the general stability of the respective jurisprudence. Compared to later cases, the numbers of *amici curiae* and prominent conservative legal movement members participating was negligible.[24] The dissents of Justices Kennedy and Scalia in *Austin*, on the other hand, were indicative of the direction and degree of criticism that members of the conservative legal support structure would begin to voice about *Austin* in its aftermath. In their impassioned dissents, the Justices in *Austin* cited the Supreme Court's decision in *First National Bank of Boston v. Bellotti* (1978) 14 times as evidence that the majority had misconstrued both Supreme Court precedent and the First Amendment in its ruling.[25]

THE FEDERALIST SOCIETY NETWORK, THE FIRST AMENDMENT, AND CAMPAIGN FINANCE

Unlike the decade following *Buckley* and *Bellotti* and preceding *Austin*, the 1990s would witness an uptick in activity and interest in campaign finance among the ever-expanding networks and organizations of the conservative legal support structure. Between 1988 and 1998, the Federalist Society's overall membership would rise from just shy of 5,000 to over 25,000 (Teles 2008, 150). Also, in 1996 the Federalist Society formed its Free Speech and Election Law Practice Group.[26] The formation of this group came on the heels of Congress's first failed attempt in 1995 to pass the sweeping campaign finance reform package that would eventually become the Bipartisan Campaign Finance Reform Act (BCRA), or McCain-Feingold.[27] In the Practice Group's very first Newsletter, published in the fall of 1996, Senator Mitch McConnell (R-KY) referred to the McCain-Feingold bill as "an unprecedented power grab" and wrote that "[f]reedom-loving Americans of all ideological persuasions should be horrified by the professional reformers' ambition to force a bureaucratic takeover of the American political process."[28] In that same issue, James Bopp, Jr. decried the FEC's "assault on the First Amendment,"[29] while Allison Hayward criticized the Supreme Court for its inconsistent application of "core" First Amendment principles in its campaign finance jurisprudence.[30] As I detail in the case analyses later in this chapter, the scholars and practitioners this Practice Group brought together both physically (through organized panels) and intellectually (through its newsletters, journal, and teleforum calls) included several key figures who factored prominently in the campaign finance litigation leading up to and including the successful challenge in *Citizens United*.

A larger group than the PEN cohering around the Second Amendment examined in the previous chapter, the group of scholars and practitioners active in discussions of campaign finance and the First Amendment within the Federalist Society network is still relatively small and tight-knit. In reviewing National Conference transcripts and Practice Group newsletters, I identified 49 individuals as active contributors to the network's dialogue on the subject. The most active contributors include current chairman of the Free Speech and Election Law Practice Group Allison Hayward, past chairman James Bopp, Jr., and legal academics Lillian BeVier, Bradley A. Smith, and John McGinnis. Several other prominent network actors contributed to this dialogue through their scholarship and advocacy, including Jan Witold Baran, Joel Gora, and Richard E. Wiley. What all these network members have in common, as Lillian BeVier explained to me in our interview in 2008, is an overarching belief in "freedom" and "liberty." Tellingly, BeVier first said "individual freedom" but then corrected herself, emphasizing that it was not just "individual freedom" but "freedom" and "liberty" more generally.[31] Federalist Society cofounder Lee Liberman Otis, who helped draft the Society's statement of principles, also formulated her response to what the network's overarching beliefs were to me in the exact same way: "I think that individual freedom, no freedom is what I would say, not individual freedom—freedom, liberty."[32] This distinction is important for members of this PEN and important for our narrative of campaign finance jurisprudence, as these members consistently have expressed the position that corporations should be entitled to many of the same liberties and freedoms guaranteed to individuals in the constitution and Bill of Rights. This is also consistent with the Federalist Society's official statement of principles, examined at length in Chapter 1, which reads, "the state exists to preserve freedom," *not* that "the state exists to preserve *individual* freedom" (emphasis added).[33]

As mentioned earlier, prior to the mid-1990s, the Federalist Society network did not appear to discuss the topic of the First Amendment and campaign finance with any frequency or intensity at National Conferences, though it did come up. At the 1986 National Meeting, for example, Milton Friedman gave a talk on "Free Markets and Free Speech," Lillian BeVier presented a campaign-finance-centric talk entitled "Hands Off the

Political Process" while Charles J. Cooper presented a similar position on campaign finance in his talk "The First Amendment, Original Intent, and the Political Process."[34] After the Free Speech and Election Law Practice Group organized in 1996, the activity and intellectual capital development was more or less centered on the Practice Group's newsletters. Between 1996 and 2000, the Practice Group published nine separate issues, featuring 38 articles by network members on topics ranging from "Taking Commercial Speech Seriously"[35] to "*Buckley v. Valeo* Revisited"[36] to a semi-regular review of relevant Supreme Court decisions in the area of campaign finance.[37] Since 2000, the Free Speech and Election Law Practice Group has hosted at least one high-profile panel at every Federalist Society National Lawyers Convention. At the 2000 National Convention, Jan Witold Baran, Michael Malbin, Steven Rosenthal, and Bradley A. Smith discussed campaign finance and the role of parties on a panel entitled "The Future of Political Parties."[38] At the 2003 National Convention, Daniel Ortiz, Trevor Potter, Kenneth Starr, David Thompson, and Fifth Circuit Judge Jerry Smith directly engaged the topic of "Campaign Finance Reform in the Supreme Court."[39] Additionally, the Federalist Society sponsored a four-panel, year-long "Election Law Series" as a "Special Project" from May through September 2006, indicating the increasing importance and institutional attention the network was giving to the subject.[40]

There have been several kinds of arguments levied by Federalist Society network members against campaign finance regulations. For example, network members warned of the chilling effect that disclosure requirements might have on speech.[41] Others made the claim that campaign finance regulations stifling the speech of corporations create undue influence by the left-liberal media and Hollywood elite.[42] Still others attempted to show that campaign finance regulations serve only to entrench incumbents and are self-serving for those in power.[43] For the purposes of this chapter, however, three arguments are worth exploring in detail. Taken together, these three arguments helped to arm the Supreme Court majority with both the intellectual capital and the judicial bravado necessary to abandon judicial restraint and *stare decisis* and radically reinterpret the constitutional framework for campaign finance in *Citizens United v. FEC* (2010). These arguments include the following: (1) the First Amendment prohibits governments from attempting to equalize speech resources, (2) there is no meaningful First Amendment distinction to be drawn between the protections of individual and corporate speech, and (3) the principles of judicial restraint and *stare decisis* should not deter Justices from correcting the constitutional mistakes of prior courts in the area of campaign finance.

The First Amendment Prohibits Governments from Attempting to Equalize Speech Resources

The crucial premise of the Supreme Court's holding in *Buckley v. Valeo* (1976), as interpreted by Federalist Society network members, is that the First Amendment forbids federal and state legislatures from attempting to equalize speech resources in order to enhance public debate. To paraphrase member Lillian BeVier's 1994 *Columbia Law Review* article (recommended by the Federalist Society's *Bibliography*),[44] this kind of government intervention in and meddling with the political process constitutes the very antithesis of freedom (BeVier 1994, 1260). This critique, to quote BeVier's article directly, runs along these lines:

> The First Amendment's negative constraints on government, which embody our traditional conception of "freedom of speech," have been instrumental in the achievement of the broadly participatory, relatively open, officially uncensored, political debate in which we take pride. It is a mistake, however, to maintain that. . . [the First Amendment's] guarantee of autonomy may be sacrificed in order "to *ensure* a well-functioning deliberative process among political equals" (emphasis in original). (BeVier 1994, 1261)

Empowering legislatures to restrict the speech rights of one portion of society (e.g., the wealthy or corporations) in order to enhance the speech rights of others, BeVier and other members contend, constitutes an unconstitutional and unauthorized redistribution of political power. Federalist Society Practice Group member and former chairman of the FEC, Bradley A. Smith, wrote in a 1997 *Georgetown Law Journal* article that the "[First] Amendment's language, which states that government 'shall not' act, makes clear that [vibrant public discussion] was to be achieved by protecting individual liberty interests against government interference" and not, Smith continued, "through an activist government role in political debate" (Smith 1997, 66). Senator Mitch McConnell (R-KY) made a variant of this same argument (albeit with far more rhetorical flourish) in front of the Federalist Society's Free Speech and Election Law Practice Group in 1999. Speaking derogatorily about the legislators promoting the McCain-Feingold bill, McConnell remarked that, "these free speech utilitarians. . . claim that it is necessary to avoid certain dangers associated with allowing some groups of citizens. . . engage in too much political speech." "And the fact is," McConnell continued, "that the First Amendment does not permit government to control the quantity or nature of political dialogue for any purpose, no matter how allegedly laudatory or necessary it may be."[45]

Paraphrasing this same argument, member John O. McGinnis remarked to his audience at the 2000 Annual Student Symposium that "[a]t its core, *Buckley* recognizes that the First Amendment provides a shield against government intervention, not a matrix for government regulation" (McGinnis 2000, 32). Moreover, McGinnis's presentation (later reprinted as a law review article) defends this core holding of *Buckley* with reference to several authorities from the Originalist canon—something the pre-Federalist Society *Buckley* Court did not do in its opinion. In the course of showing that these kinds of campaign finance regulations are "flatly inconsistent with the historic core of the First Amendment's protections," McGinnis cites the "struggle for freedom of speech in late seventeenth century England" and the battle against government restrictions on the printing press as evidence that the founding generation was wary of any attempt by government to control or regulate speech or the communication of political ideas (McGinnis 2000, 34). Additionally, quoting the Founder whose silhouette graces the Federalist Society logo, McGinnis reminded his audience that James Madison wrote in his essay *Property* that "'man had a property right in his opinions and the free communication of them'" and that "the First Amendment protects 'the communication of opinions' as well as the holding of opinions" (McGinnis 2000, 33–34). McGinnis also cited *Federalist* 10, Madison's essay on factions, as support for greater First Amendment pluralism and freedom of speech and expression. In the context of campaign finance, McGinnis warns, the "pluralistic roots of the First Amendment should make us suspicious that any attempt to restrict expenditures for political speech is actually an attempt to entrench a legislative or popular majority" (McGinnis 2000, 35).

For many Federalist Society members, this critique took on more urgency and importance in the wake of the Supreme Court's decision in *Austin v. Michigan Chamber of Commerce* (1990)—a case that expanded the scope of permissible government intervention into the political process by widening the definition of "corruption" to include "the appearance of corruption." Lillian BeVier dedicated an entire section of her 1994 *Bibliography*-endorsed law review article to examining why the Supreme Court's opinion in *Austin* was so "troublesome" and how it represents a clear "departure from *Buckley's* limiting principles" (BeVier 1994, 1270–1271). As BeVier writes, the majority opinion in *Austin* effectively "transform[ed] the most highly protected category of core political speech into an activity legitimately subject to complete prohibition" without "identify[ing] the constitutional principle" that would license such a ruling (BeVier 1994, 1271). A former vice chairman of the Federalist Society's Free Speech and Election Law Practice Group, Charles H. Bell, wrote in a 1996 Newsletter that *Austin* was a prime example of the acceptance of "a Political Nanny State" and of the liberals' "fundamental interest in realigning political and economic power, and in fixing the rules to accomplish those ends."[46] Finally, current chairman of the Federalist Society's Free Speech and Election Law Practice Group, Allison Hayward, wrote in 2008 for the Practice Group journal *Engage* that with its recent decisions (citing *Austin* as chief among them) the Supreme Court has had "a confounding effect on campaign regulation"[47] and mused that with the addition of Roberts and Alito, "now might be a good moment" for the Supreme Court to revisit its campaign finance jurisprudence.[48]

There Is No Meaningful First Amendment Distinction to Be Drawn Between the Protections of Individual and Corporate Political Speech

The authority most often cited within the Federalist Society network for the claim that the First Amendment draws no distinction between individual and corporate speech is the Supreme Court's decision in *First National Bank of Boston v. Bellotti* (1978). As I wrote earlier, in *Bellotti* the Supreme Court was considering a Massachusetts statute that made it illegal for business corporations to make contributions or expenditures to influence the outcome of a ballot initiative if the question did not materially affect the corporation's business interest. As Justice Powell wrote for the majority in *Bellotti*, the relevant constitutional question was not "whether corporations 'have' First Amendment rights" that were "coextensive with those of natural persons" but rather whether a prohibition on corporate political expenditures "abridges expression that the First Amendment was meant to protect."[49] In the case of the Massachusetts statute, the majority answered this question in the affirmative, noting that "[t]he speech proposed by appellants is at the heart of the First Amendment protections."[50] Powell also proclaimed in *Bellotti* that "'[t]he inherent worth of the speech in terms of its capacity for informing the public does not depend upon the identity of its source, whether corporation, association, union, or individual."[51]

Even though this opinion was handed down several years before the Federalist Society was founded, it became a highly valued piece of intellectual capital within the network—one that helped members justify and articulate their principled disagreement with campaign finance-favorable decisions like *Austin v. Michigan Chamber of Commerce* (1990) and *McConnell v. FEC* (2003). For example, network member Larry E. Ribstein[52] criticized the Supreme Court's decision in *Austin* in a 1992 law review article entitled "Corporate Political Speech" when he wrote that the decision was at odds with the "broad recognition of corporate First Amendment rights in Justice Powell's decision in *First National Bank v. Bellotti*" (Ribstein 1992, 109). Ribstein spent much of the article contrasting *Bellotti* with *Austin* and provided a robust First Amendment argument for the protection of corporate political speech. Member Jill E. Fisch[53] wrote in a 1991 law review article that "[e]ven superficial scrutiny of the opinion in *Austin* reveals that it stands in absolute contradiction to the principles set out in *Bellotti*" (Fisch 1991, 613), and she spent a significant portion of the article illustrating this inconsistency (Fisch 1991, 595–614, 618, 640). Lillian BeVier also cited *Bellotti* in her 1994 *Bibliography*-endorsed law review article as the principled First Amendment alternative to the Supreme Court's ruling in *Austin* (BeVier 1994, 1258). Writing for the *Cato Supreme Court Review* in 2003, Bradley A. Smith critiqued the Supreme Court's decision in *Federal Election Commission v. Beaumont* (2002)[54] both for its dubious reliance on *Austin* and because, in his view, "the opinion includes the de facto overruling of *Bellotti*" (Smith 2003, 218).

Just as Federalist Society member John O. McGinnis supplemented and bolstered *Buckley v. Valeo* (1976) with his own Originalist analysis, with their historical scholarship on the role of corporations and campaign finance, Practice Group members Allison R. Hayward and Bradley A. Smith provided support for the core holding in *Bellotti* by challenging the purported governmental interest in regulating corporations any differently from individuals or other associations of individuals for First Amendment purposes. That their scholarship was complementary was not an accident. In addition to being connected through the Federalist Society's Free Speech and Election Law Practice Group, Hayward served as the chief of staff for Smith when he was commissioner of the FEC. Hayward's scholarship has focused on debunking what she refers to as "the fable of reform," that is, the notion that campaign finance reform generally, and the corporate contribution ban specifically, was enacted because of a strongly felt need to control the undue influence of corporations and unions on the political process (Hayward 2008a, 421). Identifying Justice Felix Frankfurter's oft-cited majority opinion in *United States v. United Auto Workers* (1957)[55] as the source of this "fable," Hayward mobilized historical evidence to show how the reform movement was not necessary or natural, but rather was "dictated by political opportunism" and became an effective way to "restrict political rivals' access to financial resources" (Hayward 2008a, 422). Hayward's article mentioned several Supreme Court opinions—chief among them *McConnell v. FEC* (2003)—that relied on what she argued was a faulty or incorrect version of history presented in *Auto Workers* to justify the need for strengthening prohibitions on direct corporate contributions and reigning in corporate political activity (Hayward 2008a, 423–425). The rest of the article mobilized historical sources—both primary and secondary—that challenged the *Auto Workers* narrative of the campaign finance reform movement. Notably, Hayward published a version of this same article three years earlier as a Federalist Society White Paper under the title "Rethinking Campaign Finance Prohibitions."[56]

Bradley A. Smith's book *Unfree Speech*, published before the Supreme Court's decision in *McConnell*, made a similar argument about the misuse or mischaracterization of history by reformers looking to further regulate or restrict the political speech and influence of corporations (Smith 2001, 9, 21–24, 27, 29–30, 36). In the preface to this book, after noting that parts of the book had been presented at several different symposia, Smith thanked the Federalist Society specifically for "sponsoring many of the above lectures and panels, along with others at various lawyers' chapters around the country and before the society's E. L. Wiegand Free Speech and Election Law Practice Group" (Smith 2001, xiii). Smith also mentioned several Federalist Society network members by name in his acknowledgments (Lillian BeVier, James Bopp, Jr., John O. McGinnis, William Marshall,[57] John Norton Moore,[58] Roger Pilon,[59] and Daniel Polsby[60]), noting that he benefited greatly from discussions with them (Smith 2001, xii). As I discuss in detail in this book's final chapter, Smith's acknowledgments are but one illustration of the important role that the Federalist Society, acting as a PEN, plays in the development, nurturing, and refinement of intellectual capital and ideas for the conservative legal movement—ideas and capital that litigators, *amici curiae,* and judges use to help justify the reconstruction of constitutional frameworks. As Daniel Polsby, who is credited by Smith in the acknowledgments to *Unfree Speech,* said to me in our interview in 2008, the Federalist Society has "been very effective at creating a voice, an outlet, that meets a couple of times a year and collects people who have kindred interests in one room where they can talk about the things that interest them about current public policy on the highest plane." Polsby continued that the Federalist Society "makes it possible for people to continue to stay on course with their own research interests because they don't have the sense they are just talking to a wall."[61] Lillian BeVier, who is also credited in Smith's acknowledgments, said something very similar to me during our interview about the Federalist Society's contribution to the marketplace of ideas. Specifically, she talked about how having fellow Federalist Society members who share her ideas helped her pursue topics that were, in her own words, "completely out of the mainstream" of legal academia.[62]

The Principles of Judicial Restraint and *Stare Decisis*
Should Not Control in the Area of Campaign Finance

As I wrote in Chapter 1, the proper role of the judiciary is one of the topics consistently discussed within the Federalist Society network since its founding. Enshrined in the third part of the Federalist Society's statement of principles ("it is emphatically the province and duty of the judiciary to say what the law is, not what it should be"), within the Federalist Society network this is popularly noted as a concern with "judicial activism" or, conversely, a belief in "judicial restraint." While Federalist Society members repeatedly mentioned this topic in our interviews as one of the chief concerns and unifying principles of members within the network, Executive Director Eugene Meyer pointed out that this statement is actually "the closest thing to a controversial statement in our statement of purpose."[63] Member Richard Willard expressed a similar sentiment in our interview when asked about the principles that unify members of the network: "I would say that most people would believe in [Originalism] but, for example, on the judicial activism versus judicial restraint there are some people in the Society who feel that judges should be activist and others who are more advocates of judicial restraint."[64] In my follow-up question, I confirmed that Willard was referring to "judicial restraint" as the act of upholding settled law or constitutional doctrine, that is, as being cautious not to disrupt an area of law or overturn precedents. In this sense, "judicial restraint" means that a judge tends to abide by the doctrine of *stare decisis,* which is Latin for "to stand by things decided," and is not eager to overturn precedent. Conversely, "judicial activism" would refer to a judge who privileges what he or she would consider a correct interpretation or outcome of the case over respecting the decisions of past courts, even if this means overturning one or more precedents. The most vocal advocate of this understanding of judicial restraint within the Federalist Society network is J. Harvie Wilkinson. A Fourth Circuit judge and an active Federalist Society network member since the early 1980s, Wilkinson consistently has warned of the dangers of uprooting too many areas of settled law at too fast a pace. For example, at the 1988 Annual Student Symposium, Wilkinson warned that, regardless of what the original meaning dictated, the Supreme Court should not attempt to enact swift and broad changes to the constitutional landscape all at once: "the fortuities of uneven constitutional development must be respected, not cast aside in the illusion of reordering the landscape anew."[65]

There is, however, another understanding of "judicial activism" versus "judicial restraint" that, as one journalist recently suggested[66] and my interview data confirmed, has now become the dominant understanding within the Federalist Society network. Championed by network members such as Randy Barnett, Richard Epstein, and Justice Clarence Thomas, "judicial restraint" means simply that a judge interprets the words of the Constitution consistent with its original meaning. On the other hand, "judicial activism" is when a judge substitutes his or her own policy preferences for those of the founding generation. Understood this way, a judge is being restrained if he or she overturns precedents that were decided in a manner inconsistent with Originalism—decisions that were the products of past "judicial activism"—regardless of how long they have controlled or been considered settled law. The concern with fixing past law and aligning jurisprudence with the original meaning therefore trumps any deference to the doctrine of *stare decisis*. These two different understandings of judicial restraint and activism came head to head at the Federalist Society's 2013 National Lawyers Convention. The Sixth Annual Rosenkranz Debate pitted J. Harvie Wilkinson against Randy Barnett on this topic.[67] The resulting debate and conversation highlighted a clear preference within the Federalist Society network for the Barnett brand of judicial restraint over the Wilkinson brand.[68]

Though it might be more acceptable now within the Federalist Society network to talk openly about overruling precedents and to advocate for massively realigning constitutional jurisprudence, it is still unusual to see a group of litigators and scholars uniformly calling for the Supreme Court to abandon *stare decisis*. In fact, of all the constitutional areas that I examine in this book, this call was most pronounced in the area of campaign finance. While some members, such as Joel Gora, have called for revisiting and overruling parts of the Supreme Court's decision in *Buckley v. Valeo* (1976),[69] most of the calls for reconsidering campaign finance precedents from network members focus on decisions that, in their view, are inconsistent with the *Buckley* and *Bellotti* precedents—namely, *Austin* and *McConnell*. Unsurprisingly, these calls accelerated with the appointment of Roberts and Alito, two individuals who had proven Federalist Society credentials. For example, in his 2007 law review article entitled "The John Roberts Salvage Company: After McConnell, a New Court Looks to Repair the Constitution," Bradley A. Smith advocated overruling *Austin* outright (Smith 2007, 918–920). While recognizing that Roberts, Alito, and Kennedy are not "inclined to readily overrule precedent," Smith argues that *Austin* is "the odd case out in the post-*Buckley* jurisprudence" and that "overruling the case would not be a radical move" (Smith 2007, 920). Similarly, Allison Hayward, speaking on a panel entitled "The Supreme Court and Campaign Finance" at the 2008 National Lawyers Convention, did not hold back with her recommendations for SCOTUS. In a passage that seems directly addressed to Roberts and

Alito, who had declined to consider overruling *Austin* just a year earlier, Hayward concluded her conference remarks with a plea for the justices to disregard judicial restraint:

> Whatever appealing qualities might attach to a justice's respect for precedent and restraint in ordinary circumstances, none are found here. It is vitally important that future justices appreciate the position the Court is in, and the power the Court has to improve the law. Rather than decry judicial activism, principled Court watchers need to allow for space for future justices to repair the mistakes of the past.[70]

While we cannot know for sure the extent to which this support and encouragement from fellow network members helped Roberts and Alito join the other conservatives' campaign to "repair the mistakes of the past" in *Citizens United*, as I discuss further in Chapter 6, members of the Federalist Society network certainly believe the justices are listening. As cofounder Steven Calabresi said to me in our interview regarding the feedback or criticism that Federalist Society network members provide to Supreme Court justices, "I think it absolutely helps keep them in check. When one tries to think about what kinds of checks exist on officials as powerful as Supreme Court Justices I think the check of criticism by law schools, journalists and conservative think tanks like the Federalist Society, criticism from those quarters is something that they notice."[71] The next section will demonstrate conclusively that once these Justices decided to abandon judicial restraint and *stare decisis* in *Citizens United*, the Federalist Society network was an important source of intellectual capital that helped them justify that controversial decision.

THE FIRST AMENDMENT AND CAMPAIGN FINANCE AT THE SUPREME COURT

Nearly three decades after the Supreme Court's decision in *Buckley v. Valeo* (1976), members of Congress resolved to update the Federal Election Campaign Act of 1971. The resulting legislation was called the Bipartisan Campaign Reform Act of 2002[72] (BCRA). Cosponsored by Senators John McCain (R-AZ) and Russell D. Feingold (D-WI), the legislation sought to address two major problems. The first part of the bill, Title I, addressed "soft money," or the practice of donating to political parties, which would then pass the money on to respective candidates. Neither the original bill in 1971 nor the amendments in 1974 placed any regulations or limits on party donations. The second part, Title II, addressed the proliferation of "issue advocacy ads." Paid for by groups that were not a part of a campaign's formal organization, neither restrictions nor limits existed for the fundraising for or spending on advertisements.

Despite the careful consideration of the congressional drafters, many in the conservative-libertarian legal community felt that the legislation went too far in the proposed reforms. Senate Majority Whip, Mitch McConnell (R-KY), along with 10 other organizations, responded and filed suit, stating the legislation to be unconstitutional given First Amendment jurisprudence.[73] The Supreme Court in a special session heard the resulting litigation, *McConnell v. Federal Election Commission* (2003), on September 8, 2003. The Justices were asked to look at the constitutionality of various sections, including Section 203.[74] Prior to the passage of BCRA, the Federal Election Campaign Act §316(b)(2) simply made it "unlawful. . . for any corporation whatever, or any labor organization, to make a contribution or expenditure in connection with" certain federal elections.[75] BCRA §203 amended the definition of the term "contribution or expenditure" to include "any applicable electioneering communication."[76] This section of BCRA dealt with the proliferation of soft money, but also placed greater constraints on the First Amendment speech rights of corporations and unions.

In a sweeping and complex 272-page decision issued in December 2003, the Supreme Court in *McConnell* upheld the constitutionality of §203 by a bare 5 to 4 majority. Relying critically on *Austin v. Michigan Chamber of Commerce* (1990), the majority opinions, written by Justices Sandra Day O'Connor and John Paul Stevens, said that the federal government had a compelling and constitutionally permissible interest in regulating "the corrosive and distorting effects of immense aggregations of wealth that are accumulated with the help of the corporate form."[77] The use of *Austin* by the majority was not a popular choice with the more conservative members of the court. Indeed, the dissents in *McConnell* sent clear signals to the broader legal community that they disagreed with the way in which *Austin* was used to justify the narrowing of corporate speech rights. An opportunity to revisit the decision, these dissenting Justices indicated, would be looked upon favorably. As Justice Thomas wrote, "[b]ecause *Austin*'s definition of "corruption" is incompatible with the First Amendment, I would overturn *Austin* and hold that the potential for corporations and unions to influence voters. . . is not a form of corruption justifying any state regulation or suppression."[78]

The signals in *McConnell* were an important step in the development of the constitutional path that would culminate in *Citizens United*. More important, however, the makeup of the Supreme Court changed dramatically between 2003 and 2007. Chief Justice John Roberts replaced

Chief Justice Rehnquist in 2005 and Justice Samuel Alito replaced Justice Sandra Day O'Connor in 2006. A change in the makeup of the Supreme Court is a unique and powerful kind of signal. New members of the Court bring new philosophical approaches to the law and a shift in the voting blocs (Baird 2007, 58). Alito and Roberts were known commodities to the Federalist Society, and their presence was another indication that—given the right case—the Supreme Court would be amenable to revisiting *McConnell* and the frustrating precedent set in *Austin.* The conservative legal movement did not have to wait long to see exactly how the changed composition on the Supreme Court might influence their fortunes in the area of campaign finance. Less than a year after Justice Alito replaced Sandra Day O'Connor, the Supreme Court granted review in *Federal Election Commission v. Wisconsin Right to Life*—a case that raised a direct challenge to O'Connor's 2003 majority opinion in *McConnell.*

Federal Election Commission v. Wisconsin Right to Life (2007)

In July 2004, Wisconsin Right to Life, Inc. (WRTL), a "state nonprofit, nonstock ideological advocacy corporation,"[79] began broadcasting advertisements urging voters to contact Wisconsin senators Feingold and Kohl and ask them to oppose a planned Senate filibuster of federal judicial nominees. WRTL planned to finance the ad campaign with its general treasury funds.[80] WRTL had intended to run its ads through August 15, 2004, but recognized that this would bring it within 30 days of the Wisconsin primary, and would therefore constitute illegal "electioneering communications" under Section 203 of the BCRA. Believing it had a First Amendment right to broadcast these ads, WRTL (represented by Federalist Society member James Bopp, Jr.[81]) filed suit in the federal District Court for the District of Columbia against the FEC. Bopp made two arguments in defense of WRTL. First, he alleged that WRTL's ads were more accurately classified as "grassroots lobbying advertisements"[82] and therefore did not constitute the kind of communications that the drafters of the BCRA intended to limit. Second, he argued that the relevant portions of *McConnell v. FEC* (2003), which upheld the constitutionality of Section 203, should be overturned because they were inconsistent with the First Amendment's narrow tailoring requirement.[83]

The three-judge District Court disagreed on both grounds. It denied the motion for a preliminary injunction and dismissed WRTL's complaint. WRTL was therefore unable to air its ads during the 30-day period. WRTL appealed to the Supreme Court. On appeal, the Supreme Court found in favor of WRTL and declared that the District Court had misinterpreted and incorrectly applied the *McConnell* decision. On remand, the District Court, in an opinion authored by Richard J. Leon and joined in full by Federalist Society member and 12-time National Conference partici- pant David Sentelle[84] held that Section 203 of the BCRA was unconstitu- tional as applied to WRTL's campaign. In a 5 to 4 decision, the Supreme Court affirmed this decision, holding that WRTL's campaign constituted "issue advocacy" as opposed to "express advocacy" and that BCRA's pro- hibition on the use of corporate funds to finance these ads violated the corporation's free speech rights.[85] In the majority opinion, written by Chief Justice John Roberts, the Supreme Court ruled that as long as the speech at issue could reasonably be interpreted as anything other than "express advocacy," then the Section 203 prohibitions should not apply. Justice Scalia wrote a concurring opinion, in which Justices Thomas and Kennedy joined, arguing that the Supreme Court ought to have gone fur- ther in this case. Writing for the three Justices, Scalia outright called for overruling *Austin v. Michigan Chamber of Commerce* (1990) and reversing the relevant portion of *McConnell* that Roberts, joined by Alito, had left intact—if only barely—in his majority opinion.

As illustrated in Figure 3.1, the Federalist Society network was well rep- resented in the *Wisconsin Right to Life* litigation. Federalist Society network member and long-time co-chair of the Society's Free Speech and Election Law Practice Group, James Bopp, Jr., represented the appellee, WRTL, while 10 Federalist Society members signed on to *amicus curiae* briefs in support of Bopp's client—Charles J. Cooper, David H. Thompson,[86]

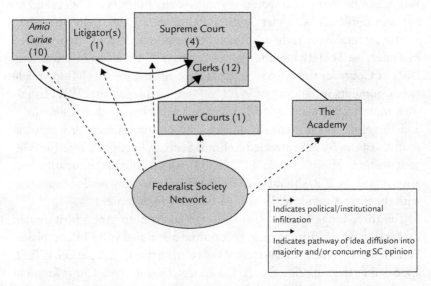

Figure 3.1 *FEC v. Wisconsin Right to Life* (2007)

Erik S. Jaffe,[87] Jan Witold Baran,[88] Jay Alan Sekulow, Laurence Gold,[89] Joel Gora,[90] Steven J. Law,[91] Steven Shapiro,[92] and Theodore Olson. As I wrote earlier, Society member and federal judge David Sentelle joined in the majority opinion ruling in favor of WRTL at the District Court level. Additionally, of the four Federalist Society members on the Supreme Court, three wrote opinions in this case. Chief Justice Roberts wrote for the majority, while Justice Scalia and Justice Alito each wrote concurring opinions. Thus, in Figure 3.1, I have indicated 12 clerks as potential conduits through which Federalist Society network intellectual capital might have been transmitted to the Justices writing in this case.

Toward the end of his majority opinion in *Wisconsin Right to Life,* Chief Justice John Roberts took a moment to acknowledge the importance of the issue of campaign finance to a wide and "diverse" set of groups and organizations:

> These cases are about political speech. The importance of the cases to speech and debate on public policy issues is reflected in the number of diverse organizations that have joined in supporting WRTL before this Court: the American Civil Liberties Union, the National Rifle Association, the American Federation of Labor and Congress of Industrial Organizations, the Chamber of Commerce of the United States of America, Focus on the Family, the Coalition of Public Charities, the Cato Institute, and many others.[93]

The organizations that Roberts lists are quite diverse in terms of their issue focus (the NRA as compared with Focus on the Family) and their political tilts (the ACLU as compared with the Chamber of Commerce). Though these groups might make for strange bedfellows, they are hardly strangers. What they have in common, apart from an interest in loosening campaign finance restrictions, is some connection to the Federalist Society network. With the exception of the Coalition of Public Charities, each of these groups was represented on brief by at least one Federalist Society network member in this litigation.[94] This fact speaks to the power of a PEN to effectively organize and cohere around discrete issues, even if its members would be ideologically and politically opposed on others. This also resonates with Ann Southworth's description of the Federalist Society as the "cross-roads" of the conservative movement and as an important "mediator organization" for the sometimes disparate constituencies that coexist within the movement (Southworth 2008).

These Federalist Society network *amici* all urged the Supreme Court to uphold Federalist Society member David Sentelle's District Court ruling that Section 203 of the BCRA was unconstitutional as applied to the broadcasts at issue in the litigation.[95] Their briefs supplemented Sentelle's opinion with intellectual capital from Federalist Society network scholarship,[96] the Originalist canon,[97] and with a generous dose of *First National Bank of Boston v. Bellotti*.[98] Going a step further than his network colleagues, WRTL counsel James Bopp, Jr., asked the Supreme Court to overturn *McConnell's* holding that Section 203 was constitutional on its face. In a section of his brief that would be echoed in Justice Scalia's concurring opinion (and later in Chief Justice Roberts's concurring opinion in *Citizens United*), Bopp argued that this case fell squarely within the Supreme Court's framework for when it was appropriate to abandon the doctrine of *stare decisis*:

> This Court has provided standards for determining when it is appropriate to overrule precedent. . . . *Stare decisis* is a "principle of policy," and not an "inexorable command.". . . Two primary rationales govern. First, "badly reasoned" or "unworkable" precedent will be overturned. . . . Second, precedent is reversed if an essential factual assumption of the prior case was inaccurate or becomes inaccurate. . . . Consistent with the above guideline, the experience in this case. . . reveals that the assumption in *McConnell* that as-applied challenges would be an adequate remedy to protect genuine issue ads has proven inaccurate and unworkable. . . . Therefore, there is clear justification for partially overturning *McConnell*.[99]

Three justices in *Wisconsin Right to Life* agreed with Bopp and were prepared to overrule Section 203 of *McConnell*. Writing in concurrence and joined by Justices Kennedy and Thomas, Scalia devotes a full three pages of his opinion to the issue of *stare decisis*, arguing (as Bopp did) that because it produced an "'unworkable' legal regime" and because the "as-applied test" failed to sufficiently safeguard First Amendment rights, the relevant portions of *McConnell* ought to be overruled.[100] In response to those who would caution against disrupting settled law and changing the constitutional landscape too quickly, Scalia argued that it was the *McConnell* decision—and before that, the *Austin* decision—that actually disrupted a body of settled law since *Buckley*: "It is not as though *McConnell* produced a settled body of law. Indeed, it is far more accurate to say that *McConnell* unsettled a body of law" (emphasis in original). Scalia's opinion insisted that the Supreme Court's "pre-*McConnell* decisions, with the lone exception of *Austin*, disapproved limits on independent expenditures. The modest medicine of restoring First Amendment protection to nonexpress advocacy-speech that was protected until three Terms ago does not unsettle an established body of law."[101]

While, according to Scalia, overruling *McConnell* would have been merely "modest medicine," the newly appointed Chief Justice Roberts and Justice Alito were not quite ready to swallow it in *Wisconsin Right to Life.* Exhibiting what I referred to earlier as the J. Harvie Wilkinson brand of judicial restraint, Roberts wrote "in deciding this as-applied challenge, we have no occasion to revisit *McConnell's* conclusion that the statute is not facially overbroad."[102] While joining the majority opinion in full, Alito wrote separately in this case. His concurrence more directly "signals" (Baird 2007) both to his colleagues on the Court and to those outside the Court that he would reconsider the holding in *McConnell* if it later proved unworkable: "I join the principal opinion because I conclude... that because § 203 is unconstitutional as applied to the advertisements before us, it is unnecessary to go further and decide whether § 203 is unconstitutional on its face." "If," Alito continued, "it turns out that the implementation of the as-applied standard set out in the principal opinion impermissibly chills political speech... we will presumably be asked in a future case to reconsider the holding in McConnell that § 203 is facially constitutional."[103] On clear display in this exchange between Roberts and Alito, on the one hand, and Scalia, Thomas, and Kennedy, on the other, are two very different understandings of judicial restraint—both of which, as I documented earlier, have constituencies within the Federalist Society network. Roberts and Alito play the role of J. Harvie Wilkinson here—resolving the issue at hand on the narrowest grounds possible so as not to disrupt the constitutional landscape too much, too quickly. The priority for Scalia et al., on the other hand, is fixing the perceived mistakes of the past—decisions like *McConnell* and *Austin*, which were not faithful to the text, history, and meaning of the First Amendment. This is the Randy Barnett–Richard Epstein–Clarence Thomas definition of judicial restraint. Within this framework, overruling these precedents is not judicial activism; it is simply, to borrow Scalia's phrase, providing some "modest medicine" for an ailing area of constitutional jurisprudence. As we see in *Citizens United,* it did not take long for Scalia to convince his new colleagues of the healing benefits of this "modest medicine" and of letting go of their concerns with *stare decisis.*

In the end, the decision in *Wisconsin Right to Life* gave the Federalist Society network the proverbial "half a loaf." Laurence Gold, Jan Witold Baran, and James Bopp, Jr., all praised the decision in *USA Today,* with Gold calling the ruling "a breath of constitutional fresh air."[104] Federalist Society cofounder Steven Calabresi was more ambivalent. He was quoted in the same edition of *USA Today* saying that while "conservatives will be happy" about the Supreme Court's ruling in *Wisconsin Right to Life,* "many conservatives will be struck by the incremental, small steps taken" by the Supreme Court.[105] To wit, Lillian BeVier wrote of *Wisconsin Right to Life* in 2007 that instead of embracing a kind of "faux judicial restraint," perhaps "judicial honor—and the rule of law—would have been fully

satisfied only by a straightforward overruling of a precedent left standing with its theoretical heart cut out and its head severed" (BeVier 2007,
105). Similarly underwhelmed with the decision, Allison Hayward wrote
that the Supreme Court's decision in *Wisconsin Right to Life* was "unfortunately unremarkable" (Hayward 2008b, 309). The article, appropriately enough, was titled "Wisconsin Right to Life: Same Song, Different
Verse." In the earlier analysis of Federalist Society speech acts, I noted
that Hayward had become especially vocal in Practice Group newsletters
and publications about abandoning judicial restraint in the wake of the
Supreme Court's decision in *Wisconsin Right to Life*. Recall, for example,
that in a 2008 passage from *Engage*, she implored fellow network members
to stop worrying about judicial activism and start worrying about giving
future Justices license "to repair the mistakes of the past."[106]

Citizens United v. Federal Election Commission (2010)

In January 2008, Citizens United, a nonprofit corporation, released
a film entitled *Hillary: The Movie* that criticized then-Senator Hillary
Clinton, who was a candidate for the Democratic Party's presidential
nomination.[107] In addition to releasing the film in theaters and on DVD,
Citizens United intended to increase distribution by making it available
to digital cable subscribers with video-on-demand. To promote the film,
Citizens United produced two 10-second ads and one 30-second ad for
Hillary: The Movie, which included a short, pejorative statement about
Senator Clinton, followed by the name of the movie and the movie's
website address. Citizens United intended to air the advertisements on
both broadcast and cable television. Because Citizens United planned to
screen the advertisements within 30 days of the 2008 primary elections, it
was subject to the restrictions outlined in the BCRA.[108] Because it feared
civil and criminal penalties under the BCRA's ban on corporate-funded
independent expenditures, outlined in section 441b, Citizens United,
which at that point was represented by James Bopp, Jr., sought declaratory and injunctive relief against the FEC in December 2007, arguing
that BCRA was unconstitutional as applied to *Hillary: The Movie*.[109] The
District Court, which consisted of Federalist Society member Circuit
Judge A. Raymond Randolph[110] and District Judges Royce Lamberth
and Richard Roberts, denied the motion for preliminary injunction and
granted the FEC's motion for summary judgment, holding that BCRA
was constitutional as applied to *Citizens United*.[111]

Citizens United, which had since secured Federalist Society stalwart
Theodore Olson as counsel, appealed to the U.S. Supreme Court, arguing

initially that the BCRA's prohibitions did not apply to documentaries like *Hillary: The Movie*. As Jeffrey Toobin would later recount in a 2012 *New Yorker* piece, "[Theodore] Olson had presented the case to the Court in a narrow way... the main issue was whether the McCain-Feingold law applied to a documentary, presented on video on demand, by a nonprofit corporation."[112] Citizens United was not asking the Supreme Court to overrule the relevant portions of the BCRA, because—the organization did not think that necessary. However, after a backdoors "private drama"[113] that involved negotiations among the conservative justices about using this case to revisit *Austin* and *McConnell*, Chief Justice Roberts agreed to order a new round of arguments for the case in the new term that would ask the parties to file new briefs directly addressing whether or not the decisions in *Austin* and *McConnell* ought to be overruled. Instead of waiting for the first Monday in October (when the Supreme Court's new term traditionally begins), the second round of oral argument in *Citizens United* was scheduled for September 9, 2009. In the final opinion, released on January 21, 2010, Justice Kennedy wrote for the five-Justice majority, holding that in barring corporations and unions from using general treasury funds to make independent expenditures that advocate the election or defeat of a candidate, the federal government violated the First Amendment by impermissibly suppressing political speech on the basis of the speaker's corporate identity. Moreover, as presaged three years earlier by the concurring bloc (Scalia, Thomas, and Kennedy) in *Wisconsin Right to Life*, this decision effectively overruled precedents established in both *Austin v. Michigan Chamber of Commerce* and *McConnell v. Federal Election Commission*.[114]

In addition to Theodore Olson, who picked up the litigating mantle from James Bopp, Jr., 13 other Federalist Society network members, several of whom were repeat players from the litigation in WRTL, participated as *amici curiae* in this case—Edwin Meese III, Bradley A. Smith,[115] Charles Cooper, David H. Thompson, Floyd Abrams,[116] James Bopp, Jr., Joel Gora, John Eastman, Laurence Gold, Steven J. Law, Steven Shapiro, Reid Alan Cox,[117] and Allison Hayward.[118] Of the four Federalist Society–affiliated Supreme Court Justices in the majority in *Citizens United*, two wrote separate, concurring opinions in the case: Chief Justice Roberts and Justice Scalia. Their eight clerks, in addition to three of Justice Kennedy's clerks who clerked for lower court Federalist Society judges, comprise the 11 Federalist Society clerk conduits indicated in Figure 3.2.

When a majority of Supreme Court justices decide they are ready to revise or reconstruct a constitutional framework, they need to justify that decision with reference to some authorities either internal to the institution (precedent) or external to it but recognized as authoritative (legal

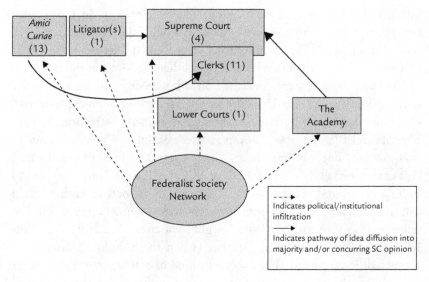

Figure 3.2 *Citizens United v. FEC* (2010)

scholarship or other interpretive authorities). Justice Kennedy, writing for the majority in *Citizens United*, relied on both. Joining a chorus of Federalist Society network members, Kennedy dusted off *First National Bank of Boston v. Bellotti* (1978) and featured it prominently in the majority's reasoning—citing it 24 times.[119] For example, Kennedy cited *Bellotti* as evidence that "[t]he Court has thus rejected the argument that political speech of corporations or other associations should be treated differently under the First Amendment simply because such associations are not 'natural persons.' "[120] As Kennedy's repeated citation to the 1978 precedent demonstrated, *Bellotti* served a critical purpose in *Citizens United*, that is, to bolster the argument that *Austin* was a departure from core First Amendment principles and "an aberration."[121] This was exactly the argument made by network member Theodore Olson in his brief for Citizens United, which referenced *Bellotti* 12 times.[122] The Olson-authored brief argued that *Austin's* logic "was rejected almost verbatim in *Bellotti*,"[123] that it cannot "be reconciled with *Bellotti's* recognition that political speech is no less valuable 'because the speech comes from a corporation rather than an individual' "[124] and that, accordingly, it was "wrongly decided and should be overruled."[125] Three Federalist Society network *amicus curiae* briefs submitted in this case also used *Bellotti* to question *Austin's* principal holding.[126]

Kennedy's majority opinion also mobilized intellectual capital and support for the majority's reasoning in *Citizens United* from Federalist Society network member scholarship. Kennedy referenced an article by member

Richard H. Fallon[127] (whose work on federal judicial procedure is recommended in the Federalist Society's *Bibliography*)[128] to defend the majority's decision to decide the broader constitutional question in *Citizens United* rather than the more narrow, as-applied challenge first stipulated by the parties in their briefs.[129] Far from being simply a technical question about federal judicial procedure, this went to the heart of what the proper judicial role was and should be (a discussion that was the focus of Chief Justice Roberts's concurrence, which we will turn to in a moment). Kennedy also relied on the historical scholarship of Federalist Society Practice Group members Bradley A. Smith and Allison R. Hayward (both of whom submitted *amicus curiae* briefs in this case) to argue against the proposition that restrictions on corporate political speech have been in practice long-standing, legitimate, or necessary. Bradley A. Smith, whose book *Unfree Speech* was cited in Kennedy's majority opinion,[130] signed on to *amicus curiae* briefs submitted by the Center for Competitive Politics[131] and by Seven Former Chairmen and One Former Commissioner of the FEC.[132] This latter brief, with fellow network member James Bopp, Jr., as counsel of record, was cited directly twice in Kennedy's majority opinion.[133] Hayward's *amicus curiae* brief[134] summarized her campaign finance scholarship and specifically directed the Court to her article "Revisiting the Fable of Reform,"[135] which was reviewed earlier in this chapter and successfully found its way into Kennedy's majority opinion twice. [136] Most notably, Hayward's brief and article were cited as direct support in the majority opinion (*901) for overruling *Austin* and abandoning *stare decisis*:

> When neither party defends the reasoning of a precedent, the principle of adhering to that precedent through *stare decisis* is diminished. *Austin* abandoned First Amendment principles, furthermore, by relying on language in some of our precedents that traces back to the *Automobile Workers* Court's flawed historical account of campaign finance laws, see Brief for Campaign Finance Scholars as *Amici Curiae;* Hayward 45 HarvJ. Legis. 421.

While Kennedy's majority opinion did offer a brief justification for abandoning *stare decisis*, the Chief Justice, who, alongside newly appointed Justice Alito, declined to consider overruling *Austin* three years earlier in *Wisconsin Right to Life*, took up the burden of fully justifying this decision in *Citizens United.*

Chief Justice Roberts's concurring opinion is a direct response to the strongly worded dissent of Justice John Paul Stevens. In his 90-page dissent, joined by Justices Ginsburg, Breyer, and Sotomayor, Stevens accused the majority of violating several tenets of judicial process: answering a question that was not presented to them properly, deciding the case on the broadest, rather than the narrowest legal grounds, and of abandoning *stare decisis*. These derelictions of judicial process, Stevens wrote, were not simply "technical defect[s] in the Court's decision" but instead demonstrated an approach to the judicial role that ran "contrary to the fundamental principle of judicial restraint."[137] In sum, Stevens charged the Court of operating "with a sledge hammer rather than a scalpel"[138] and wrote that the majority's decision cannot be the work product of a Court that was "serious about judicial restraint."[139] Roberts's defense of the majority's decision in *Citizens United* embodied a fundamentally different understanding of judicial restraint—one that privileged fidelity to constitutional principles over fidelity to principles of judicial process (*stare decisis*, etc.). As he wrote, the principle of *stare decisis* should be viewed as instrumental, not as an end in itself: "[i]ts greatest purpose is to serve a constitutional ideal—the rule of law." Roberts continued, "when fidelity to any particular precedent does more to damage this constitutional ideal than to advance it, we must be more willing to depart from that precedent."[140] This justification for abandoning *stare decisis* echoed that of Federalist Society network member Lillian BeVier who, as I recounted earlier, wrote that the *Wisconsin Right to Life* decision amounted to a kind of "faux judicial restraint" and argued that both "judicial honor" and "the rule of law" would have been better served by overruling, rather than preserving precedents (BeVier 2007, 105). While Roberts was clearly responding to the dissenting bloc in *Citizens United*, one can understand his concurring opinion as addressed to another audience: those within the Federalist Society network who would interpret it as a signal that the Chief Justice was moving closer to the Barnett-Epstein-Thomas model of judicial restraint (privileging principle) and away from the Wilkinson model (privileging process).

Finally, Federalist Society mentor Justice Scalia also wrote separately in the case. The purpose of his concurring opinion was, as he wrote, to demonstrate "the conformity of today's opinion with the original meaning of the First Amendment."[141] Specifically, Scalia was working to counter the strong assertion, articulated by Justice Stevens in his dissent, "there is not a scintilla of evidence to support the notion" that the original understanding of the First Amendment would preclude regulatory distinctions between the human and corporate form.[142] Scalia and Stevens both mobilized numerous sources from the Originalist canon, as well as scholarship on the early founding period and the role of corporations, in their attempts to persuade their audience that history and Originalism were on their side. Setting aside the question of whose Originalism trumped whose in *Citizens United*, it was plain to all audiences that Originalism

JUDICIAL ACTIVISM, INC. (87)

(and, by extension, the Federalist Society network) was the real winner. As I articulate at greater length in Chapter 6, the back-and-forth over Originalism in this case and others is evidence that the Federalist Society successfully has changed the debate and has helped to bring Originalism into the legal mainstream. As member John C. Yoo said in our personal interview (and as Stevens's dissent in *Citizens United* makes clear), now "even liberals on the Supreme Court take it seriously."[143]

IDEAS WITH CONSEQUENCES: THE FIRST AMENDMENT AND CAMPAIGN FINANCE

If *Wisconsin Right to Life* gave Federalist Society network members the proverbial "half a loaf," *Citizens United* provided a significant portion of the second half of that loaf—though it did leave some crumbs on the table. For example, Theodore Olson (arguing on behalf of Citizens United) and other *amici curiae* affiliated with the Federalist Society network were unable to persuade a majority of the justices that the disclosure requirements of McCain-Feingold were unconstitutional as applied to Citizens United.[144] As I wrote earlier, the issue of disclosure was one that had been discussed with some regularity by Federalist Society network members who worry that these requirements impermissibly chill free speech and thus violate the First Amendment.[145] Disclosure aside, Federalist Society network litigators, *amici*, and scholars celebrated the Supreme Court's decision in *Citizens United*. James Bopp, Jr., who initiated the litigation and participated as *amicus curiae*, called the ruling "a wonderful decision" and a "ringing affirmation of the protections of the First Amendment."[146] Jan Witold Baran, who submitted an *amicus* brief on behalf of the Chamber of Commerce, referred to the decision as a "breath of fresh air" and said that it would "restrain Congress from flooding us with arcane, burdensome, convoluted campaign laws that discourage political participation."[147] Ted Olson, celebrating after his client's victory, told newspapers that "the court's decision vindicates the right of individuals to engage in core political speech by banding together to make their voices heard"[148] and that "[t]he Court recognized that permitting widespread participation in the marketplace of ideas will invigorate political discourse... and, ultimately, strengthen the very foundations of our democracy."[149]

Citizens United was also a victory for the network in that it demonstrated willingness from Roberts and Alito to abandon the Wilkinson-model of judicial restraint and embrace the Barnett-Epstein-Thomas model that, as I discussed earlier in this chapter, seems to have found a significant constituency within the Federalist Society. And once these justices decided to abandon *stare decisis,* the Federalist Society network became a series of active conduits through which intellectual capital was transmitted. This intellectual capital helped the majority defend the decision to abandon *stare decisis* and rebuild the scaffolding of campaign finance jurisprudence around the First Amendment principles articulated in *Bellotti.* Moreover, constituting another win for the Federalist Society network, we saw in Stevens's dissent evidence that Originalism had taken hold as the dominant discourse on the Supreme Court. Even if the liberals or progressives on the bench disagree with it, as I return to discuss in Chapter 6, they felt compelled to respond to their conservative and libertarian counterparts in that discourse.

The question of whether the decision in *Citizens United* lived up to its perilous promise to damage the integrity of our democratic institutions and democratic process (or whether, as Justice Alito mouthed at the 2010 State of the Union Address, this is simply "not true")[150] has proven difficult to assess. Even still, the impact of *Citizens United* is already evident in a few significant areas. Just as *Heller* and *McDonald,* the Second Amendment cases examined in the previous chapter, opened the doors for more Second Amendment litigation and invigorated litigators to attempt to push their deregulation efforts further and deeper, the decision in *Citizens United* energized First Amendment campaign finance litigators to continue to chip away at both state and federal campaign finance legislation. To wit, Steve Simpson, an attorney for the Institute of Justice and a regular participant in Federalist Society discussions on campaign finance,[151] was quoted in *USA Today* saying that he was "certainly emboldened" by the decision in *Citizens United.*[152] Similarly, James Bopp, Jr., spoke of his "10-year plan to take all this [campaign finance regulation] down" and was quick to point out, after Citizens United, that "we are not done yet."[153] In its Free Speech and Election Law Practice Group Teleforum calls, its National Conferences, its lawyer chapter events, and its Student Chapter events, the Federalist Society has served as a hub of post–*Citizens United* discussion and strategic deliberation, facilitating close to 100 events on the decision and its aftermath.[154] This energetic discussion within the network already has translated into action. Spearheaded by the James Madison Center for Free Speech (with James Bopp, Jr., as General Counsel) and the Center for Competitive Politics (with Bradley Smith at the helm), lawsuits have been filed in federal courts challenging federal disclosure requirements, state electioneering disclosure requirements, federal lobbying disclosure requirements, the FEC's classification of a "political committee," soft money bans, and coordinated spending bans.[155] Most noteworthy is the recent Supreme Court litigation in *McCutcheon v. Federal Election Commission,*[156] which challenged the McCain-Feingold Act's aggregate limits on combined campaign contributions to non-candidate committees, national party committees, and candidate committees. Decided by the Supreme Court by a 5 to 4 vote on April 2, 2014, the opinion in *McCutcheon*, authored by Chief Justice Roberts, held that the aggregate limits cap did not in fact serve to further the government's compelling interest in preventing corruption. Court-watchers are referring to the case as "Citizens United II"[157] because it has the potential to both further entrench the *Citizens United* frame and to hollow out federal and state regulations on campaign finance more deeply.

There have been some significant lateral effects of the *Citizens United* decision. As Gordon Silverstein presents in *Law's Allure,* some of the most powerful effects of judicial decisions are the framing effects they can have for other areas of law. Once a new path opens up in a particular area of law, litigators who have been unsuccessful pursuing one line of reasoning can latch on to this new path, reframe their case, and potentially have better success (Silverstein 2009, 68–75). In the case of *Citizens United*, the holding that the First Amendment's protection of speech does not discriminate between human and corporate or other associational speakers has already been used by savvy litigators (many of them connected with the Federalist Society network) to argue that the same logic should apply to the First Amendment's protection of religious liberty.[158] For example, arguing before the Tenth Circuit Court of Appeals *en banc*, Federalist Society network member and counsel for the for-profit business Hobby Lobby, Kyle Duncan,[159] successfully persuaded the Court of Appeals that the corporation's free-exercise rights were protected by the First Amendment and had been violated by the Health and Human Services mandate requiring most business and entities to provide contraceptive coverage for their female employees.[160] Citing the Supreme Court's holdings in both *Citizens United* and *Bellotti*, the Tenth Circuit (in an opinion authored by Federalist Society network member Timothy Tymkovich)[161] held that "[t]he Constitution guarantees freedom of association of this kind as an indispensable means of preserving other individual liberties'" and that "the Free Exercise Clause is *not* a 'purely personal' guarantee[]. . . unavailable to corporations and other organizations because the 'historic function' of the particular [constitutional] guarantee has been limited to the protection of individuals."[162]

The Separation of Governmental Powers Is Central to Our Constitution

CHAPTER 4

Federalism and the Commerce Power

Returning to "First Principles"

U.S. Constitution, Article I, Section 8, clause 3
The Congress shall have Power...
[t]o regulate Commerce with foreign Nations,
and among the several States, and with the Indian Tribes

On January 30, 1987, Pat Buchanan sent an urgent, last-minute memo to President Ronald Reagan's chief of staff about the president's scheduled call to the fledgling Federalist Society that night: "Ken Cribb called from Justice to say Ed Meese is asking 'as a personal favor' that the Chief of Staff make the added point in his phone call to the Federalist Society tonight—about the structural tensions inside the Constitution."[1] The memo provoked anger and annoyance from the president's chief of staff, but because it was framed as a favor to Attorney General Meese, he agreed and added the talking point.[2] Two of Meese's special assistants named on the telephone message request, who had a hand in drafting the language for the last-minute addition to the president's talking points, were Federalist Society cofounders David McIntosh and Steven Calabresi.[3] The additional talking point that Meese and his special assistants felt so strongly about including in President Reagan's phone call to the Federalist Society read as follows:

The structure of government designed by the Framers protects individual liberty by ensuring against the concentration of power in any one branch or level of government. This is accomplished through a carefully-crafted system of checks and balances, which rests on the twin Constitutional doctrines of Federalism and separation of powers. . . . All three branches of the federal government—executive, legislative, and judicial—have a special obligation to maintain fidelity to these ideals, as expressed and embodied in our written Constitution—the supreme law of the land. This Bicentennial Year represents an opportunity for us all to affirm and strengthen our adherence to those ideals.[4]

This talking point neatly encapsulates how Federalist Society members understand constitutional structure and why it is so important to them. The protection of freedom as established in Chapter 1, is the key normative and principled belief of Federalist Society network members. Further, network members believe that the structure of the Constitution best preserves freedom through the separation and fragmentation of power, both vertically and horizontally. As the second prong of the Federalist Society's statement of principles states, network members believe that *the separation of governmental powers is central to our Constitution.* This chapter and the next focus on the Federalist Society's long-term efforts to revive and reinvigorate judicial enforcement of the vertical separation of powers (federalism and state sovereignty), thereby fundamentally restructuring the relationship between the federal government, the states, and the individual. Specifically, this chapter examines three landmark federalism decisions—*New York v. United States* (1992), *United States v. Lopez* (1995), *Morrison v. United States* (2000)—in which the Supreme Court enlisted the help of Federalist Society network ideas and intellectual capital to enforce limits on the federal commerce power for the first time in almost half a century.

The Supreme Court's role in policing the boundaries between federal and state power has long been a source of "ideological tension" and "high political drama" (Scheiber 2005, 322). The principal constitutional clause around which this federalist "political drama" has unfolded is the Commerce Clause (Art. 1, Sec. 8, clause 3).[5] This clause, which grants Congress the power to regulate commerce "among the several States," became the primary vehicle through which the federal government extended its regulatory reach into the states throughout the latter half of the twentieth century; and, for this, Congress had the Supreme Court to thank. After a series of controversial decisions in the early 1930s that had enforced strict limits on Congress relating to commerce power and had all but crippled President Roosevelt's New Deal plan, the Supreme Court signaled that it would no longer view the Commerce Clause as a strict limit on congressional regulatory power.[6] This new doctrinal approach reached its fullest expression in a 1946 decision,

American Power & Light v. SEC, in which the Supreme Court declared that Congress's commerce power was " 'as broad as the economic needs of the nation' required" (Scheiber 2005, 327). Needing to prove only the slightest connection between the activity being regulated and interstate commerce, Congress had used this power to pass legislation regulating everything from intrastate labor relations to wheat grown for personal consumption to private restaurants serving interstate travelers.[7]

The Supreme Court's broad interpretation of Congress's commerce power was grounded in and supported by a theory of flexible or "political safeguards" federalism that viewed the primary checks against the excessive accumulation of federal power as political ones, not legalistic or judge-centric ones (Kramer 2000). In other words, proponents of this theory believed that the boundaries of state and federal power could be negotiated politically, rather than decided legalistically through a narrow interpretation of commerce (Choper 1980). Additionally, in contradistinction to the more rigid view endorsed by the Supreme Court in the pre–New Deal era, proponents of political safeguards federalism viewed the Constitution as a broad blueprint that ought to be interpreted in light of the changing needs and politically expressed desires of society. So, rather than embracing a static, eighteenth-century constitutional understanding of commerce, advocates of the more flexible federalism approach argued that Congress's commerce power should be interpreted in light of the ever more complex and interdependent nature of national markets. Under this doctrinal approach, the Supreme Court decided that any activity "affecting interstate commerce" was within the scope of Congress's regulatory power under the Commerce Clause.

This theory and the Supreme Court's resulting hands-off approach to the Commerce Clause had been cause for political concern with Republicans from the Barry Goldwater campaign onward. As political scientists Cornell Clayton and J. Mitchell Pickerill have shown, discussions of the Tenth Amendment, state sovereignty, and limited federal power began to appear with some frequency in Republican Party platforms as early as 1976 and increased steadily from 1980 to 1988 (Clayton and Pickerill 2004, 96). Moreover, the discourse of "limited government" became something of a mantra during Ronald Reagan's presidential campaign. In his first inaugural address, President Reagan announced his New Federalism Initiative, in which he promised to "curb the size and influence of the federal government" and to restore "the distinction between the powers granted to the federal government and those reserved to the states, or to the people."[8]

In line with this political pro-federalism push, conservative and libertarian legal elites began discussing the issue of federalism with a renewed sense of urgency in the 1980s. For example, in the 1988 Reagan Justice Department report *The Constitution in the Year 2000*, principal author and Federalist Society member Stephen Markman[9] wrote that "for those who view federalism as a serious concern of the Constitution, the current state of the Supreme Court's law in this area is troubling." The report goes on to suggest that in the "1990s" the Supreme Court might "reconsider its doctrines granting Congress virtually limitless powers under the Commerce Clause" and, based on the "structure of the Constitution," it might "reverse its current course and place judicial limits" on Congress's commerce power.[10] Prior to the cases examined in this chapter, there had been one recent but short-lived attempt to enforce meaningful limits on Congress's commerce power. In the 1976 decision *National League of Cities v. Usery*, the Supreme Court relied in part on the Commerce Clause to invalidate federal wage and hour restrictions on state and government employees.[11] This precedent and the principle of limited federal power it embodied, however, was overturned within the span of a decade in *Garcia v. San Antonio Metro Transit Authority* (1985), prompting Justice Rehnquist to predict in dissent that it would not be long before the Supreme Court would have another stand-off over Congress's commerce power.[12]

THE FEDERALIST SOCIETY NETWORK ON THE COMMERCE CLAUSE

Judicial enforcement of constitutional federalism has been a salient topic of discussion at Federalist Society National Conferences. The preface to the transcript from the very first Federalist Society meeting, dedicated in its entirety to "Federalism," reveals this early enthusiasm within the network for the vertical separation of powers: "At a time when the nation's law schools are staffed largely by professors who dream of regulating from their cloistered offices every minute detail of our lives. . . the Federalists met—and proclaimed the virtues of individual freedom and of limited government."[13] Since that time, the Federalist Society has hosted dozens of panels and invited talks on the subject. A review of the agendas for Federalist Society National Conferences from 1982 to 2011, for example, revealed that no fewer than 30 panels contained the word "federalism" in their titles.[14] On those panels and in those talks, Federalist Society participants consistently have criticized the Supreme Court for half a century of lax enforcement of the constitutionally prescribed limits on Congress's commerce power. For example, at the 1988 National Lawyers Convention, scholar William Van Alstyne lamented that "'the power to regulate commerce among the states'" had been interpreted by the Supreme Court as "the power 'to regulate' period, whether or not it is commerce, whether or not it is among the states."[15] At that same conference, Federalist Society member Lynn Baker referred to the Commerce Clause in her talk as the "Hey, you-can-do-whatever-you-feel-like Clause."[16]

Federalist Society network members also have been active critics of Congress's commerce power outside Federalist Society conferences. To illustrate this point, a search that I conducted in 2009 within a subset of conservative media outlets for "federalism" revealed that nearly one in five articles published in those outlets were authored by Federalist Society network members.[17] While most of these authors expressed their federalism concerns in more general terms, 39 (21%) of them did specifically address Congress's commerce power.[18] My interviews with founding and core members of the Federalist Society also demonstrated a strong concern with limiting the scope of Congress's commerce power. For example, in my interview with Federalist Society cofounder David McIntosh, he lamented the tendency of Congress to "ignore" the original meaning of the Constitution, "because they want to use the commerce clause as their end all and be all."[19] Former Reagan appointee Douglas Kmiec also discussed the original meaning of the Commerce Clause in our interview, arguing that Justice Clarence Thomas's interpretation of that clause, which advocates radically limiting and reinterpreting the modern understanding of "commerce," in fact "comes closest to the pure Federalist Society model."[20]

In terms of the constitutional areas examined in this book, federalism and/or state sovereignty rank as the most salient topic of discussion within the Federalist Society network. In total, in looking through conference transcripts, Practice Group newsletters, and through Federalist Society recommended scholarship, I was able to identify 129 speech acts that dealt primarily with federalism and/or state sovereignty. This sample includes speech acts from 93 different actors within the Federalist Society network. It also includes repeat performances from several notable individuals, including Charles Fried, Edwin Meese III, James L. Buckley, Charles J. Cooper, Michael W. McConnell, Paul M. Bator, and Richard A. Epstein. Within this sample, Congress's commerce power is discussed explicitly in about one-third (42) of these speech acts. After a close reading of all these speech acts, I identified three general categories of argument expressed by Federalist Society network members in favor of narrowing the scope of Congress's commerce power: textual arguments supporting an originalist interpretation of the phrase "commerce... among the several states"; structural arguments relying on Madison's *Federalist* 45 that emphasize the relationship between limited governmental powers and individual freedom; and functionalist arguments for less federal regulation derived from economic theories supporting competition and free markets.

A Textualist-Originalist Interpretation of "Commerce. . . among the Several States"

The textualist-originalist argument blends textual analyses of the language of the clause itself with original understanding arguments to advocate for a narrow interpretation of Congress's commerce power. Its proponents have used it to critique several of the tests and doctrines that the Supreme Court has developed since the late 1930s that, for example, have permitted Congress to regulate activities, behaviors, or industries that, when considered in the aggregate, can be understood to have a substantial effect on interstate commerce. As Charles J. Cooper lamented at the 1994 National Lawyers Conference, "It is no exaggeration to say today that there is almost no human commercial endeavor that cannot be brought within the Congress's commerce powers as construed by the Supreme Court."[21] Advocates of the textualist-originalist interpretation of the commerce power situate the terms "commerce" and "among the several states" within an eighteenth-century framework in which the Supreme Court's modern doctrines and tests would appear, according to the argument, completely illogical. While several Federalist Society conference participants have deployed this argument for narrowing the scope of the Commerce Clause in their conference speeches,[22] the textualist-originalist arguments for narrowing the commerce power are developed most fully in Federalist Society network scholarship. Each of the sources that I examine here is also recommended reading under "federalism" and the "Commerce Clause" in the Federalist Society's *Annotated Bibliography of Conservative and Libertarian Legal Scholarship*.

In the first source recommended under the "Commerce Clause" sub-heading—Richard Epstein's 1987 *Virginia Law Review* article, "The Proper Scope of the Commerce Power"—Epstein argues that the content assigned to "commerce" must make sense with respect not only to the economic relationship between Congress and the states but also with respect to "foreign nations" and the "Indian tribes." As Epstein illustrates rhetorically, "What possible sense does it make as a matter of ordinary English to say that Congress can regulate 'manufacturing with foreign nations, or with Indian tribes'. . . ?" (Epstein 1987, 1393–1394). This textual argument is then further supported with reference to familiar historical sources from the Originalist canon such as Elliot's *Debates, The Federalist,* and the *Antifederalist* papers. From these sources, Epstein concludes that "the affirmative scope of the commerce power" should be limited to "interstate transportation, navigation and sales, and the activities closely incident to them. All else should be left to the states" (Epstein 1987, 1454).

Building on Epstein's work, legal scholar and member Randy Barnett engaged in an extensive textualist-originalist exploration of the term "commerce" in his Federalist Society–recommended 2001 law review article, "The Original Meaning of the Commerce Clause." Relying on evidence from eighteenth-century dictionaries, James Madison's notes from the Constitutional Convention, *The Federalist*, and the ratification debates, Barnett concluded that the founding generation understood "commerce" as being confined to "trade" or "exchange," and this did not include other commercial activities such as manufacture and agriculture (Barnett 2001, 112–125). Offering further intellectual support for a more restrictive reading of the Commerce Clause, Federalist Society member and Pepperdine academic Douglas W. Kmiec argued in his 2001 law review article, "Rediscovering a Principled Commerce Power," that the most "historically informed" definition of "commerce" was a relatively narrow one linked to certain principles articulated in the "Virginia Resolutions of 1787" (Kmiec 2001, 560–565).

Reinvigorating the Structural Limits on Federal Power via Madison's *Federalist* 45

The structural argument on behalf of a more limited interpretation of Congress's commerce power, often supported with reference to Madison's *Federalist* 45, is closely connected to the network's shared beliefs about the relationship between limited government and individual freedom. In this essay, Madison proclaimed that "[t]he powers delegated by the proposed Constitution to the federal government are few and defined" whereas "[t]he powers reserved to the several states will extend to all the objects which, in the ordinary course of affairs, concern the lives, liberties, and properties of the people, and the internal order, improvement, and prosperity of the State" (Rossiter 1961, 260–261). According to this structural argument, by interpreting the powers delegated to Congress via the Commerce Clause as not "few," but many, the Supreme Court has eroded one of the most important structural checks on expansive federal power and has posed a serious threat to individual liberty. The relationship between limited government (enumerated federal power) and individual liberty was articulated by Charles J. Cooper at the 1992 National Student Conference: "individual rights and enumerated powers are opposite sides of the same coin. . . . By delegating legislative power over certain subjects to the federal government, the people consented to abide by the laws enacted by the federal government which pertained to those subjects." "However," Cooper continued, "as to those subjects over which the federal government had no delegated legislative power, the people retained the right vis-a-vis the federal government to act any way they pleased."[23] At this same conference, former state legislator Pete du Pont referred to the "Commerce Clause" as "the most notable" of the "structural devices" the Founders included in the Constitution "to restrain the government." In supporting a reading of the Commerce Clause that provided only "limited power" to Congress, du Pont made specific reference to Madison's *Federalist* 45.[24] At the 1998 Federalist Society Conference, "Reviving the Structural Constitution," member John Yoo also articulated a structural argument for a government of limited and enumerated powers, recalling the oft-cited language from Madison's *Federalist* 45 to argue against the "broad sweep given to the Commerce Clause" by the "modern Court" (Yoo 1998, 2).

The structural argument for a more narrow judicial interpretation of Congress's commerce power is also evident in network scholarship recommended in the Federalist Society's *Bibliography*. In his 1987 law review article referenced earlier, Richard Epstein considered the Commerce Clause in light of the "overall constitutional structure" and concluded that when the "federal government received delegated powers from the states and the individuals within the states. . . there was clearly no sense that either grantor conferred upon the Congress the plenary power to act as a roving commission" that would be empowered to "do whatever it thought best for the common good" (Epstein 1987, 1395–1396). In light of this original understanding of a limited government empowered by "We the People," Epstein continued, any judicial interpretation that reads "the Commerce Clause" as "allow[ing] the government to regulate anything that even indirectly burdens or affects commerce does away with the key understanding that the federal government has received only enumerated powers" (Epstein 1987, 1396). Charles J. Cooper, one of the strongest and most vocal proponents of federalism and limited government, writes in his 1988 article recommended in the Federalist Society's *Bibliography*, "The Demise of Federalism," that the Supreme Court had "abdicated its constitutional responsibility" to enforce the Commerce Clause as a "structural limitation on federal governmental power." Referring to Madison's *Federalist* 45, Cooper argues that the founder whose silhouette graces the Federalist Society logo "underestimated the power of judicial interpretation" to erode the structural checks against federal power that the Constitution had put in place (Cooper 1998, 283, 249).

The Framers, Free Markets, and Functionalist Originalism

While several of the Federalist Society network actors' Commerce Clause arguments begin with this historical and structural insight about the relationship between limited government and individual freedom as important in its own right, they do not all end there. For instance, at the 1998 Student Conference, Lynn Baker argued for supplementing these more formalist or "historical insight[s]" about federalism and the Commerce Clause with a "functionalist originalism" derived from the economic logic of public choice theory.[25] As articulated by Antonin Scalia at the Society's first national meeting in 1982, this argument is derived from the libertarian belief that "the free market has the ability to order things in the most efficient manner, and generally should be allowed to operate free of government intervention."[26] This "functionalist" argument for federalism is perhaps best represented in the speech acts and scholarship of Richard Epstein. At the 1989 National Lawyers Convention, Epstein explained the relationship between federalism and public choice theory, many of whose adherents advocate competition and open markets: "The bottom line, therefore, is that separation of powers, checks and balances, should be treated as a means to an end. The only way that this end can be rightly understood is with a healthy dose of public choice theory, which should animate your coming and your going in public life." Epstein continued, emphasizing that "[w]hen most outputs of Congress are redistributive, then the best way to make government work is to see that its wheels grind slowly so that as little harm as possible is done. And that spells a great appreciation for the now neglected virtues of separation of powers."[27]

Similarly, at the 1998 National Student Conference, Epstein used this same logic to argue that "the courts should reverse the limitless reading of the Commerce Clause and reject the implicit economic logic that underlies the vast expansion of federal power."[28] Former Solicitor General Charles Fried used the same functionalist logic at the 1982 National Conference to argue that the Supreme Court's Commerce Clause jurisprudence, and its complicit role in the centralization of governmental power, had the practical effect of facilitating greater government spending: ". . . special interests can get a stronger hold at the federal level than they can at the state level; all one needs at the federal level is to find a few skillful congressmen and one senator, and one is assured a billion or so annually in the federal budget."[29] Legal scholar John McGinnis echoed the same concern, relying explicitly on public choice theory's concept of "rent-seeking" to explain the inherent dangers of the Supreme Court's Commerce Clause post-1940s jurisprudence:

> The advantage of federalism under this view is that a properly designed dual system of government can limit the total amount of rent-seeking by such interest groups more than can a unitary state. Rent-seeking from the national government is limited by giving it only limited powers, including limited powers, of taxation. Rent-seeking from state government is limited by putting those governments in competition with one another for capital, including human capital. The bridge between the two mechanisms is that the limited powers of the national government sustain the conditions for competition among the state governments.[30]

As McGinnis went on to explain at the 1997 National Student Conference, "by the early 1940s the United States Supreme Court had abandoned the constitutional limitations that prevented the federal government from directly regulating manufacturing and the conditions of labor, thereby greatly increasing special-interest power to obtain regulatory rents." Similarly, Epstein has repeatedly called for a return to a "pre-1937" approach to the Commerce Clause, insisting that the Supreme Court's jurisprudence was "more intellectually coherent" and consistent with the important precepts of public choice theory as understood by these network members.[31]

The "functionalist" argument for a limited reading of the Commerce Clause, at times relying exclusively on the language of public choice theory and at other times blending this logic with a "functionalist originalism," has appeared with some frequency in Federalist Society network scholarship. For example, a 1987 article recommended under the "federalism" section of the Federalist Society's *Bibliography* by Michael W. McConnell blends this public choice logic with an Originalist perspective to argue on behalf of the functional benefits of federalism. In "Federalism: Evaluating the Founders' Design," McConnell described how the American system of "dual sovereignty," preserved through a narrow reading of the Commerce Clause, was designed to promote three "complementary objectives: (1) 'to secure the public good,' (2) to protect 'private rights,' and (3) 'to preserve the spirit and form of popular government'" (McConnell 1987, 1492). Engaging in an extensive "examination of the founders' arguments and the modern literature," the McConnell piece catalogued the functional benefits of federalism:

> ... decentralized decision making is better able to reflect the diversity of interests and preferences of individuals in different parts of the nation. Second, allocation of decision making authority to a level of government no larger than necessary will prevent... attempts by communities to take advantage of their neighbors. And, third, decentralization allows for innovation and competition in government. (McConnell 1987, 1493)

Federalist Society member John Yoo argued that "the framers' under-standing" of federalism and limited government "anticipated some of the concerns raised in recent scholarship" by "Public choice scholars" (Yoo 1998, 37). As he wrote in a 1998 law review article, "put in pub-lic choice terms, federalism and the maintenance of a federal govern-ment of limited, enumerated powers may be a positive externality that no individual state acting individually or collectively fully internalizes." However, the Yoo article maintained that the Framers also built "delib-erate inefficienc[ies]" into the system to protect individual liberty and that these checks and balances can be seen to be "at odds with the public approach to federalism" because they do not maximize efficiency (Yoo 1998, 41–42, 43–44).

While certainly not all-inclusive or exhaustive, this sample of speech acts and published scholarship advocating for a more limited understand-ing of the Commerce Clause represents some of the Federalist Society network's shared beliefs, first outlined in Chapter 1, about limited gov-ernment, individual liberty, and the role of the judiciary in enforcing and policing the separation of powers. The next task of this chapter will be to examine how and to what extent the actual intellectual capital generated by Federalist Society members was diffused to Supreme Court decision makers in three important decisions handed down between 1992 and 2000: *New York v. United States* (1992), *United States v. Lopez* (1995), and *United States v. Morrison* (2000).[32]

THE COMMERCE CLAUSE AND
THE SUPREME COURT

Recall from the introductory section of this chapter that the Supreme Court had, for the first time in almost half a century, flirted with a more limited interpretation of Congress's commerce power in its 1976 *National League of Cities* opinion. To the chagrin of many conservatives and lib-ertarians, chief among them Justice Rehnquist, this decision was over-turned just nine years later in *Garcia*. Justice Rehnquist, who would be elevated to Chief Justice the following year, was nonetheless "confident" that the principle of limited federal power embodied in *National League of Cities* would "in time again command the support of a majority of this Court."[33] With three more conservative appointments to the Supreme Court over the next five years, two of whom were very prominent within the Federalist Society network—Justice Antonin Scalia and Justice Clarence Thomas—the odds of Rehnquist's bold prediction panning out were certainly much more favorable as of 1991.

New York v. United States (1992)

This case challenged the constitutionality of the Low-Level Radioactive Waste Policy Amendments Act.[34] An effort to ease the burden on states such as Washington, South Carolina, and Nevada that until 1980 had been accepting all of the nation's low-level radioactive waste, the original legislation mandated that each state in the union be responsible for developing a method of disposing of its waste by 1986. States were given the choice of either building their own disposal sites or joining an interstate compact. When it became clear that states were not complying, Congress passed the Amendments Act, which extended the deadline for another seven years and included three types of provisions to encourage compliance with the Act: "monetary incentives" that authorized states to collect a surcharge for accepting waste, "access incentives" that authorized states to charge multiple surcharges to states not in compliance and to deny access altogether, and a "take title" provision that would hold a state liable for all damages incurred as a result of its failure to take possession or take title of its waste in a timely manner.[35]

The State of New York had not joined a regional compact but instead identified five potential intrastate dumping sites for its waste in Allegany County and Cortland County. After intense opposition from the residents of these counties to the state's plan, New York and the two counties decided to file suit against the United States in the Northern District Court of New York claiming that the Amendments Act violated the Tenth Amendment, the Eleventh Amendment, and the Constitution's Guarantee Clause (Art. IV, 4).[36] The District Court dismissed the case, and the Second Circuit Court of Appeals affirmed the lower court's ruling. New York and its counties appealed to the Supreme Court, which granted cert and heard the case on March 30, 1992. The Supreme Court decision, handed down in June, affirmed in part and reversed in part, holding that of the three provisions in question, only the "take title" provision exceeded Congress's enumerated powers under the Commerce Clause and thus violated the doctrine of state sovereignty as protected by the Tenth Amendment.

Of the six parties filing *amicus curiae* briefs in *New York*, two were represented on brief by Federalist Society network members. Virginia Seitz[37] and Laurence Gold[38] argued on behalf of the AFL-CIO, while Carter Phillips[39] and Rex Lee[40] represented the Rocky Mountain Low-Level Radioactive Waste Compact. However, both parties were arguing to affirm the lower court ruling. Also urging the Supreme Court to affirm the lower court ruling and uphold the constitutionality of the Waste Amendments, the United States was represented on brief by

Federalist Society member Kenneth W. Starr.[41] Interestingly, then, the pro-federalism arguments were not being articulated by either Federalist Society network *amici curiae* or affiliated counsel participating in this case. However, as Figure 4.1 details, the Federalist Society network still had four active conduits through which pro-federalism intellectual capital could be diffused: Justice Antonin Scalia, Justice Clarence Thomas, and two clerks with Federalist Society ties.[42]

As I mentioned, both the District Court of Northern New York and the Second Circuit Court of Appeals dismissed the State of New York's case against the Waste Amendments. Relying on the Supreme Court's opinion in *Garcia*, the decision that had overturned in dramatic fashion the briefly resurrected principle of limited federal power articulated in *National League of Cities*, the Second Circuit majority provided a brief discussion of the tension that exists between Congress's commerce power under the Commerce Clause and the doctrine of state sovereignty embodied in the Tenth Amendment: "It is self-evident that virtually every congressional exercise of power under the *commerce clause* will limit state power over that commerce and, to that extent, will invite state objections under the *Tenth Amendment.*"[43] In determining where the balance lay between these two constitutional provisions, the Appeals Court cited *Garcia's* flexible, process-based framework that elevated the "national political process" over "the courts" as the ultimate arbiter of the limits of federal power and protector of state sovereignty.[44] Discounting the nine years during which *National League of Cities* was considered authoritative precedent,

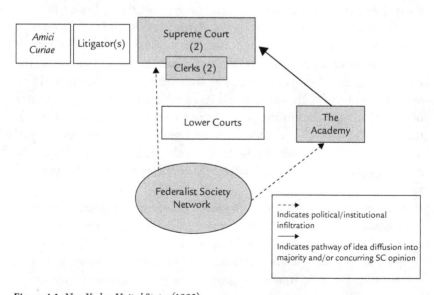

Figure 4.1 *New York v. United States* (1992)

this process-based framework or, as many Federalist Society network actors would understand it, this abdication of judicial responsibility, had provided Congress with wide-ranging regulatory power under the Commerce Clause for half a century. As long as *Garcia* and the laundry list of prior Supreme Court decisions consistent with its framework remained in force, legislation like the Waste Amendments would unquestionably continue to "pass constitutional muster" in lower courts.[45]

While the Supreme Court majority opinion in *New York*, authored by Justice Sandra Day O'Connor, did not overturn the *Garcia* framework, it did represent a bold departure from these prior cases by explicitly relying on a more "formalistic" approach to enforcing the constitutional boundaries between federal and state sovereignty:

> Much of the Constitution is concerned with setting forth the form of our government, and the courts have traditionally invalidated measures deviating from that form. The result may appear "formalistic" in a given case to partisans of the measure at issue, because such measures are typically the product of the era's perceived necessity. But the Constitution protects us from our own best intentions: It divides power among sovereigns and among branches of government precisely so that we may resist the temptation to concentrate power in one location as an expedient solution to the crisis of the day. The shortage of disposal sites for radioactive waste is a pressing national problem, but a judiciary that licensed extraconstitutional government with each issue of comparable gravity would, in the long run, be far worse.[46]

In sketching out the "constitutional line between federal and state power," the majority opinion referred to several essays from the *Federalist*, in addition to numerous excerpts from the *Records of the Federal Convention* and Elliot's *Debates*.[47] More important, the majority also cited Federalist Society network scholar Michael W. McConnell's article, "Evaluating the Founders' Design" as an authoritative statement on "the benefits of this federal structure."[48] This article and its functionalist-originalist defense of federalism, detailed in the prior section, had been cited almost verbatim in the Supreme Court's 1991 majority opinion in *Gregory v. Ashcroft*.[49] The excerpts below, first from the McConnell article and second from the majority opinion in *Gregory*, illustrate this overlap in logic and language:

> Three important advantages of decentralized decision making emerge from an examination of the founders' arguments and the modern literature. First, decentralized decision making is better able to reflect the diversity of interests and preferences of individuals in different parts of the nation. Second, allocation of decision making authority to a level of government no larger than necessary will prevent... attempts

by communities to take advantage of their neighbors. And, third, decentralization allows for innovation and competition in government.[50]

This federalist structure of joint sovereigns preserves to the people numerous advantages. It assures a decentralized government that will be more sensitive to the diverse needs of a heterogeneous society; it increases opportunity for citizen involvement in democratic processes; it allows for more innovation and experimentation in government; and it makes government more responsible by putting the states in competition for a mobile citizenry.[51]

Because the benefits of federalism had "been extensively catalogued" in *Gregory*, the majority in *New York* merely gestured to that opinion as additional support for its application of a more "formalistic" federalism framework.[52]

The three challenged provisions of the Waste Amendments, detailed earlier in this section, were considered in light of this more "formalistic" framework derived from and supported by Originalist sources and Federalist Society network member scholarship. Of the three provisions, the majority ruled that only the "take-title" provision constituted an "unconstitutionally coercive regulatory technique. . . lying outside Congress' enumerated powers" that made it "inconsistent with the federal structure of our Government established by the Constitution."[53] The Act stood as constitutional, with this provision being severable from the rest of the Amendments. However, the principle of limited federal power that had up until this point existed mostly in the speech acts and scholarship of Federalist Society actors had been articulated and defended by a majority on the Supreme Court for only the second time in half a century. Relying on the canon of Originalist sources and select Federalist Society scholarship, the majority's opinion represented a sign of hope for individuals frustrated with the Supreme Court's long history of employing a hands-off, political process–based approach to federalism. The question remained, however, whether the Supreme Court would be persistent in policing the boundaries between state and federal power based on a more "formalistic" understanding of federalism or whether *New York* would become the *National League of Cities* of the 1990s, swiftly swept aside and overturned in favor once again of a more deferential and pragmatic approach to federal regulatory power. Observers would not have long to speculate about where the Supreme Court was headed with its federalism jurisprudence. Just two years after the opinion was handed down in *New York v. United States*, the Supreme Court would hear oral argument in another case that implicated directly the limits of Congress's powers to pass legislation under the Commerce Clause.

United States v. Lopez (1995)

This case subjected the Gun-Free School Zones Act to constitutional scru-
tiny, raising the question of whether the Act constituted a valid exercise of
Congress's power to regulate interstate commerce under the Commerce
Clause. Enacted as part of the Crime Control Act of 1990, the Gun-Free
School Zones Act made it a crime for any individual knowingly to possess a firearm within 1,000 feet of a school.[54] Cosponsored by Senators
Joe Biden (D-DE) and Strom Thurmond (R-SC) and signed into law by
President George H. W. Bush, the Gun-Free School Zones Act received
strong bipartisan support in both the House and the Senate. The issue of
gun possession near schools had received some national attention after a
gun attack outside a Stockton, California, elementary school in January
1989 killed five children between the ages of six and nine.[55]

High school senior Alfonso Lopez, Jr., was charged with violating
the Gun-Free School Zones Act for having carried a concealed revolver
into his high school in San Antonio, Texas. His counsel moved to have
the case dismissed in District Court for the Western District of Texas
on the grounds that the Act exceeded Congress's congressional power
to regulate under the Commerce Clause. The District Court denied
the motion to dismiss the case, concluding that the Act was a constitutional exercise of Congress's commerce power, and subsequently
convicted Alfonso Lopez, Jr. On appeal to the United States Court
of Appeals in September 1993, the Fifth Circuit reversed the conviction, holding that the Gun-Free School Zones Act did indeed exceed
Congress's authority pursuant to the Commerce Clause. The Supreme
Court granted cert, heard oral argument on November 8, 1994, and
issued a 5 to 4 split decision affirming the Fifth Circuit Court's holding
the following April.

The litigation in *Lopez* did not attract widespread Federalist Society
network participation. The four network members identified in Figure 4.2
as *amici curiae* in this case—Randy Barnett, Henry Mark Holzer,[56] Daniel
Polsby,[57] Charles E. Rice[58]—were all signatories on the same brief (the
Academics for the Second Amendment brief). Litigating the case on behalf
of Alfonso Lopez, Jr., was advocate and Federalist Society participant
Carter Phillips. Notably, three of the clerks working for Justice Clarence
Thomas in this case—Saikrishna Prakash,[59] Caleb Nelson,[60] and John
Yoo[61]—would go on to become presenters at Federalist Society National
Conferences and prominent members within the conservative legal move-
ment. While I cannot say with any degree of certainty which of these
clerks, if any, helped pen Justice Thomas's important concurring opinion
in *Lopez*, scholarship in political science suggests that Supreme Court

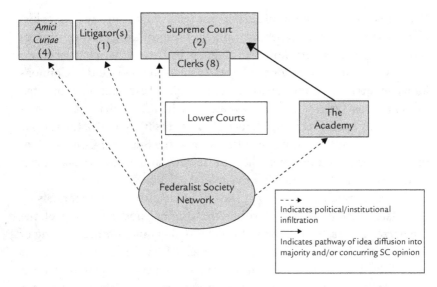

Figure 4.2 *United States v. Lopez* (1995)

clerks play an important role in crafting opinions (Peppers 2006, 83–144; Ward and Weiden 2006, 200–236) and also act as a critical bridge between the courts and the legal academy, bringing with them the latest theories, ideas, and creative legal strategies being nurtured and developed in the law schools (Atiyah and Summers 1987, 281–283).

The Supreme Court majority opinion in *Lopez*, written by Chief Justice Rehnquist, opened with a recitation of the same excerpt from Madison's *Federalist* 45 and also repeated some of the benefits of the dual federal structure as catalogued, with the help of Federalist Society scholar Michael W. McConnell, in *Gregory*:

We start with first principles. The Constitution creates a Federal Government of enumerated powers. See Art. I, § 8. As James Madison wrote, "the powers delegated by the proposed Constitution to the federal government are few and defined. Those which are to remain in the State governments are numerous and indefinite." *The Federalist* No. 45, pp. 292–293 (C. Rossiter ed. 1961). This constitutionally mandated division of authority "was adopted by the Framers to ensure protection of our fundamental liberties." *Gregory v. Ashcroft, 501 U.S. 452, 458, 115 L. Ed. 2d 410, 111 S. Ct. 2395 (1991)* (internal quotation marks omitted). Just as the separation and independence of the coordinate branches of the Federal Government serve to prevent the accumulation of excessive power in any one branch, a healthy balance of power between the states and the Federal Government will reduce the risk of tyranny and abuse from either front.[62]

Rehnquist's majority opinion did not proceed to engage in any deep or historical theorizing about federalism and the limits of Congress's commerce power. These tasks were, however, taken on by three other Justices in two separate concurring opinions in *Lopez*. Justices Kennedy and O'Connor's joint concurring opinion consisted of a thoughtful exploration, supported by numerous Originalist sources and couched in Federalist Society–friendly language, of the importance of "federalism" as one "of the various structural elements in the Constitution" and the Supreme Court's attendant "authority and responsibility" to "review" and at times strike down "congressional attempts to alter the federal balance."[63]

Federalist Society member Justice Thomas also wrote separately to articulate what he believed to be "the original understanding of the Commerce Clause."[64] Notably, in his defense of a more limited reading of "commerce," Justice Thomas incorporated Richard Epstein's argument from "The Proper Scope of the Commerce Power" (explored at great length earlier in this chapter) almost verbatim. While Thomas does not cite the 1987 Epstein article, the similarity in language and logic is unmistakable. I excerpt first from the Epstein article, and next from Justice Thomas's concurring opinion:

Similarly, one does not want a meaning of the term commerce which renders any one of these three heads of the commerce power redundant or unnecessary. The modern view which says that commerce among the several states includes all manufacture and other productive activity within each and every state. . . violates this constraint. . . . What possible sense does it make as a matter of ordinary English to say that Congress can regulate "manufacturing with foreign nations, or with the Indian tribes," or for that matter "manufacturing among the several states," when the particular fabrication or production takes place in one state, even with the goods purchased from another?. . . It is worth noting that this view of commerce as trade is consistent with the other prominent mention of the word commerce in the Constitution. Article I also states that "[n]o preference shall be given by any Regulation of Commerce or Revenue to the Ports of one State over those of another." The term "commerce" is used in opposition to the term "revenue," and seems clearly to refer to shipping and its incidental activities. . . .[65]

Moreover, interjecting a modern sense of commerce into the Constitution generates significant textual and structural problems. For example, one cannot replace "commerce" with a different type of enterprise, such as manufacturing. When a manufacturer produces a car, assembly cannot take place "with a foreign nation" or "with the Indian Tribes." Parts may come from different states or other nations and hence may have been in the flow of commerce at one time, but manufacturing takes place at a discrete site. Agriculture and manufacturing involve the production of goods; commerce encompasses traffic in such articles. The Port Preference Clause also suggests that the term "commerce" denoted sale and/or transport rather than business generally. According to that Clause, "no Preference shall be given by any Regulation of Commerce or Revenue to the Ports of one State over those of another." *U.S. Const., Art. I, § 9, cl. 6.* Although it is possible to conceive of regulations of manufacturing or farming that prefer one port over another, the more natural reading is that the Clause prohibits Congress from using its commerce power to channel commerce through certain favored ports.[66]

Thomas also mobilized several essays from the *Federalist*, excerpts from Elliot's *Debates*, and evidence from an edited volume called *A Documentary History of the Ratification of the Constitution* to implore the other members of the Supreme Court to "reconsider" its broad understanding of commerce and, "at an appropriate juncture," to "modify" its "Commerce Clause jurisprudence" to conform to the "original understanding" of the Constitution. For the time being, however, the Justice admitted that it would suffice "to say that the [Commerce] Clause does not empower Congress to ban gun possession within 1,000 feet of a school."[67]

The majority and concurring opinions in *Lopez* made it quite clear that the Supreme Court's new "formalistic" federalism framework, introduced in *Gregory* and *New York* a few years prior, would not be a *National League of Cities*–like blip on the constitutional radar screen. Indeed, the post-*Lopez* optimism that change was afoot with the Supreme Court's Commerce Clause jurisprudence was particularly evident among Federalist Society network members. Federalist Society cofounder Steven Calabresi wrote in a law review article that the *Lopez* decision marked "a revolutionary and long overdue revival of the doctrine that the federal government is one of limited and enumerated powers" and that it "must be recognized as an extraordinary event" for having "shattered forever the notion that, after fifty years of Commerce Clause precedent, we can never go back to the days of limited national power" (Calabresi 1995, 752). Similarly, John C. Yoo, who clerked for Thomas that term, wrote a few years after the *Lopez* decision that "Federalism is back, with a vengeance" (Yoo 1998, 27). The Federalist Society itself responded to this post-*Lopez* optimism by organizing its 1998 Student Conference around the topic "Reviving the Structural Constitution," at which speakers discussed and debated the rebirth of federalism, undoing the New Deal, and the advantages and disadvantages of a return to the formalist framework applied in *Lopez*.[68] As it turned out, Federalist Society network members would not have long to wait to see whether or not all this optimism surrounding a more permanent return to the "formalistic" federalism framework announced in *New York* and *Lopez* was misplaced or in fact warranted.

United States v. Morrison (2000)

The constitutional challenge in this case involved a provision of the Violence Against Women Act (VAWA), enacted pursuant to Congress's Commerce Clause authority and its remedial power under the Fourteenth Amendment. The law provided a federal civil remedy for victims of gender-motivated violence.[69] VAWA was drafted by Senator Joe Biden (D-DE) and signed into law by President Bill Clinton as part of the Violent Crime Control and Law Enforcement Act of 1994.[70] The federal legislation was supported by groups like the National Organization for Women (NOW) and viewed by proponents as an important supplement to the patchwork of state legislation in place at that time, much of which was seen as providing inconsistent and unsatisfactory remedies for victims of gender-motivated violence. For instance, under Virginia state law, rape is a "crime with a remarkably wide range of sanctions, from five years to life imprisonment" with the choice being left to "'the discretion of the court or the jury'" (Noonan 2002, 123).

In early 1995 Christy Brzonkala, a Virginia Tech freshman, filed a report to the University complaining that she had been raped by two members, Antonio Morrison and James Crawford, of the school's football team (Noonan 2002, 121). When, after a series of hearings, the University failed to sanction the two football players appropriately, Brzonkala filed suit against Morrison and Crawford in the U.S. District Court for the Western District of Virginia for damages under the Violence Against Women Act (VAWA). The United States intervened to defend the constitutionality of VAWA but to no avail. The District Court dismissed the complaint, ruling that Congress lacked the authority to enact VAWA under either the Commerce Clause or its Fourteenth Amendment remedial power. A panel of the United States Court of Appeals for the Fourth Circuit initially reversed the District Court's ruling but upon rehearing *en banc*, affirmed in a 7–4 decision. The Fourth Circuit majority opinion issued on March 5, 1999, was written by Federalist Society member Judge Michael Luttig.[71] The Supreme Court heard the appeal from the United States on January 11, 2000 and affirmed the Fourth Circuit's ruling in a 5 to 4 decision issued the following May.

Federalist Society network participation in *Morrison* reflected their post-*Lopez* excitement about the Supreme Court's recent federalism revival. Eleven members signed on to 5 of the 18 *amicus curiae* briefs submitted in *Morrison*: William H. Pryor,[72] Jeffrey Sutton,[73] John Eastman, Edwin Meese III, Phyllis Schlafly,[74] Richard Epstein, Clint Bolick, Timothy Lynch,[75] Roger Pilon,[76] Robert A. Levy, and Mary Ann Glendon.[77] Every one of these briefs was urging affirmance of the Luttig-authored Fourth Circuit majority decision. Two of the three network members listed as counsel in this case—Michael Rosman[78] and Charles Fried[79]—were also arguing for affirmance of the lower court's decision. Between the Fourth Circuit (Luttig and Wilkinson) and the Supreme Court (Scalia and Thomas), the Federalist Society network boasted four judicial decision-makers in this case. Additionally, as Figure 4.3 illustrates, there were five network-affiliated clerks identified in this case.[80] While Federalist Society network *amici curiae* and litigators referred to the Originalist canon a total of 69 times in constructing their arguments on behalf of a more narrow reading of Congress's commerce power, as this section details, the Supreme Court majority opinion in *Morrison* did not feature a single citation to these Originalist authorities. Instead, it relied on and reinforced the principle of limited federal power that had been articulated five years earlier in *Lopez*.[81] As I have argued elsewhere (Hollis-Brusky 2013), while the degree of idea diffusion from the Federalist Society network into the *Morrison* opinion is low when considered on its own, the fact that the majority is able to simply cite its previous handiwork in *Lopez* (which as we saw, was constructed with the help of Federalist Society intellectual capital) is in itself a measure of the influence of this *political epistemic network* in getting its ideas insinuated into authoritative Supreme Court precedent.

Judge Michael Luttig introduced the Circuit Court's opinion in *Morrison* with a strong and dramatically worded defense of limited

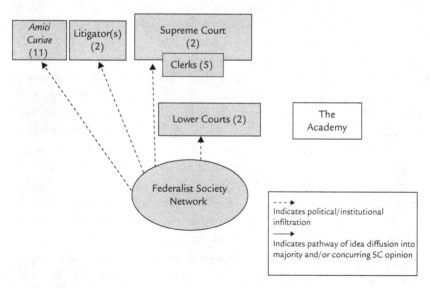

Figure 4.3 *United States v. Morrison* (2000)

government, bringing into sharp relief the shared structural belief of Federalist Society actors that the division of power between the states and the federal government is a precondition for individual liberty. "We the People, distrustful of power, and believing that government limited and dispersed protects freedom best, provided that our federal government would be one of enumerated powers, and that all power unenumerated would be reserved to the several states and to ourselves." "Thus," Luttig continued, "though the authority conferred upon the federal government be broad, it is an authority constrained by no less a power than that of the People themselves."[82] The majority proceeded to justify its conclusion that the provision of VAWA in question "simply cannot be reconciled with the principles of limited federal government upon which this Nation is founded" with reference to a string of recent decisions, like *New York* and *Lopez*, in which the Supreme Court had "incrementally, but jealously, enforced the structural limits on congressional power that inhere in Our Federalism."[83] Reaffirming the impressions of several Federalist Society network actors, the majority noted that the *Lopez* decision was indeed the "Supreme Court's most significant recent pronouncement on the Commerce Clause" and that while it did not explicitly overturn "the precise holdings" of *Garcia* and past precedents like it, *Lopez* effectively "renounced or limited some of the most sweeping reasoning and dicta of [the Supreme Court's] Commerce Clause opinions."[84]

Fourth Circuit Judge and Federalist Society member J. Harvie Wilkinson wrote separately to add his own thoughts on the recent Commerce Clause decisions that resurrected a role for the courts in enforcing the structural boundaries between federal and state power. He considered *Morrison* and past decisions like *New York* and *Lopez* to be cases that "pit the obligation to preserve the values of our federal system against the imperative of judicial restraint," in light of other periods of judicial intervention or "Judicial activism."[85] Wilkinson's concurrence echoed concerns that many Federalist Society network members share—concerns that, in fact, he himself addressed in his talk at the 1988 Student Conference. In that talk, Wilkinson warned that regardless of what the original meaning dictated, the Supreme Court should not attempt to enact swift and broad changes to the constitutional landscape all at once: "the fortuities of uneven constitutional development must be respected, not cast aside in the illusion of reordering the landscape anew."[86] In *Morrison*, Wilkinson concluded that these decisions did indeed strike a proper balance between the obligation of judges to uphold and defend the Constitution and the obligation of judges to be measured and cautious in striking down popularly enacted legislation.[87] Finally, Wilkinson noted that his "fine colleagues" in dissent might not share his views but that their Commerce Clause jurisprudence would in effect "sweep the role of the judiciary and the place of the states away" and amount to an attempt to "rewrite[] the Constitution" to their particular "taste."[88] Wilkinson also warned judges against this tendency, what he described as the truly damaging kind of judicial activism, in his 1988 Federalist Society talk: "[this] holds special hazards for judges who are mindful that the proper task is not to write their personal views of appropriate public policy into the Constitution."[89]

The Supreme Court's majority opinion, written by Chief Justice Rehnquist, relied on its holdings in *Lopez* and *City of Boerne v. Flores* to conclude that the federal civil remedy provided for under VAWA could not be sustained as a constitutional exercise of Congress's authority under either the Commerce Clause or the Fourteenth Amendment.[90] The majority opinion in *Morrison* did not engage in any novel analysis, but merely reinforced the principle of limited federal power articulated most recently in *Lopez*: "*Lopez* emphasized. . . that even under our modern, expansive interpretation of the *Commerce Clause*, Congress' regulatory authority is not without effective bounds."[91] Justice Thomas added a four-sentence concurring opinion that reiterated his view, expressed in *Lopez*, that the Supreme Court ought to align its Commerce Clause jurisprudence "with the original understanding of Congress' powers" if it does not wish to "continue to see Congress appropriating state police powers under the guise of regulating commerce."[92] The dissenting opinion composed by Justice Souter and joined by Justices Stevens, Ginsburg, and Breyer chastised the majority for its reliance on a "new" kind of "categorical formalism" in enforcing the boundaries of federalism that, in their view, had no such "constitutional warrant."[93]

IDEAS WITH CONSEQUENCES: FEDERALISM AND THE COMMERCE POWER

After *Morrison*, the question remains, then, to what extent does the Supreme Court's Commerce Clause jurisprudence reflect the shared beliefs and intellectual capital of members in the Federalist Society network?

In terms of network members' textualist-originalist arguments advocating a more limited understanding of "commerce," we saw that in *Lopez* Justice Thomas's concurrence engaged in an extensive Originalist defense of this narrow reading of "commerce," relying in part on the logic and language of fellow member Richard Epstein's 1987 law review article. While this understanding has yet to gain acceptance by a majority of the Supreme Court, Thomas reiterated in *Morrison* (and once again in dissent in *NFIB v. Sebelius* (2012))[94] his intent to continue to push his colleagues to reconsider their Commerce Clause jurisprudence in light of this evidence. The structural argument linking limited federal power to individual freedom, on the other hand, has been adopted and articulated by majorities of decision-makers on both the federal circuit and the Supreme Court. Recall that both the Fifth Circuit and Supreme Court majority opinions in *Lopez* opened with citations to Madison's *Federalist* 45 to justify what Rehnquist referred to as a return to "first principles" in their Commerce Clause jurisprudence. Similarly, in his Fourth Circuit concurring opinion in *Morrison*, an opinion littered with references to the importance of constitutional "structure" and "structural principles," J. Harvie Wilkinson relied on Madison's *Federalist* 45 to support the position that the "federal commerce power" had "identifiable and judicially enforceable boundaries."[95] Finally, while the Supreme Court has yet to consider the benefits of federalism from a pure public choice perspective, as some network members like John O. McGinnis and Richard Epstein have, it did in both *Gregory* and *New York* rely explicitly on Michael W. McConnell's functionalist-originalist defense of federalism to catalog the many benefits of the constitution's dual structure of sovereignty.

Taken together, the trilogy of Commerce Clause cases examined in this chapter were viewed by federalism proponents in the Federalist Society as serious victories for the principle of limited government. As network member Jeremy Rabkin[96] wrote in *The Weekly Standard* just weeks after the Supreme Court rounded out its constitutional reconsideration of Congress's commerce power in *United States v. Morrison*, the "remarkably unflinching" and "brusque" opinion in *Morrison* "show[ed] [that] the Court is not rattled by such [liberal scare] tactics" and that "for the Court's current majority, the Constitution really does mean something."[97] Several days earlier in the *Wall Street Journal*, Charles Fried had applauded the majority in *Lopez* and *Morrison* for its successful "attempt to breathe life into the federalism doctrine" and chastised the dissenting Justices for their refusal to draw any meaningful limits between "the national and the local."[98] Randy Barnett took the opportunity of Chief Justice Rehnquist's passing half a decade later to evaluate positively "the New Federalism" and the Supreme Court's "revival of the ideas that the judiciary should protect the role of the states within the federal system and enforce the textual limits on the powers of Congress."[99]

While the cases examined in this chapter certainly represented a long-awaited victory for the proponents of a more limited understanding of congressional commerce power, as a number of scholars have noted, the Supreme Court has refrained from targeting legislation at the heart of either party's political agenda and thus has not effectively limited the power of the federal government in any meaningful way (Shroeder 2001; Whittington 2001; Clayton and Pickerill 2004). In areas of importance to Republicans, such as drug control and federal preemption of state law, for example, the Supreme Court has "conspicuously shied away" from curbing Congress's regulatory power (Clayton and Pickerill 2004, 91). For example, in *Gonzales v. Raich* (2005) the Supreme Court upheld the federal government's power under the Commerce Clause to ban the personal use of medical marijuana, contrary to the will of the California voters.[100] In *Watters v. Wachovia* (2007), the Supreme Court (at that point populated by four Federalist Society–affiliated Justices)[101] handed another victory to the federal government in ruling that Congress had the power to regulate operating subsidiaries of national banks and, under the Commerce Clause, could preempt state regulations.[102] Finally, in a case that I will discuss at length in the next chapter, *NFIB et al. v. Sebelius* (2012), the Supreme Court ruled that the Individual Mandate portion of the Affordable Care Act was unconstitutional under the Commerce Power, but then proceeded to provide a constitutional rationale to uphold the Mandate under Congress's Taxing Power.

Still, after half a century of being on the losing end of Commerce Clause decisions, Federalist Society–network advocates of limited government have reason to be optimistic. Moreover, the Commerce Clause cases constitute only half of the story of the "triumph of federalism" that Rabkin and several other Federalist Society network actors have celebrated in the media and in law review articles.[103] The other half of this "constitutional revolution" in federalism, as Federalist Society cofounder Steven G. Calabresi has labeled it, involves a revival of state sovereignty and the Supreme Court's adoption of a novel doctrine, built in part upon the majority's reasoning in *New York v. United States*—the Anti-Commandeering Doctrine. This doctrine, codified into law in a revolutionary opinion written by Antonin Scalia, was later relied on by seven Supreme Court Justices in *NFIB et al. v. Sebelius* (2012) to strike down the Medicaid expansion provision of the Affordable Care Act as unconstitutionally "coercive" and in violation of state sovereignty.

CHAPTER 5

State Sovereignty and the Tenth Amendment

The Anti-Commandeering Doctrine

U.S. Constitution, Amendment X
The Powers not delegated to the United States by the Constitution,
nor prohibited by it to the states,
are reserved to the states respectively, or to the people.

Questions of federalism, Justice O'Connor reminded her audience in the majority opinion in *New York v. United States* (1992), "can be viewed in either of two ways." In some cases, the Supreme Court has framed its inquiry around whether a statute is authorized by "one of the powers delegated to Congress in Article I of the Constitution." In other cases, "the Court has sought to determine whether an Act of Congress invades the province of state sovereignty reserved by the Tenth Amendment." These two inquiries, O'Connor proceeds to explain, "are mirror images of one another: If a power is delegated to Congress in the Constitution, the Tenth Amendment expressly disclaims any reservation of that power to the states; if a power is an attribute of state sovereignty reserved by the Tenth Amendment, it is necessarily a power the Constitution has not conferred on Congress."[1] While the three cases reviewed in the previous chapter all framed their federalism questions around the scope and extent of Congress's enumerated power under the Commerce Clause (Art. I, sec. 8, cl. 3), this chapter examines two other revolutionary federalism cases in which the Supreme Court focused its constitutional analysis on the "mirror image" of these inquiries—beginning instead with state sovereignty and the Tenth Amendment. In its crudest formulation, the state sovereignty doctrine maintains that after the American Revolution, the sovereignty of the English Crown was "transferred" directly to the people and, through them, to the "individual states" (Nash 2005, 969). These states were authorized to act as sovereign decision-makers, except in those areas where they had, through the ratification of the Constitution, explicitly authorized the federal government to act instead. This "geometric" or formalist view of federal-state relations thus divides sovereignty into two separate spheres, with "each government" understood as "supreme in its respective sphere" (Nash 2005, 969). In terms of the constitutional text, the doctrine of state sovereignty finds its most authoritative expression in the Tenth Amendment (U.S. Const., Amend. X). The principal legacy of the Anti-Federalists, who were fearful of the concentration of power, the Tenth Amendment declares that "the powers not delegated to the United States by the Constitution, nor prohibited by it to the states, are reserved to the states respectively, or to the people."[2]

The Tenth Amendment and the state sovereignty doctrine notwithstanding, by the late 1970s most federalism scholars had pronounced the formalistic or geometric view of dual federalism described above as being "dead" (Hills 1998, 815). Cooperative federalism, a system in which federal, state, and local governments share responsibility for governance and interact cooperatively, had become the "reigning conception of American federalism" (Kincaid 1990, 139). Instead of conceiving of state and federal governments operating each within their own distinct spheres of power, cooperative federalism more accurately reflected how federalism had come to work in practice; that is, federal, state and local governments working together to fund and implement complex social and economic legislation. Beginning in the late 1950s and intensifying in the 1960s, for example, the federal government began to work with and provide funding to state and local governments to address problems of racism, health care, individual rights, poverty, and environmentalism (Kincaid 1990). While the objective of this legislation was for the federal government to work with states to alleviate serious social and economic ills, critics of this approach noted the propensity of "cooperative federalism" to degenerate into "coercive federalism," wherein the federal government imposed conditions on the states that seriously invaded state sovereignty and threatened to erode the constitutional limits of federal power (Kincaid 1990, 139).

In addition to the Supreme Court's laissez-faire approach to Congress's commerce power, the advent of cooperative/coercive federalism had become a serious concern for proponents of state sovereignty. The Tenth Amendment, in effect, had been on the losing end of constitutional and political challenges to federal power for half a century. The view that the Tenth Amendment was nothing more than "a truism" with no substantive meaning, first articulated by Justice Stone in the 1941 case *United States v. Darby*, had more or less reduced the state sovereignty doctrine to empty rhetoric—an ineffective protection against federal incursion.[3] In fact, the Supreme Court decision in *Darby* provoked a Yale law professor to announce in a 1941 law review article with some sadness that "The Tenth Amendment Retires" (Feller 1941, 223). Even in cases where the Supreme Court did pay lip service to the substantive protections for state sovereignty within the Tenth Amendment (see, e.g., *Hodel v. Virginia Surface Mining* (1981)[4] and *FERC v. Mississippi* (1982)[5]), it consistently found that the federal legislation in question did not in fact violate those protections. The one exception had been the short-lived decision in *National League of Cities v. Usery* (1976), which brought the Tenth Amendment out of retirement to help justify limiting the scope and reach of the Fair Labor Standards Act. This opinion, authored by Justice William Rehnquist, prompted state sovereignty advocates to announce with some optimism "[r]eports of the death of the Tenth Amendment have been greatly exaggerated" (Abrams 1983–1984, 723) and that "the Tenth Amendment is alive and doing well" (Percy 1976–1977, 95). However, as was chronicled in the previous chapter, the Supreme Court reversed course and overruled the *National League of Cities* decision only nine years later. Seen in this context, the Supreme Court's opinion in *New York v. United States* (1992) represented a long-awaited victory for proponents of state sovereignty. Though, as we saw in the previous chapter, the majority in *New York* ultimately relied on the Commerce Clause to strike down the take-title provision of the Low-Level Radioactive Waste Amendments, the opinion goes out of its way to give some teeth to the Tenth Amendment's implicit prohibitions on legislation that subjects states to "coercive" conditions, supporting its analysis with a multipage review of Originalist evidence surrounding the adoption of the Tenth Amendment.[6]

While *New York* signaled, for the first time, that a majority on the Supreme Court was willing to use the Tenth Amendment and its implicit prohibitions on federal "coercion" of the states as a serious limit on federal power, Federalist Society network actors had been hard at work developing the intellectual capital for this theory at conferences and in their scholarship well before this decision and continued to do so after. I will examine Federalist Society network participation and activity in two Supreme Court cases that built on and extended the logic of *New York* in developing a robust theory of state sovereignty that would come to be known as the Anti-Commandeering Doctrine: *Printz v. United States*

(1997), and *NFIB et al. v. Sebelius* (2012). As in previous chapters, I follow this up with an assessment of the extent to which the Supreme Court incorporated Federalist Society network actors' intellectual capital in articulating and/or supporting their decisions.

THE FEDERALIST SOCIETY NETWORK ON STATE SOVEREIGNTY/ANTI-COMMANDEERING

Discussions of the constitutional merits of federalism and state sovereignty have become a permanent fixture of the Federalist Society dialogue. As we should expect, discussions of Commerce Clause federalism, within the Federalist Society network, are often merged with discussions of its constitutional "mirror image"—state sovereignty and the Tenth Amendment. A review of past National Conference agendas reveal that state sovereignty has also been discussed with some frequency on its own. For example, at the very first Federalist Society Conference in 1982, Michael W. McConnell's talk that focused on the Tenth Amendment and state sovereignty was called "The Politics of Returning Power to the States."[7] At the 1994 National Lawyers Conference, panelists A. Raymond Randolph, Richard Epstein, and Stephen F. Williams discussed state sovereignty extensively on their panel "Limits on National Power and Unconstitutional [Coercive] Conditions."[8] State Sovereignty also received prime billing at the 1998 National Student Conference, "Reviving the Structural Constitution." Two speakers highlighted states' rights in the titles of their speeches (Lynn A. Baker, "The Revival of States' Rights; A Progress Report and a Proposal"; John C. Harrison, "In the Beginning Are the States"), and several others discussed the importance of state sovereignty in the broader context of federalism and the commerce power.[9] Interview data also illustrate Federalist Society members' interest in reviving a robust understanding of both the Tenth Amendment and state sovereignty. For example, in discussing the emphases and concerns of Federalist Society members and how they have changed (or not) over the life span of the organization, Charles J. Cooper was quick to point out that there is still an intense interest "within Federalist Society circles" in "restoring the structural protection" for states "to make decisions about how they will live. . . without the leveling and often times suffocating national rule" that the Supreme Court has allowed the federal government to impose on them.[10] Similarly, Loren A. Smith said that one of the "unifying" principles of the Federalist Society was "a certain concern that states have a legitimate role in the federal system and that centralization in

Washington is not the system that the Framers sought."[11] Former Reagan attorney general and early Federalist Society mentor Edwin Meese also expressed a concern that legislators, once they arrived in Washington, D.C., lost their "allegiance to maintaining the Founders' constitutional view of the states in the whole structure of government." This, Meese continued, "has enabled the administrative state" and has destroyed "the balance between state and central government."[12]

In terms of state sovereignty mentions in Federalist Society speech acts, just under half (64) of the 129 speech acts I located dealing with federalism/state sovereignty made explicit mention of the Tenth Amendment. Some of the most prominent and outspoken advocates of the Tenth Amendment and state sovereignty will be familiar from last chapter's Commerce Clause analysis—Charles J. Cooper, William Van Alstyne, and Michael W. McConnell, for example. However, this sample also includes speech acts from Federalist Society member state legislators—Pete du Pont and Malcolm Wallop, for example—who have a stake in reviving states' rights from the bottom up, rather than the top down. These members articulated an argument grounded in state sovereignty and the Tenth Amendment for limiting the federal government's reach into the states—a reach that had been seriously extended since the advent of cooperative/coercive federalism. From a close reading of all these speech acts, the arguments that Federalist Society members make on behalf of state sovereignty and reviving states' rights tend be of two kinds: Originalist arguments, relying on the Anti-Federalists and evidence from the Founding Era, that push back against the notion that the text of the Tenth Amendment merely states a "truism"; and arguments drawing on these same sources to address the more acute problem of "coercion" of the states by the federal government.

The Tenth Amendment Is Not a Mere "Truism"

Legal scholar Martin Redish opened his remarks at the 1996 Federalist Society National Lawyers Convention with the following satirical comment on the Supreme Court's century-long record of accomplishment of policing the boundaries between federal and state power:

> Well, I have decided to entitle my talk, "The Supreme Court and Constitutional Federalism: A 100 Year How-Not-To-Do-It Manual." If the Supreme Court was to have one of those Bob Vila fix-it shows about constitutional federalism—maybe we could call it "This Old House and Senate"—and people were to call in and ask

questions, and the Supreme Court was to give advice, you would want to do the exact opposite of what they said.[13]

Redish attributed the Supreme Court's poor track record on federalism in part to the fact that it had felt at liberty to continually "ignore or disregard" the Tenth Amendment as an "unimportant" and "superfluous truism." Referring to the historical record, Redish argued that the Tenth Amendment instead should be understood as a "political exclamation point" on the federal government's limited enumerated power. Several other Federalist Society network members expressed a similar unwillingness to accept the view that the Tenth Amendment, as Justice Stone famously wrote in *United States v. Darby,* communicated a mere truism. Current D.C. Circuit Judge David Sentelle confessed to an audience at the 1988 National Lawyers Conference that he "ha[d]n't gotten the word and perhaps never will. . . that the Tenth Amendment was intended to create an empty set." Sentelle continued, surmising that if "today" scholars and others see the Tenth Amendment "as an empty set, it is because we are not looking to see what is there" but rather what has resulted from "an improper treatment of the constitutional division of the powers of rule."[14]

Along the same lines, at the 1992 National Student Conference, Pete du Pont lamented the fact that the Supreme Court in *Darby* had "reduc[ed] the Tenth Amendment to a truism" and had subsequently "disavowed any judicial role in protecting the states from federal intrusion, leaving the states to fend for themselves and the national bull free to rampage through state china shops."[15] Finally, Ninth Circuit Judge Alex Kozinksi introduced a panel at the 1998 National Student Conference with a discussion of how the "rebirth of federalism" embodied in *New York* and *Lopez* would hopefully challenge the view held by "most scholars" that the Tenth Amendment was "'a mere truism' that left the states only such power as Congress chose not to exercise."[16] As mentioned earlier, many of these Federalist Society network members support their more robust understanding of Tenth Amendment state sovereignty protections with reference to founding documents. For instance, in her presentation before a Federalist Society audience at the 1998 National Student Conference, Lynn Baker relied on the "Framers' intent" and "history" to support her conclusion that "the states' ratification of the federal Constitution was predicated on the preservation of a sphere of autonomy for the states" and thus that "the Tenth Amendment" was intended "to serve as [a] real constraint on the exercise of federal power rather than as meaningless rhetoric."[17] Six years earlier, at the 1992 Federalist Society Student Conference, Charles J. Cooper relied on papers of the Anti-Federalists and records from the Federal Convention to point out how far the Supreme Court had deviated from the original understanding of the Tenth Amendment. Cooper referred to the Tenth Amendment as one of the "forgotten" Amendments that, unfortunately, had "not had the constraining influence on the federal government's appetite for power that the Founders, especially the Anti-Federalists, had hoped." After mobilizing this historical evidence, Cooper asked the Federalist Society audience rhetorically: "When was the last time the Supreme Court upheld a State's claim that a congressional enactment encroached on the State's sovereign authority in violation of the Tenth Amendment? That has happened only once in over fifty years." Cooper continued his lament, pointing out that even "[t]hat modest, almost insulting, concession to state sovereign authority did not last long."[18] Expressing a similar sense of frustration with the state of constitutional federalism over a decade earlier, at the 1982 National Conference, Theodore Olson looked to Madison's *Federalist* 39 as evidence that the Founders had intended a more robust protection of the "spheres of sovereignty" with the addition of the Tenth Amendment.[19] The *Federalist* 39, which links the Constitution's authority to "the assent and ratification of the several states, derived from the supreme authority in each State—the authority of the people themselves," was also cited by participant John S. Baker, Jr., at the 1992 Federalist Society Student Conference in his discussion of the Tenth Amendment's protections against "a newly energetic central government" that "could infringe on the powers of the states and the liberties of its citizens."[20]

Recommended reading on the Federalist Society's *Annotated Bibliography of Conservative and Libertarian Legal Scholarship*, Charles J. Cooper's 1988 article, "The Demise of Federalism," offers even more historical evidence in support of a further robust understanding of state sovereignty under the Tenth Amendment. Cooper situated James Madison's promise in *Federalist* 39 that the states would retain "a residuary and inviolable sovereignty" in the context of the laundry list of fears and concerns articulated by the Anti-Federalists, which, as he explained, ultimately "led directly to the proposal and adoption of the Bill of Rights, including the tenth amendment" (Cooper 1988, 239). This protection of state sovereignty, Cooper explained, was critical to the ratification of the Constitution:

> In almost every state's ratifying convention, opponents of the Constitution—the "Antifederalists"—echoed the concern expressed by George Mason of Virginia: "[T]he general government being paramount to, and in every respect more powerful than the state governments, the latter must give way to the former." . . . So great was the fear that the new national government would eventually consume the states that proponents of the Constitution were compelled to make assurances that

a bill of rights. . . would be considered by the First Congress. Eight states voted for
the Constitution only after proposing amendments to be adopted after ratification.
All eight of these included among their recommendations some version of what later
became the tenth amendment. (Cooper 1988, 239–243)

In other words, Cooper's article used Originalist and historical sources to
argue that the Tenth Amendment and its promise of state sovereignty, far
from being a mere "truism," was a precondition of the states' acceptance of
the new Constitution and was designed to "ensure the continued strength
of the states vis-a-vis the national government" (Cooper 1988, 244).

> "State governments are neither regional offices nor
> administrative agencies of the federal Government."

Justice O'Connor's majority opinion in *New York v. United States* (1992),[21]
which was reviewed in the previous chapter, succinctly articulates
the argument that Federalist Society members have been making at
their conferences and in their scholarship since the early 1980s against
cooperative-turned-coercive federalism. For example, at the very first
Federalist Society National Meeting in 1982 on "Federalism," Michael W.
McConnell used similar language to lament the development of cooperative (or "coercive") federalism: "the federal government has put itself in
the position of managing partner of an enterprise, rather than that of a
separate sovereignty. The States, to a very real extent, have been reduced
to the role of administering federal programs, rather than functioning as
sovereign states."[22] A few years later, responding to the Supreme Court's
flip-flop in *Garcia*, William Van Alstyne complained in his article "Second
Death of Federalism" (recommended reading on the Federalist Society's
Bibliography) that by refusing to acknowledge the Tenth Amendment as a
check on coercive federalism, the Supreme Court was complicit in creating "a plenary national power to dictate the terms of state and local government."[23] Similarly, in the 1988 Reagan Justice Department Report *The
Constitution in the Year 2000*, principal author and Federalist Society D.C.
Chapter head Stephen Markman dedicated several pages to the "troubling" issue of federal-state coercion, noting the constitutional threat this
poses to state sovereignty and the Tenth Amendment, as well as the practical problems that states face if they decide to opt out: "When Congress
seeks to control state policies by imposing conditions on grants and tax
exemptions, the states can theoretically avoid congressional control by
abstaining from the federal program." "In practice," the Report continues,
"this is highly burdensome. . . . It may therefore be all but impossible for a

state to withdraw from a federal program in response to a newly instituted condition."[24] The report continues that "[i]f the Court continues down this path, it may be expected that the role of the states in addressing public policy issues will be significantly reduced by the year 2000." On the other hand, the report states, the Court "could decide to reverse its current course and place judicial limits, derived from the Tenth Amendment and the structure of the Constitution, on the authority of Congress... to interfere in matters of state concern."[25]

That same year, in his 1988 law review article "The Demise of Federalism" (again, recommended reading by the Federalist Society), Charles J. Cooper reviewed a flood of federal legislation that places what he considered to be "coercive" conditions on the states, arguing that the "courts have acquiesced in this erosion of state power, deferring to Congress and rejecting arguments that the conditions imposed interfere with the sovereign prerogatives reserved to the states under the tenth amendment." Cooper explains that while the courts have been receptive to challenges to statutes that appeared to "coerce individuals" it has "rejected similar arguments when applied to the states."[26] Cooper echoed the same concerns with the erosion of state sovereignty and the coercion of the states by the federal government at the 1994 Federalist Society National Lawyers Conference. Speaking before that audience, Cooper argued, "[a]t the wholesale level, surely no one will deny that the states have been 'melted' into little more than administrative units of the federal government."[27] At the same 1994 Conference, reflecting on the Supreme Court's decision in *New York v. United States* (1992), U.S. senator Malcolm Wallop characterized the federal government as a "temptress," explaining that "[i]t holds out the promise of things to the states, but its promises are conditional." Wallop continues, describing the unfortunate consequences of the various ways in which the federal government invades state sovereignty and "coerces" the states: "With the modern advent of the unfunded mandate, of the overzealous bureaucrat, of coercive federal court orders and of the blackmail of states and localities through the attachment of strings to the granting of federal funds, the federal government circumvents all the protections that we thought were in place against administrative despotism." Wallop ended his talk at the 1994 National Lawyers Conference with a bold prediction: "I honestly believe we are at a sort of watershed time now.... I believe that the people will begin to take back some of the powers that the states have lost under the Tenth Amendment." Wallop continued, "You are beginning to see movements to right ourselves. And organizations such as this one will serve as the intellectual basis from which these changes are derived."[28]

THE STATE SOVEREIGNTY/
ANTI-COMMANDEERING DOCTRINE AND THE
SUPREME COURT

By the mid-1990s, the Rehnquist Court had already signaled, through its Commerce Clause opinions in *New York* and *Lopez*, that it was both willing and capable of enforcing the limits on federal power in order to protect and preserve the individual states' rights to exercise sovereign decision-making in those "area[s] to which states lay claim by right of history and expertise."[29] Still, the Tenth Amendment had been a second consideration in *New York*, as the majority's opinion and analysis turned instead on the limits of Congress's commerce power. Just one year after it handed down its decision in *Lopez*, the Supreme Court would consider a set of related but distinct questions concerning the scope of state sovereignty and the limits on federal power implicit and explicit within the structure of the Constitution. Along with the previously examined opinion in *New York*, the opinion in this case—*Printz v. United States* (1997)—would lay the groundwork for the Supreme Court's landmark decision in *NFIB et al. v. Sebelius* (2012) to strike down the Medicaid expansion provision of President Barack Obama's health care legislation.

Printz v. United States (1997)

In this case, the Supreme Court considered a challenge to an interim provision of the Brady Handgun Violence Prevention Act (Brady Act) that required law enforcement officers of certain states to carry out background checks on individuals attempting to purchase a handgun.[30] Initially proposed to Congress in 1987, the Brady Handgun Violence Prevention Act was spearheaded by Sarah Brady, the wife of President Reagan's press secretary, James S. Brady, who was shot in the assassination attempt on President Reagan in 1981 and permanently disabled. After initial setbacks and opposition, attributed to the intense lobbying efforts of the National Rifle Association (NRA), the Brady Act found a champion in President Clinton, who helped move the bill through the Senate, and signed it into law in 1993. The Brady Act mandated the establishment, by November 30, 1998, of a national system for instant criminal background checks of proposed handgun transferees in order to ensure that handguns were not being sold to a subset of violent criminals, fugitives, illegal aliens, and mentally ill persons. In the interim, in states that did not provide for handgun permits or instant background checks, the Brady Act ordered the state's chief law enforcement officers (CLEOs) to personally carry out a background check within five days of all handgun purchases and, in some cases, to provide a written report containing the reasons for authorizing or not authorizing a handgun purchase.[31]

In separate suits filed in the U.S. District Courts of Montana and Arizona, Sheriffs Jay Printz and Richard Mack, the CLEOs for their respective counties, challenged the interim provisions of the Brady Act, arguing that Congress could not constitutionally compel state officers to execute federal laws. Both District Courts agreed that the interim provisions of the Brady Act were unconstitutional but severable from the rest of the Act, leaving a voluntary system of background checks and the five-day waiting period intact. On consolidated appeal, the Ninth Circuit Court of Appeals reversed the District Court decision and held, in an opinion handed down in September 1995, that the Tenth Amendment did not prohibit Congress from enlisting the states to help carry out certain federal requirements.[32] The Supreme Court granted cert and heard the appeal on December 3, 1996. In a 5 to 4 decision handed down in June of the following year, the majority reversed the Ninth Circuit's holding and struck down the interim provisions of the Brady Act as violating the structural principles of federalism and dual sovereignty.

Federalist Society network participation was relatively scant in *Printz*. As Figure 5.1 illustrates, only two Federalist Society network members participated as *amici curiae* in *Printz* (Gale A. Norton[33] and Timothy Tymkovich[34]) and there were no Federalist Society actors listed on

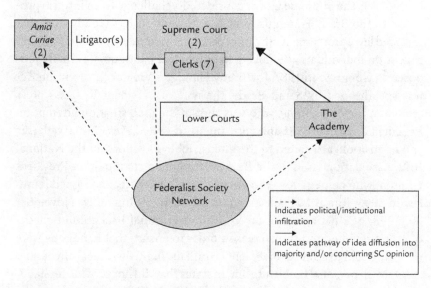

Figure 5.1 *Printz v. United States* (1997)

litigants' briefs. However, the two Federalist Society–network Justices (Scalia and Thomas) each wrote opinions in the decision. The most notable datum in *Printz* is citations to Federalist Society scholarship. Five of the 13 *amicus* briefs filed in *Printz* cited Federalist Society network scholarship in their arguments. Counsel briefs referred to two articles by network members, while the majority and concurring opinions of Supreme Court decision makers relied on five different sources of Federalist Society scholarship to help support state sovereignty arguments.

Both of the District Court opinions in *Printz* relied on Justice O'Connor's analysis in *New York*, examined in the last chapter, to conclude that the interim provisions of the Brady Act violated the Tenth Amendment.[35] Reminding his audience that analyses concerning Congress's commerce power and the Tenth Amendment are "mirror images of each other," Judge Charles C. Lovell, writing for the District Court of Montana, concluded that even though the decision in *New York* did not necessarily turn on the Tenth Amendment, the "language in the opinion made clear that the constitutional principles of state sovereignty restrict the federal government not only from compelling the states to enact a federal regulatory program, but also from administering such a program."[36] The Ninth Circuit Court of Appeals, however, found no violation of the Tenth Amendment, arguing that the District Courts' reading of *New York* was overly broad: "Mack and Printz. . . contend that. . . the federal government is now flatly precluded from commanding state officers to assist in carrying out a federal program. We do not read *New York* that broadly."[37] Accordingly, the Ninth Circuit found that there "would appear to be nothing unusually jarring to our system of federalism" in the Brady Act's interim provisions.[38] The Supreme Court majority, in an opinion authored by Justice Scalia, would come to a very different conclusion.

Justice Scalia's majority opinion in *Printz*, joined by Chief Justice Rehnquist and Justices Thomas, O'Connor, and Kennedy, is grounded not in the "text of the Constitution" but rather "in historical understanding and practice, in the structure of the Constitution, and in the jurisprudence" of the Supreme Court.[39] As would be expected, in order to tease out the historical understanding and practice, Scalia refers to several essays from *The Federalist*, as well as excerpts from the *Records of the Federal Convention*, and Joseph Story's *Commentaries*.[40] Finding that the history is not "conclusive," Scalia's opinion turned next to consider "the structure of the Constitution" in order to "discern among its 'essential postulates'. . . a principle that controls the present cases."[41] In supporting the majority's opinion that the interim provisions of the Brady Act violated principles of federalism and the structure of dual sovereignty embodied in the

Constitution and made explicit in the Tenth Amendment, Scalia relied on articles authored by four different Federalist Society network members:[42] Saikrishna Prakash, cofounder Gary Lawson,[43] cofounder Steven Calabresi, and David Schoenbrod.[44] In one notable section of the majority opinion, for example, Scalia cites an article co-authored by Federalist Society member Gary Lawson to support his reasoning that the interim provisions violate the principle of state sovereignty reflected in various constitutional provisions, not just the Tenth Amendment. I excerpt first from the Lawson piece, and subsequently from the Scalia opinion:

> In the Federalist [No. 33], Alexander Hamilton similarly argued that. . . "The propriety of a law, in a constitutional light, must always be determined by the nature of the powers upon which it is founded. . .". . . . The Tenth Amendment declares that "[t]he powers not delegated to the United States by the Constitution, nor prohibited by it to the states, are reserved to the states respectively, or to the people." This provision expressly confines the national government to its delegated sphere of jurisdiction. . . [any] law that regulates subjects outside Congress' enumerated powers is not "proper" and therefore not constitutional. The Tenth Amendment, as with the rest of the Bill of Rights, is thus declaratory of principles already contained in the unamended Constitution. . .[45]

> When a [law] violates the principle of state sovereignty reflected in the various constitutional provisions we mentioned earlier. . . it is not a "Law. . . proper. . ." and is thus, in the words of The Federalist, "merely [an] act of usurpation" which "deserves to be treated as such." The Federalist No. 33, 204 (A. Hamilton). See Lawson & Granger, The "Proper" Scope of Federal Power: A Jurisdictional Interpretation of the Sweeping Clause, 43 Duke L. J. 267, 297–326, 330–333 (1993). . . [The dissent's] argument also falsely presumes that the Tenth Amendment is the exclusive textual source of protection for principles of federalism. Our system of dual sovereignty is reflected in numerous constitutional provisions. . . and not only those, like the Tenth Amendment, that speak to the point explicitly.[46]

Mobilizing this scholarship from the Federalist Society network, in addition to a variety of sources from the Originalist canon, the majority concluded that the interim provisions of the Brady Act "offend[ed]" the "very principle of state sovereignty" and "compromise[d] the structural framework of dual sovereignty" to such an extent as to render them unconstitutional.[47] Scalia closed the majority's analysis by reiterating Justice O'Connor's defense of the Supreme Court's "formalistic" approach to federalism.[48] As we saw in the last chapter, this same approach was mobilized to defend the Supreme Court's narrowing of the federal commerce power in *New York, Lopez,* and *Morrison.*

Though they join the majority opinion, Justices O'Connor and Thomas both write separately to bring attention back to the Tenth Amendment, the constitutional provision that played a mere supporting role in Justice Scalia's majority opinion.[49] For example, Justice Thomas wrote separately "to emphasize that the *Tenth Amendment* affirms the undeniable notion that under our Constitution, the Federal Government is one of enumerated, hence limited, powers. . . . Accordingly, the Federal Government may act only where the Constitution authorizes it to do so."[50] As we saw in Chapter 2, Justice Thomas also used his concurring opinion to pen some thoughts about the original meaning of the Second Amendment's right to "keep and bear arms," musing hopefully that "perhaps, at some future date, this Court will have the opportunity to determine whether Justice Story was correct when he wrote that the right to bear arms 'has justly been considered as the palladium of the liberties of a republic.'"[51] In support of this claim, Thomas's concurring opinion referenced "a growing body of scholarly commentary" that indicated the right to bear arms was, in fact, a personal right. The string-cite of scholarship Thomas referred to was, in fact, borrowed from an *amicus* brief submitted in *Lopez*, the case examined in the previous chapter that struck down the federal Gun-Free School Zones legislation. Four Federalist Society network members were signatories on that brief: Charles E. Rice, Daniel Polsby, Henry Mark Holzer, and Randy Barnett.[52] I excerpt first from the *Lopez* brief and then from Thomas's concurring opinion in *Printz*:

> In contrast, articles accepting the Amendment as an individual right are published on their own merits and in top rank law reviews. . . Van Alstyne, "The Second Amendment and the Personal Right to Arms," *43 DUKE L. J. 1236 (1994)*, Amar, "The Bill of Rights and the Fourteenth Amendment," *101 YALE L. J. 1193, 1205– 11, 1261–2 (1992)*;. . . Cottrol & Diamond, "The Second Amendment: Toward an AfroAmericanist Reconsideration," *80 GEORGETOWN L.J. 309 (1991)*. . . Levinson, "The Embarrassing Second Amendment," *99 YALE L. J. 637 (1989)*. . . Kates, "Handgun Prohibition and the Original Meaning of the Second Amendment," *82 MICH. L. REV. 203 (1983)*. . . S. Halbrook, "THAT EVERY MAN BE ARMED": THE EVOLUTION OF A CONSTITUTIONAL RIGHT (1984). See generally, J. Malcolm, TO KEEP AND BEAR ARMS: THE ORIGINS OF AN ANGLO-AMERICAN RIGHT (Harvard U. Press, 1994), ch. 8.[53]

> Marshaling an impressive array of historical evidence, a growing body of scholarly commentary indicates that the "right to keep and bear arms" is, as the Amendment's text suggests, a personal right. See, *e.g.,* J. Malcolm, To Keep and Bear Arms: The Origins of an Anglo-American Right 162 (1994); S. Halbrook, That Every Man Be Armed, The Evolution of a Constitutional Right (1984); Van Alstyne, *The Second*

Amendment and the Personal Right to Arms, 43 *Duke L. J.* 1236 *(1994)*; Amar, The *Bill of Rights* and the *Fourteenth Amendment, 101 Yale L. J. 1193 (1992)*; Cottrol & Diamond, The *Second Amendment*: Toward an Afro-Americanist Reconsideration, *80 Geo. L. J. 309 (1991)*; Levinson, The Embarrassing *Second Amendment, 99 Yale L. J. 637 (1989)*; Kates, Handgun Prohibition and the Original Meaning of the *Second Amendment, 82 Mich. L. Rev. 204 (1983).*[54]

While neither the *Lopez* nor *Printz* decisions addressed the Second Amendment question, as I detailed in Chapter 2, this scholarship would feature prominently in Justice Scalia's landmark opinion in *District of Columbia v. Heller* (2008) over a decade later and would help to justify the Supreme Court's individual rights interpretation of the Second Amendment.[55]

Justice John Paul Stevens argued in dissent that given the long tradition of cooperation between the federal government and state and local officers "we are far truer to the historical record by applying a functional approach" to federalism that relies on the political process to safeguard the division between national and local than the majority whose decision relies on "empty formalistic reasoning of the highest order." Stevens further asserted that "perversely," the majority's ruling "seems more likely to damage than to preserve" federalism by creating incentives for the federal government "to aggrandize itself" in lieu of enlisting the help of the states.[56] For its part, the majority of the Supreme Court also did its best in *Printz* to counter the dissent's use of "sources we have usually regarded as indicative of the original understanding of the Constitution," by referring to these interpretations in various places as "a mighty leap," "untrue," "most implausible," and "most peculiar."[57]

While the number of Federalist Society network participants in *Printz* did not rival that of the previous chapter's *United States v. Morrison* (2000) case, for example, the amount of reliance on Federalist Society scholarship across the board—by *amici*, counsel, and judicial decision-makers—in this case was truly impressive. Aided and supported by this scholarship and intellectual capital, Justice Antonin Scalia constructed a state sovereignty argument that reinforced and extended the "formalistic" federalism framework that we first witnessed in the previous chapter's examination of *New York*. Relying on both the Tenth Amendment and overall "structure of the constitution," the majority and concurring opinions in *Printz* together represented a sweeping and robust statement on the importance of dual sovereignty and of states' rights. While the immediate casualties of this novel Anti-Commandeering doctrine were the interim provisions of the Brady Act, the long-term consequences and import of this intellectual capital would not be fully understood for another 15 years.

National Federation of Independent
Business et al. v. Sebelius (2012)

On March 23, 2010, after a year of highly politicized town hall meetings, summits, and a sharply divided partisan vote in Congress, President Barack Obama signed the Patient Protection and Affordable Care Act (ACA) into law. A keystone of the legislation is a provision (hereafter "the Individual Mandate") requiring that most Americans maintain "minimum essential" health care coverage.[58] Beginning in 2014, individuals who do not comply with this requirement would pay "a penalty" to the Internal Revenue Service. This provision was designed to provide near-universal coverage and to lower overall health care costs by addressing the problem of adverse selection. As Theda Skocpol and Lawrence Jacobs explain, "mandating most individuals to get insurance serves to pool the relatively small number of sick and medically expensive cases with the far larger number of healthy people" and prevents the insurance market from becoming "lopsided" (Skocpol and Jacobs 2010, 74). Another important provision of the ACA aimed to expand access to healthcare by increasing the scope of the Medicaid program, a federally subsidized and state-administered program that provides coverage for some poor people. The Act required state programs to provide Medicaid coverage to all adults with incomes up to 133 percent of the federal poverty level. This represented a significant increase, as many states currently cover disabled adults, pregnant women, and adults with children, and only if their income is considerably lower –11% of the poverty line in Alabama, for example. (Skocpol and Jacobs 2010, 76–77). A classic example of cooperative federalism, the ACA increases federal funding to cover most of the states' costs in expanding Medicaid coverage but also conditions that funding on states complying with new coverage requirements.[59] If a state refuses to comply with the new coverage requirements, it may lose not only the federal funding for those requirements, but all of its federal Medicaid funds.[60]

The conservative legal mobilization efforts against the ACA (derogatorily referred to on the legal/political right as "Obamacare") began long before the statute was signed into law. In this effort, prominent Federalist Society members led the charge. In July 2009, for example, the Federalist Society released a White Paper (co-authored by Peter Urbanowicz and Dennis G. Smith) entitled "Constitutional Implications of an 'Individual Mandate' in Health Care Reform," in which the authors outline various constitutional objections to the proposed healthcare legislation.[61] On September 18, 2009, the Federalist Society hosted an online debate as part of its series "Originally Speaking," on the constitutionality of Health Care Reform. It then hosted a follow-up debate in November specifically on the issue of the constitutionality of the Individual Mandate, in which

David B. Rivkin raised a host of constitutional objections to healthcare reform, referring to the Individual Mandate as the "Commerce Clause on steroids."[62] This conservative legal mobilization against "Obamacare" spilled over into the mainstream media. In August 2009, Federalist Society members David Rivkin and Lee Casey wrote an op-ed for the *Wall Street Journal* entitled "Illegal Health Reform."[63] Federalist Society member Randy Barnett—who would become the mastermind behind the legal strategy attacking the individual mandate—posted a follow-up article on *Politico* less than a month later, and argued that the commerce power did not and could not be understood to allow Congress to mandate the purchase of health insurance.[64] From September to December 2009, David Rivkin was busy making the rounds on Fox News and FoxNews.com, calling the proposed health care legislation "an unprecedented imposition on individual liberty."[65]

Despite these objections, the ACA became the law of the land in March 2010. As expected, shortly thereafter 26 states,[66] several individuals, and the National Federation for Independent Business (NFIB) filed suits in federal District Courts, raising a host of constitutional objections to the legislation. The challenges that the Supreme Court ultimately agreed to hear in *NFIB et al. v. Sebelius* (2012) came out of the Eleventh Circuit Court of Appeals and, before that, the United States District Court for the Northern District of Florida. The Supreme Court case involved two main constitutional issues: (1) a challenge to the Act's Individual Mandate as exceeding Congress's power to enact under the Commerce Clause; and (2) a Tenth Amendment/Anti-Commandeering challenge to the Act's Medicaid expansion provision. While the District Court and the Eleventh Circuit had both ruled that the Individual Mandate exceeded Congress's power under the Commerce Clause, the former had ruled that it was non-severable from the rest of the legislation, while the latter ruled that most of the Act could be salvaged even after striking down the mandate component.

As for the challenge to the Medicaid expansion, the Eleventh Circuit had ruled that the provision to expand Medicaid did not constitute "coercion" as the Supreme Court had defined it in *New York* and *Printz* and therefore did not violate the Tenth Amendment to the Constitution. Parties on both sides of the case appealed the Eleventh Circuit's decision to the Supreme Court: the States Attorneys General (Florida et al.) and the NFIB appealed the Eleventh Circuit's holding on the Medicaid Expansion and its decision on the severability of the Individual Mandate, respectively, and the United States Government (Department of Health and Human Services and Secretary Kathleen Sebelius) appealed the Eleventh Circuit's holding on the Individual Mandate as exceeding

Congress's power under the Commerce Clause. The Supreme Court announced that it would hear the challenges in what would become known as *NFIB et al. v. Sebelius* in November 2011 and, in a historic move signaling the importance of this case, it designated six hours of oral argument over three days (as opposed to the normal one hour) at the end of March 2012 to thoroughly consider all constitutional questions and concerns from the parties. After months of media speculation, fanfare, and election-year politicking, the Supreme Court finally announced its decision on June 28, 2012. In a fractured opinion written by Chief Justice John Roberts, the Supreme Court agreed with the Eleventh Circuit and District Court (and many members of the Federalist Society network) that the Individual Mandate exceeded Congress's power under the Commerce Clause. However, in a surprise move, the Chief Justice wrote that the Individual Mandate could still be upheld under Congress's taxing power and was therefore constitutional. On the other hand, the Supreme Court reversed the Eleventh Circuit's holding on the Medicaid expansion provision, arguing that it did in fact constitute "coercion" and therefore did violate the Tenth Amendment Anti-Commandeering Doctrine established in *New York* and *Printz*.

As I described a few paragraphs back, Federalist Society members had been invested in the litigation efforts against the ACA well before the Act was signed into law—before there was even anything concrete to litigate against. Given the enthusiasm within the network for the constitutional questions concerned (federalism/state sovereignty) and the scope and importance of the legislation itself, it should not come as a surprise that Federalist Society network participation in the litigation in *NFIB et al. v. Sebelius* (2012) was very high. As Figure 5.2 illustrates, 24 Federalist Society network members participated as *amici curiae* in this case. These 24 members were listed on 15 of the total 56 *amicus curiae* briefs submitted on behalf of the states and the NFIB. This list includes several names familiar from this chapter and Chapter 4 that I have identified as thought leaders within the Federalist Society network on the topics of federalism and state sovereignty—Edwin Meese III, Richard Epstein, and Charles J. Cooper. Additionally, eight Federalist Society members were listed as counsel on litigant's briefs, including both counsels of record. For the states (Florida et al.), Federalist Society member Paul Clement[67] was listed as counsel of record and argued the case before the Supreme Court. Also listed on the brief from the states are Federalist Society members Robert M. McKenna,[68] David B. Rivkin, Lee A. Casey, and Michael B. Wallace.[69] Counsel of record for the National Federation of Independent Business, Federalist Society member Michael A. Carvin[70] also argued his client's case before the Supreme Court at oral argument

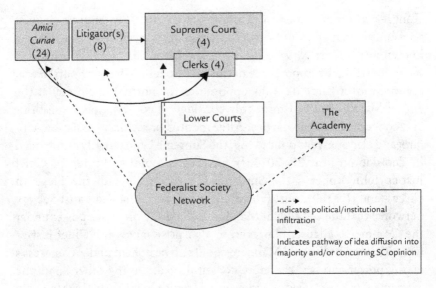

Figure 5.2 *NFIB et al. v. Sebelius* (2012)

and was aided on brief by two other Federalist Society members—
Randy Barnett and Gregory G. Katsas.[71] Finally, though neither the
District Court opinion nor the Eleventh Circuit opinion was written by
a Federalist Society member, the network was well represented at the
Supreme Court level with Chief Justice John Roberts and Justices Scalia,
Thomas, and Alito.

Although the Individual Mandate portion of the ACA was ultimately
left intact by the Supreme Court, the majority opinion in *NFIB et al.
v. Sebelius* still represented a partial victory for the Federalist Society network. Relying on the Commerce Clause cases examined in the previous
chapter—*New York, Lopez,* and *Morrison*—the majority opinion ruled
that the Individual Mandate exceeded Congress's commerce power. In
doing so, it reaffirmed the more limited understanding of the Commerce
Clause that many network members had fought for decades to get the
Supreme Court to adopt. The successful litigation strategy against the
Individual Mandate, often credited to Federalist Society member Randy
Barnett, was to draw a clear line between what the Supreme Court had
previously said Congress could regulate (commercial "activity") versus
what they argued the ACA was attempting to regulate ("inactivity").[72]
The counsel brief for the NFIB (on which Randy Barnett was a signatory) explains that "[u]nder controlling precedent, there are 'three broad
categories of activity that Congress may regulate under [that] commerce
power'. . . Yet none of those 'categories of activity' covers the inactivity
regulated by the mandate—i.e., the non-purchase of health insurance."[73]

The brief for the states (Florida et al.), on which Federalist Society member Paul Clement was counsel of record and four other network members were signatories, also advanced the activity/inactivity argument.[74] In addition, 23 of the 54 *amicus curiae* briefs submitted on behalf of NFIB and/or the states mentioned the activity/inactivity distinction a total of 90 times in their arguments. Seven of these briefs had Federalist Society network signatories.[75]

This novel activity/inactivity distinction was adopted wholesale by Chief Justice John Roberts in his majority opinion in *NFIB et al. v Sebelius*. It also featured prominently in the joint dissent of Scalia, Thomas, Alito, and Kennedy.[76] As Roberts writes, "[a]s expansive as our cases construing the scope of the commerce power have been, they all have one thing in common: They uniformly describe the power as reaching 'activity.'" He continues that, unlike previous cases, the individual mandate "does not regulate existing commercial activity:"

> It instead compels individuals to *become* active in commerce by purchasing a prod-
> uct, on the ground that their failure to do so affects interstate commerce. Construing
> the Commerce Clause to permit Congress to regulate individuals precisely *because*
> they are doing nothing would open a new and potentially vast domain to congressio-
> nal authority. Every day individuals do not do an infinite number of things. In some
> cases they decide not to do something; in others they simply fail to do it. Allowing
> Congress to justify federal regulation by pointing to the effect of inaction on com-
> merce would bring countless decisions an individual could *potentially* make within
> the scope of federal regulation, and—under the Government's theory—empower
> Congress to make those decisions for him.[77]

Roberts continues that if the Supreme Court were to accept the Individual Mandate as a valid exercise of the commerce power, then Congress could presumably also use the commerce power to mandate individuals to purchase "food, clothing, transportation, shelter, or energy" and to regulate individuals "from cradle to grave." In fact, Federalist Society member and counsel of record for the NFIB made this exact point during oral argument. "If being born is entering the market," Carvin argued, "then I can't think of a more plenary power Congress can have, because that literally means they can regulate every human being from cradle to grave."[78]

This concern with the slippery slope of governmental regulation, of the limitless power of Congress to compel individuals to engage in activity and to regulate individuals "precisely because they are doing nothing" was also an oft-cited concern by Federalist Society *amici curiae* in their briefs to the Supreme Court. For example, in his *amicus* brief, Federalist Society member Richard Epstein writes, "This Court must give a candid answer to this question: 'If the government can force us to buy health insurance, what can't it force us to do? To that question it is not an acceptable answer to say that in the name of protecting and advancing health, the commerce power allows the federal government to prescribe what individuals may eat, how they must exercise, and what medicines they may take." Epstein's brief extended this logic, arguing that "[w]ithout judicially enforceable limits on the power of Congress, only the self-restraint of transient congressional majorities can limit the reach of the federal government. History teaches, and Madison knew all too well, that in any constitutional republic, the transition to unrestrained majority rule is often an irrevocable step on the road to tyranny."[79] The language in Roberts's majority opinion also echoed the concerns of Federalist Society network members expressed in op-eds, on Fox News, and in Federalist Society–sponsored debates up to a year prior to this decision. For example, in an online debate hosted by the Federalist Society in November 2009, David B. Rivkin had argued that the Individual Mandate "does not regulate any transactions at all. It regulates human beings, simply because they exist, and orders them to engage in certain types of economic transactions."[80] Similarly, network member Ilya Somin had written earlier in 2010 in a Federalist Society–sponsored publication that while "some argue that those who choose not to purchase health insurance are not simply 'doing nothing,' . . . the individual mandate is not contingent on engaging in any. . . activities."[81]

What is so noteworthy about this wholesale adoption of the activity/inactivity distinction is the fact that the Eleventh Circuit opinion, which also found that the Individual Mandate exceeded Congress's commerce power, did not accept this distinction as dispositive. In fact, in their jointly authored majority opinion, Judges Joel Frederick Dubina (a George H. W. Bush nominee) and Frank Hull (a Clinton nominee) wrote, "Whereas the parties and many commentators have focused on this distinction. . . we are not persuaded that the formalistic dichotomy of activity and inactivity provides a workable or persuasive enough answer in this case."[82] Unlike the Supreme Court majority, the Eleventh Circuit was hesitant to adopt the kind of formalistic distinction that had plagued the Supreme Court's pre–New Deal era Commerce Clause jurisprudence—the kind of jurisprudence that Federalist Society members such as Richard A. Epstein, if we recall last chapter's discussion on the Commerce Clause, are quite eager to return to in regular practice. What is even more noteworthy about the adoption of the activity/inactivity distinction is that, according to several experts and legal commentators—Justice Ruth Bader

Ginsburg among them—because Roberts's opinion ultimately upheld the Individual Mandate as constitutional under Congress's taxing power, it was not legally necessary to address the Commerce Clause question at all.[83] So Roberts's treatise on the Commerce Clause and his adoption of the activity/inactivity distinction can arguably be construed as a way of placating those on the legal right (his fellow Federalist Society members chief among them) who would understandably be upset with him for joining the liberal bloc to uphold the Individual Mandate. If this is so, then this speaks to the power of the Federalist Society network as a "judicial audience" (Baum 2006), that is, as a check and a safeguard against conservative judges and Justices straying too far from what their intellectual and social peer group expect of them.

A second and more important way in which the opinion in *NFIB et al. v. Sebelius* can be understood as a victory for the Federalist Society network and proponents of limited government is in its ruling on the Medicaid expansion provision. To recall, this provision required states to provide Medicaid coverage to adults with incomes up to 133 percent of the federal poverty level. While the ACA increases federal funding to cover the states' costs in expanding Medicaid coverage, if a state refuses to comply with the expanded coverage requirements, it may lose not only the federal funding for those requirements, but all of its federal Medicaid funds. The states (Florida et al.), led by counsel of record and Federalist Society member Paul Clement, argued that this provision violated the principles of state sovereignty embodied in the Constitution, as well as the coercion doctrine: "The coercion doctrine is as essential... to the preservation of the integrity, dignity, and residual sovereignty of the states."[84] To make its case, the states' brief relies heavily on *New York* and *Printz*, citing these cases a combined 13 times in its Argument section. Seven other parties submitted *amicus curiae* briefs addressing the Medicaid question; three of these briefs contained Federalist Society signatories (Richard A. Epstein, Steven G. Bradbury,[85] and James F. Blumstein[86]).[87] The majority opinion, penned by Chief Justice Roberts, dutifully reviews Supreme Court precedent on "coercion" and "commandeer[ing]," focusing especially on the opinions in *New York* and *Printz* to support the proposition that it is the duty of the Supreme Court "to strike down federal legislation that commandeers a state's legislative or administrative apparatus for federal purposes."[88] After reviewing the details of the Medicaid expansion provision, the majority concludes that it crosses the line from inducement into unconstitutional coercion. In a final statement that recalls language often recited within Federalist Society network, Roberts emphasizes that, in a system of limited government and dual sovereignty, "Congress has no authority to order the states to regulate according to its instructions."[89]

Though Scalia, Alito, Thomas, and Kennedy join in the ruling that the Medicaid expansion provision is unconstitutionally coercive, they write separately in this case. In addition to agreeing with the logic of the majority opinion, the three Federalist Society network members, joined by Justice Kennedy, pen a strong defense of federalism and the separation of powers as the key "structural protections" of liberty found in the Constitution:

> The Constitution, though it dates from the founding of the Republic, has powerful meaning and vital relevance to our own times. The constitutional protections that this case involves are protections of structure. Structural protections—notably, the restraints imposed by federalism and separation of powers—are less romantic and have less obvious a connection to personal freedom than the provisions of the Bill of Rights or the Civil War Amendments. Hence they tend to be undervalued or even forgotten by our citizens. It should be the responsibility of the Court to teach otherwise, to remind our people that the Framers considered structural protections of freedom the most important ones, for which reason they alone were embodied in the original Constitution and not left to later amendment. The fragmentation of power produced by the structure of our Government is central to liberty, and when we destroy it, we place liberty at peril. Today's decision should have vindicated, should have taught, this truth; instead, our judgment today has disregarded it. [90]

As discussed in Chapter 1, it is and always has been a priority of the Federalist Society network to promote and protect federalism and the separation of powers, what several members refer to as the "twin doctrines of the structural constitution."[91] If there is a unifying principle or something that approximates orthodoxy within the Federalist Society, this is surely the belief. The joint dissent, penned by three prominent Federalist Society members, succinctly and emphatically illustrates this opinion. More important, it illustrates their disappointment with the Chief Justice, a fellow Federalist Society network member, for "disregard[ing]" this "truth" and for placing "liberty at peril" by upholding the Individual Mandate portion of the ACA. Further, in its closing section, the joint dissent accuses the majority [read Chief Justice] of "vast judicial overreaching," of "undermining state sovereignty" and of rewriting congressional legislation.[92] Unsatisfied with the partial victory on the Medicaid expansion, the dissenting Justices announce that they "would find the [Affordable Care] Act invalid in its entirety."[93]

IDEAS WITH CONSEQUENCES: STATE SOVEREIGNTY AND ANTI-COMMANDEERING

While Federalist Society network members (including the three very prominent members in dissent) expressed both frustration and disappointment with the decision of Chief Justice John Roberts to join with the liberal bloc of the Court in upholding the Individual Mandate in *NFIB et al. v. Sebelius*, this case actually represented a significant victory for this federalism-focused network, the culmination of decades of intellectual effort and investment. To wit, Federalist Society member and mastermind behind the ACA legal challenge, Randy Barnett, wrote shortly after the decision in *Sebelius* that, from his perspective, proponents of federalism and limited government had actually won, even while losing.[94] As this chapter and previous have chronicled, the ways in which proponents of federalism have "won" are in fact many.

After reading the opinions in *New York, Printz,* and *NFIB,* no legal scholar or court-watcher can reasonably declare that the Tenth Amendment is understood by the current Supreme Court to be a dead letter, a "mere truism." As we saw in both the current and previous chapter, several Justices went out of their way in both the majority and concurring opinions to breathe new life into the Tenth Amendment. Even though the Tenth Amendment had played a mere supporting role in the majority opinions in *New York* and *Printz,* through its dicta and rhetoric in those cases the Supreme Court had succeeded at, as one Federalist Society network commentator described in a February 2000 *Weekly Standard* article, "blow[ing] the dust off the Tenth Amendment."[95] While this Tenth Amendment rhetoric, undergirded in critical ways by Federalist Society network intellectual capital, would be important for supporting the Supreme Court's decision 12 years later in *NFIB,* it has also contributed to a broader revolution in state sovereignty—one that has included the Supreme Court's adoption of a novel and expansive understanding of the Eleventh Amendment's State Sovereign immunity doctrine.[96]

As I explain elsewhere, over the past 20 years the Supreme Court has used both of these doctrines in surprising ways to push back against perceived incursions into state power and state prerogative (Hollis-Brusky 2013). This robust understanding of state sovereignty and its implications for the future of federal power was on full display in former Federalist Society network advisor Justice Antonin Scalia's dissenting opinion in the controversial 2012 Arizona immigration case, *Arizona et al. v. United States.*[97] In his dissent, which was joined in part by Federalist Society–affiliated Justices Thomas and Alito, Scalia draws on the Tenth and

Eleventh Amendments to articulate an argument for an extreme version
of state sovereignty—one that, as the majority warned, if accepted would
allow "every State [to] give itself the independent authority to prosecute
federal... violations" and, in essence, create a system of 50 separate sovereigns, each with the power to enforce federal law as it saw fit.[98] While this
opinion did not command the majority of the Supreme Court in this case,
the same robust state sovereignty logic undergirding it was used by the
conservative majority to strike down Section 4 of the Voting Rights Act
in *Shelby County v. Holder* (2013).[99] In that majority opinion, Chief Justice
Roberts wrote that the Voting Rights Act of 1965 represented "a drastic
departure from basic principles of federalism" and that the coverage formula that had subjected some states and jurisdictions to a preclearance
requirement prior to enacting changes to their voting laws or procedures
represented "an equally dramatic departure from the principle that all
states enjoy equal sovereignty."[100] While this constitutional principle of
equal dignity and sovereignty of the states finds no support in the text
of the Constitution itself, it is clearly aligned with several of the cases I
have examined both in the last few chapters of this book and elsewhere
(Hollis-Brusky 2013), in which the Supreme Court has used structuralist
arguments to inflate the sphere of state sovereignty in order to push back
on what these Justices perceive to be unjustified and offensive incursions
by the federal government into state affairs.

The Anti-Commandeering Doctrine that emerged from the Supreme
Court's reasoning in *New York* and *Printz* reads like a scripted response
to the complaint articulated for over a decade prior to these decisions at
Federalist Society meetings and in network scholarship—that thanks
to the advent of cooperative federalism, the states were dangerously
close to becoming administrative units of the federal government. That
is because, in many ways, Federalist Society members wrote the script.
Once that script was written, the Supreme Court majority in *NFIB* was
able to draw on the Anti-Commandeering Doctrine to strike down the
Medicaid Expansion provision of the ACA with relative jurisprudential
ease. In fact, in holding as it did in *NFIB* that a federal law can constitute an unconstitutional command even if the states can choose not
to act, the majority in effect redefined the scope of the doctrine and
placed a completely new class of federal laws at constitutional risk. As
one scholar explains, this is "an important shift" in the doctrine that
could "jeopardize a range of federal spending programs" (Joondeph
2012). We will likely find out in the coming years whether the opinion in *NFIB* will open the door for constitutional challenges to a large
swath of cooperative federalism programs that once were thought to
be well within the scope of federal power. What is clear even at this

point is that State Senator Malcolm Wallop's prediction at the 1994 Federalist Society National Conference ("I honestly believe we are at a sort of watershed time now. . . . I believe that the people will begin to take back some of the powers that the states have lost under the Tenth Amendment") has proved to be remarkably prescient. Moreover, as this chapter and the previous have demonstrated, the Federalist Society has in fact (as Wallop also predicted) "serve[d] as the intellectual basis" for many of "these changes."[101]

It Is Emphatically the Province and Duty of the Judiciary Branch to Say What the Law Is, Not What It Should Be

CHAPTER 6

Saying What the Law Is

The Federalist Society and the
Conservative Counterrevolution

Taking a step back, the task of this final chapter is to begin to aggregate what we know about the Federalist Society network and its influence. This includes reviewing insights drawn from the analyses in this book, and situating this within a body of scholarship on constitutional change more generally, and on the role of "support structures" (Epp 1998; Southworth 2008; Teles 2008; Hollis-Brusky 2011a) in that process more specifically. Doing so will help to identify some of the critical ways in which this network and others like it (past, present, or future) can (1) shape the content, direction, and character of constitutional revolutions by supporting, developing, and diffusing ideas or intellectual capital to Supreme Court decisionmakers; and (2) help foster the conditions that facilitate those constitutional revolutions in the first place by (a) identifying, credentialing, and getting the right kinds of judges and Justices on the bench, (b) acting as a vocal and respected judicial audience to keep those judges and Justices in check once on the bench, and (c) creating an intellectual and political climate that is favorable to the desired change by reducing the stigma associated with once-radical ideas or constitutional theories. In effectively performing this dual function, the Federalist Society for Law and Public Policy Studies has had remarkable success implementing the third prong of its statement of principles: *that it is emphatically the province and duty of the judiciary to say what* [they believe] *the law is, not what* [others believe] *it should be.*

While the first function of the Federalist Society as a *political epistemic network* (PEN)—providing intellectual capital for judicial decision makers—has been detailed in this book, as well as in my prior scholarship on the topic (Hollis-Brusky 2011b, 2013), the second function—helping to foster an environment where constitutional change is possible in the first place—builds on earlier work on the Federalist Society (Hicks 2006; Paik et al. 2007; Southworth 2008; Teles 2008, 2009; Scherer and Miller 2009), and synthesizes this work with social science scholarship on the dynamics of constitutional change (Dahl 1957; Graber 1993; Epp 1998; Clayton and May 2000; Whittington 2001, 2005; Balkin and Levinson 2001, 2006; Clayton and Pickerill 2004; Gillman 2006) and judicial behavior (Baum 2006; Baird 2007). This chapter proceeds by reviewing and/or introducing evidence to illustrate two critical functions that the Federalist Society network performed in helping to bring about and shape the Supreme Court's "conservative counterrevolution."

SHAPING THE CONTENT, CHARACTER, AND DIRECTION OF SUPREME COURT DECISIONS

As the preceding chapters have demonstrated, the Federalist Society network and its members have played an important role in generating and diffusing ideas and intellectual capital to Supreme Court decision-makers in several of the most significant decisions of the "conservative counterrevolution" currently underway on the Court.[1] Acting in their professional capacities as academics, *amici curiae*, litigators, clerks, and judges, members of the Federalist Society network (like the "cognitive baggage handlers" Haas described in his classic article on epistemic communities) carried their shared beliefs, ideas, authorities, and sources to decision-makers through scholarship and, more proximately, through *amici curiae* and merits briefs filed in those cases. Because of the conditions of uncertainty associated with changing constitutional meaning—conditions that epistemic community theorists identify as important for influence (Haas 1992; Cross 2013)—the Justices relied on outside intellectual capital from Federalist Society network members to help justify their revised and reconstructed constitutional frames in these cases where *doctrinal distance* (Hollis-Brusky 2013) was meaningful and significant. For example, in Chapter 2 we saw how, with the properly framed case brought by Federalist Society–affiliated litigators and with the intellectual capital nurtured and supported through the Federalist Society network, five Justices on the Supreme Court were able to reinterpret, by some standards radically, the Second Amendment's right to keep and bear arms as a personal, not a collective right in *Heller*. While the network did not achieve its ideal constitutional result in *McDonald*— to resurrect the Privileges or Immunities clause—Justice Alito's opinion did further entrench the *Heller* individual rights holding of the Second

Amendment and, with help from several Federalist Society network members, Justice Thomas's concurrence laid the first brick on a path to possibly resurrecting the Privileges or Immunities Clause in the future.

Similarly, in Chapter 3 we saw how Federalist Society network members helped to construct and intellectually reinforce the path that led to the Supreme Court's revolutionary *Citizens United* decision, in which it held that the First Amendment protections for free speech extended to corporations and unions as well as individuals. As Justice Stevens warned in his dissent, this holding not only threatened to "undermine the integrity of elected institutions across the Nation" but it also would likely "do damage to this institution."[2] Finally, in Chapters 4 and 5, we saw Federalist Society members for decades lobbying the Supreme Court to "Reviv[e] the Structural Constitution."[3] Once the Court seemed ready and willing to consider doing so, network members again provided the intellectual capital and support to justify narrowing the long-expansive federal commerce power in *New York, Lopez,* and *Morrison*—holding that federal programs aimed at controlling waste disposal, guns near schools, and violence against women were beyond the scope of the federal commerce power. Even more critically, Justice Scalia relied on several sources of network scholarship to construct the novel "Anti-Commandeering" Doctrine in *Printz*. While the immediate casualty of *Printz* was the background-check provisions of the Brady Act, this same doctrine would empower the Supreme Court to strike down the Affordable Care Act's Medicaid Expansion in *NFIB et al. v. Sebelius*. Each of these cases persuasively demonstrates how the Federalist Society network helped to shape the content, character, and direction of these revolutionary Supreme Court decisions.

As I have written elsewhere (Hollis-Brusky 2013), and as this expanded study further demonstrates, this dynamic makes sense in the context of what we know about law and the American judicial enterprise as being both highly path-dependent and preoccupied with the problem of justifying the power of judicial review in a democratic system. The American judicial enterprise and judicial decision-making in particular, as Gordon Silverstein has written, is "distinctly different" from decision-making and policymaking in the political branches:

> . . . judicial decision-making follows different rules and is driven by different incentives, limited by different constraints, and addressed to different audiences in a different language than is the political process. The way judges articulate, explain, and rationalize their choices and the way earlier decisions influence, shape, and constrain later judicial decisions are distinctly different from the patterns, practices, rhetoric, internal rules, and driving incentives that operate in the elected branches and among bureaucrats. (Silverstein 2009, 63)

One unique constraint of the American judicial enterprise, as I wrote in Chapter 1, is the "giving reasons requirement" (Shapiro 2002). Unlike legislators who simply vote according to their policy preferences, judges and Justices are required to issue written opinions explaining, supporting, and defending their decisions. In order to persuade a similarly trained and educated legal and political audience that these decisions were well reasoned and authoritative, these opinions must situate the given decision within an established legal or constitutional framework or, alternatively, they must provide a convincing argument for why that framework should either be ignored, altered, or reconstructed entirely. In other words, judicial decision-makers can either attempt to fit the case within an "existing line of reasoning" (Silverstein 2009, 64) or, as Chief Justice Rehnquist did in *Lopez*, "begin with first principles" and instead construct an altered or new line of reasoning—a new constitutional frame—to justify their decision. In the parlance of path-dependence, when the Supreme Court decides to do the latter, we might refer to this as a new point of "critical juncture" (Mahoney 2000; Pierson 2000; Hathaway 2001; Bennet and Elman 2007; Capoccia and Kelemen 2007) in Supreme Court jurisprudence.

Of course, the less costly, lower risk option for decision-makers is to justify their decisions with reference to the existing constitutional framework, particularly if that frame and the attendant precedents have become entrenched from years of judicial reliance and authoritative citation. As former Supreme Court Justice Robert Jackson wrote in *The Struggle for Judicial Supremacy*:

> Justices are drawn only from the legal profession. The entire philosophy, interest, and training of the legal profession tend toward conservatism. . . it is much concerned with precedents, authorities, existing customs, usages, vested rights, and established relationships. Its method of thinking, accepted by no other profession, cultivates a supreme respect for the past, and its order. Justice Cardozo has well said that the "power of precedent, when analyzed, is the power of the beaten track." No lawyer sufficiently devoted to the law to know our existing rules, the history of them, and the justification for them, will depart from them lightly. (Jackson 1979, 313–314)

Again, if we want to think about Justice Jackson's observations in terms of path-dependence, once the Supreme Court starts down a path or line of reasoning and once that path is "beaten" or entrenched in doctrine, the costs of un-sticking the old line of reasoning and constructing a new one are very high (Pierson 2000, 254; Silverstein 2009). This is because the further the Supreme Court decides to move away from its established constitutional frame in a given case, the less it will be able to rely on past lines of reasoning and precedent to legitimate its ruling, and the more it will have to fish around for alternative authorities and constitutional frames to justify a decision.

I argue that it is this precise dynamic that opened the door for the Federalist Society to frame and shape the Supreme Court's legal reasoning by providing ideas, authoritative sources, and legal arguments that were used to un-stick and reconstruct the constitutional frames articulated in the cases examined in this book. Once that constitutional frame was laid down and the intellectual capital incorporated into Supreme Court doctrine, it could once again justify its rulings according to its own precedent, as we saw in *United States v. Morrison* (2000)—the case that struck down part of the Violence Against Women Act as beyond the scope of the federal commerce power. That is not to say, however, that *Morrison* and cases like it do not exhibit Federalist Society network influence. The Supreme Court, in treating the Federalist Society–constructed opinion in *Lopez* as settled law, is saying that these ideas no longer need to be defended or legitimated. They are now part of the new constitutional frame, one that has the force and authority of Supreme Court precedent backing the judgment. In many ways, then, opinions that follow on the heels of these revolutionary decisions and further entrench those decisions—as *Morrison* did after *Lopez*—exhibit the highest degree of Federalist Society influence, for they not only contain the network imprimatur but they also have the weight of Supreme Court precedent. What that constitutional frame looks like and how it is articulated is important because it influences the decision-making and policymaking of lower courts, future courts, the political branches, and other political and legal entrepreneurs. In his book *Law's Allure*, political scientist Gordon Silverstein cites Martin Shapiro on this point, emphasizing that written opinions matter since these "provide the constraining directions to the public and private decision makers who determine ninety-nine percent of conduct that never reaches the courts" (Silverstein 2009, 64).

In summary, the preceding chapters helped to illuminate the "untold ways" (to once again borrow cofounder David McIntosh's words) in which the Federalist Society network has shaped the content, character, and direction of the conservative counterrevolution. That is, it shows how—once the door for constitutional change was open and the Justices were willing—the Federalist Society network became an active series of conduits through which ideas and intellectual capital were transmitted to decision-makers looking to justify their altered or reconstructed constitutional frameworks. But, as prior scholarship on the Federalist Society has gestured at, and as scholarship on constitutional change more generally would suggest, we should also partially credit the Federalist Society network with helping to bring about that constitutional change in the first place—in helping to create (again, in the parlance of path-dependence) the "critical junctures" that it would then actively work to shape with its ideas and intellectual capital. The next section synthesizes previous research on the Federalist Society network with that of my own and integrates this with insights from scholarship on constitutional change and judicial behavior to highlight three ways in which the Federalist Society network helped to create a climate conducive to constitutional change.

HELPING TO CREATE A CLIMATE CONDUCIVE TO CONSTITUTIONAL CHANGE

In addition to exploiting the opportunities to shape constitutional meaning and direction when they have arisen, what has the Federalist Society network done to help foster and facilitate those opportunities in the first place?[4] In other words, can we identify ways in which this network has worked actively to help bring about a climate conducive to constitutional change? While there are undoubtedly many other "untold ways" in which the network and its members have had a hand in fostering a climate conducive to constitutional change, I explore three areas—grounded in and drawn from studies of constitutional change and judicial behavior in political science—where we can identify Federalist Society influence: getting the right cast of characters on the Supreme Court; acting as an effective judicial audience; and creating an intellectual climate more favorable to Originalism and conservative and libertarian legal ideas.

Getting the Right Cast of Characters on the Supreme Court

[T]he Federalist Society has a de facto monopoly on the credentialing of rising stars... on the left there are a million ways of getting credentialed; on the political right, there's only one way in these legal circles.

—Federalist Society member Michael Greve, February 12, 2008[5]

The topic of constitutional change has long fascinated and engaged the academic imagination. While explaining constitutional change has become something of a cottage industry within legal scholarship and political science, the voices that have dominated this debate have all echoed variations of the same proposition: that the "Supreme Court follows the election returns."[6] This insight finds its most robust expression in "regime politics theory" (Dahl 1957; Graber 1993; Clayton and May 2000; Balkin and Levinson 2001, 2006; Whittington 2001; Clayton and

Pickerill 2004; Gillman 2006). This theory maintains that constitutional change is ultimately driven by electoral politics—the people elect a president, who then exercises the power of appointment to pack the federal courts with judges who share his party's broad political agenda: "[w]hen Presidents are able to appoint enough judges and Justices, constitutional doctrines start to change" (Balkin and Levinson 2006, 102). While I— alongside several other scholars—have maintained that getting the right cast of characters on the bench is not a *sufficient* condition for bringing about constitutional change and revolution (see, e.g., Hollis-Brusky 2011a), it is still a *necessary* condition for enacting such change.

The founding generation of the Federalist Society was acutely aware of this concept. After all, as former Reagan Justice Department appointee and Federalist Society member Douglas Kmiec said to me in our interview, one of the key insights that founding members of the Federalist Society learned at the Reagan Justice Department (alongside "ideas have consequences") is that "policy is people."[7] So changing constitutional law and policy meant, first, getting the right people into positions of power and influence in government (where judicial nominees are vetted, selected, and confirmed) and on the bench (where these "people" can actually shape and influence "policy"). One of the earliest members of the Federalist Society, who also served in the Reagan Justice Department alongside its founders, recalls Steven Calabresi telling him that, for exactly this reason, it was "crucial to credential young conservatives. . . and to build an alternative elite."[8] Corroborating this, Steven Teles recounts in his own work on the Federalist Society that building an "informal" job placement network to rival that of the "liberal legal network" was an explicit goal of the Federalist Society's founders (Teles 2008, 140). By all measures, they have succeeded. As one member put it to me, "you cannot have a conversation in Washington about judges without the Federalist Society being part of it."[9] That is because, over the past 30 years, the Federalist Society network and its members have played a key role in recruitment, training, credentialing, and vetting nominees for federal judgeships. As Michael Greve stated emphatically in the interview excerpt above, the Federalist Society now has a "de facto monopoly on the credentialing of rising stars" within the conservative legal movement. Federalist Society member and former Student Chapter president Tony Cotto illustrated the power of the Federalist Society credential with reference to President George W. Bush's withdrawn Supreme Court nomination of Harriet Miers: "No Fed Society credentials, that's going to hurt you. It hurt Harriet [Miers] a lot.... We want credentials. We want to see you've spoken at Federalist Society conferences, we want to know you've been at dinners, gripping and grinning. Even if you're not a die-hard, we need to know you."[10]

Moreover, while it does not issue official rankings of judicial candidates like the American Bar Association, the Federalist Society network has become an important "informal" gatekeeper for vetting judicial nominees to the lower federal courts and to the Supreme Court during Republican administrations (Southworth 2008, 138–141; Teles 2008, 527–529; Hollis-Brusky 2011b). As he explained in our interview, Federalist Society member Michael Carvin believes the Federalist Society is "influencing some aspects of the judicial confirmation process" because unlike before, "conservatives have an intellectual background and set of principles that are out there and widely accepted."[11] Similarly, member Randy Barnett said that while opponents refer to the Federalist Society as a "vast right-wing conspiracy, the truth that lies behind that is that. . . the Federalist Society is the only source of conservative and libertarian legal intellectual activity in the United States." "Given that," Barnett continued, "of course Republican administrations rely on the Federalist Society as a source of talent; as a farm team."[12] Another reason that the Federalist Society credential has become so important to Republican administrations, which the Barnett quote gestures at, is that these administrations are themselves staffed with members of the Federalist Society network. For example, Teles notes that Stephen Markman, a former president of the D.C. Chapter of the Federalist Society, was responsible for judicial nominations during the second half of the Reagan administration, while Federalist Society cofounder Lee Liberman Otis was in charge of the White House counsel's work on judicial nominations during the George H.W. Bush administration (Teles 2008, 158). My own research suggests that the role of the Federalist Society as an ideological gatekeeper in vetting judicial nominees was expanded during the George W. Bush administration (Hollis-Brusky 2011a, 2011b). For example, as Federalist Society member Daniel Troy described it to me, "[e]verybody, I mean everybody who got a job [in the George W. Bush administration] who was a lawyer was involved with the Federalist Society. I mean everybody."[13] While I cannot corroborate the literal assertion that "everybody" who got a job was involved with the Federalist Society network, other members confirmed that Federalist Society network associates Fred Fielding, Rachel Brand, Bradford Berenson, and Brett Kavanaugh played key roles in selecting, vetting, and shepherding nominees through the confirmation process during the George W. Bush administration (Hollis-Brusky 2011a). The fruits of their labor include the confirmation of Federalist Society network members Barrington D. Parker, Jr. (Second Circuit), Edith Brown Clement (Fifth Circuit), Michael W. McConnell (Tenth Circuit), Jay Bybee (Ninth Circuit), Timothy Tymkovich (Tenth Circuit), Jeffrey Sutton (Sixth Circuit), Michael Chertoff (Third Circuit), Richard C. Wesley (Second Circuit), Carlos T. Bea (Ninth Circuit), William H. Pryor, Jr. (Eleventh Circuit), Diane Sykes (Seventh

Circuit), Priscilla Owen (Fifth Circuit), Janice Rogers Brown (D.C. Circuit), Thomas B. Griffith (D.C. Circuit), Debra Ann Livingston (Second Circuit), and three Supreme Court Justices with very strong and long-standing Federalist Society credentials—Chief Justice John Roberts, Justice Samuel Alito, and Justice Brett Kavanaugh.

These "Federalist Society alumni," as Federalist Society cofounder Calabresi believes, have tended to "push public policy in a libertarian-conservative direction in the way that Yale Law School alumni who have become judges have tended to push judging in a legal realist direction."[14] Calabresi's impression is supported empirically. Nancy Scherer and Banks Miller found that judges on the United States courts of appeals who are self-identified Federalist Society members decide cases in a more conservative manner than non-member Republican judges (Scherer and Miller 2009). To return to regime politics theory, bringing about constitutional change is not just about "appoint[ing] enough judges and Justices" (Balkin and Levinson 2006, 102), but rather about appointing enough of the *right* judges and Justices: individuals who have been shaped intellectually and have been professionally credentialed by a network that will, through its personal and professional ties, hold those judges and Justices accountable for being faithful to a particular view of the Constitution and of constitutional interpretation. The Federalist Society network has accomplished this, first, by carefully selecting, training, and vetting potential judicial nominees, and, second, by acting as a vocal and vigilant "judicial audience" (Baum 2006) for judges and Justices once they are on the bench. I explore this related function in the next section.

Acting as a Vigilant and Vocal Judicial Audience

I did a brief a few years ago in [*Gonzales v. Raich*] because it is part of the Federalist Society calling but it's also part of my calling to want to respect the division between that which is national and that which is local. . . [a]nd I was enormously disappointed that someone who's been great friends with me and the Federalist Society for years, Justice Scalia, would write an opinion concurring in [that] judgment. . . and I've said to him face to face that he got it wrong and he'll tell me why I got it wrong. . . [s]o that's pretty direct feedback.
—Federalist Society member Douglas Kmiec, March 14, 2008[15]

To have a serious and lasting influence on the direction of constitutional law and jurisprudence—a constitutional revolution—you need to appoint the *right* cast of characters to the courts and you need to make sure that, once appointed, they do not fall victim to the "Greenhouse Effect," or judicial drift—that is, the observed tendency for some conservative

Supreme Court appointees to moderate their beliefs during their tenure on the court, thereby drifting to the ideological center or left. Presidents and electoral politics can influence the first half of this equation—*who* gets appointed—but it is ultimately up to the "support-structure" (Epp 1998; Hollis-Brusky 2011a) to ensure that judges remain faithful to their appointing regime once on the court. As I explained in Chapter 1, the concept of judicial drift and the attempts to mitigate it can be best understood in light of political scientist Lawrence Baum's concept of a "judicial audience" (Baum 2006). In his book *Judges and Their Audiences*, Baum draws on research in social psychology to argue that judges, like all other people, seek approval or applause from certain social and professional groups and that the manner in which a judge decides cases and writes opinions may be influenced by certain "audiences" that the judge knows will be paying attention to his or her "performance" (Baum 2006, 24–49). Moreover, Baum argues, that of all the types of audiences for whom a judge might perform, "social groups and the legal community have the greatest impact on the choices of most judges" (Baum 2006, 118). The Federalist Society for Law and Public Policy, as a social and professional network extending to all levels of the legal community, can be understood as a hybrid of both of these most influential referent groups for judges.[16] As Baum writes of the Federalist Society in the context of his own work,

> [j]udges who identify with the society and participate in its activities have an attentive audience that applauds certain kinds of decisions and doctrines. In this way the organization makes more concrete and thus more salient the ideological reference groups of conservative judges. One result is to provide additional reinforcement for the kinds of conservative positions that members of the society favor. (Baum 2006, 125)

Baum adds that while, as an organization, the Federalist Society provides a strong referent for conservative judges and Justices, it is probably most effective and potent as a "personal audience" for particular judges and Justices who have connections to prominent members within the network (Baum 2006, 125).

This was evidenced throughout the case studies examined in this book. We saw examples of the Federalist Society network acting as a vigilant and vocal "judicial audience"—applauding or booing the opinions and decisions of network-affiliated Supreme Court Justices in the media and in law review articles. The "personal audience" element of the Federalist Society network was exemplified in several instances through my interviews with Federalist Society network members as well. The interview excerpt from my conversation with Federalist Society member Douglas Kmiec exemplifies the kind of personal interaction and, as he calls it, "feedback loop" that the Federalist Society network facilitates between judges, Justices, and other members of the legal community. During that interview, Kmiec expressed his disappointment with his "friend" Justice Scalia for joining the majority in *Gonzales v. Raich* (2005)[17] in holding that, under the Commerce Clause, the federal government may criminalize the production and use of medical marijuana even where states approved its use for medicinal purposes. Federalist Society member Randy Barnett, who argued *Raich* for the plaintiffs before the Supreme Court, also mentioned this case as an example of network members expressing vocal disappointment with Scalia for his perceived infidelity to Originalism and principles of limited federal government: "[Federalist Society members] totally shook their head and said, 'we can't believe it.' I mean, I think Justice Thomas's stock really went up at that point and Justice Scalia's stock took a hit. If there were a Justice trading market within the Federalist Society... I think Scalia's stock is down as a result of [*Raich*]."[18]

In addition to simply expressing their disappointment in interviews to me, or even simply writing law review articles and op-eds expressing their frustrations, many Federalist Society members also have personal relationships with and access to these Justices through formal and informal network events, dinners, and meetings. Kmiec said he has told Scalia "face-to-face" that he thought he got the *Raich* decision wrong. Similarly, Steven Calabresi, a former law clerk to Scalia, said he agrees with what Scalia decides and writes "95% of the time" but he said that he "really value[s]" the opportunity to disagree "that 5% of the time... and to explain [to him] why." When he does, Calabresi added, "I tend to think I am out-Scalia-ing Scalia, if there is such a thing."[19] The inference here is that there is a clear ideological or interpretive standard from which the Justice has deviated and the vigilant and vocal members of this judicial audience are in a position, both personally and professionally, to signal their disapproval with this instance of drift from the agreed-upon or shared understanding within the Federalist Society network.

Another way in which an attentive judicial audience like the Federalist Society can help bring about constitutional change is through paying attention to and responding appropriately to a variety of different "signals" (Baird 2007) that Supreme Court Justices send about the kinds of cases and constitutional questions they would like to hear. While the Supreme Court is not a "self-starting" institution (Hollis-Brusky 2011a) and while it cannot make a certain case or controversy appear before them "as if by magic" (Epp 1998, 18), as scholar Vanessa A. Baird explains in *Answering the Call of the Court*, the Justices can and do communicate their preferences for certain kinds of cases, questions, and policy issues through signaling:

> A justice might indicate a preference or priority change with a majority opinion, or even perhaps a concurring or dissenting opinion. The justices might indicate more or less directly what kinds of arguments or case facts they would be more or less interested in considering. They might not provide this information in a case opinion at all—they could provide cues in oral arguments for repeat players, or perhaps by saying something to a journalist or in a commencement address. There may be several justices doing or saying something that gives litigants some kind of indication of interest in a particular policy, or perhaps the clues might come from only a single justice. (Baird 2007, 44)

The effectiveness of these signals, whatever form they might take, will ultimately depend on the presence of an attentive and attuned judicial audience consisting of individuals and organizations (legal entrepreneurs) with the capacity to find, finance, and litigate the right kinds of well-framed cases and constitutional questions the signaling judges want.

We saw a very explicit example of judicial signaling in this book with Justice Clarence Thomas's concurring opinion in *Printz v. United States* (examined in Chapters 2 and 5), in which the Justice mused hopefully that "perhaps, at some future date, this Court will have the opportunity to determine whether Justice Story was correct when he wrote that the right to bear arms 'has justly been considered as the palladium of the liberties of a republic.'"[20] As I detailed in Chapter 2, when the conditions seemed favorable (i.e., after two more Federalist Society network-credentialed colleagues had joined Thomas), members of the network responded by bringing to Thomas et al. a Second Amendment challenge that would effectively and radically reinterpret the right to keep and bear arms. So if we think of this network as, among other things, facilitating "communication" among and between members of the conservative legal movement (Southworth 2008) both on and off the bench, then we can understand how the Federalist Society has helped increase the clarity, response time, and quality with which these signals are communicated and received by members of the support structure. Understanding the Federalist Society in the context of networks, signals, and communication helps shed some light on the response that Federalist Society member Gail Heriot provided when I asked her about Federalist Society influence. She paused, and simply said, "Like Verizon, 'it's the network.'"[21]

Changing the Debate and Reducing the Stigma of Once-Radical Ideas and Theories

I think certainly in my professional lifetime the debate, the dialogue, about constitutional law has shifted much more towards Originalism... even liberals on the Supreme Court take it seriously. ... I think the Federalist Society has had an amazing impact and influence on the debate when measured against its numbers. ... I mean it's sort of a crude measure, but the real impact is how the dialogue has shifted.

—Federalist Society member John C. Yoo, January 16, 2008[22]

As Steven Teles has described, in addition to engaging in *recruitment* activities, investing in *human capital*, and producing *social capital* in the form of networks, the Federalist Society also produces *cultural capital*, "in that its activities facilitate the orderly development of conservative legal ideas and their injection into the legal mainstream, reducing the stigma associated with those ideas in institutions that produce and transmit professional distinction" (Teles 2008, 136). Drawing on work by legal theorists such as Jack Balkin, Sanford Levinson, and Owen Fiss, Teles explains why this *cultural capital* is important, indeed integral, to the process of constitutional development: "for legal ideas to be taken seriously by the courts they cannot be seen as wholly novel or outside the realm of legitimate professional opinion. This is work that first must be done outside the courts" (Teles 2008, 12). Connecting this with my earlier discussion about the path-dependence of law and the importance of justifying judicial power in a democracy, when the Justices decide to alter or reconstruct a constitutional frame, the outside intellectual capital that they rely on to do so must *first* be seen as reasonable, legitimate, and authoritative within the broader legal community. In other words, the ideas, frames, and sources the Justices rely on to justify their decisions will not be accepted if large segments of the legal community believe them to be, to quote Jack Balkin, "positively loony" or "off the wall" (Balkin 2001, 1444–1445; Teles 2008, 12). While Teles cabins his examination of the production of cultural capital by the Federalist Society to the law schools and its importance within the legal profession more generally, there is evidence also to suggest a second way in which the Federalist Society network, through its media outreach and burgeoning relationship with Tea Party groups and legislators, is helping to change the constitutional culture outside the legal profession.

The Federalist Society, as Teles describes, was founded in a set of institutions that historically had been quite "hostile" to conservative and libertarian thought: "America's law schools" (Teles 2008, 137). As it grew and its law school chapters multiplied, the Federalist Society became a home for once-ostracized conservative and libertarian law students. As Federalist Society member Walter Berns said to me in our interview, "[t]he purpose of the Federalist Society was to make it clear to law students of a conservative persuasion that they were not alone in the world. And, my God, they have succeeded."[23] Similarly, Michael Horowitz, who mentored many of the fledging Federalists in the Reagan administration, said that the Federalist Society was "so important" because it "really created this forum that allowed [conservative and libertarian law students] to think and to know that they were not alone."[24] Eugene Meyer, executive director of the Federalist Society, explained to me why the Federalist Society's presence within the law schools was so important:

> . . . instead of law students going to law school and hearing only about left-wing ideas . . . students who are interested in ideas now have the opportunity at most schools to hear some counter-weight and also have the opportunity to meet other people who share those ideas. That probably would never have happened before [the Federalist Society existed] and that's a huge deal. . . . So that affects what that next generation of lawyers is like and the whole discussion in law school now pays some attention to a whole set of ideas it ignored before. It's still a minority, but it's in the game.[25]

In a similar vein, Steven Calabresi explained:

> The Federalist Society made it okay to be a conservative and a libertarian and kind of fortified the outspokenness of conservatives and libertarians in different law schools on different faculties spread across the country. . . so I think the Federalist Society helped to change the legal culture by giving conservatives and libertarians a sense of belonging and feeling that there was a home.[26]

Steven Teles has observed that, by helping conservative and libertarian law students realize that their "identity is not shameful and that there are others out there like them," the Federalist Society helped transform a previously "stigmatized" identity and set of ideas into "a badge of pride" (Teles 2008, 166–167). For example, Federalist Society member Michael Rappaport credits the Federalist Society with helping him formulate thoughts on Originalism, on which he is now a leading theorist, before it became an acceptable topic to discuss in mainstream legal scholarship:

> I will say this, that I think that it's had just enormous effects, not by pulling any strings but just in the very ordinary way of being a vehicle; allowing people to debate issues, allowing people to just constantly, every year having several conferences

which get ideas out which would not otherwise be considered. So, now, for example on Originalism, there's a good deal of stuff outside of the Federalist Society being done on Originalism. But, for a long time, there wouldn't have been so it allows there to be intellectual interest in the ideas. It allows there to be intellectual debate about the ideas. It allows people to know about one another. In the Academy, it's extremely important. My guess is that it's also important at the level of practicing lawyers, especially for people who are politically minded.[27]

Because law students eventually graduate and go on to pursue careers in the legal profession, the transformation that started in the law schools has carried over (and has been institutionalized by the Federalist Society through its Lawyers Chapters and practice groups) into the legal profession at large. As former attorney general and early mentor to the founding generation of Federalists, Edwin Meese III, explained to me in our interview, the Federalist Society "has contributed a great deal to the legal profession as a whole because it went beyond law schools. As people graduated from law schools and liked what they were doing in the Federalist Society, they formed lawyers chapters. And so as a result it's been a material factor in the whole legal profession."[28] Thirty years removed from the Federalist Society's founding, there are now several generations of lawyers who have come up through the ranks of the Federalist Society network, who have been trained to take Originalism and conservative and libertarian legal ideas seriously, and who are not afraid "to show their ideological stripes" (Teles 2008, 166) for fear of persecution or professional penalty. Indeed, within the legal academy and in legal scholarship, there is no question that Originalism has become far more acceptable than it was in the early 1980s. Two indications of its growing acceptance within the legal community is that there has been a push among legal progressives to co-opt Originalism,[29] and that, as Federalist Society member John C. Yoo mentioned in the opening excerpt to this section, "even liberals on the Supreme Court take it seriously."

The Federalist Society founders, several of whom had worked in the Reagan Justice Department under Attorney General Meese (Teles 2010; Hollis-Brusky 2011b), have long understood the importance of shaping not just the legal debate, but also the broader political and public debate about the role of government and the Constitution. However, this is not anything the Federalist Society had devoted institutional resources to until fairly recently. When I interviewed him in 2008, Federalist Society Executive Director Eugene Meyer twice mentioned the Society's then-recent institutional efforts to promote their members as experts and encourage them to speak to the media, go on television, and do outreach in state and federal governments—that is, to make a concerted effort to have an impact on the debate and discussion "beyond just the legal community." Here is an excerpt from that interview:

> A third thing we're beginning to do is with our people who have developed real expertise in these areas, getting them out into the media. Not to speak on behalf of the Federalist Society, not to give a position, but what we've tried to do is give them some media training and some help getting placed so that the broad ideas that we talk about get out there beyond just the legal community. That happened a lot in the Supreme Court nomination battles. We're trying to do that in the states to some degree; to get some discussion out there of what the rule of law means, what courts should be doing, what state courts should be doing, how do some of these battles apply and if we're thinking about it this way, what sorts of questions apply.[30]

Around the time of our conversation, the Federalist Society added to its website a PDF document entitled "Journalist's Guide to Legal Policy Experts."[31] This 59-page document provides the names and contact information of hundreds of Federalist Society–affiliated experts on over 200 different topics, ranging from Anti-Trust Law[32] to Political Correctness,[33] from the Line Item Veto[34] to School Vouchers,[35] and from Fundamental Rights[36] to Land Use.[37] While I have not investigated the extent to which these particular members have appeared in the media since the publication of this list, in the preceding chapters we did see some evidence of Federalist Society network media presence. Randy Barnett is a particularly noteworthy illustration. Listed on the Journalists' Guide as an expert under "Constitutional Law," "Federalism," "Fundamental Rights," "Gun Control," and six other topics,[38] Barnett wrote about the *McDonald* decision in the *Wall Street Journal*,[39] the "New Federalism" Revolution and William Rehnquist's legacy in the *Wall Street Journal*,[40] and the *NFIB* decision in the *Washington Post*.[41] Barnett,[42] along with fellow network member David B. Rivkin[43] and Federalist Society cofounder David McIntosh,[44] also appeared on Fox News to discuss high-profile constitutional cases and issues such as the Affordable Care Act, gun control, immigration, and voting rights.

A more recent avenue that the Federalist Society looks to be exploring in order, as Eugene Meyer stated, to influence the dialogue and debate beyond the legal community, has been to bring itself into dialogue with the Tea Party movement and its leadership in Congress. For example, the 2010 Federalist Society National Lawyers Convention was organized around the topic "Controlling Government: The Framers, the Tea Parties, and the Constitution." The convention description is instructive of the very exploratory nature of the developing relationship between the Federalist Society "elites" and the "tea parties" formed by "the people":

We have come a long way since the framing of the Constitution when our Founding Fathers struggled with the question of how to install a government strong enough to govern and limited enough to leave the people with the maximum practical degree of freedom. That question is perennial and highlighted by recent events. Indeed, some of our citizens recalled the passions that led to independence and the Constitution by forming tea parties. That movement today is seeking ways to limit government in practice. At the same time, other forces view such proposals as not only impracti-cal, but undesirable. Some believe that elites need to help the people to avoid many of the problems and pitfalls of society. Others take a more Burkean view about the leavening of direct democracy. Many interesting questions arise here, and we hope to explore them through four Showcase panels which address attempts to limit gov-ernment and also include some discussion of the dangers and problems of the people exercising overly direct control of the government.[45]

The Republican senator from Utah, Mike S. Lee, gave one of the keynote addresses at that conference. In addition to being a prominent member of the Senate Tea Party Caucus, when at law school he served as president of the Brigham Young University Law School Chapter of the Federalist Society.[46] Lee was invited back to the Federalist Society's Thirtieth Anniversary Convention in 2012, where he and fellow Tea Party Caucus colleague, Senator Ted Cruz (R-TX) gave back-to-back addresses in the Grand Ballroom of the Mayflower Hotel in Washington, D.C.[47] As another (non-institutional) example of this kind of continuing outreach outside the legal community, in January 2011 former Federalist Society advisor and mentor Justice Scalia was invited by then-Representative Michelle Bachman (R-MN) to lead a seminar on constitutional interpre-tation to the House Tea Party Caucus.

While there is certainly ambivalence about aligning themselves institutionally with the Tea Party, illustrated very clearly by the 2010 conference description, as well as some apparent disinterest on the part of non-lawyer Tea Party legislators and voters about "high-level" constitutional theorizing,[48] this kind of outreach is consistent with Meyer's stated goal to have an influence "beyond just the legal com-munity." It is also consistent with what I heard from certain members of the Federalist Society network during interviews in 2008. For exam-ple, cofounder and former Indiana Congressman David McIntosh said to me that it was "discouraging that Congress doesn't pay attention to its constitutional role" and said that he thought Congress "could ben-efit from an educational program" that would instruct them on "what the constitution expects [of them] and would show them how to think about it."[49] Bringing Tea Party legislators into the fold and having them speak with and learn from mainstream Federalist Society elites at conferences is certainly one way of attempting to shape the thinking and constitutional dialogue beyond the legal community. Additionally, the "educational program" McIntosh described to me in 2008 might have had its pilot run with Justice Scalia at the Tea Party House Caucus in 2011. But, as McIntosh recognized, there are real limits to getting legislators and voters to engage in the constitutional debate in the way that the Federalist Society has: "you go home to your district and you talk to your voters and they don't really want to hear that you've spent your time in Washington thinking about what the Constitution says. . . so being a lawyer. . . and being part of the Federalist Society were not things I advertised when I was running for office."[50] While there are real challenges to convincing legislators and voters to seriously engage in the kind of constitutional discourse that happens in and around the Federalist Society, by distilling their ideas and disseminating them in newspapers, on Fox News, and by reaching out early on to the newly minted class of Tea Party legislators, the Federalist Society and its members have certainly contributed to the legitimating of Originalism and of conservative and libertarian legal positions outside the legal community. Taken together, these efforts both inside and outside the legal profession have acted like, to borrow Federalist Society member Lillian BeVier's language, "dripping water,"[51] slowly wearing away at the dominance of liberal legal thought and effectively changing the dialogue about the Constitution and constitutional culture. To bring this back to our focus on constitutional change, nurturing and supporting this kind of *cultural capital* (Teles 2008) is important for bringing about constitutional revolutions because, as I have said before, the Supreme Court's only power lies with its ability to persuade an audience of similarly educated elites inside the legal profession *and* "We the people" at large that its decisions are well-reasoned and legitimate—that it is, in fact, saying *what the law is* and not simply what they think *it should be*.

An Agenda for Future Research

Looking Back, Looking Forward

This book has examined what the Federalist Society for Law and Public Policy *does*—by providing a framework that we as students and observers of American politics can use to make sense of its influence and by providing evidence of that influence in concrete cases. This book has not conclusively answered the question of what the Federalist Society *is*. Is it, as several Federalist Society members suggested to me in our conversations, *sui generis*?[1] Or is the Federalist Society, as Lawrence Baum has written, simply a more "formalize[d]" or stylized version of the kind of informal elite networks that have always operated within the legal community? (Baum 2006, 126)? As evidence, Baum points to the Franklin Roosevelt–era Justices, who—as other scholars have documented—maintained strong links with liberals in the academy, in the executive branch, and with judges on other courts:

> There were strong links between some of Franklin Roosevelt's Supreme Court appointees and other liberals in the New Deal era (Lash 1975; Newman 1997; Jackson 2003). Liberal Justices on the Court and the federal court of appeals for the District of Columbia interacted with each other and with like-minded people who held other positions in the 1960s and 1970s. Indeed, the dining room of a liquor warehouse in Washington served as something of a "salon" for liberals in and out of the judiciary during that era. (Barbash 1981; Clines and Weaver 1982; Baum 2006, 126)

What Baum and other scholars are documenting is what Teles referred to as the genesis of the "Liberal Legal Network," whereby "a generation of New Deal lawyers, informed by legal realism and experienced in government, created new kinds of law and new kinds of lawyering, and became in the process an integral part of America's legal elite" (Teles 2008, 24–25). As Teles documents and my research further illustrates, the founders of the Federalist Society were conscious of the Roosevelt-era model and sought to build a counter-network that would rival what the left built from the 1930s onward (Teles 2008, 137–142). Moreover, this period witnessed several seismic shifts in constitutional jurisprudence: the demise of *Lochner* era jurisprudence (Gillman 1993), the rise of a sociological jurisprudence that justified the expanding role of government in the economy (Irons 1982; Horwitz 1992; Duxbury 1995; Cushman 1998), and the Warren Court's "rights revolution" (Epp 1998; Horwitz 1999). If we follow the logic that I outlined earlier about "critical junctures" and *doctrinal distance*, these eras would seem ripe for a PEN analysis. Perhaps such an analysis would corroborate what Baum suggests: that is, that the Federalist Society for Law and Public Policy is simply a more "formalize[d]" version of the kinds of elite networks that have long-existed within the legal "support structure" (Epp 1998) to aid and influence the work of judges and Justices.

Alternatively, it might reveal something else. Perhaps the Federalist Society's innovation—the act of formalizing and institutionalizing these once-informal networks—itself represents something of a "critical juncture" within the legal community. That is, the Federalist Society model, though inspired by the "Liberal Legal Network," is viewed now by many within the legal community as strategically superior to its prototype. The informal networks and processes that successfully helped support and implement the "rights revolution" on the left are now seen as insufficient counterweights to the more formalized and organized Federalist Society network. The best evidence that the Federalist Society has indeed altered the rules of engagement around the battle for constitutional understanding was the founding in 2001 of a progressive counterpart to the Federalist Society—the American Constitution Society (ACS). The ACS is the "mirror image" of the Federalist Society (Southworth 2008, 185) in its institutional machinery, with an emphasis on creating a community of legal elites who share a particular legal and constitutional philosophy, networking these elites, and supporting their professional development. Its mission, as articulated on the organization's website, "promote[s] the vitality of the U.S. Constitution and the fundamental values it expresses: individual rights and liberties, genuine access to justice, democracy and the rule of law."[2] Like its philosophical foil, ACS boasts a growing number of lawyer and student chapters. It sponsors conferences, debates, colloquia, and networking events, and supports a number of working groups that develop litigation strategies on issues such as federalism, executive power, and judicial nominations. As founding executive director of ACS Lisa Brown explained to me in an interview in 2008, "the ultimate goal [of ACS] is to further a progressive vision of law and policy, to get ideas out there and have them be acted on and implemented. . . over time as people go into different positions of all sorts and different jobs in government and judging, then you actually see more of the. . . realizing of the ideas." Brown continued to say that the ideas were important, but it was the "ideas connected to the people. . . the network" that had been the Federalist Society's formula for success—a formula the ACS has been doing its best to try to imitate.[3]

While I cannot pretend to have captured the Federalist Society's precise formula for success in these pages, future scholarship might use the dimensions of Federalist Society influence I have outlined here in this book as a starting point for evaluating how far the ACS, at just over 10 years of age, is from having the kind of influence its founders hoped it would. So, future scholarship might investigate: (1) the extent to which a PEN or mini-PENs have cohered around the ACS in order to evaluate whether members of this network are poised to take advantage of and shape "critical junctures" in constitutional development; and (2) the extent to which members of the ACS network are successfully working to bring those "critical junctures" about by (a) getting the right cast of characters on the bench, (b) functioning as a vigilant and vocal judicial audience, and (c) recapturing the debate over constitutional interpretation. While a systematic examination of these critically important questions will undoubtedly be the subject of future studies, I will close by offering some preliminary thoughts and insights, gleaned from my interviews with some of the leadership of the ACS, as well as from interviews with Federalist Society members about its progressive counterpart in 2008.

In 1988, then-newly appointed Supreme Court Justice Antonin Scalia delivered a lecture in honor of William Howard Taft. The lecture, entitled "Originalism: The Lesser Evil," succinctly illustrates what I believe to be the single greatest challenge for the ACS:

> . . . nonoriginalism confronts a practical difficulty reminiscent of the truism of elective politics that "You can't beat somebody with nobody." It is not enough to demonstrate that the other fellow's candidate (originalism) is no good; one must also agree upon another candidate to replace him. Just as it is not meaningful for a voter to vote "non-Reagan," it is not very helpful to tell a judge to be a "non-originalist." If the law is to make any attempt at consistency and predictability, surely there must be general agreement not only that judges reject one exegetical approach (originalism), but that they adopt another. And it is hard to discern any emerging consensus among the nonoriginalists as to what this might be.[4]

One of the reasons that the Federalist Society network has been so successful in shaping constitutional understanding has been the identifiable PENs that cohered around various doctrinal areas within the organization. These PENs share a set of beliefs, a canon of authoritative sources, and employ a clear method of interpreting the Constitution: Originalism.

One of the critical questions for ACS will be the extent to which it has managed effectively to generate consensus among progressives about the non-originalist interpretive alternative—that is, to borrow Scalia's phrase, the "non-Reagan" of constitutional interpretation. Every member with whom I spoke in 2008 identified this as the key challenge for the ACS moving forward. For example, Lisa Brown, the former executive director of ACS, said of the state of ideological coherence within the organization at that time, "I think on a broad level there's agreement. What there isn't yet is an 'Originalism.'"[5] Similarly, board member Goodwin Liu said that one of goals of the ACS is "to capture the intuitive set of ideas that progressives sort of take for granted in terms of how they see the world. Progressives always think, 'well I know what I think but it's hard to articulate it.' So, we're trying to articulate it."[6] As evidence that the ACS is taking this task seriously, Brown, Liu, and other members I interviewed pointed to the "Constitutional Interpretation and Change Issue Group," whose mission has been to work toward developing and articulating a progressive alternative to Originalism. Pulling together big name progressive and liberal legal scholars such as Pamela Karlan, Jack Balkin, Robert Post, Reva Siegel, Cass Sunstein, Mark Tushnet, Geoffrey Stone, Laurence Tribe, and Bruce Ackerman (among others), the aim of this Issue Group is to "promote persuasive and accessible methods of interpretation that give full meaning to the guarantees contained in the Constitution" and to "debunk[] the purportedly neutral theories of originalism and strict construction."[7]

In terms of intellectual production, over the past five years, this working group has produced dozens of issue briefs and three book-length explorations of what progressive constitutional interpretation is and how it is applied. Future scholarship might mine these sources, alongside ACS member speech acts at National Conferences and other ACS publications such as *Advance* and the *Harvard Law and Policy Review* to examine whether these institutional investments in developing something like Originalism for progressives have paid dividends. Is there an emerging consensus in terms of how members talk about and employ constitutional interpretation? Is there a shared canon of authorities members consistently cite? This ideological coherence, the development of an interpretive consensus, and the ability to shape and socialize its members accordingly will be important for ACS if it hopes to be in a position to influence the content and character of the next [progressive] "critical juncture" in constitutional development.

In terms of helping bring that progressive "critical juncture" about, as I explained earlier, one of the necessary conditions (though not a sufficient condition) for a constitutional revolution is having the right cast of characters on the court. An important element in that process is in the identification, credentialing, and vetting of potential judicial candidates. As leaders within both the ACS and the Federalist Society recognize, this is the portion of the Federalist Society formula that its counterpart will have the most difficulty replicating. In part, this has to do with the plethora of institutions on the legal left (including, but not limited to, elite law schools like Harvard, Yale, and Stanford) where aspiring progressive lawyers can be credentialed. To paraphrase Federalist Society member Michael Greve's words cited earlier in this chapter, on the legal left there are "a million ways to get credentialed," but on the legal right, "there is only one." Federalist Society member Dan Troy expressed a similar sentiment about the limited utility of the ACS network when it comes to getting clerkships, judgeships, and other jobs in government:

> If you want to be a judge, which a lot of lawyers want to be, and the Federalist Society has been very good for that kind of network, or you want a government job and you have a choice between getting involved in the [American Bar Association] or getting deeply involved in the American Constitution Society, if I were a liberal I'd bet on the ABA. . . . I think I'm going to make more contacts and I think they're going to be more prestigious. . . . So, I just don't see the same need for it.[8]

Leaders within the ACS acknowledge the improbability of making their organizational credential a *sine qua non* for prestigious jobs and judgeships. While recognizing that it will not have a de facto monopoly on the credentialing of progressive legal talent, former executive director Lisa Brown said that she thought the ACS credential would still be viewed as "a positive, a plus" for Democratic administrations looking to appoint strong progressives into judgeships and government positions.[9] While those I interviewed in 2008 could simply speculate, we now have six years of nominations under a Democratic administration to examine for ACS influence. After the selection of ACS board member Eric Holder as attorney general, the *New York Times* published an article touting the influence the organization seemed to have early on in the Obama administration, noting in particular appointments to the executive branch.[10] On the other hand, Obama's two Supreme Court nominees—arguably the most important appointments in terms of influencing constitutional law and policy—do not seem to have strong ties to the ACS network. Justice Sonia

Sotomayor was a virtual unknown to progressives within the ACS network and, according to at least one source, her appointment initially made liberals and progressives "unhappy."[11] Justice Elena Kagan was a speaker and participant in ACS conferences in 2005, 2007, and 2008, although, as Obama noted on her confirmation, she also frequently participated in and received "standing ovations" from "the Federalist Society."[12] Future studies might more closely inspect the DNA of all the Obama administration's executive branch and judicial appointees and evaluate whether or not the ACS credential factors prominently in some or all of these appointees.

One high-profile blow dealt to both the Obama administration and the ACS was the failed battle to appoint board member Goodwin Liu to the Ninth Circuit Court of Appeals after his nomination was filibustered successfully by Senate Republicans in 2011.[13] In his Senate hearing, Liu was asked about his involvement with ACS by Senator Jon Kyl (R-AZ), who equated Liu's involvement with and promotion of the mission of ACS with a desire to usurp the political process and engage in an agenda of judicial activism. A short excerpt from the transcript of that hearing illustrates this:

SENATOR KYL. Thank you, Madam Chairman, and for your patience. I want to get back to this question of agenda that I was talking about before we had our little break. You, in a broadcast earlier this year, January 3rd, on NPR, were discussing how the Obama administration represented a new opportunity for the American Constitution Society. You said that Obama administration, "that ACS had the opportunity to actually get our ideas and the progressive vision of the Constitution and of law and policy into practice." What did you mean by "our ideas" and your "progressive vision" of the Constitution and law and policy?

PROFESSOR LIU. Senator, I think that was a reference to the ideas that underpin the American Constitution Society. I think, as the mission statement of that organization reads, it's a dedication to certain basic principles of our Constitution: genuine equality, liberty, access to the courts, and a broad commitment to the rule of law.

. . .

SENATOR KYL. Well, the way you described it was "the opportunity to actually get our ideas and the progressive vision of the Constitution and of law and of policy into practice," so I assume you subscribe to these views when you talked about "our ideas."

PROFESSOR LIU. I have—I think, as I think the record shows, Senator, I have been deeply involved in the American Constitution Society.

SENATOR KYL. Yes.

PROFESSOR LIU. I have served on the board, I have chaired the board.

SENATOR KYL. There's nothing wrong with having views that are wrong. [Laughter.]

SENATOR KYL. No. OK. But I mean, so that's what you meant by "the opportunity to actually get our ideas and progressive vision of the Constitution and law and policy into practice." But I guess the follow-up question is, obviously I guess you would say you were speaking in a policy way, not through the judicial process. Is that the way—

PROFESSOR LIU. I think—well, Senator, the short answer is yes. In addition, I think that—look, I mean, I think every President has his or her own views of what vision they would like to enforce as a President. I think—I don't think I was meaning anything more than just that basic prerogative of the President.

SENATOR KYL. Policy through the appropriate ways of implementing policy.

PROFESSOR LIU. Absolutely. Yes.[14]

How should we interpret the failed battle to confirm Liu who, in many ways, is the embodiment of the American Constitution Society's progressive jurisprudence and approach to the law? Further, did this high-profile failure create a stigmatizing effect among legal progressives? Alternatively, as the failed nomination of Robert Bork to the Supreme Court in 1987 did for the fledgling Federalists working at the Reagan Justice Department, will this have a rallying and mobilizing effect within the ACS? These questions and more will be important for scholars to think about and study in detail in the future.

Even if we do see evidence of the ACS gene playing a prominent role in Obama's judicial nominations, is this society poised and positioned to act as a vigilant and vocal judicial audience (Baum 2006), keeping its members in line with the progressive judicial philosophy that the network advocates? In many ways, the answer to this question will depend on whether or not, per the PEN criterion, ACS has developed an identifiable, shared interpretive philosophy, and a set of beliefs that members could in fact use as a baseline for measuring the performance of ACS-affiliated judges and Justices. I asked Goodwin Liu in 2008 how, given that the progressive vision seemed to encompass so many different intellectual touchstones and strands, folks within the ACS would be able to identify and hold someone accountable to that broad vision. He paused for quite a while and then said that he would look for "the unique quality of people who are progressive in their orientation. . . which is that these kind of majestic generalities in the constitution need to be made practical for people in their everyday lives."[15] Future studies might investigate whether Liu's baseline for evaluating the performance of progressive judges resonates within the network at large or whether there are one or several varied criteria among the members of ACS. Beyond that, how well are ACS members positioned to respond vocally to perceived drifts or deviations from the progressive standard (and is there a feedback loop to the Justices, as there clearly is within the Federalist Society network)? A more systematic evaluation of how vocal, vigilant, and unified members of the ACS network have been in applauding and booing Supreme Court decisions and how consistent they have been in terms of the criteria they use to talk about and evaluate the performance of progressive judges in the media (along with an examination of which media outlets members are using to disseminate their ideas) would go a long way toward helping evaluate the ACS network as an effective (or potentially effective) "judicial audience" (2006).

Finally, how successful has the ACS been in recapturing the debate over constitutional interpretation, in reducing the stigma of (or rebranding) the "living constitution" approach to constitutional interpretation? The phrase "living constitution," once associated with the judicial philosophies of prestigious judges and Justices such as John Marshall, Oliver Wendell Holmes, Louis Brandeis, and Thurgood Marshall, has been redefined successfully over the past few decades by those on the legal and political right as synonymous with "judicial activism" and as an excuse to write one's own social and moral values into the Constitution. As David A. Strauss writes in his book *The Living Constitution,* the standard critique of the "living constitution" usually proceeds along these lines:

> A living constitution is, surely, a manipulable constitution. If the Constitution is not constant—if it changes from time to time—then someone is changing it. And that someone is changing it according to his or her own ideas about what the Constitution should look like. The "someone," it's usually thought, is some group of judges. So a living constitution would not be the Constitution at all. . . [rather] a collection of gauzy ideas that appeal to the judges who happen to be in power at a particular time and that they impose on the rest of us.[16]

Strauss also notes that these critiques have been so effective that scholars who write about constitutional interpretation avoid using it, unless they are using it derisively (Strauss 2010, 2). Justice Scalia is a clear example of the latter. In the fall of 2011, Scalia told a Senate committee that he hoped the "living constitution would die" and, more recently, in a 2013 talk at Southern Methodist University, Scalia reportedly became exasperated with those who believe in the "living Constitution," emphatically insisting that "[i]t's not a living document. It's dead, dead, dead."[17] Given its explicit mission of countering and "debunking" Originalism, how successful has the ACS been at recapturing the debate over constitutional interpretation—of burying the dead constitution of Originalism and breathing new life into the notion of a "living constitution?"

It should be noted that the parameters of what the ACS considers its battleground over constitutional meaning are drawn more narrowly than were those of its rival organization at its founding. Liberals and progressives still largely claim the legal Academy and the legal profession as their intellectual territory. As ACS board member and Yale Law School professor Robert Post explained to me, "we are still hegemonic within the law schools, most law professors are liberal, most students are liberal." The implication of this, Post explained, is that "ACS is coming in on the back of an extremely well developed tradition of liberal legal thinking that has endless supporters in the law schools," and unlike its counterpart, it does not have to engage in "idea generation." Rather, Post insisted, the principal task of ACS is "idea dissemination and distribution."[18] As former executive director Lisa Brown also said, the "gap" the founders of ACS noticed was not in the law school dialogue or debate, but rather "it was that the public dialogue had become so lop-sided and that there was a sense of needing a progressive voice in the public dialogue." Brown continued that the real work of ACS is to "communicate" and "synthesize" all the work that has been done on "progressive constitutional interpretation in the Academy" and make it accessible to a public or political audience.[19] Whether they call it "living constitutionalism" or something else, many of the leading liberal lights in the Academy still practice and preach something very similar, so how is ACS distilling and repackaging this progressive constitutional vision for public consumption?

One of the aforementioned book projects to emerge from the ACS's "Constitutional Interpretation and Change Issue Group" exemplifies one such approach to rebranding the "living constitution." *Keeping Faith with the Constitution*, written by Goodwin Liu, Pamela Karlan, and Christopher Schroeder and available for free on the ACS website as a PDF download,[20] rebrands "living constitutionalism" as "constitutional fidelity," co-opting the term that Edwin Meese III and other prominent intellectuals on the right used in the 1980s to define Originalism in contradistinction to the "living constitution" approach.[21] Even though the book's authors do not once use the phrase "living constitution," an excerpt from the introduction locates their approach squarely within this tradition:

> Interpreting the Constitution, we argue, requires adaptation of its text and principles to the conditions and challenges faced by successive generations. The question that properly guides interpretation is not how the Constitution would have been applied at the Founding, but rather how it should be applied today in order to sustain its vitality in light of the changing needs, conditions, and understandings of our society.[22]

Moreover, the authors of the book define their approach as a "richer" and more constitutionally faithful alternative to Originalism.[23] This is consistent with the ACS's stated goal of "debunking" Originalism.[24]

Potentially complicating the achievement of this objective, there are those deeply connected with and involved in ACS, such as Yale Law professor Jack Balkin, who are instead attempting to co-opt Originalism for progressives. In 2008 at the ACS's National Convention, Jack Balkin appeared on a panel with Federalist Society stalwart Randy Barnett and Goodwin Liu and argued for the merits of a progressive Originalism. Shortly after that panel, I asked Liu what he thought of Balkin's move to Originalism. Liu responded that "to call Jack Balkin an Originalist is just to empty the word Originalism of very much meaning. I mean Jack Balkin's Originalism is not that far from Justice Brennan's appeal to contemporary values. . . if Originalism is able to accommodate that kind of evolving understanding, then I just don't understand what the debate is about anymore."[25] Despite the reservations of Liu and others about this being a disingenuous strategy, Balkin's campaign to convert liberals and progressives within the ACS network to Originalism did not stop there. In 2011, Balkin gave a talk before the University of Chicago Law School Chapter of ACS entitled "Why Liberals Should Be Originalists."[26] Professor Balkin's conversion to Originalism is explained and justified in greater detail in his 2011 book, *Living Originalism* (Belknap: 2011), where he makes the case that "living constitutionalism" and "Originalism" are actually compatible interpretive theories. Future research might investigate which of these strategies is actually dominant among members of the ACS network (using surveys and/or analyzing network members' conference speech acts, intellectual/academic production, and print and media appearances) and whether the tension between the two will be productive or ultimately will hinder the ability of ACS to reclaim the public and political debate over constitutional interpretation.

In closing, in addition to these important empirical questions that warrant further investigation, I think there are also normative questions that merit some consideration. If the Federalist Society model and the rise of its rival, the ACS, does represent a "critical juncture" within the legal profession, that is, a new model of identifying, training, promoting, and disciplining lawyers on both the right and the left from professional cradle (law school) to professional grave (retirement), then what consequences might this have for the legal profession specifically and for the politicization of law, more generally? By governing the ideological socialization of young law professionals and plugging them into a political network that creates professional incentives for students and lawyers aspiring to top clerkships, positions in the national bureaucracy, and federal judgeships, some fear that these legal-hybrid organizations have further blurred the crucial divide, however tenuous, between law and politics and have contributed negatively to the polarization of the law.[27] Others, such as George Washington University law professor Orin Kerr, say this is an improvement on the old model of networking within the legal profession based on school credentials or family ties: "Now the networking is more open."[28] These normative concerns will be important for scholars, students, and practitioners of American politics and law to think about and engage with as we seek to understand and evaluate the mechanisms, old and new, by which "ideas" *can* and *do* "have consequences."[29]

List of Interviews
(CPHS Protocol #2007-7-5)

1. Charles J. Cooper (founding member and chairman of Cooper & Kirk, PLLC; assistant attorney general for the Office of Legal Counsel (1985–1988)) in discussion with the author, June 2, 2008.
2. Carter Phillips (managing partner, Sidley Austin, LLP) in discussion with the author, January 30, 2008.
3. Daniel Troy (attorney, Sidley Austin, LLP; special assistant, Office of Legal Counsel (1984–1988)) in discussion with the author, January 30, 2008.
4. Daniel Ortiz (professor of law, University of Virginia Law School) in discussion with the author, February 6, 2008.
5. Daniel Polsby (dean and professor of law, George Mason Law School) in discussion with the author, February 11, 2008.
6. David McIntosh (partner, Meyer, Brown and Platt; member of Congress (1995–2001); cofounder, Federalist Society) in discussion with the author, January 25, 2008.
7. Donald Devine (vice-chairman, American Conservative Union; director, U.S. Office of Personnel Management under President Ronald Reagan) in discussion with the author, February 7, 2008.
8. Douglas W. Kmiec (professor of law, Pepperdine University; Office of Legal Counsel under Presidents Ronald Reagan and George H. W. Bush) in discussion with the author, March 14, 2008.
9. Edwin W. Meese, III (U.S. attorney general under President Ronald Reagan (1985–1988); Fellow, Heritage Foundation) in discussion with the author, February 5, 2008.
10. Eugene Meyer (president, Federalist Society) in discussion with the author, February 8, 2008.

11. Fred L. Smith (president and founder, Competitive Enterprise Institute) in discussion with the author, January 16, 2008.

12. Gail Heriot (professor of law, University of San Diego; commissioner, United States Commission on Civil Rights) in discussion with the author, March 18, 2008.

13. Goodwin Liu (professor of law, University of California, Berkeley Law School; Board of Directors, American Constitution Society; nominee to Ninth Circuit Court of Appeals) in discussion with the author, June 27, 2008.

14. Gregory Maggs (senior associate dean for Academic Affairs and professor of law, George Washington University Law School) in discussion with the author, January 22, 2008.

15. John C. Yoo (professor of law, University of California, Berkeley Law School; former law clerk to Judge Laurence H. Silberman and Justice Clarence Thomas; general counsel, U.S. Senate Judiciary Committee (1995–1996); deputy assistant attorney general, Office of Legal Counsel (2001–2003)) in discussion with the author, January 16, 2008.

16. John T. Noonan (senior circuit judge, Ninth Circuit Court of Appeals) in discussion with the author, January 14, 2008.

17. Loren A. Smith (judge, U.S. Court of Federal Claims; chairman, Administrative Conference of the United States (1981–1985)) in discussion with the author, January 24, 2008.

18. Laurence Claus (professor of law, University of San Diego; former John M. Olin Fellow at Northwestern University School of Law) in discussion with the author, March 18, 2008.

19. Lee Liberman Otis (Office of Legal Counsel, George H. W. Bush Administration; general counsel (2001–2005); cofounder, Federalist Society) in discussion with the author, June 4, 2008.

20. Lillian BeVier (professor of law, University of Virginia Law School) in discussion with the author, February 1, 2008.

21. Linda Chavez (chairman, the Center for Equal Opportunity; staff director, U.S. Commission on Civil Rights (1983–1985)) in discussion with the author, January 29, 2008.

22. Lisa Brown (executive director, American Constitution Society (2001–2008)) in discussion with the author, June 19, 2008.

23. Louis Michael Seidman (professor of constitutional law, Georgetown Law School) in discussion with the author, February 15, 2008.

24. Michael Carvin (partner, Jones Day; deputy assistant attorney general, Civil Rights Division (1985–1987); deputy assistant attorney general, Office of Legal Counsel (1987–1988)) in discussion with the author, January 28, 2008.

25. Michael Greve (director of the Federalism Project, American Enterprise Institute) in discussion with the author, February 12, 2008.

26. Michael Horowitz (Senior Fellow, Hudson Institute; general counsel, Office of Management and Budget under President Ronald Reagan) in discussion with the author, January 22, 2008.

27. Michael Rappaport (professor of law, University of San Diego Law School; special assistant, Office of Legal Counsel under President Ronald Reagan) in discussion with the author, March 17, 2008.

28. Randy Barnett (professor of legal theory, Georgetown University Law School) in discussion with the author, June 10, 2008.

29. Richard K. Willard (partner, Steptoe and Johnson, LLP; assistant attorney general, Civil Rights Division under President Ronald Reagan) in discussion with the author, January 31, 2008.

30. Robert Post (dean and professor of Law, Yale Law School; Board of Directors, American Constitution Society) in discussion with the author, June 12, 2008.

31. Roger Clegg (president and general counsel, Center for Equal Opportunity; assistant attorney general, Civil Rights Division (1987–1991); assistant to the solicitor general (1985–1987)) in discussion with the author, January 29, 2008.

32. Spencer Abraham (U.S. senator from Michigan (1994–2001); U.S secretary of Energy (2001–2004); cofounder, *Harvard Journal of Law and Public Policy*) in discussion with the author, June 3, 2008.

33. Steven Calabresi (professor of law, Northwestern University; cofounder, Federalist Society) in discussion with the author, April 3, 2008.

34. Thomas A. Smith (professor of law, University of San Diego Law School; senior counsel, President Reagan's Council of Economic Advisors) in discussion with the author, March 19, 2008.

35. Tony Cotto (former student chapter president at George Washington University Law School, the Federalist Society) in discussion with the author, January 31, 2008.

36. Walter Berns (Resident Scholar, American Enterprise Institute) in discussion with the author, January 24, 2008.

NOTES

INTRODUCTION

1. Richard S. Weaver, *Ideas Have Consequences* (Chicago, IL: University of Chicago Press, 1948).
2. Leonard S. Leo, "Welcome Address." Showcase Panel I: Federalism and Federal Power. 2012. Federalist Society National Lawyers Convention, November 19, 2012 (accessed June 13, 2013), http://www.fed-soc.org/publications/detail/federalism-and-federal-power-event-audiovideo.
3. Antonin Scalia was a faculty advisor to the Federalist Society when it was a student group at the University of Chicago and presented at the very first Federalist Society Conference. See Antonin Scalia, "The Two Faces of Federalism," *Harvard Journal of Law and Public Policy* 6 (1982): 19–22. Clarence Thomas has also been a frequent participant at Federalist Society events and conferences since the late 1980s. See Clarence Thomas, "The Higher Law Background of the Privileges or Immunities Clause of the Fourteenth Amendment." *Harvard Journal of Law and Public Policy* 12, no. 1 (1989): 63–70. John G. Roberts, Jr., was plugged into the Federalist Society network through his work in the Reagan Justice Department, alongside many of its founders. Roberts also delivered the Barbara K. Olson Memorial Lecture at the Federalist Society's 2007 25th Anniversary National Lawyers Convention, accessed June 13, 2013, http://www.fed-soc.org/publications/detail/7th-annual-barbara-k-olson-memorial-lecture-event-audiovideo.
4. See "About Us" (accessed June 13, 2013), http://www.fed-soc.org/aboutus/.
5. 124 Stat. 119.
6. Leonard S. Leo, "Welcome Address." Showcase Panel I: Federalism and Federal Power. 2012. Federalist Society National Lawyers Convention. November 19, 2012 (accessed June 13, 2013), http://www.fed-soc.org/publications/detail/federalism-and-federal-power-event-audiovideo.

CHAPTER 1

1. David McIntosh, (partner, Meyer, Brown and Platt; member of Congress (1995–2001); cofounder, Federalist Society) in discussion with the author, January 25, 2008.
2. Steven Calabresi, (professor of law, Northwestern University; cofounder, Federalist Society) in discussion with the author, April 3, 2008.
3. See, for example, interview with Carter Phillips (managing partner, Sidley Austin, LLP) in discussion with the author, January 30, 2008: "*Sui generis* is probably as good of a description as you can come up with in terms of what that organization is."; interview with Gregory Maggs (senior associate dean for Academic Affairs and professor of law, George Washington University Law School) in discussion with the author, January

22, 2008: " I think it is really *sui generis* and if you think about why it was formed you sort of understand why that is"; interview with Michael Carvin (partner, Jones Day; deputy assistant attorney general, Civil Rights Division (1985–1987); deputy assistant attorney general, Office of Legal Counsel (1987–1988)) in discussion with the author, January 28, 2008: "... it's got characteristics of [a think tank and an interest group] but I would call it a think tank slash debating society... their contribution to the market-place of ideas comes a lot more from these structured conferences and their speakers... so I would think they're *sui generis* in that respect."; interview with Richard K. Willard (partner, Steptoe and Johnson, LLP; assistant attorney general, Civil Rights Division under President Ronald Reagan) in discussion with the author, January 31, 2008: "I think it's pretty *sui generis*..."

4. I have actually called the Federalist Society an "epistemic community" in earlier writing on the subject (see Hollis-Brusky 2010, 2013). I figured that even if it did not work perfectly, the research approach and logic of the epistemic community model was right for investigating Federalist Society influence. However, various reviewers, scholars, and epistemic community theorists have persuaded me since that early time that instead of stretching the epistemic community construct to fit the Federalist Society network, I ought to acknowledge the very important ways in which the model does not fit and perhaps develop a related construct that can be applied to networks like the Federalist Society with a strong political valence. That is what this section attempts to accomplish.

5. See Federal Society Organization, About Us page, accessed February 16, 2009, www.fed-soc.org/aboutus.

6. I coded the speaker lists for the entire set of presenters at Federalist Society National Meetings from 1982 to 2011. Speakers were coded for their occupation at the time they were participating in the event. For instance, Kenneth Starr, who participated in nine Federalist Society National Meetings, was coded three different ways during three periods of his career history: as Executive Branch (U.S. solicitor general); Private Practice (Kirkland & Ellis); and Academic (Dean Pepperdine Law School). For some, the speaker's current occupation was listed on the program agenda or in the footnote section of the reprinted transcript of their talk. For others, I had to investigate. If it was unclear as to what the speaker was doing at the exact time of his or her talk, a very small set of instances, I coded the individual for the occupational role I could find that was closest to the tenure of the talk. Of the 1,957 speakers coded, the breakdown of raw data with percentages (rounded up to nearest whole number) were as follows: Legal Academics (717, or 37%); Think Tank or Interest Group (253, or 13%); Federal Judge (247, or 13%); Private Practice (249, or 13%); Executive Branch (187, or 10%); Corporate or Corporate Counsel (73, or 4%); Other (73, or 4%); Press and Media (58, or 3%); State or Local Politicians (55, or 3%); and Legislative Branch (45, or 2%).

7. Interview with Gail Heriot (professor of law, University of San Diego; commissioner, United States Commission on Civil Rights) in discussion with the author, March 18, 2008.

8. I borrow the phrase "boots on the ground" from Federalist Society member and American Enterprise Institute Scholar Michael Greve. Interview with Michael Greve (director of the Federalism Project, American Enterprise Institute) in discussion with the author, February 12, 2008.

9. See Federal Society Organization, About Us page, accessed February 16, 2009, www.fed-soc.org/aboutus.

10. Fusionism, sometimes described as "libertarian means to conservative or traditional ends," is a philosophy of American conservatism most closely associated with

conservative intellectual and *National Review* editor Frank S. Meyer, the father of Federalist Society executive director Eugene Meyer. In his book *In Defense of Freedom: A Conservative Credo* (1962), Meyer outlined what he understood to be a uniquely American variant of conservatism that blended traditional conservative emphases on values and virtue with a libertarian focus on freedom and political liberty.

11. Based on content analysis of a sample of just over 200 speech acts from Federalist Society National Meetings from 1982–2008, *The Federalist Papers* were the most often cited authoritative source, receiving 173 specific mentions. Within that sample, *Federalist 10*, *Federalist 78*, and *Federalist 51* received the most mentions by name.

12. Roger Clegg (president and general counsel, Center for Equal Opportunity; assistant attorney general, Civil Rights Division (1987–1991); assistant to the solicitor general (1985–1987)) in discussion with the author, January 29, 2008.

13. See, for example, Interview with Douglas Kmiec (professor of law, Pepperdine University; Office of Legal Counsel under Presidents Ronald Reagan and George H. W. Bush) in discussion with the author, March 14, 2008: ". . . during the Reagan administration we cared a lot about the separation of powers [and] part of the Federalist Society is to defend the separation of powers and the. . . horizontal structure of the Constitution"; Interview with John Yoo (professor of law, University of California, Berkeley Law School; former law clerk to Judge Laurence H. Silberman and Justice Clarence Thomas; general counsel, U.S. Senate Judiciary Committee (1995–1996); deputy assistant attorney general, Office of Legal Counsel (2001–2003)) in discussion with the author, January 16, 2008: "I could tell you the Federalist Society [stands for] Originalism and the strict separation of powers."; Interview with Steven Calabresi (professor of law, Northwestern University; cofounder, Federalist Society) in discussion with the author, April 3, 2008: "The Society has always been consistently interested in promoting. . . a greater respect for the separation of powers."

14. See, for example, Interview with Charles J. Cooper (founding member and chairman of Cooper & Kirk, PLLC; assistant attorney general for the Office of Legal Counsel (1985–1988)) in discussion with the author, June 2, 2008: "I am among those [in the Federalist Society] who prefer a consistent and principled view towards state sovereignty. . . I believe that the principles of federalism are robust enough to stand up for decisions I don't like as well as those I do."; Interview with Carter Phillips (managing partner, Sidley Austin, LLP) in discussion with the author, January 30, 2008: "I've always viewed the federalism part of [the Federalist Society] as the most significant. . . I always thought that respect for states' rights was one of the original driving forces of it."; Interview with Loren Smith, (judge, U.S. Court of Federal Claims; chairman, Administrative Conference of the United States (1981–1985)) in discussion with the author, January 24, 2008: "I guess that would be one element of federalism that unifies [the Federalist Society]. . . another idea that federalism connotes to me is a certain concern that states have a legitimate role in the federal system and that centralization in Washington is not the system that the Framers sought. . . it infringes too much on individual liberties."

15. *Marbury v. Madison*, 5 U.S. 137 (1803) was a landmark Supreme Court decision that established the principle of judicial review. In his majority opinion, Chief Justice John Marshall famously wrote: "It is emphatically the province and duty of the judicial department to say what the law is. Those who apply the rule of particular cases, must of necessity expound and interpret that rule. If two laws conflict with each other, the courts must decide on the operation of each."

16. Interview with Charles J. Cooper (founding member and chairman of Cooper & Kirk, PLLC; assistant attorney general for the Office of Legal Counsel (1985–1988)) in discussion with the author, June 2, 2008.

17. See, for example, Interview with Douglas Kmiec (professor of law, Pepperdine University; Office of Legal Counsel under Presidents Ronald Reagan and George H. W. Bush) in discussion with the author, March 14, 2008: "So, it would be the standard things like federal-state relations and the separation of powers, the nature of the judicial function, [these are the] stand-bys."; Interview with Gail Heriot (professor of law, University of San Diego; commissioner, United States Commission on Civil Rights) in discussion with the author, March 18, 2008: "One thing, the most unifying... is that the judiciary's job is not to make law but to say what the law is. That is something that just about everyone agrees with up to a point."; Interview with Laurence Claus (professor of law, University of San Diego; former John M. Olin Fellow at Northwestern University School of Law) in discussion with the author, March 18, 2008: "I just don't think that judges should be pretending the constitution says something about them when it doesn't; that unelected judges should be trumping majorities in areas where the law doesn't give them a man-date to do it."; Interview with Lee Liberman Otis (Office of Legal Counsel, George H. W. Bush administration; general counsel (2001–2005); cofounder, Federalist Society) in discussion with the author, June 4, 2008: "... the main feeling was that the courts are deciding a lot of questions without reference to anything that the American people had authorized them to decide and that is not what should be happening."; Interview with Lillian BeVier (professor of law, University of Virginia Law School) in discussion with the author, February 1, 2008: "... the over-arching principle is the rule of law... being neces-sary to restrain the Court who seemed to think that they could make it up."; Interview with Michael Carvin (partner, Jones Day; deputy assistant attorney general, Civil Rights Division (1985–1987); deputy assistant attorney general, Office of Legal Counsel (1987–1988)) in discussion with the author, January 28, 2008: "I started reading these opinions and realized they were intellectually bankrupt and started getting firmer in my views about the need for a limited judiciary. So I was probably typical of the people who were attached to the Federalist Society in the beginning."; Interview with Michael Rappaport (professor of law, University of San Diego Law School; special assistant, Office of Legal Counsel under President Ronald Reagan) in discussion with the author, March 17, 2008: "If you come from a libertarian slash conservative perspective... you would never believe that judges should be able to rewrite the law to pursue their policy objectives. I mean, the law was the limit on the state. You would never allow the state to rewrite it."

18. See, 1984 National Student Conference: "A Symposium on Judicial Activism: Problems and Responses"; 1987 National Lawyers Conference: "Changing the Law: The Role of Lawyers, Judges, and Legislatures"; 1993 National Student Conference: "Symposium on Judicial Decision Making"; "Symposium on Judicial Decisionmaking: The Role of Text, Precedent, and the Rule of Law" (Transcript reprinted in *Harvard Journal of Law and Public Policy* 17, no. 1 (1994); 1999 National Lawyers Conference: "The Rule of Law, Modern Culture, and the Courts at Century's End"; 2001 National Lawyers Convention: "Judicial Decision-Making"; 2008 National Lawyers Convention: "The People and the Judiciary"; 2008 National Student Conference: "The People and the Courts."

19. See, for example, Interview with Daniel Troy, January 30, 2008: "So I'm sure that some-time during my second year [of law school].... I read Judge Bork's seminal *Indiana Law Journal* article.... So I quickly became a Borkean not only because I was clerking for Judge Bork but because it really spoke to me. And he really sort of articulated my dis-satisfaction [with the courts]."; Interview with Daniel Ortiz, February 6, 2008: "... there had been articles, very influential articles, written in law reviews before that time [on Originalism]. The most famous was probably Bork's piece in the *Indiana Law Journal*."; Interview with Lee Liberman Otis (Office of Legal Counsel, George H. W. Bush administration; general counsel (2001–2005); cofounder, Federalist Society) in discussion with the author, June 4, 2008: "I think initially probably an awful lot of us

started out with Bork's critique of the courts as usurping democracy."; Interview with Lillian BeVier (professor of law, University of Virginia Law School) in discussion with the author, February 1, 2008: "... when I first started teaching in 1970 and I started reading law scholarship and I was interested in constitutional theory, in constitutional structure and the legitimacy of decision-making by the Court in particular, the idea that the Supreme Court can overstep its constitutional boundaries by making things up, making constitutional rights up. I just became interested in that idea... [and], at some point I must've read Robert Bork's 1971 *Indiana Law Journal* piece."; Interview with Michael Carvin (partner, Jones Day; deputy assistant attorney general, Civil Rights Division (1985–1987); deputy assistant attorney general, Office of Legal Counsel (1987–1988)) in discussion with the author, January 28, 2008: "I read Bork's *Indiana Law Journal* article just sort of by accident and it made unbelievable sense to me. And, as I said, part of me becoming more and more conservative was reading these opinions and they were just not intellectually coherent and if you want[ed] some meat you were drawn to people like Bork and Scalia who were making coherent arguments and they were brilliant men and... incredibly persuasive writers. So it just made a lot more sense to me."

20. Interview with Loren A. Smith (judge, U.S. Court of Federal Claims; chairman, Administrative Conference of the United States (1981–1985)) in discussion with the author, January 24, 2008.
21. Interview with Eugene Meyer (president, Federalist Society) in discussion with the author, February 8, 2008.
22. See 1995 National Student Conference: "Originalism, Democracy, and the Constitution" and 2005 National Lawyers Convention: "Originalism."
23. Co-authored by members Roger Clegg and Michael DeBow, the Web-published *Annotated Bibliography of Conservative and Libertarian Legal Scholarship* explains its selection of sources and scholarship in the following manner: "As to what is 'conservative' or 'libertarian' we relied most heavily on the Founders' ideals for guidance. With respect to constitutional law, for example, we searched for works that endeavored to interpret the Constitution according to its text and original meaning."
24. This edited volume, published by Regnery Press (2007) and available from the Federalist Society's online store, contains excerpts from five select panel debates on Originalism from Federalist Society conferences. It also features an introduction by cofounder Steven Calabresi, a foreword by Supreme Court Justice Antonin Scalia, and an epilogue by former Solicitor General Theodore B. Olson and includes famous speeches about Originalism by former Attorney General Edwin Meese, III, Judge Robert H. Bork, and President Ronald Reagan. The website's promotional blurb (see www.fed-soc.org/store/id.471/default.asp) reads: "What did the Constitution mean at the time it was adopted? How should we interpret today the words used by the Founding Fathers? In *Originalism: A Quarter-Century of Debate*, these questions are explained and dissected by the very people who continue to shape the legal structure of our country."
25. See, for example, Interview with Edwin Meese, III (U.S. attorney general under President Ronald Reagan (1985–1988); Fellow, Heritage Foundation) in discussion with the author, February 5, 2008: "I think [the Federalist Society represents] a commitment to the rule of law and a commitment to the Constitution, and from that kind of a body of philosophical principles—Originalism is a part of that."; Interview with Eugene Meyer (president, Federalist Society) in discussion with the author, February 8, 2008: "So those are the two things I think more than anything else that we have done; Originalism and helping to create a broader debate in the law schools and ultimately the legal community at large."; Interview with Michael Rappaport (professor of law, University of San Diego Law School; special assistant,

Office of Legal Counsel under President Ronald Reagan) in discussion with the author, March 17, 2008: "So, now, for example on Originalism there's a good deal of stuff outside of the Federalist Society being done on Originalism but, for a long time, there wouldn't have been so it allows there to be an intellectual interest in the ideas."; Interview with Randy Barnett (professor of legal theory, Georgetown University Law School) in discussion with the author, June 10, 2008: "Once I made the move to Originalism, and not only that, became one of the leading theoretical spokespeople and defenders of the method we had a lot more in common and my relationship to the Federalist Society became much closer after that."; Interview with Richard K. Willard (partner, Steptoe and Johnson, LLP; assistant attorney general, Civil Rights Division under President Ronald Reagan) in discussion with the author, January 31, 2008: "I think there are probably many different viewpoints on a lot of issues within the Society but I would think that most members would believe in Originalism as a school of thought."; Interview with Michael Greve (director of the Federalism Project, American Enterprise Institute) in discussion with the author, February 12, 2008: "Obviously the one thing that Originalism as a theory did for the Federalist Society was it gave them an agenda and a platform."

26. Interview with Daniel Troy (attorney, Sidley Austin, LLP; special assistant, Office of Legal Counsel (1984–1988)) in discussion with the author, January 30, 2008 (Washington, DC).

27. Interview with John Yoo (professor of law, University of California, Berkeley Law School; former law clerk to Judge Laurence H. Silberman and Justice Clarence Thomas; general counsel, U.S. Senate Judiciary Committee (1995–1996); deputy assistant attorney general, Office of Legal Counsel (2001–2003)) in discussion with the author, January 16, 2008 (Berkeley, CA).

28. Interview with Steven Calabresi (professor of law, Northwestern University; cofounder, Federalist Society) in discussion with the author, April 3, 2008 (Chicago, IL).

29. See Federal Society Organization, About Us page, accessed February 16, 2009, www. fed-soc.org/aboutus.

30. Interview with Thomas Smith (professor of law, University of San Diego Law School; senior counsel, President Reagan's Council of Economic Advisors) in discussion with the author, March 19, 2008.

31. Ibid.

32. See, e.g., Brigham 1987; McCann 1994, 1996; Sarat and Kearns 1998; Scheingold 2004.

33. See www.fed-soc.org/events for a small sampling of all the events the Federalist Society sponsors each year.

34. See, for example, personal interview with Michael Greve (director of the Federalism Project, American Enterprise Institute) in discussion with the author, February 12, 2008 (calls Federalist Society Conferences important for the "credentialing of rising stars"); Interview with Tony Cotto (former Student Chapter president at George Washington University Law School, the Federalist Society) in discussion with the author, January 31, 2008 (in the context of why the Federalist Society stalwarts did not accept Harriet Myers as a Supreme Court nominee): "She's not a true believer... [The Federalist Society stalwarts] want credentials, they want to see you've spoken at Fed Society conferences, they want to know you've been at dinners and luncheons, gripping and grinning."

35. Participant observations at a Federalist Society Student Chapter Happy Hour, Recessions Bar, Washington, D.C. February 12, 2008.

36. Sources exhaustively examined include transcripts of National Student Conferences reprinted in the *Harvard Journal of Law and Public Policy*; audio and written transcripts

of National Lawyer Conferences; scholarly articles and books recommended in the Federalist Society's *Annotated Bibliography of Conservative and Libertarian Legal Scholarship*, accessed May 23, 2012, at http://www.fed-soc.org/resources/page/conservative-libertarian-legal-scholarship-annotated-bibliography; scholarly articles and books published by Federalist Society members; Federalist Society Practice Group Newsletters (1996–2000); *Engage* Journal of the Federalist Society Practice Groups (2002–2012); Federalist Society White Papers; relevant other multimedia from events accessible through the Federalist Society's online archive (www.fed-soc.org). In determining network members' shared beliefs, I also relied on data gathered from personal interviews with Federalist Society members in 2008 and archival data gathered from the Ronald Reagan Presidential Library in Simi Valley, CA, in 2008.

37. Individuals clerking for a Supreme Court Justice are not likely to appear at a Federalist Society National Conference as a speaker prior to or concurrent with their clerkship. However, given the important role that clerks play in the researching and writing of Supreme Court opinions (see, e.g., Peppers 2006; Ward and Weiden 2006), I did note their presence as a possible conduit for idea diffusion if the clerk would later go on to become a prominent member of the Federalist Society (John C. Yoo, Sakrishna Prakash, and Paul Cassell, for example, are individuals who were involved with the society prior to clerking but would not be invited to speak at a National Conference until later in their careers) or if they had previously clerked for a lower court judge who is a prominent Federalist Society member (J. Michael Luttig and Laurence Silberman, for example).

38. See http://www.atlasti.com/index.html.

39. To clarify, it was not enough to show that the Supreme Court opinion was in some general sense "Originalist." To count in terms of influence, these Originalist sources, references, or lines of argumentation required proof that they were in fact diffused through a Federalist Society member participating in the litigation and/or through Federalist Society members' published scholarship. If the idea could not be traced to an identifiable source of Federalist Society member scholarship and/or through a brief or lower court opinion authored by a Federalist Society member, it was not considered an indicator of influence.

CHAPTER 2

1. Robert A. Sprecher, "The Lost Amendment." *American Bar Association Journal* 51 (1965): 667.
2. U.S. Const., Amend. II ("A well regulated Militia being necessary for the security of a free State, the right of the People to keep and bear arms shall not be infringed").
3. *United States v. Cruikshank*, 92 U.S. 542 (1876); *Presser v. Illinois*, 116 U.S. 252 (1886); *Miller v. Texas*, 153 U.S. 535 (1894).
4. *Barron v. Baltimore*, 32 U.S. 243 (1833).
5. *United States v. Miller*, 307 U.S. 174 (1939): *178.
6. See, e.g., *Cases v. United States* (1942) (First Circuit), *United States v. Warin* (1976) (Sixth Circuit), and *United States v. Oakes* (1984) (Tenth Circuit).
7. See Federalist Society Organization, About Us page, www.fed-soc.org/aboutus.
8. *Printz v. United States* 521 U.S. 898, (1997): *938.
9. Interview with Loren Smith (judge, U.S. Court of Federal Claims; chairman, Administrative Conference of the United States (1981–1985)) in discussion with the author, January 24, 2008.
10. Interview with David McIntosh (partner, Meyer, Brown and Platt; member of Congress (1995–2001); cofounder, Federalist Society) in discussion with the author, January 25, 2008.

11. See, e.g., Walter Berns, "On Madison and Majoritarianism: A Response to Professor Amar," *Harvard Journal of Law and Public Policy* 15 (1992): 113; Thomas W. Merrill, "The Role of Institutional factors in Protecting Individual Liberties," *Harvard Journal of Law and Public Policy* 15 (1992): 85; Frank H. Easterbrook, "Bills of Rights and Regression to the Mean," *Harvard Journal of Law and Public Policy* 15 (1992): 71; Theodore Olson, "How Effective are Bills of Rights in Protecting Individual Freedoms," *Harvard Journal of Law and Public Policy* 15 (1992): 53.

12. Thomas W. Merrill, "The Role of Institutional Factors in Protecting Individual Liberties," *Harvard Journal of Law and Public Policy* 15 (1992): 85.

13. 107 Stat. 1536. The Brady Act instituted a federal background check system for the purchase of firearms.

14. Alan Gura, *Gun Rights Litigation Update*, Sponsored by the Criminal Law and Procedures Practice Group of the Federalist Society for Law and Public Policy. August 16, 2012, 12:00 EST.

15. Thomas W. Merrill, "The Role of Institutional factors in Protecting Individual Liberties," *Harvard Journal of Law and Public Policy* 15 (1992): 85.

16. Nelson Lund had been featured as a presenter at four Federalist Society National Conferences. See, e.g., 1999 National Lawyers Convention, Civil Rights Group Panel, "Firearms Litigation, Tort Liability, and the Second Amendment"; 2001 National Lawyers Convention, Panel II, "Judicial Decisionmaking: The Case of Judicial Oversight of the Political Process"; 2008 National Lawyers Convention, Civil Rights Panel, "The Heller Case"; 2011 National Student Symposium, Panel I, "Economic Theory, Civic Virtue and the Meaning of the Constitution."

17. Nelson Lund, "The Past and Future of the Individual's Right to Bear Arms," *Georgia Law Review* 31, no. 1 (1996–1997): 2.

18. Eugene Volokh has been a featured presenter nine times at Federalist Society National Conferences. See, e.g., 1999 Annual National Student Symposium, "Freedom of Speech about Political Candidates: The Unintended Consequences of Three Proposals" (transcript reprinted in *Harvard Journal of Law and Public Policy* 24, no. 1 (2000): 47–70); 2001 National Lawyers Convention, Free Speech and Election Law Panel, "The Bartnicki Case and Privacy"; 2002 National Lawyers Convention, Free Speech and Election Law Panel, "Arguing the Slippery Slope"; 2004 National Lawyers Convention, Free Speech and Election Law Panel, "First Amendment: Regulation of False Statements of Fact"; 2005 National Lawyers Convention, Free Speech and Election Law Panel, "What Is the 'Free Press?'"; 2007 National Lawyers Convention, Free Speech and Election Law Panel, "Restricting Parental Speech"; 2008 National Lawyers Convention, Free Speech and Election Law Panel, "Freedom of Speech vs. Anti-Discrimination Laws"; 2008 National Lawyers Convention, Showcase Panel IV, "Showcase Panel IV: Regulation of Judicial Conduct: Silencing Judges or Avoiding Improper Influence"; 2010 National Lawyers Convention, Religious Liberties Panel, "Christian Legal Society v. Martinez."

19. Eugene Volokh, "The Commonplace Second Amendment," *New York University Law Review* 73 (1998): 793, 795.

20. Eugene Volokh, "The Commonplace Second Amendment," *New York University Law Review* 73 (1998): 793, 795.

21. Randy Barnett has been a featured presenter at 12 Federalist Society National Conferences. See, e.g., 1986 Federalist Society National Meeting, "Are Enumerated Constitutional Rights the Only Rights We Have? The Case of Associational Freedom" (transcript reprinted in *Harvard Journal of Law and Public Policy* 10, no. 1 (1987) 101–116; 1988 Annual National Federalist Society Symposium, "Two Conceptions of the Ninth Amendment" (transcript reprinted in *Harvard Journal of Law and Public Policy*

12, no. 1 (1989): 29–42); 1991 National Lawyers Convention, Panel III: The Death of Contract and the Rise of Tort, "Some Problems with Contract as Promise" (transcript reprinted in *Cornell Law Review* 77, no. 5 (1992): 1022–1033); 1995 National Student Symposium, Panel V: Is Originalism Possible? Historical Indeterminacy, "The Relevance of the Framers' Intent" (transcript reprinted in *Harvard Journal of Law and Public Policy* 19, no. 2 (1996): 403–410); 2004 National Lawyers Convention, Federalism and Separation of Powers Panel, "Gay Marriage and Amending the Constitution"; 2005 National Lawyers Convention, Showcase Panel IV, "The Original Meaning of the Commerce, Spending and Necessary & Proper Clauses"; 2007 National Lawyers Convention, Showcase Panel II, "Is American Different from Other Major Western Democracies?"; 2007 Annual Student Symposium, "What Is Morality? The Philosophical and Theological Foundations of Moral Debate"; 2009 National Lawyers Convention, "Constitutional Interpretation and the Bill of Rights"; 2010 Annual Student Symposium, Panel II, "Originalism and Construction: Does Originalism Always Provide the Answer?"; 2010 National Lawyers Convention, Showcase Panel I, "Enumerated Powers: The Tenth Amendment, and Limited Government"; 2011 Annual Student Symposium, "Debate: Economic Freedoms and the Constitution." Barnett also confirmed to me in our personal interview that since he made the move to Originalism, he has found a welcome and receptive home within the Federalist Society network and has strengthened his personal and professional ties with its members (Personal interview with Randy Barnett (professor of legal theory, Georgetown University Law School) in discussion with the author, June 10, 2008).

22. Don Kates is an active member of the Federalist Society Civil Rights Practice Group, who often speaks on issues relating to criminology and Gun Rights. See, e.g., "Discussion about the DC Gun Ban and Its Road to the Supreme Court," George Mason Student Chapter, September 19, 2007, and "Gun Laws & the Heller Case," San Diego Lawyers & Student Chapter, February 20, 2008.

23. Randy Barnett and Don Kates, "Under Fire: The New Consensus on the Second Amendment," *Emory Law Journal* 45 (1996): 1139, 1207.

24. Nelson Lund, "The Past and Future of the Individual's Right to Bear Arms," *Georgia Law Review* 31, no. 1, (1996–1997): 20.

25. For a transcript of the panel discussion, see *Civil Rights Practice Group Newsletter* 3, no. 1 (Spring 1999).

26. See, e.g., Barnett and Kates, supra note 23: 1177–1178; Lund, supra note 24: 12–15, 60–61; and Volokh, supra note 20: 806.

27. See, e.g., Lund supra note 24: 33 and Barnett and Kates, supra note 23: 1208–1209.

28. See, e.g., Barnett and Kates, supra note 23: 1169–1172, 1175–1176, and 1213.

29. Barnett and Kates, supra note 23: 1177–1178 (quoting 3 William Blackstone, Commentaries: 4).

30. Lund, supra note 24: 33.

31. Nelson Lund, "To Keep and Bear Arms." Heritage Guide to the Constitution.

32. "nor shall any State deprive any person of life, liberty, or property, without due process of law."

33. John Harrison, who interviewees confirm was one of the first generation of young Federalist Society members coming out of the Reagan Justice Department (interview with Daniel Troy (attorney, Sidley Austin, LLP; special assistant, Office of Legal Counsel (1984–1988)) in discussion with the author, January 30, 2008), has also been a presenter at eight Federalist Society National Conferences. See, e.g., 1998 National Student Symposium, Panel IV: Federalism in Constitutional Context, "In the Beginning Are the States" (transcript reprinted in *Harvard Journal of Law and Public Policy* 22, no. 1 (1998): 173–180); 1988 National Symposium, Panel IV: The

Role of Legislative and Executive Branches in Interpreting the Constitution (transcript reprinted in *Cornell Law Review* 73, (1988): 371–374); 1991 National Student Symposium, Debate: Should Congress Pass Legislation Overruling the Supreme Court's Decision in the Peyote Case?, "The Free Exercise Clause as a Rule about Rules" (transcript reprinted in *Harvard Journal of Law and Public Policy* 15, no. 1 (1992): 169–180); 2002 National Student Symposium, Panel II: Originalism and Historical Truth, "Forms of Originalism and the Study of History" (transcript reprinted in *Harvard Journal of Law and Public Policy* 26, no. 1 (2003): 83–94); 2005 National Lawyers Convention, Showcase Panel I: Originalism and Unenumerated Constitutional Rights; 2006 Annual Student Symposium, Panel: Enforceablity of International Tribunals' Decisions in the U.S.; 2009 Annual Student Symposium, Panel IV: The Administrative State and the Constitution; 2010 Annual Student Symposium, Panel IV: Does the Originalism of the Fourteenth Amendment Guarantee Justice for All?

34. Michael Kent Curtis has been a featured presenter at two National Conferences. See, e.g., 1988 National Federalist Society Symposium, "Privileges or Immunities, Individual Rights, and Federalism" (transcript reprinted in *Harvard Journal of Law and Public Policy* 12, no. 1 (1989): 53–62); 1999 National Lawyers Convention, Showcase Panel: Back to the Future—What 21st Century Legal Culture Can Learn from the 19th Century's First Amendment.

35. "No State shall make or enforce any law which shall abridge the privileges or immunities of citizens of the United States."

36. "Firearms Litigation, Tort Liability, and the Second Amendment—A Symposium." *Civil Rights Practice Group Newsletter* 3, no. 3 (February 1, 2000).

37. Lund, supra note 24: 50.

38. Thomas Burrell, "Is There Anything 'Fundamental' in the Right to Keep and Bear Arms? A Call for Parity in the Incorporation Doctrine." *Engage* 9, no. 1 (February 2008): 26.

39. Ibid., 22.

40. John Harrison, "Reconstructing the Privileges or Immunities Clause." *Yale Law Journal 101* (1992): 1385, 1465.

41. 83 U.S. 36 (1873).

42. For a more detailed account of this case and its implications for the Privileges Or Immunities Clause, see Charles Black, *A New Birth of Freedom: Human Rights Named and Unnamed* (New Haven, CT: Yale University Press, 1997), 41–85.

43. John Harrison, "Reconstructing the Privileges or Immunities Clause." *Yale Law Journal 101* (1992): 1385.

44. Barnett and Kates, supra note 23: 1156.

45. Panel III: Federalism and the Scope of the Federal Criminal Law (James L. Buckley, William Van Alstyne, David B. Sentelle, Joseph E. diGenova, G. Robert Blakey). Transcript reprinted in *American Criminal Law Review* 26 (1988–1989): 1737–1778.

46. William Van Alstyne, "The Second Amendment and the Personal Right to Arms." *Duke Law Journal 43* (1993–1994): 1236.

47. Ibid., 1251–1252 ("[t]he immunities of citizens with respect to rights previously secured only from abridging acts of Congress were recast in the Fourteenth Amendment as immunities secured also from any similar act by any state. It was precisely in this manner that the citizen's right to keep and bear arms, formerly protected only from acts of Congress, came to be equally protected from abridging acts of the sates as well").

48. Michael Kent Curtis, *No State Shall Abridge: The Fourteenth Amendment and the Bill of Rights* (Durham, NC: Duke University Press, 1987), 104.

49. Transcript reprinted in *Harvard Journal of Law and Public Policy* 12 (1989): 53–61.

50. Ibid., 53.

51. *Printz v. United States,* 521 U.S. 898, Thomas, J. concurring: *938–939.
52. DC ST § 7-2501.01 et seq.
53. Council Act No. *694 1–142, Hearing and Disposition before the House Committee on the District of Columbia, 94th Cong., 2d Sess., on H. Con. Res. 694, Ser. No. 94–24, p. 25 (1976).
54. D.C. Code Ann. Tit. 22, §§93201–3217, Arts. 50–56 (D.C. Police Regulations).
55. D.C. Code § 7-2507.02.
56. (Council Act No. *694 1–142), 25.
57. Paul Duggan, "Lawyer Who Wiped Out D.C. Ban Says It's about Liberties, Not Guns." *Washington Post,* March 18, 2007, A01.
58. Adam Liptak, "Carefully Plotted Course Propels Gun Case to Top." *New York Times,* December 3, 2007, 16.
59. 311 F.Supp.2d 103.
60. F.3d, 2012 WL 1450561.
61. See 478 F. 3d 370 (Silberman, J, majority).
62. Since Justice Scalia is notorious for only selecting clerks with Federalist Society credentials, and since there were no concurring or separate opinions in *Heller,* in Figure 2.1 I have noted Justice Scalia's four law clerks at the time as conduits through which Federalist Society intellectual capital might have been diffused (Aditya Bamzai, John F. Bash III, Bryan M. Killian, and Rachel P. Kovner). All but one (Bryan M. Killian) also previously clerked for a Federalist Society–affiliated lower court judge.
63. See, e.g., 1989 National Lawyers Convention, Panel I, "Agency Autonomy and the Unitary Executive" (transcript reprinted in *Washington University Law Quarterly* 68, no. 3 (1990): 495–499); 1992 National Lawyers Convention, Luncheon Address, "The Clarence Thomas Confirmation: A Retrospective" (transcript reprinted in *Cumberland Law Review* 23, no. 1 (1993): 141–154); 1994 Annual Student Symposium, Panel IV: "Feminism, Children, and the Family" (transcript reprinted in *Harvard Journal of Law and Public Policy* 18, no. 2 (1995): 501–503); 1995 National Lawyers Convention, Address, "The D.C. Circuit Task Force on Gender, Race, and Ethnic bias: Political Correctness Rebuffed" (transcript reprinted in *Harvard Journal of Law and Public Policy* 19, no 3 (1996): 759–766); 2002 National Lawyers Convention, Convention Luncheon Speaker; 2009 Annual Student Symposium, Banquet Keynote Speaker.
64. In addition to being actively involved in the Federalist Society's Civil Rights Practice Group, Clark Neily was invited to present on gun rights at the 2008 National Lawyers Convention. See Civil Rights Panel, "The Heller Case."
65. In addition to being on the Federalist Society's Board of Visitors, Robert Levy has been an invited presenter at three Federalist Society National Conferences. See, e.g., 2002 National Lawyers Convention, Civil Rights Panel, "Privacy in the Post-September 11 World"; 2003 National Lawyers Convention, Special Session, "Civil Liberties and the War on Terror"; 2004 National Lawyers Convention, "Litigation: Regulation Through Litigation."
66. Alan Gura is an active member of the Federalist Society's Civil Rights Practice Group and has participated in dozens of lawyer chapter events on the Second Amendment and gun rights. See, e.g., Federalist Society Debate, "Parker v. District of Columbia: DC Gun Ban Case," August 31, 2007; "D.C. v. Heller and the Future of Gun Control Legislation," Fordham Student Chapter, January 22, 2009; "Reception and Remarks with Alan Gura," Minnesota Lawyers Chapter, January 23, 2013.
67. Brief for Amici Curiae Former Senior Officials of the Department of Justice in Support of Respondent, 2008 WL 405551 (U.S.) (Charles J. Cooper, Edwin Meese III, William P. Barr, George J. Terwilliger III, Robert H. Bork, Viet Dinh, Timothy E. Flanigan, Douglas W. Kmiec, Jack Goldsmith, and Richard K. Willard); Brief Amicus Curiae of

the Heartland Institute in Support of Respondent, 2008 WL 405555 (U.S.) (Richard K. Willard, Eugene Volokh); Brief of the Second Amendment Foundation as Amicus Curiae Supporting Respondent, 2008 WL 383529 (Nelson Lund); Amicus Brief of the American Center for Law and Justice in Support of Respondent, 2008 WL 383518 (Jay Alan Sekulow); Amicus Curiae Brief of the Goldwater Institute in Support of Respondent, 2008 WL 405566 (U.S.) (Clint Bolick, Bradford A. Berenson); Brief of the States of Texas, Alabama, Alaska, Arkansas, Colorado, Florida, Georgia, Idaho, Indiana, Kansas, Kentucky, Louisiana, Michigan, Minnesota, Mississippi, etc., 2008 WL 40558 (R. Ted Cruz, Steve Carter, Michael A. Cox, Robert M. McKenna); Brief of Criminologists, Social Scientists, Other Distinguished Scholars at the Claremont Institute as Amici Curiae (Don B. Kates); Amicus Curiae Brief of the Libertarian National Committee, Inc. In Support of Respondent (2008 WL 391284 (Bob Barr)).

68. As several interviewees confirmed, Ed Meese III was one of the earliest patrons of the fledgling Federalist Society group, hiring many of its founding members into the Department of Justice as special assistants in the 1980s and providing some institutional support and legitimacy for the group in its early years. I have documented these ties extensively in Hollis-Brusky 2011b.

69. See Federal Society Website, May 23, 2013, http://www.fed-soc.org/publications/page/civil-rights-practice-group-executive-committee-contact-information.

70. 2008 WL 405551 (U.S.) (Appellate Brief).

71. Edwin Meese III, Richard K. Willard, Charles J. Cooper, and Douglas Kmiec were involved in the drafting of this brief at the time I interviewed them. Each one mentioned it to me, unsolicited, as an example of the way in which the Federalist Society network had kept them in contact with one another after leaving the Reagan Justice Department and facilitated their collaborative efforts on this brief in particular.

72. Interview with Edwin Meese III (U.S. attorney general under President Ronald Reagan (1985–1988); Fellow, Heritage Foundation) in discussion with the author, February 5, 2008.

73. Interview with Douglas Kmiec (professor of law, Pepperdine University; Office of Legal Counsel under Presidents Ronald Reagan and George H. W. Bush) in discussion with the author, March 14, 2008.

74. *Heller,* *577.

75. Ibid., *584–585 (Scalia, J., majority) (citing Eugene Volokh, State Constitutional Rights to Keep and Bear Arms, *Texas Review of Law and Politics* 11 (2006): 191).

76. .Ibid., *597 (Scalia, J., majority).

77. Ibid., *587 (Scalia, J., majority) ("And the phrases used primarily in those military discussions include not only 'bear arms' but also 'carry arms,' 'possess arms,' and 'have arms'—though no one thinks that those *other* phrases also had special military meanings. See Barnett, "Was the Right to Keep and Bear Arms Conditioned on Service in an Organized Militia?" *Texas Law Review* 83 (2004): 237, 261).

78. See Brief of the Second Amendment Foundation as Amicus Curiae Supporting Respondent, 2008 WL 383529 (Nelson Lund): *14.

79. Interview with Randy Barnett (professor of legal theory, Georgetown University Law School) in discussion with the author, June 10, 2008.

80. 130 S. Ct. 3020 (2010).

81. Chicago, Ill., Municipal Code § 8-20-050 et seq.

82. Chicago, Ill., Journal of Proceedings of the City Council 10049 (1982).

83. Fred Barbash, "Illinois Suburb Inspires a National Drive for Handgun Controls," *Washington Post*, March 1, 1982, A9.

84. Lea Donosky et al., "A New Push for Gun Control," *Newsweek*, March 15, 1982, 22.

85. 130 S. Ct. 3026–27.

86. Ibid.
87. Ibid.
88. Ibid.
89. *NRA, Inc. v. Village of Oak Park*, 617 F. Supp. 2d 752, 753 (N.D. Ill. 2008) (citing *Quilici v. Village of Morton Grove*, 695 F.2d 261 (7th Cir. 1982)).
90. 92 U.S. 542 (1876).
91. 116 U.S. 252 (1886).
92. 153 U.S. 535 (1894).
93. *Slaughter-House Cases*, 16 Wall. 36, 21 L.Ed. 394.
94. *McDonald*, 130 S.Ct. 3027.
95. Ibid., 3028.
96. Ibid.
97. Ibid., 3025, 3036.
98. Amicus Curiae Brief of the American Center for Law and Justice in Support of Petitioners, WL 4049146 (Jay Alan Sekulow), Brief of the States Texas, Ohio, Arkansas, Georgia, Alabama, Alaska, Arizona, Colorado, etc., 2009 WL 4378909 (James C. Ho, Richard Corday, Michael A. Cox, Robert M. McKenna); Brief Amicus Curiae of Cato Institute and Pacific Legal Foundation in Support of Petitioners, 2009 WL 4030387 (Robert A. Levy); Brief Amicus Curiae of Center for Constitutional Jurisprudence in Support of Petitioners, 2009 WL 4049148 (John C. Eastman, Edwin Meese III); Brief of Constitutional Law Professors as Amici Curiae in Support of Petitioners, 2009 WL 4099504 (Douglas T. Kendall); Brief for the Goldwater Institute, Scharf-Norton Center for Constitutional Government, and Wyoming Liberty Group as Amici Curiae Supporting Petitioners, 2009 WL 4247970 (Clint Bolick); Brief of Amicus Curiae Institute for Justice in Support of Petitioners, 2009 WL 4099506 (Clark M. Neily III).
99. In addition to being an active member of the Federalist Society's Civil Rights Practice Group, Clint Bolick has been a presenter at four National Conferences. See 1990 Annual Symposium, Panel V: New Frontiers in Civil Rights, "Unfinished Business: A Civil Rights Strategy for America's Third Century" (transcript reprinted in *Harvard Journal of Law and Public Policy* 114, no. 1 (1991): 137–141); 1996 Annual Student Symposium, Panel II: Justice for All? "Civil Rights and the Criminal Justice System" (transcript reprinted in *Harvard Journal of Law and Public Policy* 20, no. 2 (1997): 391–396); 2006 National Lawyers Convention, Civil Rights Panel, "Civil Rights in the 21st Century"; 2004 National Lawyers Convention, Showcase Panel IV, "Brown and School Choice."
100. John C. Eastman has been an invited presenter at seven Federalist Society National Conferences. See 2001 National Lawyers Convention, Showcase Panel I, "Judicial Decisionmaking: The Case of Life, Liberty and Property in the Modern Technological Age"; 2003 National Lawyers Convention, "Environmental Law and Property Rights"; 2004 National Lawyers Convention, "Federalism and Separation of Powers: Gay Marriage and Amending the Constitution"; 2007 National Lawyers Convention, "Federalism: Religion, Early America and the Fourteenth America"; 2008 National Lawyers Convention, "Federalism: The Roberts Court and Federalism"; 2009 National Lawyers Convention, "Federalism and the Economic Crisis"; 2010 National Lawyers Convention, "Federalism: Is There Any Remaining Limit to Federal Power."
101. In addition to clerking for Federalist Society members Judge Laurence H. Silberman and Justice Antonin Scalia, Paul Clement has been a presenter at four Federalist Society National Conferences. See 2001 National Lawyers Convention, Showcase Panel II, "Judicial Decisionmaking: The Case of Judicial Oversight of the Political Process"; 2005 National Lawyers Convention, "Address"; 2006 National Lawyers Convention, "Welcome and Opening Address"; 2008 National Lawyers Convention, "The Roberts Court and Federalism."

102. Kevin Martin has been a participant in three Federalist Society National Conventions. See 2004 National Lawyers Convention, "Telecommunications: Emerging Technologies and the Role of the Federal and State Regulators"; 2005 National Lawyers Convention, "Address"; 2008 National Lawyers Convention, "Telecommunications: The FCC and the First Amendment."

103. Of the seven, the only brief that did not lobby for the privileges or immunities path was Brief of the States Texas, Ohio, Arkansas, Georgia, Alabama, Alaska, Arizona, Colorado, etc., 2009 WL 4378909 (James C. Ho, Richard Corday, Michael A. Cox, Robert M. McKenna).

104. See Amicus Brief for Academics for the Second Amendment in Support of the Petitioners, 2009 WL 4099518 (Prof Joseph Edward Olson and David T. Hardy, Counsels of Record); Brief of the American Civil Rights Union, Let Freedom Ring, Committee for Justice, and the Family Research Council, as Amici Curiae in Support of Petitioners, 2009 WL 4099513 (Peter J. Ferrara, Counsel of Record).

105. *National Rifle Association of America, Inc., v. City of Chicago, Illinois, and Village of Oak Park, Illinois*, 567 F. 3d 856 (2009) (Seventh Circuit): *858–860.

106. See Federalist Society Statement of Principles, May 21, 2013, http://www.fed-soc.org/aboutus/page/our-background.

107. See "A Symposium on Judicial Activism: Problems and Responses" (transcript reprinted in *Harvard Journal of Law and Public Policy* 7, no. 1 (1984): 87–100); "The First Annual Federalist Society Lawyers Convention" (transcript reprinted in *Harvard Journal of Law and Public Policy* 11, no. 1 (1988): 59–66); "Symposium on Judicial Decisionmaking: The Role of Text, Precedent, and the Rule of Law" (transcript reprinted in *Harvard Journal of Law and Public Policy* 17, no. 1 (1994): 61–70); 2001 National Lawyers Convention: "Judicial Decisionmaking" (audio available at www.fed-soc.org) 2008 National Lawyer's Convention: "The People and the Judiciary" (audio available at www.fed-soc.org); 2008 Annual Student Symposium: "The People and the Courts" (audio available at www.fed-soc.org).

108. See, e.g., "A Symposium on Judicial Activism: Problems and Responses" (transcript reprinted in *Harvard Journal of Law and Public Policy* 7, no. 1 (1984): 1–176); "The First Annual Federalist Society Lawyers Convention" (transcript reprinted in *Harvard Journal of Law and Public Policy* 11, no. 1 (1988): 1–110); "Symposium on Judicial Decisionmaking: The Role of Text, Precedent, and the Rule of Law" (transcript reprinted in *Harvard Journal of Law and Public Policy* 17, no. 1 (1994); 1–156); "Federalism and Judicial Mandates" (transcript reprinted in *Arizona State Law Journal* 28, no. 1 (1996): 17–222); 1999 Federalist Society National Lawyers Conference: "The Rule of Law, Modern Culture, and the Courts at Century's End"; (Federalist Society National Lawyers Conference, 1999); 2001 National Lawyers Convention: "Judicial Decisionmaking" (audio available at www.fed-soc.org) 2008 National Lawyer's Convention: "The People and the Judiciary" (audio available at www.fed-soc.org); 2008 Annual Student Symposium: "The People and the Courts" (audio available at www.fed-soc.org).

109. In asking 34 key members of the Federalist Society network to identify a unifying principle or set of principles within the Federalist Society, a belief in Originalism received the most mentions (31) and a belief in judicial restraint received the second-most mentions (25).

110. Interview with Gail Heriot (professor of law, University of San Diego; Commissioner, United States Commission on Civil Rights) in discussion with the author, March 18, 2008. See also, e.g., Interview with Charles J. Cooper (founding member and chairman of Cooper & Kirk, PLLC; assistant attorney general for the Office of Legal Counsel (1985–1988)) in discussion with the author, June 2, 2008 ("[The Federalist Society] was founded on some beliefs that, philosophical beliefs or premises, that I

very much shared. A belief in a restrained judiciary, in the importance of adhering
to the original meaning. . . . I was and still am very opposed to and concerned about
the judicial activism and its consequences."); see also Interview with Douglas Kmiec
(professor of law, Pepperdine University; Office of Legal Counsel under Presidents
Ronald Reagan and George H. W. Bush) in discussion with the author, March 14, 2008
(". . . the standard things like federal-state relations and the separation of powers, the
nature of the judicial function, there are some stand-bys. . ."); Interview with Loren
Smith (judge, U.S. Court of Federal Claims; chairman, Administrative Conference
of the United States (1981–1985)) in discussion with the author, January 24, 2008. ("I
think [the Federalist Society] has made it respectable to debate whether government
has gotten too big and whether judges, by their decisions, are undermining the constitution."); Interview with Lee Liberman Otis (Office of Legal Counsel, George H. W.
Bush Administration; general counsel (2001–2005); cofounder, Federalist Society) in
discussion with the author, June 4, 2008; (". . . the main feeling was that the courts are
deciding a lot of questions without reference to anything that the American people had
authorized them to decide and that is not what should be happening."); Interview with
Lillian BeVier, February 1, 2008 ("I think that consistent throughout is the rule of law.
. . being necessary to restrain the Court who seemed to think that they could make it
up.").

111. *McDonald*, supra note 94: *3029 (Alito, J, majority).
112. Ibid., *3030–3031.
113. Calabresi and Agudo, "Individual Rights under State Constitutions When the
Fourteenth Amendment Was Ratified in 1868: What Rights Are Deeply Rooted in
American History and Tradition?" *Texas Law Review* 87 (2008): 7, 50.
114. *McDonald*, supra note 94: *3042 (Alito, J., majority).
115. Ibid., *3050 (Scalia, J., concurring).
116. *McDonald, supra* note 94: *3118–3119 (Stevens, J., dissenting) ("Justice Scalia's method
invites not only bad history, but also bad constitutional law. . . . Not only can historical
views be less than completely clear or informative, but they can also be wrong. Some
notions that many Americans deeply believed to be true, at one time, turned out not
to be true. Some practices that many Americans believed to be consistent with the
Constitution's guarantees of liberty and equality, at one time, turned out to be inconsistent with them. The fact that we have a written Constitution does not consign this
Nation to a static legal existence. Although we should always 'pa[y] a decent regard
to the opinions of former times,' it 'is not the glory of the people of America' to have
'suffered a blind veneration for antiquity.' *The Federalist No. 14*, p. 99, 104 (C. Rossiter
ed. 1961) (J. Madison). It is not the role of federal judges to be amateur historians.
And it is not fidelity to the Constitution to ignore its use of deliberately capacious language, in an effort to transform foundational legal commitments into narrow rules of
decision.").
117. See Steven G. Calabresi (ed.), *Originalism: A Quarter-Century Debate* (Washington,
DC: Regnery: 2007), 43–45.
118. See Antonin Scalia, "Foreword," in Steven G. Calabresi (ed.), *Originalism: A Quarter
Century Debate* (Washington, DC: Regnery, 2008), See also 1985 Federalist Society
National Meeting, Antonin Scalia, "Morality, Pragmatism, and the Legal Order"
(transcript reprinted at *Harvard Journal of Law and Public Policy* 9, no. 1 (1986): 123).
See also the Seventh Annual National Federalist Society Symposium in 1988, Antonin
Scalia, "Is There an Unwritten Constitution?" (transcript reprinted in *Harvard Journal
of Law and Public Policy* 12, no. 1 (1989): 1).
119. *McDonald, supra* note 94: *3057–3058 (Scalia, J., concurring).
120. Ibid., *3088 (Thomas, J., concurring).

121. Ibid., *3071 ("Evidence from the political branches in the years leading to the Fourteenth Amendment's adoption demonstrates broad public understanding that the privileges and immunities of United States citizenship included rights set forth in the Constitution. . . . M. Curtis, No State Shall Abridge: The Fourteenth Amendment and the Bill of Rights 57 (1985) (hereinafter Curtis))" (Thomas J. concurring); *3075 ("There is much else in the legislative record. Many statements by Members of Congress corroborate the view that the Privileges or Immunities Clause enforced constitutionally enumerated rights against the states. See Curtis 112 (collecting examples))" (Thomas J. concurring); *3076 ("Even opponents of Fourteenth Amendment enforcement legislation acknowledged that the Privileges or Immunities Clause protected constitutionally enumerated individual rights. . . see Curtis 166–170 (collecting examples)"); *3078, and *3087 ("Cruikshank's holding that blacks could look only to state governments for protection of their right to keep and bear arms enabled private forces, often with assistance of local governments, to subjugate the newly freed slaves and their descendants through a wave of private violence designed to drive blacks from the voting booth and force them into peonage, an effective return to slavery. Without federal enforcement of the inalienable right to keep and bear arms, these militias and mobs were tragically successful in waging a campaign of terror against the very people the Fourteenth Amendment had just made citizens. . . Curtis 156") (Thomas, J., concurring).

122. See Amicus Curiae Brief of the American Center for Law and Justice in Support of Petitioners, WL 4049146 (Jay Alan Sekulow): 18–19; Brief Amicus Curiae of Cato Institute and Pacific Legal Foundation in Support of Petitioners, 2009 WL 4030387 (Robert A. Levy): 3, 15, 17–18, 23; Brief Amicus Curiae of Center for Constitutional Jurisprudence in Support of Petitioners, 2009 WL 4049148 (John C. Eastman, Edwin Meese III): 7, 33; Brief of Constitutional Law Professors as Amici Curiae in Support of Petitioners, 2009 WL 4099504 (Douglas T. Kendall) 6, 20, 25, 33; Brief for the Goldwater Institute, Scharf-Norton Center for Constitutional Government, and Wyoming Liberty Group as Amici Curiae Supporting Petitioners, 2009 WL 4247970 (Clint Bolick): 21; Brief of Amicus Curiae Institute for Justice in Support of Petitioners, 2009 WL 4099506 (Clark M. Neily III): 9; Petitioner Brief, 2009 WL 4378912 (Alan Gura): 14.

123. Amicus Curiae Brief of the American Center for Law and Justice in Support of Petitioners, WL 4049146 (Jay Alan Sekulow).

124. See 2007 Federalist Society National Lawyers Convention, "Shining City upon a Hill: American Exceptionalism," (accessed May 28, 2013), http://www.fed-soc.org/publications/pubID.452/pub_detail.asp.

125. Amicus Curiae Brief of the American Center for Law and Justice in Support of Petitioners, WL 4049146 (Jay Alan Sekulow): *3–8.

126. *McDonald*, supra note 94: *3063–3064 (Thomas, J., concurring).

127. Interview with Douglas Kmiec (professor of law, Pepperdine University; Office of Legal Counsel under Presidents Ronald Reagan and George H. W. Bush) in discussion with the author, March 14, 2008.

128. Interview with Randy Barnett (professor of legal theory, Georgetown University Law School) in discussion with the author, June 10, 2008 (Washington, DC) ("So when you ask me who are the big figures, Scalia is obviously because he's a Supreme Court Justice, because he writes opinions that fire people up and because a lot of people agree with him or want to agree. People need, everybody needs icons, everybody needs heroes. He serves that role, Justice Thomas serves that role for many people too. But, because he's quieter and not as caustic and not as combative, he doesn't get the attention that Justice Scalia does").

129. Randy Barnett, "The Second Amendment and the states." *Wall Street Journal (Online)*, March 2, 2010.

130. Robert A. Levy, "Second Amendment Aftermath." *Washington Times*, July 3, 2008, A22.

131. George F. Will, "Reinventing the Second Amendment." *Washington Post*, November 23, 2008, B07.

132. Federalist Society Teleforum Call, "Gun Rights Litigation Update with Professor Nelson Lund and Mr. Alan Gura." August 16, 2012.

133. Judge Diane Sykes is a six-time Federalist Society National Conference Participant (2007 National Lawyer's Convention; 2007 Annual Student Symposium; 2008 National Lawyer's Convention; 2009 National Lawyer's Convention; 2010 Annual Student Symposium; 2011 Annual Student Symposium).

134. *Ezell v. City of Chicago*, 7th Circuit 10-3525 (2011) (Sykes, J., majority).

135. Judge Richard Posner is a three-time Federalist Society National Conference Participant and, in fact, was an invited participant at the very first Federalist Society National Meeting in 1982 (First Federalist Society National Meeting—A Symposium on Federalism (1982); Federalist Society Sixth Annual Symposium (1988); 2008 National Lawyer's Convention). Interestingly, Posner wrote a rather scathing review of Justice Scalia's majority opinion in *Heller*, in the *New Republic*, accusing the Justice of misusing history and misapplying Originalism in his opinion. See Richard A Posner, "In Defense of Looseness," *The New Republic*, August 27, 2008 (accessed May 29, 2013), http://www.newrepublic.com/article/books/defense-looseness#.

136. *Moore v. Madigan*, 7th Cir. 12-1269, 12-1788 (2012) (Posner, J., majority).

137. As Adam Winkler noted in a Federalist Society Teleforum debating the merits of the Seventh Circuit decision, "in the wake of the Heller case the vast majority of courts have been eager to uphold challenged gun control laws. In fact, there's been something like 400 lower court decisions on the constitutionality of gun control laws since the Heller case was decided in 2008, the vast majority of those cases—all but six or seven of them—have upheld the challenged law and where the law has been struck down, it's usually been an extreme outlier law." Federalist Society Teleforum Call, "Controlling Gun Control?: The Seventh Circuit Steps In with Kenneth A. Klukowski, Adam Winkler, Dean A. Reuter." March 20, 2013.

138. Randy Barnett, "The Supreme Court's Gun Showdown." *Wall Street Journal*, June 30, 2010, 15.

139. Ibid.

140. Ibid.

141. Lillian BeVier has been an invited speaker at 15 Federalist Society National Conferences. See, e.g., 1986 National Meeting, "Hands off the Political Process" (transcript reprinted in *Harvard Journal of Law and Public Policy* 10, no. 1 (1987): 11–14); 1988 National Symposium, "What Privacy Is Not" (transcript reprinted in *Harvard Journal of Law and Public Policy* 12, no. 1 (1989): 99–104); 1993 Annual Student Symposium, Panel I: The Enterprise of Judging, "Judicial Restraint: An Argument from Institutional Design" (transcript reprinted in *Harvard Journal of Law and Public Policy* 17, no. 1 (1994): 7–12); 1994 Annual Student Symposium, Panel II: The Constitution on Sex, "Thoughts from a 'Real' Woman" (transcript reprinted in *Harvard Journal of Law and Public Policy* 18, no. 2 (1995): 457–464); 1995 Annual Student Symposium, Panel II: Constitutionalism and Originalism, "The Integrity and Impersonality of Originalism" (transcript reprinted in *Harvard Journal of Law and Public Policy* 19, no. 2 (1996): 283–292); 1997 Annual Student Symposium, Panel I: What Is the "Law" in Law and Economics?, "Law, Economics, and the Power of the State" (transcript reprinted in *Harvard Journal of Law and Public Policy* 21, no. 1 (1997): 5–10); 1998 Annual Student Symposium, Panel II: Congress and the Judiciary, "Religion in Congress and the

Courts: Issues of Institutional Competence" (transcript reprinted in *Harvard Journal of Law and Public Policy* 22, no. 1 (1998): 59–66); 2000 National Lawyers Convention, "Special Forum: The State of Legal Education"; 2001 National Lawyers Convention, Free Speech and Election Law Panel, "The Bartnicki Case and Privacy"; 2004 National Lawyers Convention, "Professional Responsibility: Congressional Evaluation of Judicial Nominees"; 2005 National Lawyers Convention, Free Speech and Election Law Panel, "What Is the 'Free Press?'"; 2007 Annual Student Symposium, "Government Promotion of Moral Issues"; 2008 National Lawyers Convention, Free Speech and Election Law Panel, "Freedom of Speech vs. Anti-Discrimination Laws"; 2010 National Lawyers Convention, Showcase Panel IV, "Ideas for Structural Change: Term Limits, Revving the Right to Civil Jury Trial, Moving Administrative Law Judges to Article III, and Others"; 2011 Annual Student Symposium, "Welcome and Opening Remarks."

142. Interview with Lillian BeVier (professor of law, University of Virginia Law School) in discussion with the author, February 1, 2008.

CHAPTER 3

1. 558 U.S. 310 (2010).
2. Kenneth P. Vogel, "Supreme Court Opens Floodgates for Corporate, Union Political Contributions." *St. Paul Pioneer Press*, January 20, 2010.
3. Editorial, "Judicial Activism Inc.: The Supreme Court Tosses Out Reasonable Limits on Campaign Finance." *The Washington Post*, January 22, 2010.
4. Jess Bravin, "Court Kills Limits on Corporate Politicking." *Wall Street Journal*, January 22, 2010.
5. See, e.g., Robert Barnes, "Alito's State of the Union Moment." *The Washington Post*, January 27, 2010. Available at http://voices.washingtonpost.com/44/2010/01/alito-mouths-not-true-at-obama.html.
6. Ibid.
7. House Subcommittee on the Constitution, Civil Rights, and Civil Liberties, Committee on the Judiciary. "First Amendment and Campaign Finance Reform After Citizens United." Wednesday, February 3, 2010.
8. Ibid., 1.
9. Jeffrey Toobin, "Money Unlimited." *The New Yorker*, May 21, 2012. Available at http://www.newyorker.com/reporting/2012/05/21/120521fa_fact_toobin?currentPage=5 (accessed January 3, 2014).
10. 424 U.S. 1 (1976).
11. 435 U.S. 765 (1978).
12. 494 U.S. 652 (1990).
13. U.S. Const., Amend. I ("Congress shall make no law... abridging the freedom of speech").
14. See, e.g., Silverstein 2009, 167 ("[the phrase 'money is speech'] appears not in support of the majority's conclusions, but in a partial *dissent* by Justice Byron White. The argument that 'money is speech,' Justice White writes, is one that 'proves entirely too much,' because there are so many activities that the government regulates that do, in some sense, have an effect on speech").
15. *First Nat. Bank of Boston v. Bellotti*, 435 U.S. 765, 786 (1978).
16. Ibid.
17. A Lexis Nexis Academic Search performed on May 22, 2013, for "*First National Bank v. Bellotti*" in All News Sources revealed only two mentions of the case the year it was handed down: "Corporate Free Speech Backed." *Facts on File World News Digest*, May 12, 1978, U.S. Affairs; Richard E Cohen, "New Lobbying Rules May Influence Grass-Roots Political Action." *The National Journal*, May 27, 1978.

18. See, e.g., Linda Greenhouse "Over the Cliff." *New York Times Blogs (Opinionator)*, August 24, 2011. ("I fell into a Supreme Court time warp the other day. Preparing to teach a seminar this fall on the court under Chief Justice Warren E. Burger—the court of the 1970s and mid-'80s—I picked up for the first time in many years a decision from 1978, *First National Bank of Boston v. Bellotti*. The case is not well-known today, although it should be. It was the decision that really opened the door to corporate money in politics, leading 32 years later to a very well-known case: *Citizens United*").

19. "The Big Question: What's the Most Important Supreme Court Case No One's Ever Heard of?" *The Atlantic*, May 2013. Available at http://www.theatlantic.com/maga zine/archive/2013/05/the-big-question/309290/. (accessed January 7, 2014).

20. See, e.g., *Federal Election Com. v. Central Long Island Tax Reform Immediately Committee*, 616 F. 2d 45 (Second Circuit) (1980); *Marshall v. Stevens People & Friends for Freedom*, 669 F. 2d 171 (Fourth Circuit) (1981); *Taxation with Representation v. Regan*, 676 F. 2d 715 (D.C. Circuit) (1982); *Federal Election Co. v. Massachusetts Citizens for Life, Inc.*, 769 F. 2d 13 (First Circuit) (1985) *William E Brock v. Local 375*, 860 F. 2d (1988).

21. See "Symposium: The 1986 Federalist Society National Meeting" (transcript reprinted in *Harvard Journal of Law and Public Policy* 10, no. 1 (1987): 1–26 and 53–74).

22. 494 U. S. 652.

23. *Austin*, supra note 22, at 660.

24. The ACLU with Joel Gora as the counsel of record and a group filing of the AMA, National Association of Realtors, American Insurance Association, with Carter Phillips as the counsel of record.

25. See, e.g., 494 U.S. 652 (1990). Kennedy, J. dissenting, at *699–700 ("[t]he protection afforded core political speech is not diminished because the speaker is a nonprofit cor- poration. Even in the case of a for-profit corporation, we have upheld the right to speak on ballot issues. The Bellotti Court stated: 'If the speakers here were not corporations, no one would suggest that the State could silence their proposed speech. . .'")

26. For a catalogue of this Practice Group's Newsletters from 1996 to 2000, see http://www. fed-soc.org/publications/page/free-speech-election-law-practice-group-newsletters (accessed May 22, 2013).

27. See Urofsky 2005, 109 ("The original version of the BCRA had been introduced as senate Bill 1219 in the 104th Congress in September 1995. . . The bill never made it out of committee, but at each succeeding session of Congress, Senators John McCain (R-Ariz.) and Russell D Feingold (D-Wis.) reintroduced a version of their bipartisan campaign proposal").

28. Mitch McConnell, "Campaign Finance 'Reform': A View from Capitol Hill." *Free Speech & Election Law Practice Group Newsletter 1*, no. 1 (Fall 1996). Available at http://www. fed-soc.org/publications/detail/campaign-finance-reform-a-view-from-capitol-hill (accessed January 8, 2014).

29. James Bopp, Jr., "The FEC's Assault on the First Amendment." *Free Speech & Election Law Practice Group Newsletter 1*, no. 1 (Fall 1996). Available at http://www.fed-soc.org/publi- cations/detail/the-fecs-assault-on-the-first-amendment (last accessed January 8, 2014).

30. Allison R. Hawyard, "Free Speech and the 1995–96 Term: A Mixed Message." *Free Speech & Election Law Practice Group Newsletter 1*, no. 1 (1996). Available at http:// www.fed-soc.org/publications/detail/free-speech-and-the-1995-96-term-a- mixed-message (last accessed January 8, 2014).

31. See interview with Lillian BeVier (professor of law, University of Virginia Law School) in phone discussion with the author, February 1, 2008.

32. See interview with Lee Liberman Otis (Office of Legal Counsel, George H. W. Bush Administration; general counsel (2001–2005); cofounder, Federalist Society) in dis- cussion with the author, February 1, 2008.

33. See http://www.fed-soc.org/aboutus/ (last accessed January 7, 2014).

34. See *Harvard Journal of Law and Public Policy* 10, no. 1 (1987): 1–20.

35. Daniel E. Troy, "Taking Commercial Speech Seriously." *Free Speech and Election Law Practice Group Newsletter 2*, no. 2 (Spring 1998). Available at http://www.fed-soc.org/publications/detail/taking-commercial-speech-seriously (last accessed January 8, 2014).

36. Joel M. Gora, "*Buckley v. Valeo* Revisited." *Free Speech and Election Law Practice Group Newsletter 3*, no. 3 (Winter 2000). Available at http://www.fed-soc.org/publications/detail/buckley-v-valeo-revisited (last accessed January 8, 2014).

37. See, e.g., Allison R. Hayward, "Free Speech and the 1995–96 Term: A Mixed Message." *Free Speech & Election Law Practice Group Newsletter 1*, no. 1 (Fall 1996). Available at http://www.fed-soc.org/publications/detail/free-speech-and-the-1995-96-term-a-mixed-message (last accessed January 8, 2014). See also, Allison R. Hayward, "Election Law Observer." *Free Speech and Election Law Practice Group Newsletter 2*, no. 2 (Summer 1998). Available at http://www.fed-soc.org/publications/detail/election-law-observer-2 (last accessed January 8, 2014).

38. 2000 National Lawyers Convention, Free Speech and Election Law Group, "The Future of Political Parties." See http://www.fed-soc.org/publications/page/2000-national-lawyers-convention-the-presidency (last accessed January 8, 2014).

39. 2003 National Lawyers Convention, Free Speech and Election Law Group, "Campaign Finance Reform in the Supreme Court." See http://www.fed-soc.org/publications/page/2003-national-lawyers-convention-international-law-and-american-sovereignty (last accessed January 8, 2014).

40. See http://www.fed-soc.org/publications/spdetail/election-law-series (last accessed January 8, 2014).

41. See, e.g., Stephen R. Klein, "A Cold Breeze in California: *Protect Marriage* Reveals the Chilling Effect of Campaign Finance Disclosure on Ballot Measure Issue Advocacy." *Engage 10*, no. 3 (2009): 68–73; James Bopp, Jr., "The FEC's Assault on the First Amendment." *Free Speech and Election Law Practice Group Newsletter 1*, no. 1 (Fall 1996); Bradley A. Smith, "Should 'Committing Politics' Be a Crime? The Case for Deregulating Campaign Finance." *Free Speech and Election Law Practice Group Newsletter 1*, no. 2 (July 1997).

42. See, e.g., John O McGinnis, "Against the Scribes: Campaign Finance Reform Revisited." *Harvard Journal of Law and Public Policy 24*, no. 1 (2000): 25–46; Joel M Gora, "Buckley v. Valeo Revisited." *Free Speech and Election Law Practice Group Newsletter 3*, no. 3 (Winter 2000); Mitch McConnell, "Campaign Finance 'Reform': A View from Capitol Hill." *Free Speech and Election Law Practice Group Newsletter 1*, no. 1 (Fall 1996).

43. See, e.g., John R. Lott, "Empirical Evidence in the Debate on Campaign Finance Reform." *Harvard Journal of Law and Public Policy* 24, no. 1 (2000): 9–16; Boyden Gray, "Afternoon Address." *Cumberland Law Review 23*, no. 1 (1992): 49–60; Michael W. McConnell, "A Constitutional Campaign Finance Plan." *Free Speech and Election Law Practice Group Newsletter 2*, no. 1 (May 1998); Charles R. Spies, "Michigan Issue Ad Ruling Reinforces Constitutional Protections." *Free Speech and Election Law Practice Group Newsletter 2*, no. 3 (December 1998).

44. See http://www.fed-soc.org/resources/page/conservative-libertarian-legal-scholarship-constitutional-law (last accessed January 6, 2014).

45. Mitch McConnell, "It's a Matter of Principle." *Free Speech and Election Law Practice Group Newsletter 3*, no. 1 (Spring 1999).

46. Charles H. Bell, "A Practitioner's View of *Colorado Republican Federal Campaign Committee v. Federal Election Commission*." *Free Speech and Election Law Practice Group Newsletter 1*, no. 1 (Fall 1996).

47. Allison R. Hayward, "The Supreme Court and Campaign Finance." *Engage* 9, no. 3 (October 2008): 61.

48. Ibid., 63.

49. *Bellotti*, supra note 15, at *776.

50. Ibid., *776.

51. Ibid., *777.

52. Ribstein is a professor of law at Illinois College of Law and has participated in Federalist Society faculty conferences (see, e.g., 12th Annual Faculty Conference, "Bankruptcy or Bailout," January 8, 2010) and Debates (see, e.g., Debate, "*Citizens United v. FEC*: A Roundtable Discussion," February 3, 2010).

53. Fisch presented a talk on "The New Federal Regulation of Corporate Governance" at the 2004 Annual Student Symposium (transcript reprinted in *Harvard Journal of Law and Public Policy* 28, no. 1 (Fall 2004): 39–50).

54. 539 U.S. 146 (2003) (held that applying the direct contribution prohibition to non-profit advocacy corporations is consistent with the First Amendment). Notably, this case was argued by Federalist Society member James Bopp, Jr.

55. 352 U.S. 567 (1957) (upheld a criminal conviction of a union for using union dues to sponsor commercial television broadcasts designed to influence the electorate in connection with national elections pursuant to 18 U.S.C.S. Section 610. Though the Supreme Court declined to consider the broader constitutional question of whether the ban was constitutional, Justice Felix Frankfurter mobilized historical evidence to demonstrate how this statute was consistent with a long series of congressional efforts calculated to avoid the deleterious influences of corporations and unions on the political process).

56. See Allison R. Hayward, "Rethinking Campaign Finance Prohibitions." Available at http://www.fed-soc.org/doclib/20070403_campfin.pdf (last accessed January 21, 2014).

57. Marshall, a professor at University of North Carolina School of Law, has participated in four Federalist Society National Conferences. See, e.g., 1998 Annual Student Symposium, Panel III: Constitutional Federalism Reborn, "American Political Culture and the Failures of Process Federalism" (transcript reprinted in *Harvard Journal of Law and Public Policy* 22, no. 1 (1998): 139–155); 2004 National Lawyers Convention, Showcase Panel IV, "Brown and School Choice"; 2008 National Lawyers Convention, Showcase Panel I, "Judicial Selection: Federal and State"; 2011 Annual Student Symposium, Panel III, "The Welfare State and American Exceptionalism."

58. Moore, the director of the Center for National Security Law at the University of Virginia, has presented at two Federalist Society National Conferences. See, e.g., 2000 National Lawyers Convention, Showcase Roundtable III, "What Should Shape a President's Perspective on Foreign Policy?"; 2002 National Lawyers Convention, Showcase Panel III, "Fighting Fairly: The Laws of Armed Conflict."

59. Pilon, the founder and director of Cato Institute's Center for Constitutional Studies, has presented at six Federalist Society National Conferences. See, e.g., 2001 National Lawyers Convention, Environmental Law and Property Rights, "Property Rights Protection: Judicial Activism or a Return to First Principles"; 2003 National Lawyers Convention, Criminal Law and Procedure, "Victims' Rights"; 2005 National Lawyers Convention, Telecommunications, "Expansion of Indecency Regulation"; 2006 National Lawyers Convention, Federalism, "Executive Power in Wartime"; 2008 National Lawyers Convention, Litigation, "Civil Litigation under the Roberts Court"; 2010 National Lawyers Convention, Labor, "Regulatory Power Unleashed?"

60. Polsby, who is the dean of George Mason Law School, has presented at three Federalist Society National Conferences. See, e.g., 1994 Annual Student Symposium, Panel IV: Feminism, Children and the Family, "Ozzie and Harriet Had It Right" (transcript

reprinted in *Harvard Journal of Law and Public Policy* 18, no. 2 (1995): 531–536); 1995 Annual Student Symposium, Panel I, "Originalism and the Dead Hand" (transcript reprinted in *Harvard Journal of Law and Public Policy* 19, no. 2 (1996): 243–244); 1999 Annual Student Symposium, Panel IV: Does Consumer Choice Need to be Managed, "Should Government Attempt to Influence Consumer Preference" (transcript reprinted in *Harvard Journal of Law and Public Policy* 23, no. 1 (1999): 197–202).

61. See interview with Daniel Polsby (dean and professor of law, George Mason Law School) in discussion with the author, February 11, 2008.

62. See interview with Lillian BeVier (professor of law, University of Virginia Law School) in discussion with the author, February 1, 2008 ("[The Federalist Society's principal contribution has been] opening debate. For me what that opening debate has meant, the ideas that I share with other people who are members of the Federalist Society have been able to be injected and people have found them persuasive. I can't tell you how often I've given talks at law schools and it's a topic completely out of the mainstream because that's what I seem to do and people come up to me and say, 'I never looked at it that way. I never thought about that.'")

63. Personal Interview with Eugene Meyer (president, Federalist Society) in discussion with the author, February 8, 2008.

64. Personal interview with Richard Willard (partner, Steptoe and Johnson, LLP; assistant attorney general, Civil Rights Division under President Ronald Reagan) in discussion with the author, January 31, 2008.

65. See J. Harvie Wilkinson, "The Fourteenth Amendment Privileges and Immunities Clause." *Harvard Journal of Law and Public Policy* 43, no. 12 (1989): 51–52.

66. See Ian Millhiser, "How Conservatives Abandoned Judicial Restraint, Took over the Courts, and Radically Transformed America." *Think Progress*, November 19, 2013. Available at http://thinkprogress.org/justice/2013/11/19/2944371/tedcruzification-judiciary/ (last accessed January 26, 2014).

67. See http://www.fed-soc.org/publications/detail/sixth-annual-rosenkranz-debate-resolved-courts-are-too-deferential-to-the-legislature-event-audiovideo (last accessed January 26, 2014).

68. See Ian Millhiser, "How Conservatives Abandoned Judicial Restraint, Took over the Courts, and Radically Transformed America." *Think Progress*, November 19, 2013. Available at http://thinkprogress.org/justice/2013/11/19/2944371/tedcruzification-judiciary/ (last accessed January 26, 2014).

69. See, e.g., Joel Gora, "*Buckley v. Valeo* Revisited." *Free Speech and Election Law Practice Group Newsletter* 3, no. 3 (Winter 2000).

70. Allison R. Hayward, "The Supreme Court and Campaign Finance." *Engage* 9, no. 3 (October 2008): 63.

71. Personal interview with Steven Calabresi (cofounder of the Federalist Society, professor of law, Northwestern University) in discussion with the author, April 3, 2008.

72. 116 Sat. 81 (2002).

73. See, e.g., *Senator Mitch McConnell v. Federal Election Commission*, Civ. No. 02-0582.

74. Sections 201 and 202 were also charged with being unconstitutional. I chose to highlight §203 as it proves to be the major point of contention in *Federal Election Commission v. Wisconsin Right to Life, Inc.*, 551 U.S. 449 (2007), the next case in my analysis, and the case that sets up the judicial paths that were picked up by the court in *Citizens United v. Federal Election Commission*, 558 U.S. 08-205 (2010).

75. 2 U.S.C. §441b(a) (2000 ed.).

76. 2 U.S.C.A. §441b(b)(2) (Supp. 2003).

77. *Austin v. Michigan Chamber of Commerce*, 494 U.S. 652, 658 (1990).

78. McConnell, 540 U.S. 93, at 13 (Thomas, J., concurring in part and dissenting in part).

79. 546 U.S. 410, 126 S.Ct. 1016.
80. 551 U.S. 449, 127 S.Ct. 2652.
81. Bopp, who is general counsel for the James Madison Center for Free Speech, was the co-chairman for Federalist Society's Free Speech and Election Law Group from 1996 to 2005. He has also presented at two Federalist Society National Conferences. See 2004 National Lawyers Convention, Free Speech and Election Law Panel, "First Amendment: Regulation of False Statements of Fact"; and 2010 National Lawyers Convention, Professional Responsibility Panel, "The Bloody Crossroads: *Republican Party of Minnesota v. White* Runs into *Caperton v. Massey.*"
82. 546 U.S. 410, 126 S.Ct. 1016.
83. Brief for Appellee, 2007 WL 868545 (U.S.) (Appellate Brief), *25.
84. Sentelle's earliest appearance at a Federalist Society National Conference was in 1987. See "Second Annual Lawyers Convention of the Federalist Society: The Constitution and Federal Criminal Law," Panel III: Federalism and the Scope of the Federal Criminal Law (transcript reprinted in *American Criminal Law Review* 26, no. 4 (1988–1989): 1737–1778).
85. 551 U.S. 449, 127 S.Ct. 2652.
86. Thompson, who is a managing partner at Cooper and Kirk alongside fellow network member Charles J Cooper, appeared at the 2003 National Lawyers Convention to speak on the issue of Free Speech and Election Law. See 2003 National Lawyers Convention, Free Speech and Election Law Group, "Campaign Finance Reform in the Supreme Court."
87. Jaffe, a constitutional litigator and former clerk to Justice Clarence Thomas, has participated in dozens of Federalist Society events. For a small sample of his network participation since 2006, see https://www.fed-soc.org/publications/author/erik-s-jaffe (last accessed January 27, 2014).
88. Baran, who is a litigator for Wiley Rein with extensive expertise in First Amendment and Campaign Finance law, presented at the 2000 National Student Symposium on "Political Parties and Spending Limits" (transcript reprinted in *Harvard Journal of Law and Public Policy* 24, no. 1 (2000): 83–90).
89. See, e.g., 2000 National Lawyers Convention, Labor and Employment Group Panel, "Regulatory Enforcement of Labor and Employment Law: What the Future Holds."
90. Gora, a law professor at Brooklyn Law School, has been an active member of the Federalist Society's Free Speech and Election Law Practice Group since at least 1999. See, e.g., "*Buckley v. Valeo* Revisited: Remarks of Professor Joel M. Gora at the Federalist Society's September 1999 Conference." *Free Speech and Election Law Practice Group Newsletter* 3, no. 3 (Winter 2000). Available at: http://www.fed-soc.org/publications/detail/buckley-v-valeo-revisited (last visited January 2, 2014).
91. Law, who at this time was the chief legal officer and general counsel for the U.S. Chamber of Commerce, is now the president and CEO of American Crossroads. He has presented at two Federalist Society National Conferences. See 2004 National Lawyers Convention, Labor Panel, "Globalization: Labor Challenges for the 21st Century" and 2009 National Lawyers Convention, Labor Panel, "Wall Street, Labor Unions, and the Obama Administration: A New Paradigm for Capital and Labor?"
92. Shapiro, who is the former national legal director for the ACLU, participated in the 1999 National Lawyers Convention on the Free Speech and Election Law Group's Panel, "Freedom of Speech and Criminal Facilitation."
93. *Wisconsin Right to Life, supra* note 85, *481.
94. See, e.g., "Brief Amicus Curiae of the American Civil Liberties Union in Support of Appellee" (Joel M. Gora and Steven R Shapiro, Counsel of Record). 2007 WL 894817 (U.S.) (Appellate Brief); "Brief of Amicus Curiae National Rifle Association" (Charles

J. Cooper, Counsel of Record) 2007 WL 894818 (U.S.) (Appellate Brief); "Brief of the American Federation of Labor and Congress of Industrial Organizations as Amicus Curiae in Support of Appellee" (Laurence Gold, Counsel of Record) 2007 WL 894819 (U.S.) (Appellate Brief); "Brief of Amicus Curiae Chamber of Commerce of the United States of America in Support of Appellee" (Jan Witold Baran, Counsel of Record) 2007 WL 894812 (U.S.) (Appellate Brief); "Brief Amici Curiae of the American Center for Law and Justice and of Focus on the Family in Support of Appellee" (Jay Alan Sekulow, Counsel of Record) 2007 WL 894822 (U.S.) (Appellate Brief); "Brief for Amici Curiae the Center for Competitive Politics, the Institute for Justice, Reason Foundation, The Individual Rights Foundation, and the Cato Institute, in Support of Appellees" (Erik S Jaffe, Counsel of Record) 2007 WL 922218 (U.S.) (Appellate Brief).

95. 466 F. Supp. 2d 195 (2006) (held Section 203 of the Bipartisan Campaign Reform Act unconstitutional as applied to three broadcast advertisements that Wisconsin Right to Life intended to run within 30 days of a federal general election).

96. See, e.g., "Brief of United States Senator Mitch McConnell as Amicus Curiae in Support of Appellee" (Theodore Olson, Counsel of Record) 2007 WL 894813 (U.S.) (Appellate Brief), at *14 (citing Bradley A. Smith and Jason R. Owen, "Boundary Based Restrictions in Unbounded Broadcast Media Markets: McConnell v. FEC's Underinclusive Overbreadth Analysis." *Stanford Law and Policy Review* 18 (2007)); "Brief for Amici Curiae the Center for Competitive Politics, the Institute for Justice, Reason Foundation, The Individual Rights Foundation, and the Cato Institute, in Support of Appellees" (Erik S. Jaffe, Counsel of Record) 2007 WL 922218 (U.S.) (Appellate Brief), at *15 (citing Bradley A. Smith and Jason R. Owen, "Boundary Based Restrictions in Unbounded Broadcast Media Markets: McConnell v. FEC's Underinclusive Overbreadth Analysis." *Stanford Law and Policy Review* 18 (2007)), *6 and *23 (citing Erik S. Jaffe, "*McConnell v. FEC*: Rationing Speech to Prevent "Undue" Influence, 2003–2004." *Cato Supreme Court Review* 245 (2004)); *17 (citing Ilya Somin, "Political Ignorance and the Countermajoritarian Difficulty: A New Perspective on the Central Obsession of Constitutional Theory." *Iowa Law Review* 89 (2004): 1287).

97. See, e.g., "Brief for Amici Curiae the Center for Competitive Politics, the Institute for Justice, Reason Foundation, The Individual Rights Foundation, and the Cato Institute, in Support of Appellees," supra note 96, *5, *24 (citing *Federalist* No. 10, *The Federalist Papers*); "Brief of United States Senator Mitch McConnell as Amicus Curiae in Support of Appellee" supra note 96, *11 (citing Continental Congress, "Address to the Inhabitants of the Province of Quebec" (Oct. 26, 1774), in *Journal of the Continental Congress* 1 (1904 ed.): 104); "Brief Amici Curiae of the American Center for Law and Justice and of Focus on the Family in Support of Appellee" (Jay Alan Sekulow, Counsel of Record) 2007 WL 894822 (U.S.) (Appellate Brief), *6–7 (citing 1628 Petition of Right, 3 Chas.1 c.1), *7–8 (citing 1689 Bill of Rights, 1 W. & M., Sess. 2, ch. (1689)), *9 (citing "An Act Prohibiting Trade and Intercourse with America," 16 Geo. III., c. 5 and Declaration and Resolves, First Continental Congress, October 14, 1774), *10 (citing Annals of Congress, House of Representatives, 1st Congress, 1st Sess., 451 (June 8, 1789)).

98. See, e.g., "Brief Amicus Curiae of the American Civil Liberties Union in Support of Appellee" (Joel M. Gora and Steven R Shapiro, Counsel of Record) 2007 WL 894817 (U.S.) (Appellate Brief), *25; "Brief of United States Senator Mitch McConnell as Amicus Curiae in Support of Appellee" supra note 96, *13, *16, *18, *22; "Brief of Amicus Curiae National Rifle Association" (Charles J. Cooper, Counsel of Record) 2007 WL 894818 (U.S.) (Appellate Brief), *19; "Brief of the American Federation of Labor and Congress of Industrial Organizations as Amicus Curiae in Support of Appellee" (Laurence Gold, Counsel of Record) 2007 WL 894819 (U.S.) (Appellate Brief), *22–*23.

99. Brief for Appellee, 2007 WL 868545 (U.S.) (Appellate Brief), *68.

100. *Wisconsin Right to Life,* supra note 85 (Scalia, J., concurring), *502–503.

101. Ibid., *502.

102. *Wisconsin Right to Life,* supra note 85 (Roberts, C.J., majority), *476.

103. *Wisconsin Right to Life,* supra note 85 (Alito, J., concurring), *482–483.

104. Richard Wolf and David Jackson, "Shackles Off 'Issue Ads' Naming Candidates, but Who Benefits Up for Debate." *USA Today,* June 26, 2007.

105. Joan Biskupic, "Court's Newcomers Lead a Measured Push to the Right; 5-4 Ruling Suggest That Roberts and Alito Will Reverse Prior Decisions—To a Point." *USA Today,* June 26, 2007.

106. Allison R. Hayward, "The Supreme Court and Campaign Finance." *Engage* 9, no. 3 (October 2008): 63.

107. 558 U.S. 310, 130 S.Ct. 876.

108. 2 U.S.C.A. § 434 (f)(3)(A)(i).

109. 558 U.S. 310, 130 S.Ct. 876, *321.

110. Randolph, a federal judge on the D.C. Circuit Court of Appeals, has been on the program at Federalist Society national conferences an impressive 19 times. His first appearance was as a moderator at the 1992 National Lawyers Conference, Panel IV, "Who Controls the Administrative State? A Debate on the Relationship Between Congress and Government Agencies" (transcript reprinted in *Cumberland Law Review* 23, no. 1 (1993): 125–140).

111. 530 F.Supp.2d 274 (D.D.C.2008) 558.

112. Jeffrey Toobin, "Money Unlimited." *The New Yorker,* May 21, 2012. Available at http://www.newyorker.com/reporting/2012/05/21/120521fa_fact_toobin?currentPage=5 (last accessed January 31, 2014).

113. Ibid., 5.

114. 558 U.S. 310, 130 S.Ct. 876.

115. Smith, who served as the chairman of the Federal Election Commission under George W. Bush between 2000 and 2005, currently serves as an advisor for the Federalist Society's Free Speech and Election Law Practice Group. Additionally, he has presented at two Federalist Society National Conferences. See 2000 National Lawyers Convention, Free Speech and Election Law Panel, "The Future of Political Parties" and 2010 National Lawyers Convention, "Free Speech: Anonymity and the First Amendment."

116. Abrams, a prominent First Amendment attorney, spoke on civil liberties at two of the earliest Federalist Society National Conferences. See 1986 Federalist Society National Meeting, "Content Neutrality: Some Thoughts on Words and Music" (transcript reprinted in *Harvard Journal of Law and Public Policy* 10, no. 1 (1987): 61–70) and 1987 First Annual Federalist Society Lawyers Convention, "The Ninth Amendment and the Protection of Unenumerated Rights" (transcript reprinted in *Harvard Journal of Law and Public Policy* 11, no. 1 (1988): 93–96).

117. Cox, who serves as a chairman for the Federalist Society's Free Speech and Election Law Practice Group, also presented at the 2002 National Lawyers Convention on the Telecommunications Panel, "Privacy, Telecommunications and Technology: Does Emerging Technology Force New Privacy Considerations?"

118. Hayward, a former professor at George Mason Law School and current vice president of Policy at the Center for Competitive Politics, is the chairman of the Federalist Society's Free Speech and Election Law Practice Group.

119. See, e.g., *Citizens United,* supra note 1 (Kennedy, J., majority), *898–*899 ("Prohibited, too, are restrictions distinguishing among different speakers, allowing speech by some but not others. See *First Nat. Bank of Boston v Bellotti"*); *899 ("The Court has

recognized that First Amendment protection extends to corporations. Bellotti, supra, at 778); *900 ("Under the rationale of these precedents, political speech does not lose First Amendment protection 'simply because its source is a corporation' Bellotti, supra, 784... The Court has thus rejected the argument that political speech of corporations or other associations should be treated differently under the First Amendment simply because such associations are not 'natural persons.' Ibid., 776").

120. Ibid., *900.

121. Ibid., *907.

122. See "Brief for Appellant" (Theodore Olson, Counsel of Record) 2009 WL 61467 (U.S.) (Appellate Brief), *14, 29, 30, 31, 43, 45, 47, 55.

123. Ibid., *31.

124. Ibid., *30.

125. Ibid.

126. See "Brief of the American Federation of Labor and Congress of Industrial Organizations as Amicus Curiae in Support of Appellant" (Laurence Gold, Counsel of Record) 2009 WL 2365216 (U.S.) (Appellate Brief), *12; "Brief of Amicus Curiae Center for Competitive Politics in Support of Appellant" (Stephen M. Hoerstring, Counsel of Record with Bradley A. Smith, Reid Alan Cox) 2009 WL 132719 (U.S.) (Appellate Brief), *24; "Brief of Amicus Curiae Chamber of Commerce of the United States of America in Support of Appellant" (Jan Witold Baran, Counsel of Record) 2009 WL 154011 (U.S.) (Appellate Brief), *15, 17, 18, 20.

127. Fallon, a professor at Harvard Law School, has presented at three Federalist Society National Conferences and has spoken on the topic of the judicial role. See, e.g., 1993 Annual Student Symposium, Panel IV: Non-Legal Theory in Judicial Decisionmaking, "Non-Legal Theory in Judicial Decisionmaking" (transcript reprinted in *Harvard Journal of Law and Public Policy* 17, no. 1 (1994): 87–100).

128. See http://www.fed-soc.org/resources/page/conservative-libertarian-legal-scholarship-federal-courts ("Richard H. Fallon, Jr., *Judicially Manageable Standards and Constitutional Meaning*, 119 Harv. L. Rev., 1274 (2006). This article flushes out how courts have defined 'judicially manageable standards,' which result in nonjusticiable political questions. Professor Fallon then identifies a series of criteria that guide courts, but concludes that the ultimate test is so discretionary that it could be considered judicially unmanageable.") (last accessed February 3, 2014).

129. *Citizens United,* supra note 1 (Kennedy, J., majority), *893 ("The parties cannot enter into a stipulation that prevents the Court from considering certain remedies if those remedies are necessary to resolve a claim that has been preserved. Citizens United has preserved its First Amendment challenge to 441b as applied to the facts of its case; and given all the circumstances, we cannot easily address that issue without assuming a premise—the permissibility of restricting corporate political speech—that is itself in doubt. See Fallon, As-Applied and Facial Challenges and Third-Party Standing, 113 Harv. L. Rev. 1321 (2000): 1339").

130. See, *Citizens United, supra* note 1 (Kennedy, J., majority), *900 ("At least since the latter part of the 19th century, the laws of some States and of the United States imposed a ban on corporate direct contributions to candidates. See B. Smith, Unfree Speech: The Folly of Campaign Finance Reform 23 (2001)").

131. "Brief of Amicus Curiae Center for Competitive Politics in Support of Appellant" (Stephen M Hoerstring, Counsel of Record) 2009 WL 132719 (U.S.) (Appellate Brief).

132. "Brief Amici Curiae of Seven Former Chairmen and One Former Commissioner of the Federal Election Commission Supporting Appellant on Supplemental Question" (James Bopp, Jr., Counsel of Record) 2009 WL 2349018 (U.S.) (Appellate Brief).

133. See *Citizens United, supra* note 1 (Kennedy, J., majority), *895 ("Third is the primary importance of speech itself to the integrity of the election process. As additional rules are created for regulating political speech, any speech arguably within their reach is chilled. See Part II-A, *supra*. Campaign finance regulations now impose 'unique and complex rules' on '71 distinct entities.' Brief for Seven Former Chairmen of FEC et al. as *Amici Curiae* 11–12. These entities are subject to separate rules for 33 different types of political speech. Ibid., 14–15, n. 10. The FEC has adopted 568 pages of regulations, 1,278 pages of explanations and justifications for those regulations, and 1,771 advisory opinions since 1975. See ibid., 6, n. 7."); *897–898 ("PACs have to comply with these regulations just to speak. This might explain why fewer than 2,000 of the millions of corporations in this country have PACs. See Brief for Seven Former Chairmen of FEC et al. as *Amici Curiae* 11 (citing FEC, Summary of PAC Activity 1990–2006, online at http://www. fec. gov/press/press 2007/ 20071009pac/sumhistory.pdf); IRS, Statistics of Income: 2006, Corporation Income Tax Returns 2 (2009) (hereinafter Statistics of Income) (5.8 million for-profit corporations filed 2006 tax returns). PACs, furthermore, must exist before they can speak. Given the onerous restrictions, a corporation may not be able to establish a PAC in time to make its views known regarding candidates and issues in a current campaign.")

134. "Brief of Amicus Campaign Finance Scholars in Support of Appellant, Citizens United" (Allison R. Hayward, Counsel of Record) 2009 WL 2365206 (U.S.) (Appellate Brief).

135. Ibid., *9 and *17.

136. See *Citizens United, supra* note 1 (Kennedy, J., majority) at *901 (discussing *United States v. Automobile Workers,* "The Court did not get another opportunity to consider the constitutional question in that case; for after a remand, a jury found the defendants not guilty. See Hayward, Revisiting the Fable of Reform, 45 *Harv J. Legis.* 421(463) (2008)"), *912.

137. *Citizens United, supra* note 1 (Stevens, J. dissenting), *932.

138. Ibid., *933–934.

139. Ibid., *938.

140. *Citizens United, supra* note 1 (Roberts, C. J., concurring), *920-921.

141. *Citizens United, supra* note 1 (Scalia, J., concurring), *929.

142. *Citizens United, supra* note 1 (Stevens, J., dissenting), *948.

143. Interview with John C. Yoo (professor of law, University of California, Berkeley Law School; former law clerk to Judge Laurence H. Silberman and Justice Clarence Thomas; general counsel, U.S. Senate Judiciary Committee (1995–1996); deputy assistant attorney general, Office of Legal Counsel (2001–2003)) in discussion with the author, January 16, 2008.

144. See, *Citizens United, supra* note 1(Kennedy, J., majority), *916 ("Last, Citizens United argues that disclosure requirements can chill donations to an organization by exposing donors to retaliation. Some amici point to recent events in which donors to certain causes were blacklisted, threatened, or otherwise targeted for retaliation. See Brief for Institute for Justice as Amicus Curiae 13–16; Brief for Alliance Defense Fund as Amicus Curiae 16–22").

145. See, e.g., Stephen R. Klein, "A Cold Breeze in California: *Protect Marriage* Reveals the Chilling Effect of Campaign Finance Disclosure on Ballot Measure Issue Advocacy." *Engage 10*, no. 3 (2009): 68–73; James Bopp, Jr., "The FEC's Assault on the First Amendment." *Free Speech and Election Law Practice Group Newsletter 1*, no. 1 (Fall 1996); Bradley A. Smith, "Should 'Committing Politics' Be a Crime? The Case for Deregulating Campaign Finance." *Free Speech and Election Law Practice Group Newsletter 1*, no. 2 (July 1997).

146. Howard Greninger, "High Court Removes Campaign Funding Restrictions." *Tribune-Star,* January 23, 2010.

147. Michael R. Wolford, "Commentary: What's behind the 'Citizens' Brouhaha?" *Daily Record of Rochester,* February 4, 2010.

148. "Editorial: Transparency Is the Answer to Political Spending." *Foster's Daily Democrat,* Dover, NH, January 25, 2010.

149. John O'Brien, "U.S. SC Overturns Campaign Spending Law, Infuriates Obama." *Madison County Record,* January 22, 2010.

150. See, e.g., Robert Barnes, "Alito's State of the Union Moment." *Washington Post,* January 27, 2010. Available at http://voices.washingtonpost.com/44/2010/01/alito-mouths-not-true-at-obama.html.

151. See, e.g., http://www.fed-soc.org/search/default.asp?q=steve+simpson&x=0&y=0 (last accessed February 9, 2014).

152. Fredreka Schouten, "Campaign-Finance Fights Not Over; High Court's Ruling on Spending Limits Was Just One Case." *USA Today,* January 27, 2010.

153. David Kirkpatrick, "A Quest to End Spending Rules for Campaigns." *New York Times,* January 25, 2010.

154. For a sampling of all the events the Federalist Society has facilitated on *Citizens United,* see the following search results for "citizens united" on the Society's website (which number close to 100): http://www.fed-soc.org/search/default.asp?q=citizens+united&x=0&y=0 (last accessed February 9, 2014).

155. See, generally, The Campaign Legal Center, http://www.clcblog.org/blog_item-329.html (last accessed February 6, 2014).

156. *Shaun McCutcheon, et al., v. Federal Election Commission,* No. 12-536 (proceedings and orders available at http://www.supremecourt.gov/Search.aspx?FileName=/docket files/12-536.htm (last accessed February 5, 2014).

157. See, e.g., http://prospect.org/article/mccutcheon-oral-arguments-point-way-backward-and-forward (last accessed February 6, 2014).

158. U.S. Const. Amend. I ("Congress shall make no law respecting an establishment of religion, or prohibiting the free exercise thereof").

159. Duncan, who presented at the 2014 National Lawyers Convention on "Religious Liberty and Conflicting Moral Visions" has also participated in the Religious Liberties Practice Group events and Lawyers Chapter events for the Federalist Society. See http://www.fed-soc.org/publications/author/kyle-duncan (last accessed February 6, 2014).

160. 78 Fed. Reg. 39870 (July 2, 2013); 42 U.S.C. Sec 300bb-13(a)(4) (a regulation under the Patient Protection and Affordable Care Act that requires non-exempt entities to provide insurance coverage for all FDA-approved contraceptive methods).

161. Tymkovich has been a presenter at three Federalist Society National Conferences. See 2004 National Lawyers Convention, Environmental Law Panel, "Turning Private Property into Public Trusts"; 2007 Annual Student Symposium, "Moral Choices and the Eighth Amendment"; 2008 National Lawyers Convention, Labor Panel, "Labor Initiatives in the New Administration."

162. *Hobby Lobby Stores, Inc v. Kathleen Sebelius* (U.S. Court of Appeals, Tenth Circuit) (2013), 37.

CHAPTER 4

1. Document obtained from the Ronald Reagan Presidential Library in Simi Valley, CA, on March 12, 2008. See "Memo from Pat Buchanan for the Chief of Staff," January 30, 1987. Presidential Handwriting File, Series IV, File 173.

2. Document obtained from the Ronald Reagan Presidential Library in Simi Valley, CA, on March 12, 2008. See "Memo from David Chew to Donald T. Regan, January 30, 1987." Presidential Handwriting File, Series IV, File 173. 459153SS: "We agreed on one

extra talking point, numbered #5 in the attached revised talking points. Unfortunately, the President got the talking points last night. Now we have to go back to him and give him a new set. You know how much he hates that. I feel these last minute add-ons should be turned down. They don't add much and annoy the President. But given it is a Meese request and that you agree, I have made the changes."

3. Document obtained from the Ronald Reagan Presidential Library in Simi Valley, CA, on March 12, 2008. See "Telephone Message Request from the Office of the Attorney General," January 29, 1987, 3 pm. Presidential Handwriting File, Series IV, File 173.

4. Document obtained from the Ronald Reagan Presidential Library in Simi Valley, CA, on March 12, 2008. See "Topics of Discussion," Talking Point #5. Presidential Handwriting File, Series IV, File 173, 459153SS.

5. "The Congress shall have Power. . . To regulate Commerce with foreign Nations, and among the several states, and with the Indian Tribes."

6. For a good summary of what is often referred to in Supreme Court lore as "the switch in time that saved nine" and the constitutional revolution in federal power that followed, see Barry Cushman, *Rethinking the New Deal Court: The Structure of a Constitutional Revolution* (New York: Oxford University Press, 1998), 11–32.

7. *NLRB v. Laughlin Jones & Laughlin Steel Co.*, 301 U.S. 1 (1937) (upheld the National Labor Relations Act of 1935 and held that Congress could use its Commerce Power to pass wage and hour restrictions on intrastate labor); *Wickard v. Filburn*, 317 U.S. 111 (1942) (held that the Agricultural Adjustment Act could be applied to control the production of wheat, even if grown for personal consumption only); *Heart of Atlanta Motel Inc. v. United States*, 379 U.S. 241 (held that based on the fact that even local establishments served out-of-state customers, Congress could use its commerce power to apply the 1964 Civil Rights Act to private establishments who refused to serve African Americans).

8. President Reagan, Inaugural Address, Washington, DC, January 20, 1981.

9. Stephen Markman was the president of the D.C. Lawyers Chapter for the Federalist Society and involved in the early years through connections at the Reagan Justice Department. See, e.g., 1988 Annual Student Symposium, "The Amendment Process of Article V: A Microcosm of the Constitution" (transcript reprinted in *Harvard Journal of Law and Public Policy* 12, no. 1 (1989): 112–122). For a detailed examination of Markman and other fledgling Federalist Society members' roles in providing the intellectual capital for the Reagan Justice Department's long-range legal and constitutional agenda, see Amanda Hollis-Brusky, "Helping Ideas Have Consequences: Political and Intellectual Investment in the Unitary Executive Theory, 1981–2000." *Denver University Law Review*, 89, no. 1 (2011): 197–244. See also Steven Teles, "Transformative Bureaucracy: Reagan's Lawyers and the Dynamics of Political Investment," *Studies in American Political Development* 23, no. 1 (2009): 61–83.

10. See The Office of Legal Policy, U.S. Department of Justice, Report to the Attorney General, *The Constitution in the Year 2000: Choices Ahead in Constitutional Interpretation* (1988), 138 (hereafter *Constitution in the Year 2000*). A number of interviewees linked these reports to Stephen Markman, who had also been serving as the president of the D.C. Lawyers Chapter of the Federalist Society (Teles 2008, 145). See, e.g., Interview with Daniel Troy (attorney, Sidley Austin, LLP; special assistant, Office of Legal Counsel (1984–1988)) in discussion with the author, January 30, 2008: "Obviously you had Steve Markman at the Office of Legal Policy who was writing these great pieces which you should definitely go back and read about legislative history and about Originalism. He's got this sourcebook, I mean go back and look at what OLP was putting out then."; Interview with Douglas Kmiec (professor of law, Pepperdine University; Office of Legal Counsel under Presidents Ronald Reagan and George H. W. Bush) in discussion with the author, March 14, 2008: "Steve Markman was the

head of [the Office of Legal Policy] in the second term. . . here's a memo from Steven Markman, February 1, 1989, 'Report on Adverse Inferences from Silence.' So I mean these are things I actually still consult from time to time. . ."; Interview with Richard Willard (partner, Steptoe and Johnson, LLP; assistant attorney general, Civil Rights Division under President Ronald Reagan) in discussion with the author, January 31, 2008: "When Meese was Attorney General, Steve Markman worked for him and headed up the Office of Legal Policy which was like a think tank within the Justice Department and published a lot of monographs on constitutional law and things like that"; Interview with Steven Calabresi (professor of law, Northwestern University; cofounder, Federalist Society) in discussion with the author, April 3, 2008: "All the papers on various subjects about Originalism and so forth, my impression is that Steve Markman as the head of the Office of Legal policy really came up with the idea of putting together those papers and publishing them." For a summary of the content of these Office of Legal Policy reports, see Dawn Johnsen, "Ronald Reagan and the Rehnquist Court on Congressional Power: Presidential Influences on Constitutional Change," 78 *Indiana Law Journal* 363 (2003): 363–412.

11. *National League of Cities v. Usery*, 426 U.S. 833 (1976).
12. See *Garcia v. San Antonio Metro.* Transit Authority, 469 U.S. 528 (1985) (*Hereafter Garcia*), Justice Rehnquist dissenting **580 ("But under any one of these approaches the judgment in these cases should be affirmed, and I do not think it incumbent on those of us in dissent to spell out further the fine points of a principle that will, I am confident, in time again command the support of a majority of this Court.").
13. George Hicks, "The Conservative Influence of the Federalist Society on the Harvard Law School Student Body." *Harvard Journal of Law and Public Policy* 29 (2006): 652.
14. See, e.g., 1982 Symposium, Charles Fried, "Federalism: Why Should We Care?"; 1988 National Lawyers Convention, "Federalism and the Scope of Federal Criminal Law" (James L. Buckley, William Van Alstyne, David Sentelle, Joseph E. diGenova, and G. Robert Blakey); 1989 National Student Symposium, Michael Kent Curtis, "Privileges or Immunities, Individual Rights, and Federalism"; 1992 National Student Symposium, "From Federal Union to National Monolith: Mileposts in the Demise of American Federalism"; 1998 National Student Symposium, Panel IV: "Federalism in Constitutional Context" (Max Boot, Roderick M. Hills, Jr., John C. Yoo, and Evan H. Caminker); 1999 National Student Symposium, Panel II: "International Law and Federalism: What Is the Reach of Regulation?" (Alan J. Meese, Alan O. Sykes, and Diane P. Wood); 2002 National Lawyers Convention, "Corporations, Securities and Antitrust: Competition and Regulatory Federalism" (Timothy Muris, R. Hewitt Pate, and Diarmuid O'Scannlain); 2002 National Lawyers Convention, "Showcase Roundtable IV: Wither Federalism? The Impact of Globalization and the War on Terror" (Ron Cass, John McGinnis, Randy Moss, William Pryor, Ken Wainstein, Ronald Weich, Richard Willard, and Alex Azar); 2004 National Lawyers Convention, "Federalism and Separation of Powers: Gay Marriage and Amending the Constitution" (Randy Barnett, Gerard V. Bradley, John Eastman, Jesse H. Choper, and Anthony Picarello); 2005 National Lawyers Convention, "Labor: Contending with Diverse State Employment Laws in a Global Economy, or What's So Great about Federalism?" (George H. Cohen, Randel K. Johnson, John S. Irving, and Amy Laura Wax).
15. William Van Alstyne, 1988 National Lawyers Convention, Panel II: "Federalism and the Scope of the Federal Criminal Law" (transcript reprinted in *American Criminal Law Review* 26 (1989): 1737).
16. Lynn A. Baker, 1998 National Student Symposium, "Reviving the Structural Constitution," Panel III: "Constitutional Federalism Reborn" (transcript reprinted in *Harvard Journal of Law and Public Policy* 22 (1998–1999): 95).

17. Search conducted on January 21, 2009, using LexisNexis Academic. Exact search dates were 01.01.1981–12.12.2008. I selected the *Wall Street Journal, National Review, American Spectator,* and the *Weekly Standard,* and the total combined search of all four sources yielded 1,059 hits for "federalism"; 185 of the articles returned under the "federalism" search (17%) were authored by participants in Federalist Society national meetings.

18. Media search included the *National Review, Wall Street Journal, American Spectator,* and the *Weekly Standard,* initially filtered—as detailed earlier—for mentions of "federalism" and "separation of powers" from 1.1.1981 to 12.12.2008. A database search for "commerce" within the returned results for "federalism" revealed 39 articles written by Federalist Society network actors. See, e.g., Terry Eastland, "Bookshelf: Keeping the Federal Government in Its Place," *Wall Street Journal,* August 19, 1987; Jeremy Rabkin, "State Your Business," *American Spectator,* July 1995; Steven G. Calabresi, "A Constitutional Revolution," *Wall Street Journal,* July 10, 1997; Jeremy Rabkin, "Bill's Fickle Feminists," *American Spectator,* May 1998; Michael W. McConnell, "Let the States Do It, Not Washington," *Wall Street Journal,* March 29, 1999; Daniel E. Troy, "Electing the Supreme Court," *Weekly Standard,* May 10, 1999; Michael Greve, "Federalism Is More Than States' Rights," *Wall Street Journal,* July 1, 1999; R. Alexander Acosta, "In 2000, Supreme Court Is at Stake Too," *Wall Street Journal,* August 23, 1999; Theodore B. Olson, "Aaaand They're Off! The Justices Go to Work," *Wall Street Journal,* Oct 4, 1999; Jeremy Rabkin, "Federalism v. Feminism: The Supreme Court Is Likely to Side with the Federalists," *The American Spectator,* Dec 1999/Jan 2000; Charles Fried, "Opponents of Federalism Are Mired in a Time Warp," *Wall Street Journal,* May 16, 2000; Michael S. Greve, "A Federalism Worth Fighting For," *Weekly Standard,* January 29, 2001; Jeremy Rabkin, "The Ducks Stop Here," *American Spectator,* February 2001; Douglas W. Kmiec, "Screening Judges," *National Review,* September 5, 2001; Jonathan H. Adler, "The Framers' Design," *National Review,* November 1, 2001; Robert A. Levy, "None of Their Business," *National Review,* May 22, 2002; Ronald D. Rotunda, "Federalizing the Windy City," *National Review,* June 18, 2002; Richard A. Epstein, "A Federal Case," *National Review,* October 28, 2002; Terry Eastland, "The Estrada Pinata," *Weekly Standard,* February 24, 2003; Jonathan H. Adler, "Suicidal Folly," *National Review,* August 19, 2004; John Engler, C. Boyden Gray, and Kenneth Starr, "Phony Federalists," *Wall Street Journal,* June 1, 2004; Christopher Cox, "The Marriage Amendment Is a Terrible Idea," *Wall Street Journal,* September 28, 2004; Jonathan H. Adler, "High Court Anxiety," *National Review,* December 1, 2004; John Engler, C. Boyden Gray, and Kenneth Starr, "High-Tech Federalism," *National Review,* April 27, 2005; Jonathan H. Adler, "Federalism, Up in Smoke?" *National Review,* June 7, 2005; Randy E. Barnett, "The Ninth Circuit's Revenge," *National Review,* June 9, 2005; Terry Eastland, "Reading Roberts' Mind," *Weekly Standard,* August 1, 2005; Randy E. Barnett, "William Rehnquist," *Wall Street Journal,* September 6, 2005; Richard E. Epstein, "Still Defending the New Deal Program," *Wall Street Journal,* September 7, 2005; Terry Eastland, "Farewell to the Chief: William H. Rehnquist," *Weekly Standard,* September 26, 2005; Nelson Lund, "Putting Federalism to Sleep," *Weekly Standard,* October 31, 2005; Jonathan Adler, "Environmental Enemy #1," *National Review,* January 3, 2006; Hadley Arkes, "Servatius Redux," *National Review,* January 27, 2006; John O. McGinnis, "Bookshelf: A Justices Is Weighed in the Balance," *Wall Street Journal,* January 31, 2006; Jonathan H. Adler, "How Conservative Is This Court?" *National Review,* July 5, 2007; John O. McGinnis, "One Blueprint for Obama," *Wall Street Journal,* July 15, 2008.

19. Interview with David McIntosh (partner, Meyer, Brown and Platt; member of Congress (1995–2001); cofounder, Federalist Society) in discussion with the author, January 25, 2008, Washington, DC.

20. Interview with Douglas Kmiec (professor of law, Pepperdine University; Office of Legal Counsel under Presidents Ronald Reagan and George H. W. Bush) in discussion with the author, March 14, 2008.

21. See Charles J. Cooper, "The Federal Judiciary, Life Tenure, and Self-Government." 1994 National Lawyers Conference (transcript reprinted in *Cornell Journal of Law and Public Policy* 2, no. 4 (1995): 499).

22. See, e.g., Gary S. Lawson, 1992 National Lawyers Conference, "The Congress: Representation, Accountability and the Rule of Law." Panel III: "Congress, the Court, and the Bill of Rights" (transcript reprinted in *Cumberland Law Review* 23, no. 1 (1992–1993): 91–124; Charles J. Cooper, 1992 Student Symposium, "Independent of Heaven Itself: Differing Federalist and Anti-Federalist Perspectives on the Centralizing Tendency of the Federal Judiciary" (transcript reprinted in *Harvard Journal of Law and Public Policy* 16, no. 1 (1993): 119–128); Richard Epstein, 1998 National Student Symposium, "Reviving the Structural Constitution," Panel V: "Undoing the New Deal?" (transcript reprinted in *Harvard Journal of Law and Public Policy* 22 no. 1 (1998–1999): 209).

23. Charles J. Cooper, 1992 National Student Symposium, "The Legacy of the Federalist Papers," Panel V: "The Anti-Federalists After 200 Years: Pundits or Prophets?" (transcript reprinted in *Harvard Journal of Law and Public Policy* 19 (1993): 119).

24. Pete du Pont, 1992 National Student Symposium, "The Legacy of the Federalist Papers," Epilogue: Federalism in the Twenty-First Century: Will States Exist? (transcript reprinted in *Harvard Journal of Law and Public Policy* 19 (1993): 137).

25. Lynn A. Baker, 1998 National Student Symposium, "Reviving the Structural Constitution," Panel III: "Constitutional Federalism Reborn" (transcript reprinted in *Harvard Journal of Law and Public Policy* 22 (1998–1999): 95).

26. Antonin Scalia, 1982 National Symposium: A Symposium on Federalism. "The Two Faces of Federalism" (transcript reprinted in *Harvard Journal of Law and Public Policy* 6 (1982–1983): 19).

27. Richard A. Epstein, 1989 National Lawyers Convention, "A Federalist Society Symposium on the Presidency and Congress." (transcript reprinted in *Washington University Law Quarterly* 68, no. 3 (1990): 567–574.

28. Richard A. Epstein, 1998 National Student Symposium, "Reviving the Structural Constitution," Panel V: "Undoing the New Deal?" (transcript reprinted in *Harvard Journal of Law and Public Policy* 22 (1998–1999): 209).

29. Charles Fried, 1982 National Symposium: A Symposium on Federalism, "Federalism—Why Should We Care" (transcript reprinted in *Harvard Journal of Law and Public Policy* 6 (1982–1983): 1).

30. John O. McGinnis, 1997 National Student Symposium, "Law and Economic and the Rule of Law," Panel VI: "Public Choice and the Structural Constitution" (transcript reprinted in *Harvard Journal of Law and Public Policy* 21 (1997–1998): 195).

31. Richard A. Epstein, 1998 National Student Symposium, "Reviving the Structural Constitution," Panel V: "Undoing the New Deal?" Transcript reprinted in *Harvard Journal of Law and Public Policy* 22 (1998–1999): 209.

32. *New York v. United States*, 505 U.S. 144 (1992) (hereafter *New York*), United States v. Lopez, 514 U.S. 549 (1995) (hereafter *Lopez*), *United States v. Morrison*, 529 U.S. 598 (2000) (hereafter *Morrison*).

33. *Garcia*, **580.

34. 42 USCS 2021b et seq.

35. See Summary of *New York v. United States* on lexis nexis.

36. The Tenth Amendment provides that "[t]he powers not delegated to the United States by the Constitution, nor prohibited by it to the states, are reserved to the states respectively, or to the people" (U.S. Const., Amend X); The Eleventh Amendment provides that "[t]he Judicial power of the United States shall not be construed to extend to any suit in law or equity, commenced or prosecuted against one of the United States by Citizens of another State, or by Citizens or Subjects of any Foreign State" (U.S. Const., Amend. XI); and the Guarantee Clause provides that "[t]he United States shall guarantee to every State in this Union a Republican Form of Government, and shall protect each of them against Invasion; and on Application of the Legislature, or of the Executive (when the Legislature cannot be convened) against domestic violence" (U.S. Const., Art. IV, S 4).

37. See, e.g., 1992 National Lawyers Convention, Panel III: "Congress, the Court, and the Bill of Rights" (transcript reprinted in *Cumberland Law Review* 23, no. 1 (1993): 97–104).

38. See, e.g., 2000 National Lawyers Convention, Labor and Employment Group Panel, "Regulatory Enforcement of Labor and Employment Law: What the Future Holds."

39. While Phillips was described to me in interviews as not being a "true believer" in terms of the Federalist Society, he has participated in National Conferences and is not a "token liberal," so he was included. See Speaker Agenda for 2008 Federalist Society National Lawyers Conference on "The People and the Judiciary" (available at www.fed-soc.org). Phillips participated on a panel with, among others, Roger Pilon, Jerry Smith, and Ken Starr. I also interviewed Phillips (managing partner, Sidley Austin, LLP) on January 30, 2008, for this research. He described himself as "somewhat more conservative" than most law school faculty. He also mentioned that he had a close relationship with at least one of the founding members, Peter Keisler, and a working relationship with others, such as Samuel Alito and Charles J. Cooper. Phillips also demonstrated a thorough grasp of the Federalist Society's unifying principles and beliefs, stating that he believed "federalism" and "respect for states' rights" were the "driving forces" of the Federalist Society.

40. Rex Lee, who served as President Reagan's solicitor general from 1981–1985, participated in some of the Federalist Society's earliest conferences and meetings. See, e.g., 1984 Symposium on Judicial Activism, "Legislative and Judicial Questions" (transcript reprinted in *Harvard Journal of Law and Public Policy* 7, no. 1 (1984): 35–42).

41. Kenneth Starr has been a presenter at nine Federalist Society National Conferences. See 1989 Federalist Society Symposium, Panel V, "The Role of the Courts in Separation of Powers Disputes" (transcript reprinted in *Washington University Law Quarterly* 68, no. 3 (1990): 667–706); 1992 National Lawyers Convention, "Commentary: Here and There" (transcript reprinted in *Cumberland Law Review* 23, no. 1 (1993): 193–196); 2000 National Lawyers Convention, Religious Liberties Panel, "First Amendment Roundup: Freedom of Speech, Expression, and Association and the Recent Rehnquist Court"; 2001 National Lawyers Convention, Showcase Panel III, "Judicial Decisionmaking: Judicial Enforcement of the Boundaries of the Government's Power"; 2002 National Lawyers Convention, "Barbara K Olson Memorial Lecture"; 2003 National Lawyers Convention, Free Speech and Election Law Panel, "Campaign Finance Reform in the Supreme Court"; 2004 National Lawyers Convention, Annual Convention Luncheon Speaker; 2005 National Lawyers Convention, Religious Liberties Panel, "Hyde-Weldon Amendment/Conscience Clauses"; 2008 National Lawyers Convention, "Civil Litigation under the Roberts Court."

42. Stuart Banner and Austin Schlick.

43. *The State of New York, The County of Allegany, New York and The County of Cortland, New York v. The United States of America* et al. 942 F.2D 114 (1991) (hereafter *New York Circuit*): *119.

44. Ibid., *119 (citing majority opinion in *Garcia*).
45. Ibid., *121.
46. *New York*, supra note 32, at, *187–188.
47. Ibid., *155 ("In 1788, in the course of explaining to the citizens of New York why the recently drafted Constitution provided for federal courts, Alexander Hamilton observed: 'The erection of a new government, whatever care or wisdom may distinguish the work, cannot fail to originate questions of intricacy and nicety; and these may, in a particular manner, be expected to flow from the establishment of a constitution founded upon the total or partial incorporation of a number of distinct sovereignties.' *The Federalist* No. 82, p. 491 (C. Rossiter ed. 1961)"; **157 ("Interstate commerce was an established feature of life in the late 18th century. See, *e.g., The Federalist* No. 42, p. 267 (C. Rossiter ed. 1961) ('The defect of power in the existing Confederacy to regulate the commerce between its several members [has] been clearly pointed out by experience')"; **164 ("The Convention generated a great number of proposals for the structure of the new Government, but two quickly took center stage. Under the Virginia Plan, as first introduced by Edmund Randolph, Congress would exercise legislative authority directly upon individuals, without employing the states as intermediaries. 1 Records of the Federal Convention of 1787, p. 21 (M. Farrand ed. 1911). Under the New Jersey Plan, as first introduced by William Paterson, Congress would continue to require the approval of the states before legislating, as it had under the Articles of Confederation. 1 *id.,* 243–244. These two plans underwent various revisions as the Convention progressed, but they remained the two primary options discussed by the delegates. One frequently expressed objection to the New Jersey Plan was that it might require the Federal Government to coerce the states into implementing legislation. As Randolph explained the distinction, 'the true question is whether we shall adhere to the federal plan [*i.e.,* the New Jersey Plan], or introduce the national plan. The insufficiency of the former has been fully displayed. . . . There are but two modes, by which the end of a General Government can be attained: the 1st is by coercion as proposed by Mr. Paterson's plan[, the 2nd] by real legislation as proposed by the other plan. Coercion [is] *impracticable, expensive, cruel to individuals. . . .* We must resort therefore to a national *Legislation over individuals.'* 1 *id.,* 255–256 (emphasis in original). Madison echoed this view: 'The practicability of making laws, with coercive sanctions, for the states as political bodies, had been exploded on all hands.' 2 *id., 9*"); and **165 ("In the end, the Convention opted for a Constitution in which Congress would exercise its legislative authority directly over individuals rather than over states; for a variety of reasons, it rejected the New Jersey Plan in favor of the Virginia Plan. 1 *id.,* 313. This choice was made clear to the subsequent state ratifying conventions. Oliver Ellsworth, a member of the Connecticut delegation in Philadelphia, explained the distinction to his State's convention: 'This Constitution does not attempt to coerce sovereign bodies, states, in their political capacity. . . . But this legal coercion singles out the. . . individual.' 2 J. Elliot, Debates on the Federal Constitution 197 (2d ed. 1863). Charles Pinckney, another delegate at the Constitutional Convention, emphasized to the South Carolina House of Representatives that in Philadelphia 'the necessity of having a government which should at once operate upon the people, and not upon the states, was conceived to be indispensable by every delegation present.' 4 *id., 256.*").
48. *New York*, **157.
49. *Gregory v. Ashcroft*, 501 U.S. 452 (1991) (hereafter *Gregory*).
50. Michael McConnell, "Federalism: Evaluating the Founders' Design," *University of Chicago Law Review 54* (1987): 1484, 1493.
51. *Gregory*, **458.

52. *New York,* **157 ("The benefits of this federal structure have been extensively cata-
    loged elsewhere, see, *e.g., Gregory v. Ashcroft, 501 U.S. 457–460;* Merritt, The Guarantee
    Clause and State Autonomy: Federalism for a Third Century, *Colum. L. Rev.* 88, no. 1
    (1988): 3–10; McConnell, Federalism: Evaluating the Founders' Design, *U. Chi.
    L. Rev.* 54 (1987): 1484, 1491–1511, but they need not concern us here. Our task would
    be the same even if one could prove that federalism secured no advantages to anyone.
    It consists not of devising our preferred system of government, but of understanding
    and applying the framework set forth in the Constitution").
53. *New York,* **176–177.
54. 18 USCS 922 (q)(1)(A).
55. See, "Five Children Killed as Gunman Attacks a California School," *New York Times,*
    January 18, 1989. http://www.nytimes.com/1989/01/18/us/five-children-killed-as-
    gunman-attacks-a-california-school.html (last accessed June 17, 2014).
56. See, e.g., 1986 Federalist Society Symposium, "The True *Reynolds v. United States*" (tran-
    script reprinted in *Harvard Journal of Law and Public Policy* 10, no. 1 (1986): 43–46).
57. Dean of George Mason Law School, Daniel Polsby has been a speaker at three
    Federalist Society National Conferences. See 1994 National Symposium, Panel
    IV: Feminism, Children and the Family, "Ozzie and Harriet Had It Right" (tran-
    script reprinted in *Harvard Journal of Law and Public Policy* 18, no. 2 (1995): 531–
    536); 1995 Annual Student Symposium, Panel I: Originalism and the Dead Hand,
    "Introduction" (transcript reprinted in *Harvard Journal of Law and Public Policy* 19,
    no. 2 (1996): 243–244); 1999 Annual Student Symposium, Panel IV: Does Consumer
    Choice Need to Be Managed? "Should Government Attempt to Influence Consumer
    Preference" (transcript reprinted in *Harvard Journal of Law and Public Policy* 23 no. 1
    (1999): 197–202).
58. See, e.g., 1984 National Symposium, "Withdrawing Jurisdiction from the Federal
    Courts" (transcript reprinted in *Harvard Journal of Law and Public Policy* 7, no. 1
    (1984): 13–16).
59. Prakash, who clerked for Clarence Thomas in this case, would go on to become a law pro-
    fessor (University of San Diego and University of Virginia Law School) and has also pre-
    sented at three National Conferences. See 2006 Annual Student Symposium, "How Does
    International Law Limit the War on Terror?"; 2008 Annual Student Symposium, "Bator
    Award Presentation"; 2010 Annual Student Symposium, "Originalism: A Rationalization
    for Conservatism or a Principled Theory of Interpretation?"
60. Nelson, who clerked for Clarence Thomas in this case, would go on to become a
    law professor at the University of Virginia Law School and present at two National
    Conferences. See 2001 National Lawyers Convention, Showcase Roundtable IV,
    "Judicial Decisionmaking: Precedent and Constitutional Meaning"; 2010 Annual
    Student Symposium, Panel II, "Originalism and Construction: Does Originalism
    Always Provide the Answer?"
61. As Table 1.2 in Chapter 1 illustrates, having presented at 15 Federalist Society National
    events, John C. Yoo ranks as one of most frequently invited presenters at these events.
    Per our interview, Yoo confirmed that he had been involved with the organization from
    his first year of law school at Yale Law School and describes himself as a "second gener-
    ation Federalist." Interview with John Yoo (professor of Law, University of California,
    Berkeley Law School; former law clerk to Judge Laurence H. Silberman and Justice
    Clarence Thomas; General Counsel, U.S. Senate Judiciary Committee (1995–1996);
    deputy assistant attorney general, Office of Legal Counsel (2001–2003)) in discussion
    with the author; ("I think of myself as second generation because I wasn't there when
    it was created or founded but I was someone who I think it served the purpose it for

which it was originally created; to provide this alternative, this forum of alternative views in law school for law students. So, I guess in my case it kind of worked").

62. *Lopez,* **552.

63. *Lopez,* **575.

64. *Lopez,* **584.

65. Richard Epstein, "The Proper Scope of the Commerce Clause," *Virginia Law Review* 73 (1987): 1393–1395.

66. *Lopez,* **586–587.

67. *Lopez,* **601–602.

68. See, generally, "Reviving the Structural Constitution," *Harvard Journal of Law and Public Policy* 22, no. 3 (1998–1999): 3–246.

69. The Fourteenth Amendment reads: ". . . No State shall make or enforce any law which shall. . . deprive any person of life, liberty, or property, without due process of law; nor deny to any person within its jurisdiction the equal protection of the laws. . . . The Congress shall have power to enforce, by appropriate legislation, the provisions of this article." (U.S. Const., Amend. XIV, sec. 5).

70. See Title IV of Public Law, 103–322.

71. According to several interviewees, Michael Luttig, who resigned from the Fourth Circuit Court of Appeals in 2006 over a high-profile dispute with the Bush administration regarding the litigation over Jose Padilla's detention (see, e.g., Jess Bravin and J. Lynn Lunsford, "Breakdown of Trust Led Judge Luttig to Clash with Bush" *Wall Street Journal*, May 11, 2006 (available online at http://online.wsj.com/news/articles/SB114727449814548996)), had been a permanent fixture at Federalist Society conferences prior to his resigning. Moreover, Luttig made headlines when he admitted to only hiring Federalist Society–affiliated law clerks. See, e.g., Amy Bach, "Movin' on Up with the Federalist Society," *The Nation*, October 1, 2001 ("Judge Michael Luttig on the Court of Appeals for the Fourth Circuit, for example, hires only students with membership in the Federalist Society or comparable credentials on their resumes. And almost all of Judge Luttig's clerks go on to clerkships at the Supreme Court. His unheard-of batting average is sustained because Judge Luttig diverts clerks who don't land a clerkship with other Justices to Justice Scalia (whom Luttig himself clerked for) and Justice Clarence Thomas").

72. As Table 1.2 in Chapter 1 illustrates, with 14 National Conference presentations, William H. Pryor, former state attorney general for Alabama and current Eleventh Circuit Court of Appeals judge, ranks among the most frequent Federalist Society participants in National Conferences. See, e.g., Pryor's first appearance, 1999 National Lawyers Convention, Corporations, Securities, and Antitrust Group, "Should Business Support Federalism?" and his most recent, 2010 National Lawyers Convention, Religious Liberties Panel, "Christian Legal Society v. Martinez."

73. Sutton, who is now a Sixth Circuit Court of Appeals Judge, has presented at five National Conferences from 2004 to the present. See, e.g., 2004 National Lawyers Convention, Litigation Panel, "Regulation Through Litigation" and 2010 National Lawyers Convention, Federalism Panel, "Is There Any Remaining Limit to Federal Power?"

74. Schlafly, who is the founder and executive director of the Eagle Forum, presented at four National Conferences between 1991 and 2007. See, e.g., 1991 National Lawyers Convention, Panel II: Family Law and Individual Responsibility, "The Public School System as an Instrument of Power" (transcript reprinted in *Cornell Law Review* 77, no. 5 (1992): 1000–1004).

75. Lynch, director of the Cato's Project on Criminal Justice, presented at both the 1999 National Lawyers Convention (see Criminal Law and Procedure Group, "The Future of Miranda and the Exclusionary Rule") and the 2004 National Lawyers Convention (see Criminal Law Panel, "The Patriot Act: A Three Year Retrospective").

76. Pilon, the founder and director of Cato's Center for Constitutional Studies, presented at four National Conferences between 2001 and 2010. See, e.g., 2006 National Lawyers Convention, Federalism Panel, "Executive Power in Wartime."
77. Glendon, who is a law professor at Harvard, presented at the 1992 Federalist Society Annual Student Symposium (transcript reprinted in *Harvard Journal of Law and Public Policy* 16, no. 1 (1993): 23–32).
78. Rosman, who is general counsel for the Center for Individual Rights, has also been a presenter at two National Conferences. See 2001 National Lawyers Convention, Civil Rights Panel, "The Future of Racial Preferences: Is the Issue on the Brink of Resolution at Last?"; 2006 National Lawyers Convention, Labor Panel, "Law Firm Hiring Practices and Diversity."
79. In addition to being a participant in the very first Federalist Society National Conference, Harvard law professor, and former Reagan solicitor general, Charles Fried has presented at 13 total National Conferences. See, e.g., his first (1982 Symposium on Federalism, "Federalism—Why Should We Care?" (transcript reprinted in *Harvard Journal of Law and Public Policy* 6, no. 1 (1982): 1–6)) and his most recent (2010 National Lawyers Convention, Litigation Panel, "Debating the Constitutionality of the Federal Health Care Legislation") appearances.
80. For Chief Justice Rehnquist, writing for the majority, Jay T. Jorgensen; For Justice Thomas, writing in concurrence, Steven Coltreau, C. Kevin Marshall, Kristen Silverberg, and Sanford Weisburst.
81. See, e.g., *United States v. Morrison*, 529 U.S. 598 (2000), at *606.
82. *Christy Brzonkala v. Virginia Polytechnic Institute and State University*, 169 F.3D 820 (1999) (hereafter *Morrison Circuit*), *825.
83. *Morrison Circuit*, *826.
84. Ibid., *854.
85. Ibid., *889.
86. See J. Harvie Wilkinson, "The Fourteenth Amendment Privileges and Immunities Clause," *Harvard Journal of Law and Public Policy* 12, no. 1 (1989): 43–52.
87. *Morrison Circuit*, *897.
88. Ibid., *897.
89. See J. Harvie Wilkinson, "The Fourteenth Amendment Privileges and Immunities Clause," *Harvard Journal of Law and Public Policy* 12, no. 1 (1989): 43–52.
90. *City of Boerne v. Flores*, 521 U.S. 507 (1997). This case struck down the Religious Freedom Restoration Act (RFRA) and, in doing so, was seen to limit the power of Congress severely enough to pass legislation under Section 5 of the Fourteenth Amendment. Petitioners in *Morrison* made a similar claim of congressional power under Section 5 and the Court rejected it, foreclosing another avenue for Congress to pass legislation that applies against the states.
91. *Morrison*, **606.
92. Ibid., *627.
93. Ibid., *644–645 ("If we now ask why the formalistic economic/noneconomic distinction might matter today, after its rejection in *Wickard*, the answer is not that the majority fails to see causal connections in an integrated economic world. The answer is that in the minds of the majority there is a new animating theory that makes categorical formalism seem useful again. Just as the old formalism had value in the service of an economic conception, the new one is useful in serving a conception of federalism. It is the instrument by which assertions of national power are to be limited in favor of preserving a supposedly discernible, proper sphere of state autonomy to legislate or refrain from legislating as the individual states see fit. The legitimacy of the Court's current emphasis on the noncommercial nature of regulated activity, then, does not turn on any logic serving the text of the *Commerce Clause* or on the realism of the majority's view of the national

economy. The essential issue is rather the strength of the majority's claim to have a constitutional warrant for its current conception of a federal relationship enforceable by this Court through limits on otherwise plenary commerce power").

94. See *NFIB et al. v. Sebelius,* 567 U.S. _____ (2012), Thomas, J. dissenting ("I dissent for the reasons stated in our joint opinion, but I write separately to say a word about the Commerce Clause. . . . I adhere to my view that 'the very notion of a 'substantial effects' test under the Commerce Clause is inconsistent with the original understanding of Congress' powers and with this Court's early Commerce Clause cases' ").

95. *Morrison Circuit,* **899.

96. Rabkin, who is currently a professor of law at George Mason University, has presented at nine Federalist Society National Conferences. See, 1984 National Meeting, "Public Interest Law: Is It in the Public Interest?" (transcript reprinted in *Harvard Journal of Law and Public Policy* 8, no. 2 (1985): 341–348); 1989 National Symposium, Panel II: Property and the Constitution, "Private Property and Public Office" (transcript reprinted in *Harvard Journal of Law and Public Policy* 13, no. 1 (1990): 54–59); 2000 National Lawyers Convention, Showcase Roundtable II, "What Should Shape a President's Perspective on Foreign Policy?"; 2003 Annual Student Symposium, "What We Can Learn about Human Dignity from International Law" (transcript reprinted in *Harvard Journal of Law and Public Policy* 27, no. 1 (2003): 145–168); 2003 National Lawyers Convention, Showcase Panel II, "Unilateralism, Multilateralism and American Sovereign Interests"; 2006 Annual Student Symposium, "What Is an International Rule of Law? Competing Perspectives on Its Meaning, Feasibility, and Desirability"; 2008 National Lawyers Convention, Environmental Law Panel, "The Policy Implications of the Reaction to Climate Change"; 2009 National Lawyers Convention, International Panel, "International Law: Agreements Between Sovereigns or World Government?"; 2011 Annual Student Symposium, Panel III, "The Welfare State and American Exceptionalism."

97. Jeremy Rabkin, "Sex, Violence, and the Supreme Court: The Constitution Prevails over Congressional Pandering to Feminists." *Weekly Standard,* May 29, 2000.

98. Charles Fried, "Opponents of Federalism Are Mired in a Time Warp." *Wall Street Journal,* May 16, 2000.

99. Randy E. Barnett, "William Rehnquist." *Wall Street Journal,* September 6, 2005.

100. *Gonzales v. Raich,* 545 U.S. 1 (2005) (held that under the Commerce Clause Congress may ban the use of medical marijuana even where states have approved it for medicinal use).

101. Chief Justice John Roberts, Justice Samuel Alito, Justice Clarence Thomas, and Justice Antonin Scalia. Justices Roberts and Scalia were in dissent in *Wachovia;* Justice Alito ruled with the majority; Justice Thomas did not participate in the decision.

102. *Watters v. Wachovia Bank,* 550 U.S. 1 (2007) (held that Congress had the power to preempt state regulations on subsidiaries of national banks operating within particular states).

103. Jeremy Rabkin, "Sex, Violence, and the Supreme Court: The Constitution Prevails over Congressional Pandering to Feminists." *Weekly Standard,* May 29, 2000. See also Steven G. Calabresi, "A Constitutional Revolution." *Wall Street Journal,* July 10, 1997; Terry Eastland, "Farewell to the Chief: William H. Rehnquist." *Weekly Standard,* September 26, 2005. See also Steven G. Calabresi, " 'A Government of Limited and Enumerated Powers': In Defense of United States v. Lopez," *Michigan Law Review* 94, no. 3 (1996): 752; Steven G. Calabresi, "The Era of Big Government Is Over," *Stanford Law Review* 50, no. 3 (1998):1015; Lino A. Graglia, "United States v. Lopez: Judicial Review under the Commerce Clause," *Texas. Law Review.* 74, no. 4 (1996): 719; John C. Yoo, "Defining Federalism in the 1990s," *Indiana. Law. Review* 32, no. 1 (1998): 27.

CHAPTER 5

1. *New York v. United States*, 505 U.S. 144, Opinion of O'Connor, J., *156.

2. U.S. Const., Amend X.

3. See *United States v. Darby*, 312 U.S. 100 (1941), *123–124 ("Our conclusion is unaffected by the Tenth Amendment. . . [which] states but a truism that all is retained which has not been surrendered. There is nothing in the history of its adoption to suggest that it was more than declaratory of the relationship between the national and state governments as it had been established by the Constitution before the amendment or that its purpose was other than to allay fears that the new national government might seek to exercise powers not granted, and that the states might not be able to exercise fully their reserved powers").

4. 452 U.S. 264 (1981) (holding that the Surface Mining Control and Reclamation Act of 1977, which promulgated a federal regulatory program to control the adverse effects of surface coal mining operations, did not exceed Congress's commerce power, nor did it violate the Tenth Amendment).

5. 456 U.S. 742 (1982) (holding that the Public Utility Regulatory Policies Act of 1978, which empowered the Federal Energy Regulatory Commission to promulgate rules and regulatory standards to be adopted by state utility regulatory commissions, did not exceed Congress's power under the Commerce Clause and hence did not violate the Tenth Amendment's state sovereignty protections).

6. *New York*, Opinion of O'Connor, J. *162–167.

7. Michael W. McConnell, "The Politics of Returning Power to the States." *Harvard Journal of Law and Public Policy* 6, no. 1 (1982–1983): 103.

8. For transcript, see *Cornell Journal of Law and Public Policy* 4, no. 2 (1995): 457–481.

9. For transcript, see *Harvard Journal of Law and Public Policy* 22, no. 1 (1998): 1–246.

10. Interview with Charles J. Cooper (founding member and chairman of Cooper & Kirk, PLLC; assistant attorney general for the Office of Legal Counsel (1985–1988)) in discussion with the author, June 2, 2008.

11. Interview with Loren A. Smith (judge, U.S. Court of Federal Claims; chairman, Administrative Conference of the United States (1981–1985)) in discussion with the author, January 24, 2008.

12. Interview with Edwin Meese, III (U.S. attorney general under President Ronald Reagan (1985–1988); Fellow, Heritage Foundation) in discussion with the author, February 5, 2008.

13. Martin Redish, 1996 National Lawyers Convention, Panel III: "Disciplining Congress: The Boundaries of Legislative Power" (transcript reprinted in *The Journal of Law and Politics* 13 (1997): 585).

14. David Sentelle, 1988 National Lawyers Convention, Panel III: "Federalism and the Scope of Federal Power" (transcript reprinted in *American Criminal Law Review* 26 (1989): 1737).

15. Pete du Pont, 1992 National Student Symposium, "The Legacy of the Federalist Papers," Epilogue: "Federalism in the Twenty-First Century: Will States Exist?" (transcript reprinted in *Harvard Journal of Law and Public Policy* 19 (1993): 137).

16. Alex Kozinski, 1998 National Student Symposium, "Reviving the Structural Constitution," Panel III: "Constitutional Federalism Reborn" (transcript reprinted in *Harvard Journal of Law and Public Policy* 22 (1998–1999): 93).

17. Lynn A. Baker, 1998 National Student Symposium, "Reviving the Structural Constitution," Panel III: "Constitutional Federalism Reborn" (transcript reprinted in *Harvard Journal of Law and Public Policy* 22, (1998–1999): 95).

18. Charles J. Cooper, 1992 National Student Symposium, "The Legacy of the Federalist Papers," Panel V: "The Anti-Federalists After 200 Years: Pundits or Prophets?" (transcript reprinted in *Harvard Journal of Law and Public Policy* 19 (1993): 119).

19. Theodore Olson, 1982 National Conference, "A Symposium on Federalism" (transcript reprinted in *Harvard Journal of Law and Public Policy* 6 (1982–1983): 7).

20. John S. Baker, Jr., 1992 National Student Symposium, "The Legacy of the Federalist Papers," Panel III: "Liberty and Constitutional Architecture" (transcript reprinted in *Harvard Journal of Law and Public Policy* 19 (1993): 59).

21. *New York,* Opinion of O'Connor, J. *188.

22. Michael W. McConnell, 1982 National Symposium: A Symposium on Federalism. "The Politics of Returning Power to the States" (transcript reprinted in *Harvard Journal of Law and Public Policy* 6 (1982–1983): 103).

23. William Van Alstyne, "The Second Death of Federalism." *Michigan Law Review 83,* no. 1709 (1985): 1716.

24. *Constitution in the Year 2000,* Justice Department Office of Legal Policy (1989), 137.

25. *Constitution in the Year 2000,* supra note 24: 139.

26. Charles J. Cooper, "The Demise of Federalism." *Urban Lawyer 20,* no. 2 (1988): 239–283.

27. Charles J. Cooper, 1994 National Lawyers Convention: Reinventing Self-Government, Can We Still Have Limits on National Power? Panel III: "The Federal Judiciary and Self-Government" (transcript reprinted in *Cornell Journal of Law and Public Policy* 4, (1994–1995): 500).

28. Malcolm Wallop, 1994 National Lawyers Convention: Reinventing Self-Government, Can We Still Have Limits on National Power? Panel III: "The Federal Judiciary and Self-Government" (transcript reprinted in *Cornell Journal of Law and Public Policy* 4 (1994–1995): 500).

29. *Lopez,* *583 (Justices Kennedy and O'Connor concurring).

30. See 18 U.S.C.S. 921.

31. Summary from LexisNexis, *Printz v. United States.*

32. See *Richard Mack v. United States of America; Jay Printz v. United States of America,* 66 F. 3D 1025 (1995) (hereafter *Printz Circuit*).

33. Norton, who served as the secretary of the Interior under George W. Bush, from 2011 to 2006, has been a speaker at four Federalist Society National Conferences. See 1989 National Symposium, Panel III: Regulation and Property—Allies or Enemies? "Takings Analysis of Regulations" (transcript reprinted in *Harvard Journal of Law and Public Policy* 13, no. 1 (1990): 84–90); 2000 National Lawyers Convention, Criminal Law and Procedure Group Panel, "The Migration of Responsibility and Punishment from the Wrongdoer to the Politically Correct"; 2001 National Lawyers Convention, "Address"; 2002 National Lawyers Convention, Speaker, "Twentieth Anniversary Lawyers Gala."

34. Tymkovich, a federal judge on the United States Court of Appeals for the Tenth Circuit, has presented at three National Conferences. See 2004 National Lawyers Convention, Environmental Law Panel, "Turning Private Property into Public Trusts"; 2007 Annual Student Symposium, "Moral Choices and the Eighth Amendment"; 2008 National Lawyers Convention, Labor Panel, "Labor Initiatives in the New Administration."

35. *Mack v. United States,* 856 F. Supp. 1372 (D. Ariz 1994); *Printz v. United States,* 854 F. Supp 1503 (D. Mont. 1994) (Hereafter *Printz District*).

36. *Printz District,* *1513.

37. *Printz Circuit,* *1030.

38. Ibid., 1029.

39. *Printz,* *905.

40. See, e.g., *Printz,* *915–917 ("In addition to early legislation, the Government also appeals to other sources we have usually regarded as indicative of the original understanding of the Constitution. It points to portions of The Federalist which reply to criticisms that Congress's power to tax will produce two sets of revenue officers—for example, "Brutus's" assertion in his letter to the New York Journal of December 13,

1787, that the Constitution "opens a door to the appointment of a swarm of revenue and excise officers to prey upon the honest and industrious part of the community, eat up their substance, and riot on the spoils of the country," reprinted in 1 Debate on the Constitution 502 (B. Bailyn ed. 1993). "Publius" responded that Congress will probably "make use of the State officers and State regulations, for collecting" federal taxes, The Federalist No. 36, p. 221 (C. Rossiter ed. 1961) (A. Hamilton; hereinafter The Federalist), and predicted that "the eventual collection [of internal revenue] under the immediate authority of the Union, will generally be made by the officers, and according to the rules, appointed by the several states," *id.,* No. 45, 292 (J. Madison). The Government also invokes the Federalist's more general observations that the Constitution would "enable the [national] government to employ the ordinary magistracy of each [State] in the execution of its laws," *id.,* No. 27, 176 (A. Hamilton), and that it was "extremely probable that in other instances, particularly in the organization of the judicial power, the officers of the states will be clothed in the correspondent authority of the Union," *id.,* No. 45, 292 (J. Madison). However, none of these statements necessarily implies—what is the critical point here—that Congress could impose these responsibilities *without the consent of the states....* It is interesting to observe that Story's Commentaries on the Constitution, commenting upon the same issue of why state officials are required by oath to support the Constitution, uses the same "essential agency" language as Madison did in Federalist No. 44, and goes on to give more numerous examples of state executive agency than Madison did; all of them, however, involve not state administration of federal law, but merely the implementation of duties imposed on state officers by the Constitution itself: "The executive authority of the several states may be often called upon to exert Powers or allow Rights given by the Constitution, as in filling vacancies in the senate during the recess of the legislature; in issuing writs of election to fill vacancies in the house of representatives; in officering the militia, and giving effect to laws for calling them; and in the surrender of fugitives from justice." 2 Story, Commentaries on the Constitution of the United States 577 (1851)... Even if we agreed with JUSTICE SOUTER's reading of the Federalist No. 27, it would still seem to us most peculiar to give the view expressed in that one piece, not clearly confirmed by any other writer, the determinative weight he does. That would be crediting the most expansive view of federal authority ever expressed, and from the pen of the most expansive expositor of federal power. Hamilton was "from first to last the most nationalistic of all nationalists in his interpretation of the clauses of our federal Constitution." C. Rossiter, Alexander Hamilton and the Constitution 199 (1964). More specifically, it is widely recognized that "The Federalist reads with a split personality" on matters of federalism. See D. Braveman, W. Banks, & R. Smolla, Constitutional Law: Structure and Rights in Our Federal System 198–199 (3d ed. 1996). While overall The Federalist reflects a "large area of agreement between Hamilton and Madison," Rossiter, *supra,* 58, that is not the case with respect to the subject at hand, see Braveman, *supra,* 198–199. To choose Hamilton's view, as JUSTICE SOUTER would, is to turn a blind eye to the fact that it was Madison's—not Hamilton's—that prevailed, not only at the Constitutional Convention and in popular sentiment, see Rossiter, *supra,* 44–47, 194, 196; 1 Records of the Federal Convention (M. Farrand ed. 1911) 366, but in the subsequent struggle to fix the meaning of the Constitution by early congressional practice, see *supra,* 5–10.").

41. *Printz,* *918.
42. See *Printz,* *921 ("The dissent, reiterating JUSTICE STEVENS' dissent in *New York,* 505 U.S. 210–213, maintains that the Constitution merely *augmented* the pre-existing power under the Articles to issue commands to the states with the additional power to make demands directly on individuals. See *post,* 7–8. That argument, however, was squarely rejected by the Court in *New York, supra, 161–166,*

and with good reason. Many of Congress's powers under Art. I, § 8, were copied almost verbatim from the Articles of Confederation, indicating quite clearly that 'where the Constitution intends that our Congress enjoy a power once vested in the Continental Congress, it specifically grants it.' Prakash, Field Office Federalism, *Va. L. Rev. 79, 957, 1972 (1993)*"): *923 ("We have thus far discussed the effect that federal control of state officers would have upon the first element of the 'double security' alluded to by Madison: the division of power between State and Federal Governments. It would also have an effect upon the second element: the separation and equilibration of powers between the three branches of the Federal Government itself. . . The Brady Act effectively transfers this responsibility to thousands of CLEOs in the 50 States, who are left to implement the program without meaningful Presidential control (if indeed meaningful Presidential control is possible without the power to appoint and remove). The insistence of the Framers upon unity in the Federal Executive—to insure both vigor and accountability—is well known. See The Federalist No. 70 (A. Hamilton); 2 Documentary History of the Ratification of the Constitution 495 (M. Jensen ed. 1976) (statement of James Wilson); see also Calabresi and Prakash, The President's Power to Execute the Laws, *104 Yale L. J.* 104, no. 541 (1994): 541–666. That unity would be shattered, and the power of the President would be subject to reduction, if Congress could act as effectively without the President as with him, by simply requiring state officers to execute its laws."); and *924 ("What destroys the dissent's Necessary and Proper Clause argument, however, is not the *Tenth Amendment* but the Necessary and Proper Clause itself. When a 'Law. . . for carrying into Execution' the *Commerce Clause* violates the principle of state sovereignty reflected in the various constitutional provisions we mentioned earlier, *supra, 19–20,* it is not a 'Law. . . *proper* for carrying into Execution the *Commerce Clause*,' and is thus, in the words of The Federalist, 'merely [an] act of usurpation' which 'deserves to be treated as such.' The Federalist No. 33, 204 (A. Hamilton). See Lawson & Granger, The 'Proper' Scope of Federal Power: A Jurisdictional Interpretation of the Sweeping Clause, *Duke L. J.* 43, (1993): 267, 297–326, 330–333"); and *Printz*, *927 ("The Government's distinction between 'making' law and merely 'enforcing' it, between 'policymaking' and mere 'implementation,' is an interesting one. It is perhaps not meant to be the same as, but it is surely reminiscent of, the line that separates proper congressional conferral of Executive power from unconstitutional delegation of legislative authority for federal separation-of-powers purposes. . . . This Court has not been notably successful in describing the latter line; indeed, some think we have abandoned the effort to do so. See. . . Schoenbrod, The Delegation Doctrine: Could the Court Give It Substance? *Mich. L. Rev.* 83, (1985): 1223, 1233. We are doubtful that the new line the Government proposes would be any more distinct.").

43. Though Lawson is not often credited as one of the three principal cofounders of the Federalist Society (Lee Liberman Otis, David McIntosh, and Steven Calabresi), he was mentioned by several network actors as one of the critical, early contributors in terms of developing the philosophy and libertarian side of the statement of principles of the Federalist Society. See interview with David McIntosh (partner, Meyer, Brown and Platt; member of Congress (1995–2001); cofounder, Federalist Society) in discussion with the author, January 25, 2008 ("[Gary] was one of the early people that put on the first symposium in the Yale chapter."); Interview with Douglas Kmiec (professor of law, Pepperdine University; Office of Legal Counsel under Presidents Ronald Reagan and George H. W. Bush) in discussion with the author, March 14, 2008 ("Gary would be someone who is very active in the Federalist Society today. . . [and] had systematically studied Hayek and would come out on that side of the spectrum"); Interview with Steven

Calabresi (professor of law, Northwestern University; cofounder, Federalist Society) in discussion with the author, April 3, 2008 ("One of our first chapter events at Yale Law School, we had a poster that said 'sponsored by the Federalist Society' and one of our members wrote an asterisk next to 'Society' and wrote at the bottom 'spontaneous collection of individuals acting together.' I thought that was kind of funny in terms of people caring about that. When we were first forming the chapter the same individual, Gary Lawson... when we were founding the Society he was in a Randian libertarian phase and he initially wanted us to call the Society the Ludwig von Mises Society...."). Lawson is also on record as participating in 8 Federalist Society National Conference Events.

44. Schoenbrod, a professor at New York Law School and a Visiting Scholar at the American Enterprise Institute, would not be considered a Federalist Society "true believer" or line up with many core members on various constitutional and legal issues. However, his work on delegation and the separation of powers is recommended in the Federalist Society *Bibliography* and he has spoken at two Federalist Society National Conferences on this topic. See 1989 National Lawyers Convention, Panel II, "Vetoes, Line Item Vetoes, Signing Statements, Executive Orders, and Delegations of Rulemaking Authority" (transcript reprinted in *Washington University Law Quarterly* 68, no. 3 (1990): 533–560); 1999 National Lawyers Convention, Administrative Law and Regulation Group Panel, "The Non-Delegation Doctrine Lives!"

45. Gary Lawson and Patricia Granger, "The Proper Scope of Federal Power." *Duke Law Journal* 43 (1993): 267, 299, 330.

46. *Printz v. United States,* 521 U.S. 898, *923.

47. *Printz,* *932.

48. See *Printz,* *933 (quoting *New York v. United States*) ("'Much of the Constitution is concerned with setting forth the form of our government, and the courts have traditionally invalidated measures deviating from that form. The result may appear 'formalistic' in a given case to partisans of the measure at issue, because such measures are typically the product of the era's perceived necessity. But the Constitution protects us from our own best intentions: It divides power among sovereigns and among branches of government precisely so that we may resist the temptation to concentrate power in one location as an expedient solution to the crisis of the day.'").

49. See *Printz,* *936 (Justice O'Connor concurring) ("Our precedent and our Nation's historical practices support the Court's holding today. The Brady Act violates the [*936] *Tenth Amendment* to the extent it forces states and local law enforcement officers to perform background checks on prospective handgun owners and to accept Brady Forms from firearms dealers."); and *936–937 (Justice Thomas concurring) ("The Court today properly holds that the Brady Act violates the *Tenth Amendment* in that it compels state law enforcement officers to 'administer or enforce a federal regulatory program.' See *ante,* 25. Although I join the Court's opinion in full, I write separately to emphasize that the *Tenth Amendment* affirms the undeniable notion that under our Constitution, the Federal Government is one of enumerated, hence limited, powers... Accordingly, the Federal Government may act only where the Constitution authorizes it to do so.").

50. *Printz,* *936–937.

51. Ibid., *938.

52. See Amicus Brief on Behalf of Academics for the Second Amendment, 1993 U.S. Briefs 1260; 1994 U.S.S.Ct. Briefs LEXIS 275 (hereafter *Academics Brief*).

53. *Academics Brief,* *13–16.

54. *Printz,* *939.

55. See *District of Columbia v. Heller,* 554 U.S. 570 (2008), J. Scalia writing for the majority.

56. *Printz,* *952.

57. *Printz,* *913, 912, 914, 915.

58. 26 U.S.C.S. § 5000A.
59. See 42 U.S.C.S. § 1396d(y)(1).
60. See §1396c.
61. Available at http://www.fed-soc.org/doclib/20090710_Individual_Mandates.pdf (last accessed July 23, 2012).
62. Erwin Chemerinsky and David B. Rivkin, "Individual Health Care Insurance Mandate Debate." November 3, 2009–November 6, 2009 http://www.fed-soc.org/debates/dbtid.35/default.asp (accessed July 23, 2012).
63. David B. Rivkin and Lee A. Casey, "Illegal Health Reform." *Wall Street Journal*, Opinion. August 22, 2009, http://www.washingtonpost.com/wp-dyn/content/article/2009/08/21/AR2009082103033.html (accessed July 23, 2012).
64. Randy Barnett, "Healthcare: Is 'Mandatory Insurance' Unconstitutional?" *Politico*, September 18, 2009. Available at http://www.politico.com/arena/perm/Randy_Barnett_8256A4EF-01E6-4207-B4E8-C761F2FDB5BF.html (last accessed July 23, 2012).
65. Jim Angle, "Health Care Mandate Sparks Constitutional Debate."September. FoxNews.com, September 29, 2009, http://www.foxnews.com/politics/2009/09/29/health-care-mandate-sparks-constitutional-debate/July.
66. Florida, South Carolina, Nebraska, Texas, Utah, Louisiana, Alabama, Colorado, Michigan, Pennsylvania, Washington, Idaho, South Dakota, Indiana, Mississippi, Nevada, Arizona, Georgia, Alaska, North Dakota, Wisconsin, Iowa, Ohio, Kansas, Wyoming, and Maine.
67. Clement, who served as the solicitor general from 2005 to 2008, has been a featured speaker at four Federalist Society National Conferences. See 2001 National Lawyers Convention, Showcase Panel II, "Judicial Decisionmaking: The Case of Judicial Oversight of the Political Process"; 2005 National Lawyers Convention, "Address"; 2006 National Lawyers Convention, "Welcome and Opening Address"; 2008 National Lawyers Convention, Federalism Panel, "The Roberts Court and Federalism."
68. McKenna was an invited speaker at the 2000 National Lawyers Convention. See Administrative Law and Regulation Group Panel, "The Rise of Government by Agency Guidance."
69. Wallace was a speaker at the 2004 National Lawyers Convention. See Professional Responsibility Panel, "Congressional Evaluation of Judicial Nominees."
70. Even though he does not appear as a speaker at a National Conference until 2000 (see 2000 National Lawyers Convention, Civil Rights Group Panel, "The Use and Misuse of Statistics in Civil Rights Litigation"), Michael Carvin, whom I interviewed for this book in 2008, was involved early on in the Federalist Society during his time in the Reagan Justice Department. Carvin had the following to say about how and when he became involved with the Federalist Society: "[the Founders of the Federalist Society] all worked at the Justice Department so I knew them. . . and it was mostly through those guys that I became aware of it. . . I went to some of the D.C. Lawyers lunches in the mid-80s. . . I think I started out in law school as what you'd call a 'middle of the road Republican' and then I started reading these opinions and they were intellectually bankrupt and I started getting firmer in my views about the need for a limited judiciary. So I was probably typical of the people who were attached to the Federalist Society in the beginning."
71. Katsas, who worked in the Civil Division at the Justice Department under George W. Bush, has also presented at three National Conferences. See 2003 National Lawyers Convention, Administrative Law and Regulation Panel, "Immigration and the War on Terror"; 2008 National Lawyers Convention, Litigation Panel, "Civil Litigation under the Roberts Court"; 2011 Annual Student Symposium, Panel II, "Federalism and Interstate Competition."

72. Although this proposed distinction is novel, it also represents a measured approach to the case. In other words, by developing the activity/inactivity distinction, the parties are offering the Supreme Court a means to strike down the Individual Mandate without dismantling some of its most far-reaching and long-standing Commerce Clause precedents (see, e.g., *Wickard v. Filburn* (1942) and *Gonzales v. Raich* (2005)).

73. Brief for Private Respondents on the Individual Mandate, 2012 WL 379586, 15.

74. See Brief for State Respondents on the Minimum Coverage Provision, 2012 WL 392550, 7–8.

75. See Brief of Amicus Curiae Texas Public Policy Foundation Supporting Respondents on the Individual Mandate (Richard Epstein), 2012 WL 504607, *33–34; Brief for Amici Curiae Economists in Support of Respondents Regarding Individual Mandate (Steven G Bradbury), 2012 WL 504611, *27; Amicus Brief on Behalf of Citizens and Legislators in the Fourteen Health Care Freedom States in Support of Respondents (Clint Bolick), 2012 WL 504613, *8–9; Brief Amicus Curiae of the Commonwealth of Virginia Ex Rel Attorney General Kenneth T. Cuccinelli, II, in Support of Respondents (Kenneth T. Cuccinelli, II), 2012 WL 504623, *19–21; Brief of Amicus Curiae Landmark Legal Foundation in Support of Respondents on the Individual Mandate (Mark Levin, Miahel J. O'Neill), 2012 WL 484060, *11, *17; Amicus Curiae Brief of the American Center for Law & Justice (Jay Alan Sekulow, Walter M. Weber), 2012 WL 441264, *7, *12, *15; Brief of Amicus Curiae Partnership for America in Support of Respondents on Minimum Coverage Issue (Charles J. Cooper, David H. Thompson), 2012 WL 484065, *11–12, *15.

76. See, e.g., *NFIB et al. v. Sebelius*, 567 U.S. ____ (2012). Dissent of Scalia, Alito, Thomas, and Kennedy, J., 234–235 ("It is true enough that Congress needs only a ' "rational basis" for concluding that the *regulated activity* substantially affects interstate commerce,' *ante*, 15 (emphasis added). But, it must be *activity* affecting commerce that is regulated, and not merely the failure to engage in commerce. And one is not now purchasing the health care covered by the insurance mandate simply because one is likely to be purchasing it in the future. Our test's premise of regulated activity is not invented out of whole cloth, but rests upon the Constitution's requirement that it be commerce that is regulated. If all inactivity affecting commerce is commerce, commerce is everything. Ultimately, the dissent is driven to saying that there is really no difference between action and inaction, *ante*, 26, a proposition that has never recommended itself, neither to the law nor to common sense. To say, for example, that the inaction here consists of activity in 'the self-insurance market,' Ibid., seems to us wordplay. By parity of reasoning the failure to buy a car can be called participation in the non-private-car-transportation market. Commerce becomes everything.").

77. *NFIB et al. v. Sebelius*, 567 U.S. ____ (2012). Opinion of Roberts, C.J., 45.

78. Michael Carvin, Oral Argument, March 27, 2012. *Department of Health and Human Services, et al. v. Florida, et al.*, 2012 WL 1017220.

79. Brief of Amicus Curiae Texas Public Policy Foundation Supporting Respondents on the Individual Mandate, 2012 WL 504607, 34–35.

80. David B. Rivkin, "The Federalist Society Online Debate Series: Individual Health Care Insurance Mandate Debate," November 3, 2009, http://www.fed-soc.org/debates/dbtid.35/default.aspJuly (accessed July 30, 2012).

81. Ilya Somin, "The Individual Health Insurance Mandate and the Constitutional Text." *Engage: The Journal of the Federalist Society Practice Groups 11*, no. 1 (2010): 50.

82. *State of Florida et al. v. United States Department of Health and Human Services*, 648 F.3d 1235 (Eleventh Circuit), Opinion of Dubina and Hall, 1285–1286.

83. See e.g., *NFIB*, Opinion of Roberts, C.J. 86–87 ("JUSTICE GINSBURG questions the necessity of rejecting the Government's commerce power argument, given that

§5000A can be upheld under the taxing power, *Post,* 37. But the statute reads more naturally as a command to buy insurance than as a tax, and I would uphold it as a command if the Constitution allowed it. It is only because the Commerce Clause does not authorize such a command that it is necessary to reach the taxing power question. And it is only because we have a duty to construe a statute to save it, if fairly possible, that §5000A can be interpreted as a tax. Without deciding the Commerce Clause question, I would find no basis to adopt such a saving construction.").

84. Brief of the State Petitioners on Medicaid, 2012 WL 105551, 27–28.
85. Bradbury, who has received some notoriety for authoring several controversial opinions on enhanced interrogation techniques during his time at the Office of Legal Counsel under George W. Bush, also presented at the 1999 National Lawyers Convention (see Intellectual Property Group Panel, "The Internet and Property Rights in the Digital Age").
86. Blumstein gave a talk at the 1994 National Lawyers Convention entitled "On Prudence in Health Care Reform" (transcript reprinted in *Cornell Journal of Law and Public Policy* 4, no. 2 (1995): 422–431). Notably, David Rivkin was also featured on this panel as a moderator.
87. Brief of Amici Curiae Texas Public Policy Foundation and 36 Texas State Legislators Supporting Petitioners on Medicaid (Richard A. Epstein); Brief for Amici Curiae Economists in Support of State Petitioners Regarding Medicaid Expansion (Steven G Bradbury); Brief of James F. Blumstein, as Amicus Curiae in Support of Petitioners (James F. Blumstein).
88. *NFIB,* Opinion of Roberts, C.J., 91.
89. Ibid., 111.
90. *NFIB,* Dissenting opinion of Scalia, Thomas, Alito, and Kennedy, JJ, 318–319.
91. "Memo from Pat Buchanan for the Chief of Staff," January 30, 1987. Presidential Handwriting File, Series IV, File 173. Document obtained from the Ronald Reagan Presidential Library in Simi Valley, CA, on March 12, 2008.
92. *NFIB,* Dissenting opinion of Scalia, Kennedy, Thomas, and Alito, JJ, 317, 318, and 316.
93. Ibid., 319.
94. See, e.g., Randy Barnett, "We Lost on Health Care. But the Constitution Won." *Washington Post,* June 29, 2012, http://www.washingtonpost.com/opinions/randy-barnett-we-lost-on-health-care-but-the-constitution-won/2012/06/29/gJQAzJuJCW_story.html (accessed July 6, 2012).
95. Timothy Lynch, "Criminal Theory." *Weekly Standard,* February 14, 2000.
96. U.S. Const., Amend. XI ("The Judicial power of the United States shall not be construed to extend to any suit in law or equity, commenced or prosecuted against one of the United States by Citizens of another State, or by Citizens or subjects of any Foreign State"). For more on how members of the Federalist Society network helped to provide the Supreme Court with the intellectual capital for an expansive understanding of the State Sovereign Immunity Doctrine, see Hollis-Brusky, "It's the Network: The Federalist Society as a Supplier of Intellectual Capital for the Supreme Court." *Studies in Law, Politics, and Society 61,* (2013): 137–178.
97. 567 U.S. ___ (2012) (hereafter *Arizona*).
98. *Arizona,* 10. Opinion of Kennedy, J.
99. 570 U.S. ____ (2013) (held that Section 4 of the Voting Rights Act is unconstitutional because it violated the principle of state sovereignty embedded in the Constitution and offended the equal sovereignty and dignity of the states).
100. Ibid., at 1.
101. Malcolm Wallop, 1994 National Lawyers Convention: Reinventing Self-Government, Can We Still Have Limits on National Power? Panel III: "The Federal Judiciary and

Self-Government" (transcript reprinted in *Cornell Journal of Law and Public Policy* 4 (1994–1995): 500).

CHAPTER 6

1. Parts of this section first appeared in Amanda Hollis-Brusky, " 'It's the Network': The Federalist Society as a Supplier of Intellectual Capital for the Supreme Court." *Studies in Law, Politics, and Society* 61 (2013): 164–166.
2. *Citizens United v. FEC*, 558 U.S. 310 Stevens, J. dissenting, *396.
3. See, e.g., 1998 Federalist Society National Student Symposium, "Reviving the Structural Constitution." Transcript reprinted in *Harvard Journal of Law & Public Policy* 22 (1998–1999): 3–246.
4. Parts of this section first appeared in Amanda Hollis-Brusky, "Support Structures and Constitutional Change: Teles, Southworth, and the Conservative Legal Movement." *Law and Social Inquiry* 36, no. 2 (2011): 527–531.
5. Interview with Michael Greve (director of the Federalism Project, American Enterprise Institute) in discussion with the author, February 12, 2008.
6. Peter Finley Dunne, *Mr. Dooley's Opinions* (New York: R. H. Russell, 1901) ("[N]o matter whether th' constitution follows th' flag of not, th' supreme court follows th' iliction returns").
7. Interview with Douglas Kmiec (professor of law, Pepperdine University; Office of Legal Counsel under Presidents Ronald Reagan and George H. W. Bush) in discussion with the author, March 14, 2008.
8. Interview with Thomas Smith (professor of law, University of San Diego Law School; senior counsel, President Reagan's Council of Economic Advisors) in discussion with the author, March 19, 2008.
9. Interview with Tony Cotto (former Student Chapter president at George Washington University Law School, the Federalist Society) in discussion with the author, January 31, 2008.
10. Ibid.
11. Interview with Michael Carvin (partner, Jones Day; deputy assistant attorney general, Civil Rights Division (1985–1987); deputy assistant attorney general, Office of Legal Counsel (1987–1988)) in discussion with the author, January 28, 2008.
12. Interview with Randy Barnett (professor of legal theory, Georgetown University Law School) in discussion with the author, June 10, 2008.
13. Interview with Dan Troy (attorney, Sidley Austin, LLP; special assistant, Office of Legal Counsel (1984–1988)) in discussion with the author, January 30, 2008.
14. Interview with Steven Calabresi (professor of law, Northwestern University; cofounder, Federalist Society) in discussion with the author, April 3, 2008.
15. Interview with Douglas Kmiec (professor of law, Pepperdine University; Office of Legal Counsel under Presidents Ronald Reagan and George H. W. Bush) in discussion with the author, March 14, 2008.
16. I should note that Lawrence Baum, in his own work, classifies the Federalist Society as a "Policy Group" (see, e.g., Baum 2006, 123–126). However, as I mention here, I would classify it as a hybrid "social group" and "legal community" group.
17. 545 U.S. 1 (2005).
18. Interview with Randy Barnett (professor of legal theory, Georgetown University Law School) in discussion with the author, June 10, 2008.
19. Interview with Steven Calabresi (professor of law, Northwestern University; cofounder, Federalist Society) in discussion with the author, April 3, 2008.

20. *Printz,* *938.
21. Interview with Gail Heriot (professor of law, University of San Diego; commissioner, United States Commission on Civil Rights) in discussion with the author, March 18, 2008.
22. Interview with John C. Yoo (professor of law, University of California, Berkeley Law School; former law clerk to Judge Laurence H. Silberman and Justice Clarence Thomas; general counsel, U.S. Senate Judiciary Committee (1995–1996); deputy assistant attorney general, Office of Legal Counsel (2001–2003)) in discussion with the author, January 16, 2008.
23. Interview with Walter Berns (resident scholar, American Enterprise Institute) in discussion with the author, January 24, 2008.
24. Interview with Michael Horowitz (senior fellow, Hudson Institute; general counsel, Office of Management, and Budget under President Ronald Reagan) in discussion with the author, January 22, 2008.
25. Interview with Eugene Meyer (president, Federalist Society) in discussion with the author, February 8, 2008.
26. Interview with Steven Calabresi (professor of law, Northwestern University; cofounder, Federalist Society) in discussion with the author, April 3, 2008.
27. Interview with Michael Rappaport (professor of law, University of San Diego Law School; special assistant, Office of Legal Counsel under President Ronald Reagan) in discussion with the author, March 17, 2008.
28. Interview with Edwin Meese, III (U.S. attorney general under President Ronald Reagan (1985–1988); Fellow, Heritage Foundation) in discussion with the author, February 5, 2008.
29. Perhaps the best example of movement to co-opt Originalism for Liberals/Progressives is Jack M. Balkin, *Living Originalism* (Harvard, MA: Belknap Press, 2011).
30. Interview with Eugene Meyer (president, Federalist Society) in discussion with the author, February 8, 2008.
31. Federalist Society website (accessed June 7, 2013), http://www.fed-soc.org/for_press/page/journalists-guide-to-legal-policy-experts-2.
32. Experts listed as of June 7, 2013, include George Bittlingmayer, Ronald Cass, Carolyn F. Graglia, Lino A. Graglia, John S. Irving, David B. Kopel, Robert A. Levy, Stephen R. McAllister, John O. McGinnis, and Gregory J. Sidak.
33. Experts listed as of June 7, 2013, include Larry Alexander, Francis J. Beckwith, Roger Clegg, Donald A. Daugherty, George W. Dent, Jr., Robert L. Freedman, Philip K. Howard, Kris W. Kobach, Michael I. Krauss, Curt A. Levey, Henry Manne, Douglas D. McFarland, John O. McGinnis, Cleta Mitchell, Mike Thompson, Gerald Walpin, Russell L. Weaver, C. Douglas Welty, Laurence H. Winer, and Ronald A. Zumbrun.
34. Experts listed as of June 7, 2013, include Kris W. Kobach, Nelson Lund, David N. Mayer, John O. McGinnis, Ronald D. Rotunda, and Mark I. Shublak.
35. Experts listed as of June 7, 2013, include Dana Berliner, Clint Bolick, Laurence D. Cohen, Donald A. Daugherty, George W. Dent, Jr., David N. Mayer, Charles E. Rice, Ronald D. Rotunda, Abigail Thernstrom, Eugene Volokh, Gerald Walpin, Russell L. Weaver, and Christopher Wolfe.
36. Experts listed as of June 7, 2013, include Randy Barnett, Kris W. Koback, Andrew W. Lester, David N. Mayer, Roger Pilon, Ronald D. Rotunda, Russell L. Weaver, C. Douglas Welty, and Ronald A. Zumbrun.
37. Experts listed as of June 7, 2013, include James S. Burling, Michael A. Carvin, Michael DeBow, and Gregory J. English.
38. "Contract Law," "Criminal Justice," "Economic Freedom," "Judicial Confirmation," "Miranda," and "Term Limits."
39. Randy Barnett, "The Supreme Court's Gun Showdown." *Wall Street Journal,* June 30, 2010, 15.

40. Randy E. Barnett, "William Rehnquist." *Wall Street Journal*, September 6, 2005.

41. See, e.g., Randy Barnett, "We Lost on Health Care. But the Constitution Won." *Washington Post*, June 29, 2012, http://www.washingtonpost.com/opinions/randy-barnett-we-lost-on-health-care-but-the-constitution-won/2012/06/29/gJQAzJuJCW_story.html.

42. See March 23, 2012 (on Healthcare), available on You Tube at http://www.youtube.com/watch?v=2rJcAxauinY (accessed June 7, 2013).

43. See, e.g., October 25, 2009 (on Healthcare), available on YouTube http://www.you-tube.com/watch?v=mB1D02rv0-Y; December 28, 2010 (on Immigration Ruling), available on YouTube http://www.youtube.com/watch?v=xPAd1Bq4w5g; January 16, 2013 (on Gun Control), available on YouTube http://www.youtube.com/watch?v=scx1oy-ClM4. On his personal website, Rivkin links to videos of 69 distinct media appearances, http://www.davidrivkin.com/media-gallery/media-gallery (accessed June 7, 2013).

44. See June 25, 2010 (on Immigration), available on You Tube at http://www.youtube.com/watch?v=9X31CH9_txw (accessed June 7, 2013).

45. See http://www.fed-soc.org/publications/page/2010-national-lawyers-convention-controlling-government-the-framers-the-tea-parties-and-the-constitution (accessed June 7, 2013).

46. See Address by Senator Elect Michal S. Lee, November 19, 2010 (Introduction by Leonard Leo), http://www.fed-soc.org/publications/detail/address-by-senator-elect-michael-s-lee-event-audiovideo.

47. For speaker agenda, see http://www.fed-soc.org/events/page/2012-nation al-lawyers-convention-schedule (accessed June 7, 2013).

48. See, e.g., David G. Savage and Kathleen B. Hennessey, "Scalia Appears at 'Tea Party' House Meeting." *Los Angeles Times*, January 24, 2011 (quoting seminar attendee Rep. January Schakowsky (D-IL) "'This is a discussion going on at a very, very high level right now—lots of Latin phrases from lawyers that I'm not sure what they are,' Schakowsky said. 'This was pretty dry, actually.'"

49. Interview with David McIntosh (partner, Meyer, Brown and Platt; member of Congress (1995–2001); cofounder, Federalist Society) in discussion with the author, January 25, 2008.

50. Ibid.

51. Phone Interview with Lillian BeVier (professor of law, University of Virginia Law School) in discussion with the author, February 1, 2008; ("A lot of times it's just like dripping water. You know it can wear away a stone but it takes a lot of drips. So it's just a question of getting these ideas out [there]").

EPILOGUE

1. See, for example, interview with Carter Phillips (managing partner, Sidley Austin, LLP) in discussion with the author, January, 30, 2008: "*Sui generis* is probably as good of a description as you can come up with in terms of what that organization is."; interview with Gregory Maggs (senior associate dean for Academic Affairs and professor of law, George Washington University Law School) in discussion with the author, January 22, 2008: " I think it is really *sui generis* and if you think about why it was formed you sort of understand why that is"; interview with Michael Carvin (partner, Jones Day; deputy assistant attorney general, Civil Rights Division (1985–1987); deputy assistant attorney general, Office of Legal Counsel (1987–1988)) in discussion with the author, January 28, 2008: "… it's got characteristics of [a think tank and an interest group] but I would call it a think tank slash debating society… their contribution to the market-place of ideas comes a lot more from these structured conferences and their speakers…

so I would think they're *sui generis* in that respect."; interview with Richard Willard (partner, Steptoe and Johnson, LLP; assistant attorney general, Civil Rights Division under President Ronald Reagan) in discussion with the author, January 31, 2008: "I think it's pretty *sui generis*. . ."

2. See "Mission" (accessed June 12, 2013), http://www.acslaw.org/about/mission.

3. Interview with Lisa Brown (executive director, American Constitution Society (2001–2008)) in discussion with the author, June 19, 2008.

4. Antonin Scalia, "Originalism: The Lesser Evil." *University of Cinncinatti, Law, Review,* 57 (1988–1989): 849–866, 855.

5. Interview with Lisa Brown (executive director, American Constitution Society (2001–2008)) in discussion with the author, June 19, 2008.

6. Interview with Goodwin Liu (professor of law, University of California, Berkeley Law School; Board of Directors, American Constitution Society; nominee to Ninth Circuit Court of Appeals) in discussion with the author, June 27, 2008.

7. See ACS Law website (accessed June 11, 2013), http://www.acslaw.org/issues/constitutional-interpretation-and-change.

8. Interview with Dan Troy (attorney, Sidley Austin, LLP; special assistant, Office of Legal Counsel (1984–1988)) in discussion with the author, January 30, 2008 (Washington, DC).

9. Interview with Lisa Brown (executive director, American Constitution Society (2001–2008)) in discussion with the author, June 19, 2008.

10. Charlie Savage, "Liberal Legal Group Is Following New Administration's Path to Power." *New York Times,* December 10, 2008 (noting the appointments of Executive Director Lisa Brown as White House staff secretary, Melody Barnes as director of the Domestic Policy Council, and Ronald Klain as Joe Biden's chief of staff).

11. See, e.g., David Fontana, "Sonia Sotomayor: How She Became the Public Face of the Supreme Court's Liberal Wing" *The New Republic.* June 29, 2011. Available at http://www.newrepublic.com/article/politics/91013/sonia-sotomayor-supreme-court-liberal-voice ("When Sotomayor was nominated to the Supreme Court in 2009, many liberals were unhappy. This unease was only magnified by her confirmation hearings. *The Washington Post* said there was 'little for liberals' in the hearings, and former University of Chicago Law School Dean Geoffrey Stone argued that they 'did serious damage to the cause of progressive thought in constitutional law.' ").

12. See ACS Law website (accessed June 11, 2013), http://www.acslaw.org/acsblog/marking-kagans-confirmation-obama-notes-acs-lauds-historic-moment.

13. See James Oliphant, "Obama Court Nominee Goodwin Liu Withdraws after Filibuster." *Los Angeles Times,* May 25, 2011, http://articles.latimes.com/2011/may/25/nation/la-na-0526-goodwin-liu-20110526.

14. See Senate Judiciary Committee Hearing Transcript for Goodwin Liu, April 16, 2010 (accessed June 11, 2013), http://www.judiciary.senate.gov/nominations/Materials112thCongress.cfm.

15. Interview with Goodwin Liu (professor of law, University of California, Berkeley Law School; Board of Directors, American Constitution Society; nominee to Ninth Circuit Court of Appeals) in discussion with the author, June 27, 2008.

16. David A. Strauss, *The Living Constitution* (Oxford: Oxford University Press, 2010), 2.

17. See Jeremy Leaming, "Scalia Misses Again with 'Dead' Constitution Refrain." *American Constitution Society Blog.* January 29, 2013, http://www.acslaw.org/acsblog/scalia-misses-again-with-%E2%80%98dead%E2%80%99-constitution-refrain.

18. Interview with Robert Post (Dean and Professor of Law, Yale Law School; Board of Directors, American Constitution Society) in discussion with the author, June 12, 2008.

19. Interview with Lisa Brown (executive director, American Constitution Society (2001–2008)) in discussion with the author, June 19, 2008.

20. See ACS Law website, June 12, 2013, http://www.acslaw.org/publications/books/ keeping-faith-with-the-constitution.

21. See, e.g., Edwin Meese, "Reagan Upheld the Rule of Law." *Washington Times*, February 2, 2011 ("Ronald Reagan was committed to restoring the concept of constitutional fidelity. Judges, he maintained, should base their decisions on the original meaning of the Constitution. . ."). See also Interview with Edwin Meese III (U.S. attorney general under President Ronald Reagan (1985–1988); Fellow, Heritage Foundation) in discussion with the author, February 5, 2008, ("I think it's a commitment to the rule of law and a commitment to the Constitution, and from that kind of a body of philosophical principles. . . is all kind of mixed in there but I think fidelity to the Constitution is a guiding principle").

22. Goodwin Liu, Pamela S. Karlan, and Christopher H. Schroeder, *Keeping Faith with the Constitution* (Oxford: Oxford University Press, 2010), xvi–xvii.

23. Ibid., xvi.

24. See ACS Law website, June 12, 2013, http://www.acslaw.org/about ("The American Constitution Society is also debunking conservative buzzwords such as "originalism" and "strict construction" that use neutral-sounding language but all too often lead to conservative policy outcomes. Using both traditional and new media to communicate with policymakers, judges, lawyers and the public at large, ACS presents a compelling vision of core constitutional values such as genuine equality, liberty, justice and the rule of law.").

25. Interview with Goodwin Liu (professor of law, University of California, Berkeley Law School; Board of Directors, American Constitution Society; nominee to Ninth Circuit Court of Appeals) in discussion with the author, June 27, 2008.

26. See ACS Law website, June 12, 2013, http://www.acslaw.org/events/2011-05-05/ jack-balkin-why-liberals-should-be-originalists.

27. See, e.g., Charlie Savage, "Liberal Legal Group Is Following New Administration's Path to Power." *New York Times*, December 10, 2008. ("Some law professors privately bemoan the rise of both societies, saying they are helping to polarize the law by making ambitious students think they have to pick sides early—before their thinking may have matured, and in a public way that affects which judges will hire them as clerks").

28. Ibid.

29. An allusion to an oft-quoted book within conservative legal circles by Richard S. Weaver, *Ideas Have Consequences* (Chicago, IL: University of Chicago Press, 1948).

REFERENCES

CASES CITED

Arizona et al. v. United States, 567 U.S. ___ (2012).

Austin v. Michigan Chamber of Commerce, 494 U.S. 652 (1990).

Barron v. Mayor and City Council of Baltimore, 32 U.S. 243 (1833).

Buckley v Valeo, 424 U.S. 1 (1976).

Cases v. United States, 131 F.2d 916 (1942).

Christy Brzonkala v. Virginia Polytechnic Institute and State University, 169 F.3D 820 (1999).

Citizens United v. FEC, 558 U.S. 310 (2010).

City of Boerne v. Flores, 521 U.S. 507 (1997).

District of Columbia v. Heller, 554 U.S. 570 (2008).

Ezell v. City of Chicago, 7th Circuit 10-3525 (2011).

Federal Election Commission v. Beaumont, 539 U.S. 146 (2003).

FERC v. Mississippi, 456 U.S. 742 (1982).

First National Bank of Boston v. Bellotti, 435 U.S. 765 (1978).

Garcia v. San Antonio Metro. Transit Authority, 469 U.S. 528 (1985).

Gonzales v. Raich, 545 U.S. 1 (2005).

Gregory v. Ashcroft, 501 U.S. 452 (1991).

Griswold v. Connecticut, 381 U.S. 479 (1965).

Heart of Atlanta Motel Inc. v. United States, 379 U.S. 241 (1964).

Hodel v. Virginia Surface Mining, 452 U.S. 264 (1981).

Lawrence v. Texas, 539 U.S. 558 (2003).

Mack v. United States, 856 F. Supp. 1372 (D. Ariz 1994).

Marbury v. Madison, 5 U.S. 137 (1803).

McDonald v. City of Chicago, 130 S. Ct. 3020 (2010).

Miller v. Texas, 153 U.S. 535 (1894).

Moore v. Madigan, 7th Cir. 12-1269, 12-1788 (2012).

National League of Cities v. Usery, 426 U.S. 833 (1976).

National Rifle Association Inc. v. Village of Oak Park, 617 F.Supp.2d 752, 753 (N.D.Ill. 2008).

National Rifle Association of America Inc., v. City of Chicago, Illinois and Village of Oak Park, Illinois, 567 F. 3d 856 (2009).

New York v. United States, 505 U.S. 144 (1992).

NFIB et al. v. Sebelius, 567 U.S. ____ (2012).

NLRB v. Laughlin Jones & Laughlin Steel Co., 301 U.S. 1 (1937).

Parker v. District of Columbia, 311 F. Supp. 2d 103, 109 (2004).

Perry v. Schwarzenegger, 704 F. Supp. 2d 921 (2010).

Presser v. Illinois, 116 U.S. 252 (1886).

Printz v. United States, 854 F. Supp 1503 (D. Mont. 1994).

Printz v. United States, 521 U.S. 898 (1997).

Quilici v. Village of Morton Grove, 695 F.2d 261 (7th Cir. 1982).

Richard Mack v. United States of America; Jay Printz v. United States of America, 66 F. 3D 1025 (1995).

Roe v. Wade, 410 U.S. 113 (1973).

Shelby County v Holder, 570 U.S. ___(2013).

Shelly Parker et al. v. District of Columbia, 478 F.3d 370, D.C. Cir. (2007).

State of Florida et al. v. United States Department of Health and Human Services, 648 F.3d 1235 (2011).

The Slaughter-House Cases, 83 U.S. 36 (1873).

The State of New York, The County of Allegany, New York and The County of Cortland, New York v. The United States of America et al., 942 F.2D 114 (1991).

United States v Auto Workers, 352 U.S. (1957).

United States v. Cruikshank, 92 U.S. 542 (1876).

United States v. Darby, 312 U.S. 100 (1941).

United States v. Lopez, 2 F.3D 1342 (1993).

United States v. Lopez, 514 U.S. 549 (1995).

United States v. Miller, 307 U.S. 174 (1939).

United States v. Morrison, 529 U.S. 598 (2000).

United States v. Oakes, 564 F.2d 384 (1977).

United States v. Warin, 530 F.2d 103 (1976).

Watters v. Wachovia Bank, 550 U.S.1 (2007).

Wickard v. Filburn, 317 U.S. 111 (1942).

Wisconsin Right to Life v. FEC, 551 U.S. 449 (2007).

WORKS CITED

Abrams, Kathryn. "On Reading and Using the Tenth Amendment." *Yale Law Journal* 93 (1983–1984): 723.

Acosta, R. Alexander. "In 2000, Supreme Court Is at Stake Too." *The Wall Street Journal*, August 23, 1999, sec. A15.

Adler, John. "How Conservative Is This Court?" *National Review*, July 5, 2007: Available at http://www.nationalreview.com/articles/221499/how-conservative-court/jonathan-h-adler (last accessed: June 4, 2014).

——. "Environmental Enemy #1." *National Review*, January 3, 2006. Available at http://www.nationalreview.com/articles/216385/environmental-enemy-1/jonathan-h-adler (last accessed: June 4, 2014).

——. "Federalism, Up in Smoke?" *National Review*, June 7, 2005. Available at http://www.nationalreview.com/articles/214630/federalism-smoke/jonathan-h-adler (last accessed: June 4, 2014).

——. "High Court High Anxiety." *National Review*, December 1, 2004. Available at http://www.nationalreview.com/articles/213030/high-court-high-anxiety/jonathan-h-adler (last accessed: June 4, 2014).

——. "Suicidal Folly." *National Review*, August 19, 2004. Available at http://www.nationalreview.com/articles/211921/suicidal-folly/jonathan-h-adler (last accessed: June 4, 2014).

——. "The Framers' Design." *National Review*, November 1, 2001.

——. "How Scalia-esque will Donald Trump's Supreme Court nominee be?" The Volokh Conspiracy at *The Washington Post*. January 26, 2017.

Arkes, Hadley. "Servatius Redux." *National Review*, January 27, 2006. Available at http://www.nationalreview.com/articles/216620/servatius-redux/hadley-arkes (last accessed: June 4, 2014).

Avery, Michael, and Danielle McLaughlin. *The Federalist Society: How Conservatives Took the Law Back from Liberals*. Nashville, TN: Vanderbilt University Press, 2013.

Bailyn, Bernard. *The Debate on the Constitution: Federalist and Antifederalist Speeches, Articles, and Letters during the Struggle over Ratification: Part One, September 1787–February 1788*. New York: Literary Classics of the United States, 1993.

Baird, Vanessa. *Answering the Call of the Court: How Justices and Litigants Set the Supreme Court Agenda*. Charlottesville: University of Virginia Press, 2007.

Baker, John. "'The Legacy of the Federalist Papers' from Panel III: Liberty and Constitutional Architecture from the 1992 National Student Symposium." *Harvard Journal of Law and Public Policy* 19, no. 1 (1993): 59.

Baker, Lynn. "'The Revival of States' Rights: A Progress Report and Proposal' from the 1998 National Student Conference." *Harvard Journal of Law and Public Policy* 22, no. 1 (1998–1999): 95–106.

Balkin, Jack. "Bush v. Gore and the Boundary Between Law and Politics." *Yale Law Journal* 110, no. 8 (2001): 1407–1458.

——. *Living Originalism*. Cambridge, MA: Belknap Press, 2011.

Balkin, Jack, and Sanford Levinson. "Understanding the Constitutional Revolution." *Virginia Law Review* 87 (2001): 1045–1109.

——. "The Processes of Constitutional Change: From Partisan Entrenchment to the National Surveillance State." *Fordham Law Review*, 75, no. 1 (2006): 101–145.

Barbash, Fred. "Illinois Suburb Inspires a National Drive for Handgun Controls." *The Washington Post*, March 1, 1982, sec. A9.

Barnett, Randy. "Healthcare: Is 'Mandatory Insurance' Unconstitutional?" *Politico*, September 18, 2009. http://www.politico.com/arena/perm/Randy_Barnett_8256A4EF-01E6-4 207-B4E8-C761F2FDB5BF.html.

——. "The Ninth Circuit's Revenge." *National Review*, June 9, 2005. Available at http://www. nationalreview.com/articles/214646/ninth-circuits-revenge/randy-barnett (last accessed: June 4, 2014).

——. "The Original Meaning of the Commerce Clause." *University of Chicago Law Review* 68 (2001): 101.

——. "The Second Amendment and the states." *Wall Street Journal (Online)*, March 2, 2010. Available at http://online.wsj.com/news/articles/SB10001424052748704548 60457509781165766325 (last accessed: June 4, 2014).

——. "The Supreme Court's Gun Showdown." *Wall Street Journal*, June 30, 2010. Available at http://online.wsj.com/news/articles/SB10001424052748703964104575335060436777670 (last accessed: June 4, 2014).

——. "Was the Right to Keep and Bear Arms Conditioned on Service in an Organized Militia?" *Texas Law Review* 83 (2004): 237–261.

——. "We Lost on Health Care. But the Constitution Won." *Washington Post*, June 29, 2012. http://www.washingtonpost.com/opinions/randy-barnett-we-lost-on-health-c are-but-the-constitution-won/2012/06/29/gJQAzJuJCW_story.html.

——. "William Rehnquist." *The Wall Street Journal*, September 6, 2005. Available at http:// online.wsj.com/news/articles/SB112596560700032247 (last accessed: June 4, 2014).

Barnett, Randy, and Don Kates. "Under Fire: The New Consensus on the Second Amendment." *Emory Law Journal* 45 (1996): 1139–1259.

Baum, Lawrence. *Judges and Their Audiences: A Perspective on Judicial Behavior*. Princeton, NJ: Princeton University Press, 2006.

Bennett, Andrew, and Colin Elman. "Case Study Methods in the International Relations Subfield." *Comparative Political Studies* 40, no. 2 (2007): 170–195.

——. "Qualitative Methods: The View from the Subfields." *Comparative Political Studies* 40, no. 2 (2007): 111–121.

Berenson, Tessa. 2018. "Inside Trump's Plan to Dramatically Reshape U.S. Courts." *Time Magazine*. February 8, 2018. Retrieved from http://time.com/5139118/inside-trumps-plan-to-dramatically-reshape-us-courts/ (accessed December 10, 2018).

Berns, Walter. "On Madison and Majoritarianism: A Response to Professor Amar." *Harvard Journal of Law and Public Policy* 15, no. 1 (1992): 113–118.

BeVier, Lillian. "Campaign Finance Reform: Specious Arguments, Intractable Dilemmas." *Columbia Law Review* 94 (1994): 1258–1280.

——. "First Amendment Basics Redux: Buckley v. Valeo to FEC v. Wisconsin Right to Life." *Cato Supreme Court Review* (2007): 77–113.

Black, Charles. *A New Birth of Freedom: Human Rights Named and Unnamed*. New Haven, CT: Yale University Press, 1997.

Blackstone, William. *Commentaries on the Laws of England*, 1765.

Bork, Robert. "Neutral Principles and Some First Amendment Problems." *Indiana Law Journal* 47, no. 1 (1971): 1–35.

Braveman, Daan, William Banks, and Rodney Smolla. *Constitutional Law: Structure and Rights in Our Federal System*. 3rd edition. New York: Matthew Bender, 1996.

Brigham, John. *The Cult of the Court*. Philadelphia, PA: Temple University Press, 1987.

Buckley, James, William Van Alstyne, David Sentelle, Joseph diGenova, and G. Robert Blakey. "Panel III: Federalism and the Scope of the Federal Criminal Law'." *American Criminal Law Review* 26 (1988–1989): 1737–1778.

Burrell, Thomas. "Is There Anything 'Fundamental' in the Right to Keep and Bear Arms? A Call for Parity in the Incorporation Doctrine." *Engage* 9, no. 1 (February 2008): 22–28.

Calabresi, Steven. "A Constitutional Revolution." *Wall Street Journal*, July 10, 1997, sec. A14.

——. "'A Government of Limited and Enumerated Powers': In Defense of United States v. Lopez." *Michigan Law Review* 94 (1995): 752.

——, ed. *Originalism: A Quarter-Century of Debate*. Washington, DC: Regnery Press, 2007.

——. "The Era of Big Government Is Over." *Stanford Law Review* 50, no. 3 (1998): 1015–1053.

Calabresi, Steven, and Sarah Agudo. "Individual Rights under State Constitutions When the Fourteenth Amendment Was Ratified in 1868: What Rights Are Deeply Rooted in American History and Tradition?" *Texas Law Review* 87, no. 1 (2008): 7–120.

Calabresi, Steven, and Saikrishna Prakash. "The President's Power to Execute the Laws." *Yale Law Journal* 104, no. 3 (1994): 541.

Capoccia, Giovanni, and R. Daniel Keleman. "The Study of Critical Junctures: Theory, Narrative, and Counterfactuals in Historical Institutionalism." *World Politics* 59, no. 3 (2007): 341–369.

Choper, Jesse H. *Judicial Review and the National Political Process: A Functional Reconsideration of the Role of the Supreme Court*. Chicago: University of Chicago Press, 1980.

Clayton, Cornell, and David May. "The New Institutionalism and Supreme Court Decision-Making: Toward a Political Regime Approach." *Polity* 32 (2000): 233–252.

Clayton, Cornell, and J. Mitchell Pickerill. "Guess What Happened on the Way to Revolution? Precursors to the Supreme Court's Federalism Revolution." *Publius* 34, no. 3 (2004): 85–114.

Cooper, Charles. "The Demise of Federalism." *Urban Lawyer* 20, no. 2 (1988): 239–283.

——. "'Independent of Heaven Itself: Differing Federalist and Anti-Federalist Perspectives on the Centralizing Tendency of the Federal Judiciary' from the 1992 Student Symposium." *Harvard Journal of Law and Public Policy* 16, no. 1 (1993): 119.

——. "'Reinventing Self-Government, Can We Still Have Limits on National Power?' from Panel III: The Federal Judiciary and Self-Government from 1994 National Lawyers Convention." *Cornell Journal of Law and Public Policy* 4, no. 2 (1995): 500.

——. "'The Federal Judiciary, Life Tenure, and Self-Government' from 1994 National Lawyers Conference." *Cornell Journal of Law and Public Policy* 2 (1995): 499.

———. " 'The Legacy of the Federalist Papers' from Panel V: The Anti-Federalists after 200 Years: Pundits or Prophets? from the 1992 National Student Symposium." *Harvard Journal of Law and Public Policy* 19 (1993): 119.

Cornell, Saul. *A Well-Regulated Militia: The Founding Fathers and the Origins of Gun Control in America.* New York: Oxford University Press, 2006.

Cox, Christopher. "The Marriage Amendment Is a Terrible Idea." *The Wall Street Journal,* September 28, 2004. Available at http://online.wsj.com/news/articles/SB109632714491429481 (last accessed: June 4, 2014).

Cross, Mai'a. "Rethinking Epistemic Communities Twenty Years Later." *Review of International Studies* 39, no. 1 (2013): 137–160.

Curtis, Michael. *No State Shall Abridge: The Fourteenth Amendment and the Bill of Rights.* Durham, NC: Duke University Press, 1987.

———. " 'Privileges or Immunities, Individual Rights, and Federalism.' " *Harvard Journal of Law and Public Policy* 12 (1989): 53–61.

Cushman, Barry. *Rethinking the New Deal Court: The Structure of a Constitutional Revolution.* New York: Oxford University Press, 1998.

Dahl, Robert. "Decision-Making in a Democracy: The Supreme Court as a National Policy-Maker." *Journal of Public Law* 6 (1957): 279–295.

Donosky, Lea, Michael Reese, Pamela Abramson, Elaine Shannon, and Gloria Borger. "A New Push for Gun Control." *Newsweek,* March 15, 1982: 22.

Dotterwiech, Lisa. "Who Knows What?: A Study of the Role of Epistemic Communities in the Making of the No Child Left Behind Act." Palmer House Hotel, Chicago, IL, 2008.

Du Pont, Pete. " 'Epilogue: Federalism in the Twenty-First Century: Will States Exist?' from the 1992 National Student Symposium." *Harvard Journal of Law and Public Policy* 19 (1993): 137.

Dumoulin, David. "Local knowledge in the hands of transnational NGO networks: a Mexican viewpoint." *International Social Sciences Journal* 178 (2003): 593–605.

Duggan, Paul. "Lawyer Who Wiped Out D.C. Ban Says It's about Liberties, Not Guns." *Washington Post,* March 18, 2007. Available at http://www.washingtonpost.com/wp-dyn/content/article/2007/03/17/AR2007031701055.html (last accessed: June 4, 2014).

Dunne, Finley Peter. *Mr. Dooley's Opinions.* New York: R. H. Russell, 1901.

Duxbury, Neil. *Patterns of American Jurisprudence.* New York: Oxford University Press, 1995.

Easterbrook, Frank. "Bills of Rights and Regression to the Mean." *Harvard Journal of Law and Public Policy* 15, no. 1 (1992).

Eastland, Terry. "Bookshelf: Keeping the Federal Government in Its Place." *Wall Street Journal,* August 19, 1987: 15.

———. "Farewell to the Chief: William H. Rehnquist." *Weekly Standard,* September 26, 2005. Available at http://www.weeklystandard.com/Content/Public/Articles/000/000/006/037vtngt.asp (last accessed: June 4, 2014).

———. "Reading Roberts' Mind." *Weekly Standard,* August 1, 2005. Available at http://www.weeklystandard.com/Content/Public/Articles/000/000/005/873nqkja.asp (last accessed: June 4, 2014).

———. "The Estrada Pinata." *Weekly Standard,* February 24, 2003. Available at http://staging.weeklystandard.com/Content/Protected/Articles/000/000/002/253lgyyd.asp (last accessed: June 4, 2014).

Edwards, Lee. *The Conservative Consensus: Frank Meyer, Barry Goldwater, and the Politics of Fusionism.* Vol. 8. First Principles Series. Washington, DC: The Heritage Foundation, 2007.

Elliot, Jonathan. *Debates on the Federal Constitution.* 2nd ed., 1863.

Engler, John, C. Boyden Gray, and Kenneth Starr. "Phony Federalists." *Wall Street Journal*, June 1, 2004. Available at http://online.wsj.com/news/articles/SB108605009909825376 (last accessed: June 4, 2014).

———. "High-Tech Federalism." *National Review*, April 27, 2005. Available at http://www.nationalreview.com/articles/214292/high-tech-federalism/gov-john-engler-c-boyden-gray (last accessed: June 4, 2014).

Epp, Charles. *The Rights Revolution: Lawyers, Activists, and Supreme Courts in Comparative Perspective*. Chicago: University of Chicago Press, 1998.

Epstein, Richard. "A Federal Case." *National Review*, October 28, 2002: 50.

———. "Still Defending the New Deal Program." *Wall Street Journal*, September 7, 2005, sec. A17.

———. "The Proper Scope of the Commerce Clause." *Virginia Law Review* 73 (1987): 1387–1455.

———. "'In Praise of Divided Government' from the 1989 National Lawyers Convention." *Washington University Law Quarterly* 68, no. 3 (Fall 1990): 567.

———. "'Reviving the Structural Constitution' from Panel V: Undoing the New Deal? from the 1998 National Student Symposium." *Harvard Journal of Law and Public Policy* 22, no. 1 (1998–1999): 209.

Farrand, Max, ed. *The Records of the Federal Convention of 1787*. Vol. 1. New Haven, CT: Yale University Press, 1911.

Feldman, Noah. 2018. "Democrats Can't Stop Brett Kavanaugh's Confirmation." *Bloomberg*. September 4, 2018. Retrieved from https://www.bloomberg.com/opinion/articles/2018-09-04/kavanaugh-hearings-federalist-society-is-so-close-to-victory (accessed December 10, 2018).

Feller, A. H. "The Tenth Amendment Retires." *American Bar Association* 27 (1941): 223.

Fisch, Jill E. "Frankenstein's Monster Hits the Campaign Trail: An Approach to Regulation of Corporate Political Expenditures." *William and Mary Law Review* 32 (1991): 587–643.

Fish, Stanley. *Is There a Text in this Class?* Cambridge, MA: Harvard University Press, 1980.

———. *Doing What Comes Naturally: Change, Rhetoric and the Practice of Theory in Literary and Legal Studies*. Durham, NC: Duke University Press, 1989.

Fleck, Ludwik. *Genesis and Development of a Scientific Fact*. Chicago: University of Chicago Press, 1979.

Fontana, David. "Sonia Sotomayor: How She Became the Public Face of the Supreme Court's Liberal Wing." *The New Republic*, June 29, 2011. Available at http://www.newrepublic.com/article/politics/91013/sonia-sotomayor-supreme-court-liberal-voice (last accessed: June 4, 2014).

Fried, Charles. "'Federalism- Why Should We Care?' from the 1982 National Symposium: A Symposium on Federalism." *Harvard Journal of Law and Public Policy* 22 (1982–1983): 1.

———. "Opponents of Federalism Are Mired in a Time Warp." *Wall Street Journal*, May 16, 2000, sec. A29.

Gerstein, Josh. 2017. "Gorsuch takes victory lap at Federalist dinner." *Politico*. November 16, 2017. Retrieved from https://www.politico.com/story/2017/11/16/neil-gorsuch-federalist-society-speech-scotus-246538 (accessed December 10, 2018).

Gillman, Howard. "Regime Politics, Jurisprudential Regimes, and Unenumerated Rights." *University of Pennsylvania Journal of Constitutional Law* 9, no. 1 (2006): 107–120.

Gough, Claire and Simon Shackley. "The Respectable Politics of Climate Change: The Epistemic Communities and NGOs." *International Affairs* 77, no. 2 (2001): 329–345.

Graber, Mark. "The Non-Majoritarian Problem: Legislative Deference to the Judiciary." *Studies in American Political Development* 7 (1993): 35–73.

Graglia, Lino. "United States v. Lopez: Judicial Review under the Commerce Clause." *Texas Law Review* 74 (1996): 719–771.

Grayer, Annie. 2018. "Brett Kavanaugh was concerned with his Federalist Society member-ship in 2001, emails show." *CNN.* August 19, 2018. Retrieved from https://www.cnn.com/2018/08/19/politics/brett-kavanaugh-federalist-society-emails/index.html (accessed December 10, 2018).

Greve, Michael. "Federalism Is More Than States' Rights." *Wall Street Journal,* July 1, 1999, sec. A22.

——. "A Federalism Worth Fighting For." *Weekly Standard,* January 29, 2001. Available at http://www.weeklystandard.com/Content/Protected/Articles/000/000/011/515tqfvi.asp (last accessed: June 4, 2014).

Haas, Peter. "Introduction: Epistemic Communities and International Policy Coordination." *International Organization* 46, no. 1 (1992): 1–35.

Harrison, John. "Reconstructing the Privileges or Immunities Clause." *The Yale Law Journal* 101, no. 7 (May 1992): 1385–1474.

——. " 'In the Beginning Are the States' from the 1998 National Student Conference." *Harvard Journal of Law and Public Policy* 22, no. 1 (1998–1999).

Hathaway, Oona. "Path Dependence in the Law: The Course and Pattern of Legal Change in a Common Law System." *The Iowa Law Review* 86, no. 2 (2001).

Hayward, Allison R. "Revisiting the Fable of Reform." *Harvard Journal on Legislation* 45 (2008a): 421–470.

——. "Wisconsin Right to Life: Same Song, Different Verse." *St. Louis University Public Law Review* 27 (2008b): 309–318.

Hicks, George. "The Conservative Influence of the Federalist Society on the Harvard Law School Student Body." *Harvard Journal of Law and Public Policy* 29 (2006): 623–717.

Hills, Roderick. " 'Panel IV: Federalism in Constitutional Context' from 1998 National Student Symposium: Reviving the Structural Constitution." *Harvard Journal of Law and Public Policy* 22, no. 1 (1998–1999): 815.

Hohmann, James. 2016. "Donald Trump urged to name Utah senator to high court." *The Washington Post.* April 7, 2016.

Hollis-Brusky, Amanda. "The Federalist Society and the Structural Constitution: An Epistemic Community at Work." (Unpublished doctoral dissertation) University of California, Berkeley, 2010.

——. "Support Structures and Constitutional Change: Teles, Southworth, and the Conservative Legal Movement." *Law and Social Inquiry* 36, no. 2 (2011a): 551–574.

——. "Helping Ideas Have Consequences: Political and Intellectual Investment in the Unitary Executive Theory, 1981–2000." *Denver University Law Review* 89, no. 1 (2011b): 197–244.

——. "It's the Network: The Federalist Society as a Supplier of Intellectual Capital for the Supreme Court." *Studies in Law, Politics, and Society* 61 (2013): 137–178.

Horwitz, Morton. *The Transformation of American Law 1870–1960.* New York: Oxford University Press, 1992.

——. "In What Sense Was the Warren Court Progressive?" *Widener Law Symposium Journal* 4 (1999): 95–99.

Irons, Peter. *The New Deal Lawyers.* Princeton, NJ: Princeton University Press, 1982.

Jackson, Robert. *The Struggle For Judicial Supremacy: A Study of a Crisis in American Power Politics.* New York: Octagon Books, 1979.

Jacobs, Lawrence, and Theda Skocpol. *Health Care Reform and American Politics: What Everyone Needs to Know.* New York: Oxford University Press, 2010.

Johnsen, Dawn. "Ronald Reagan and the Rehnquist Court on Congressional Power: Presidential Influences on Constitutional Change." *Indiana Law Journal* 78, no. 1 (2003).

Kincaid, John. "From Cooperative to Coercive Federalism." *Annals of the American Academy of Political and Social Science* 509 (May 1990): 139–152.

Kmiec, Douglas. "Screening Judges." *National Review,* September 5, 2001. Available at http://www.nationalreview.com/comment/comment-kmiec090501.shtml (last accessed June 4, 2014).

Kozinski, Alex. "'Reviving the Structural Constitution' from Panel III: Constitutional Federalism Reborn from the 1998 National Student Symposium." *Harvard Journal of Law and Public Policy* 22, no. 1 (1998–1999): 93.

Kramer, Larry. "Putting the Politics Back into Political Safeguards Federalism." *Columbia Law Review* 100, no. 1 (2000): 215–293.

Kruse, Michael. 2018. "The Weekend at Yale That Changed American Politics." *Politico Magazine.* September/October. Retrieved from https://www.politico.com/magazine/story/2018/08/27/federalist-society-yale-history-conservative-law-court-219608 (accessed December 10, 2018).

Kuhn, Thomas. *The Structure of Scientific Revolutions.* Chicago: University of Chicago Press, 1970.

Langbein, Laura, and Mark Lotwis. "The Political Efficacy of Lobbying and Money: Gun Control and the U.S. House, 1986." *Legislative Studies Quarterly* 15, no. 3 (1990): 413–440.

Lawson, Gary. "'The Congress: Representation, Accountability and the Rule of Law,' Panel III: Congress, the Court, and the Bill of Rights, from the 1992 National Lawyers Conference." *Cumberland Law Review* 23 (1993): 103–108.

Lawson, Gary, and Patricia Granger. "The 'Proper' Scope of Federal Power: A Jurisdictional Interpretation of the Sweeping Clause." *Duke Law School* 43, no. 2 (1993): 267–336.

Leonard S. Leo, "Welcome Address." Showcase Panel I: Federalism and Federal Power. 2012. Federalist Society National Lawyers Convention. November 19, 2012 (accessed June 13, 2013), http://www.fed-soc.org/publications/detail/federalism-and-federal-power-event-audiovideo

Levinson, Sanford. "Raoul Berger Pleads for Judicial Activism: A Comment." *Texas Law Review* 74 (1995–1996): 773.

Levy, Robert. "None of Their Business." *National Review,* May 22, 2002. Available at http://www.freerepublic.com/focus/news/687642/posts (last accessed June 4, 2014).

———. "Second Amendment Aftermath." *Washington Times,* July 3, 2008, sec. A22.

Liptak, Adam. "Carefully Plotted Course Propels Gun Case to Top." *New York Times,* December 3, 2007. Available at http://www.nytimes.com/2007/12/03/us/03bar.html (last accessed: June 4, 2014).

Liu, Goodwin, Pamela Karlan, and Christopher Schroeder. *Keeping Faith with the Constitution.* New York: Oxford University Press, 2010. http://www.acslaw.org/publications/books/keeping-faith-with-the-constitution.

Lund, Nelson. "Putting Federalism to Sleep." *Weekly Standard,* October 31, 2005. Available at http://www.weeklystandard.com/Content/Protected/Articles/000/000/006/245khuly.asp (last accessed: June 4, 2014).

———. "The Past and Future of the Individual's Right to Bear Arms." *Georgia Law Review* 31 (1996–1997): 1–76.

Lund, Nelson, and Alan Gura. "Gun Rights Litigation Update with Professor Nelson Lund and Mr. Alan Gura." Federalist Society Teleforum Call, August 16, 2012.

Lynch, Timothy. "Criminal Theory." *Weekly Standard,* February 14, 2000.

Mahoney, James. "Path Dependence in Historical Sociology." *Theory and Society* 29, no. 4 (August 2000): 507–548.

Malcolm, John. 2017. "How Trump Changed the Courts in 2017." *Heritage Foundation.* December 27, 2017. Retrieved from https://www.heritage.org/courts/commentary/how-trump-changed-the-courts-2017 (accessed December 10, 2018).

Maldonado, Alma. "An Epistemic Community and Its Intellectual Networks: The Field of Higher Education in Mexico." Doctoral dissertation, Boston College, 2004.

Markman, Stephen. *The Constitution in the Year 2000.* Washington, DC: Justice Department, 1988.

McCann, Michael. "Causal Versus Constitutive Explanations (or, On the Difficulty of Being so Positive...)." *Law and Social Inquiry* 21, no. 2 (1996): 457–482.

——. *Rights at Work: Pay Equity Reform and the Politics of Legal Mobilization.* Chicago: University of Chicago Press, 1994.

McConnell, Michael. "Federalism: Evaluating the Founders' Design." *University of Chicago Law Review* 54 (1987): 1493.

——. "Let the States Do It, Not Washington." *Wall Street Journal*, March 29, 1999, sec. A27.

——. "'The Politics of Returning Power to the States' from the 1982 Federalist Society Conference." *Harvard Journal of Law and Public Policy* 6, no. 1 (1982–1983): 103.

McGinnis, John. "Bookshelf: A Justice Is Weighed in the Balance." *Wall Street Journal*, January 31, 2006, sec. D8.

——. "One Blueprint for Obama." *Wall Street Journal*, July 15, 2008. Available at http://online. wsj.com/news/articles/SB121607859603852623 (last accessed: June 4, 2014).

——. "'Public Choice and the Structural Constitution' from the 1997 National Student Symposium." *Harvard Journal of Law and Public Policy* 21 (1997–1998): 195.

Meese, Edwin. "Reagan Upheld the Rule of Law." *Washington Times*, February 3, 2011. Available at http://www.washingtontimes.com/news/2011/feb/3/meese-reagan-upheld-the-rule-of-law/ (last accessed: June 4, 2014).

Merrill, Thomas. "The Role of Institutional Factors in Protecting Individual Liberties." *Harvard Journal of Law and Public Policy* 15, no. 1 (1992): 85–92.

Merritt, Deborah. "The Guarantee Clause and State Autonomy: Federalism for a Third Century." *Columbia Law Review* 88 (1988): 3–10.

Meyer, Frank. *In Defense of Freedom: A Conservative Credo.* Chicago: Henry Regnery Company, 1962.

Nash, A.E. Keir. "State Sovereignty And States' Rights," in *The Oxford Companion to the Supreme Court of the United States*, ed. Kermit L. Hall. New York: Oxford University Press, 2005.

Noonan, John. *Narrowing the Nation's Power: The Supreme Court Sides with the States.* Berkeley: University of California Press, 2002.

O'Neill, Jonathan. *Originalism in American Law and Politics.* Baltimore, MD: John Hopkins University Press, 2005.

Oliphant, James. "Obama Court Nominee Goodwin Liu Withdraws after Filibuster." *Los Angeles Times*, May 25, 2011. http://articles.latimes.com/2011/may/25/nation/la-na-0526-goodwin-liu-20110526.

Olson, Theodore. "Aaaand They're Off! The Justices Go to Work." *Wall Street Journal*, October 4, 1999, sec. A43.

——. "How Effective Are Bills of Rights in Protecting Individual Freedoms." *Harvard Journal of Law and Public Policy* 15, no. 1 (1992): 53–55.

——. "'A Symposium on Federalism' from the 1982 National Conference." *Harvard Journal of Law and Public Policy* 6, no. 1 (1982–1983): 7.

Paik, Anthony, Ann Southworth, and John Heinz. "Lawyers of the Right: Networks and Organization." *Law and Social Inquiry* 32, no. 4 (2007): 883–917.

Peppers, Todd. *Courtiers of the Marble Palace: The Rise and Influence of the Supreme Court Law Clerk.* Stanford, CA: Stanford University Press, 2006.

Percy, Billups. "National League of Cities v. Usery: The Tenth Amendment Is Alive and Doing Well." *Tulane Law Review* 51 (1976–1977): 95.

Pierson, Paul. "Increasing Returns, Path Dependence, and the Study of Politics." *The American Political Science Review* 94, no. 2 (2000): 251–267.

Posner, Richard. "In Defense of Looseness." *The New Republic*, August 27, 2008. http://www.newrepublic.com/article/books/defense-looseness#.

Prakash, Saikrishna. "Field Office Federalism." *Virginia Law Review* 79, no. 8 (1993): 1957–2037.

Rabkin, Jeremy. "Bill's Fickle Feminists." *American Spectator*, May 1998: 60–61.

———. "Federalism v. Feminism: The Supreme Court Is Likely to Side with the Federalists." *American Spectator*, December 1999: 60–61.

———. "Sex, Violence, and the Supreme Court; The Constitution Prevails over Congressional Pandering to Feminists." *Weekly Standard*, May 29, 2000. Available at http://staging. weeklystandard.com/Content/Protected/Articles/000/000/011/040zagxr.asp (last accessed: June 4, 2014).

———. "State Your Business." *American Spectator*, July 1995: 55–56.

———. "The Ducks Stop Here." *American Spectator*, February 2001: 14–15.

Randolph, Raymond, Richard Epstein, and Stephen Williams. "'Limits on National Power and Unconstitutional [Coercive] Conditions' from the 1994 National Lawyers Conference." *Cornell Journal of Law and Public Policy* 4, no. 1 (1994–1995): 457.

Redish, Martin. "'Panel III: Disciplining Congress: The Boundaries of Legislative Power' from the 1996 National Lawyers Convention." *The Journal of Law and Politics* 13, no. 1 (1997): 585.

Ribstein, Larry E. "Corporate Political Speech." *Washington and Lee Law Review* 49 (1992): 109–159.

Rivkin, David, and Lee Casey. "Illegal Health Reform." *Washington Post*, August 22, 2009, sec. Opinion. http://www.washingtonpost.com/wp-dyn/content/article/2009/08/21/ AR2009082103033.html.

Rossiter, Cinton, ed. *The Federalist Papers*. New York: Signet, 1961.

———. *Alexander Hamilton and the Constitution*. New York: Harcourt Trade Publishers, 1964.

Rotunda, Ronald. "Federalizing the Windy City." *National Review*, June 18, 2002. Available at http://www.nationalreview.com/comment/comment-rotunda061802.asp (last accessed June 4, 2013).

Sarat, Austin, and Thomas Kearns. *Law in the Domains of Culture*. Ann Arbor: University of Michigan, 1998.

Savage, Charlie. "Liberal Legal Group Is Following New Administration's Path to Power." *New York Times*, December 10, 2008. Available at http://www.nytimes.com/2008/12/11/ us/politics/11network.html?pagewanted=all (last accessed: June 4, 2014).

Savage, David, and Kathleen Hennessey. "Scalia Appears at 'Tea Party' House Meeting." *Los Angeles Times*, January 24, 2011. Available at http://articles.latimes.com/2011/jan/24/ nation/la-na-scalia-tea-party-20110125 (last accessed: June 4, 2014).

Scalia, Antonin. "The Two Faces of Federalism," *Harvard Journal of Law and Public Policy* 6 (1982): 19–22.

———. "Foreword." In *Originalism: A Quarter-Century of Debate*. Washington, DC: Regnery Publishing, 2007.

———. "Originalism: The Lesser Evil." *University of Cincinnati Law Review* 57 (1989 1988): 849–866.

———. "'Is There an Unwritten Constitution?' from the Seventh Annual National Federalist Society Symposium in 1988." *Harvard Journal of Law and Public Policy* 12, no. 1 (1989): 1–2.

———. "'Morality, Pragmatism, and the Legal Order' from 1985 Federalist Society National Meeting." *Harvard Journal of Law and Public Policy* 9, no. 1 (1986): 123–127.

———. "'The Two Faces of Federalism' from the 1982 National Symposium: A Symposium on Federalism." *Harvard Journal of Law and Public Policy* 6 (1982–1983): 19.

Scheiber, Harry. "Federalism." In *The Oxford Companion to the Supreme Court of the United States*, edited by Kermit Hall. New York: Oxford University Press, 2005: 321–332.

Scheingold, Stuart. *The Politics of Rights*. Ann Arbor: University of Michigan, 2004.

Scherer, Nancy, and Banks Miller. "The Federalist Society's Influence on the Federal Judiciary." *Political Research Quarterly* 62, no. 2 (n.d.): 366–378.

Schoenbrod, David. "The Delegation Doctrine: Could the Court Give It Substance?" *Michigan Law Review* 83, no. 5 (1985): 1223–1290.

Schroeder, Christopher. "Causes of the Recent Turn in Constitutional Interpretation." *Duke Law Journal* 51, no. 1 (2001): 307–361.

Sebenius, James. "Challenging Conventional Explanations of International Cooperation: Negotiation Analysis and the Case of Epistemic Communities." *International Organization* 46, no. 1 (1992): 323–365.

Sentelle, David. "'Panel III: Federalism and the Scope of Federal Power' from the 1988 National Lawyers Convention." *American Criminal Law Review* 26, no. 1 (1989): 1737.

Shapiro, Martin, and Alec Sweet, eds. *On Law, Politics, and Judicialization*. New York: Oxford University Press, 2002.

Silverstein, Gordon. *Law's Allure: How Law Shapes, Constrains, Saves, and Kills Politics*. New York: Cambridge University Press, 2009.

Smith, Bradley A. "Money Talks: Speech, Corruption, Equality, and Campaign Finance." *Georgetown Law Journal* 86 (1997): 45–99.

——. *Unfree Speech*. Princeton, NJ: Princeton University Press, 2001.

——. "Campaign Finance Reform: Searching for Corruption in All the Wrong Places." *Cato Supreme Court Review* (2003): 187–222.

——. "The John Roberts Salvage Company: After *McConnell*, a New Court Looks to Repair the Constitution." *Ohio State Law Journal* 68 (2007): 891–923.

Somin, Ilya. "The Individual Health Insurance Mandate and the Constitutional Text." *Engage: The Journal of the Federalist Society Practice Groups* 11, no. 1 (2010): 50.

Southworth, Ann. *Lawyers of the Right: Professionalizing the Conservative Coalition*. Chicago: University of Chicago Press, 2008.

Spitzer, Robert. *The Right to Bear Arms: Rights and Liberties under the Law*. Santa Barbara, CA: ABC-CLIO, 2001.

Sprecher, Robert. "The Lost Amendment." *American Bar Association Journal* 51, (1965): 665–669.

Stern, Seth and Stephen Wermiel. 2010. *Justice Brennan: Liberal Champion*. Houghton Mifflin Harcourt. New York, NY.

Story, Joseph. *Commentaries on the Constitution of the United States*. Vol. 2. 2nd edition. Boston, MA: Cambridge University Press, 1851.

Strauss, David. *The Living Constitution*. New York: Oxford University Press, 2010.

Sundstrom, Mikael. "A Brief Introduction: What is an Epistemic Community." Unpublished paper. 2000. Available at http://citeseerx.ist.psu.edu/viewdoc/download;jsessionid =C796FF2548D2BFAA2DD86A7AA8635BB2?doi=10.1.1.137.6119&rep=rep1& type=pdfhttp://citeseerx.ist.psu.edu/viewdoc/download;jsessionid=C796FF254 8D2BFAA2DD86A7AA8635BB2?doi=10.1.1.137.6119&rep=rep1&type=pdf (last accessed May 15, 2014).

Swoyer, Alex. 2018. "Kavanaugh ready for Senate questions about his ties to the Federalist Society." *The Washington Times*. September 2, 2018. Retrieved from https://www.washingtontimes.com/news/2018/sep/2/brett-kavanaugh-ready-for-senate-questions-about-h/ (accessed December 10, 2018).

Teles, Steven. *The Rise of the Conservative Legal Movement: The Battle for Control of the Law*. Princeton, NJ: Princeton University Press, 2008.

——. "Transformative Bureaucracy: Reagan's Lawyers and the Dynamics of Political Investment." *Studies in American Political Development* 23, no. 1 (2009): 61–83.

Thomas, Clarence. "The Higher Law Background of the Privileges or Immunities Clause of the Fourteenth Amendment." *Harvard Journal of Law and Public Policy* 12, no. 1 (1989): 63–70.

Toke, Dave. "Epistemic Communities and Environmental Groups." *Politics* 19 no. 2 (1999): 97–102.

Toobin, Jeffrey. 2017. "The Conservative Pipeline to the Supreme Court." *The New Yorker.* April 17, 2017.

Tortorella, John. "Reining in the Tenth Amendment: Finding a Principled Limit to the Non-Commandeering Doctrine of United States v. Printz." *Seton Hall Law Review* 28 (1998–1997): 1365.

Troy, Daniel. "Electing the Supreme Court." *Weekly Standard*, May 10, 1999. Available at http://www.weeklystandard.com/Content/Protected/Articles/000/000/010/354llmrd.asp# (last accessed: June 4, 2014).

Urofsky, Melvin. *Money and Free Speech: Campaign Finance Reform and the Courts.* Lawrence: University Press of Kansas, 2005.

Van Alstyne, William. "The Second Amendment and the Personal Right to Arms." *Duke Law Journal* 43, no. 6 (1993–1994): 1236.

——. "The Second Death of Federalism." *Michigan Law Review* 83, no. 7 (1985): 1709–1733.

——. "1988 National Lawyers Convention, Panel II: Federalism and the Scope of the Federal Criminal Law." *American Criminal Law Review* 26 (1989): 1737.

Volokh, Eugene. "State Constitutional Rights to Keep and Bear Arms." *The Texas Review of Law and Politics* no. 11 (2006): 191–217.

——. "The Commonplace Second Amendment." *New York University Law Review* 73, no. 3 (1998): 793–821.

Wallop, Malcolm. "'Can We Still Have Limits on National Power?' from Panel III: The Federal Judiciary and Self-Government from 1994 National Lawyers Convention: Reinventing Self-Government." *Cornell Journal of Law and Pubic Policy* 4, no. 1 (1994–1995): 500.

——. "'Reinventing Self-Government, Can We Still Have Limits on National Power?' from Panel III: The Federal Judiciary and Self-Government from 1994 National Lawyers Convention." *Cornell Journal of Law and Public Policy* 4, no. 1 (1995 1994): 500.

Ward, Artemus, and David Weiden. *Sorcerers' Apprentices: 100 Years of Law Clerks at the United States Supreme Court.* New York: New York University Press, 2006.

Weaver, Richard. *Ideas Have Consequences.* Chicago: University of Chicago Press, 1948.

Whittington, Keith. "Taking What They Give Us: Explaining the Court's Federalism Offensive." *Duke Law Journal* 51, no. 1 (2001): 477–520.

Wiber, Melanie. "An Epistemic Community's Work Is Never Done." *Paper presented at the annual meeting of The Law and Society Association*, Berlin, Germany, 2007. Available at http://citation.allacademic.com/meta/p_mla_apa_research_citation/1/7/7/1/7/p177173_index.html?phpsessid=ud3rtbdgpnqnpro9ok4vqfkq56 (last accessed June 4, 2014).

Wilkinson, J. Harvie. "The Fourteenth Amendment Privileges and Immunities Clause." *Harvard Journal of Law and Public Policy* 12 (1989): 51.

Will, George. "Reinventing the Second Amendment." *Washington Post*, November 23, 2008, sec. B07.

Williams, David. *The Mythic Meanings of the Second Amendment: Taming Political Violence in a Constitutional Republic.* New Haven, CT: Yale University Press, 2003.

Yee, Albert. "The Causal Effects of Ideas on Policies." *International Organization* 50, no. 1 (1996): 69–108.

Yoo, John. "Defining Federalism in the 1990s." *Indiana Law Review* 32 (1998): 27.

INDEX